Instructor's Manual and Test Bank

to accompany

World Politics
in a
New Era
Second Edition

Steven L. Spiegel
University of California at Los Angeles

Fred L. Wehling
Monterey Institute of International Studies

Prepared by

Fred L. Wehling

and

Elizabeth Matthews

Harcourt Brace College Publishers
Fort Worth   Philadelphia   San Diego   New York   Orlando   Austin   San Antonio
Toronto   Montreal   London   Sydney   Tokyo

ISBN: 0-15-505654-9

Address for Orders
Harcourt Brace College Publishers, 6277 Sea Harbor Drive, Orlando, FL 32887-6777
1-800-782-4479

Address for Editorial Correspondence
Harcourt Brace College Publishers, 301 Commerce Street, Suite 3700, Fort Worth, TX 76102

Web Site Address
http://www.hbcollege.com

Printed in the United States of America

8 9 0 1 2 3 4 5 6 7   129   9 8 7 6 5 4 3 2 1

Harcourt Brace College Publishers

Instructor's Manual

Contents

How to Use This Manual ▬▬▬▬▬▬▬▬▬▬▬

Steven Spiegel and Fred Wehling's text *World Politics in a New Era*, second edition, is designed to help students in their first year of college or junior college acquire the skills and background knowledge necessary for a basic understanding of how international affairs affect all of our lives. When used as the main textbook for an introductory course in international relations, it will show students why world history is not a chronicle of marginally relevant events distant in both time and space, but a vital, dynamic process that has shaped the contemporary world; how the world economy has a direct and immediate impact on our environment, lifestyles and jobs; and why one needs an understanding of concepts of international relations such as power, security, sovereignty, and interdependence in order to act as an informed citizen of a democratic society. In short, *World Politics in a New Era* introduces students to the basic ideas and skills that will enable them to take an active interest in global affairs.

The text uses a "building-block" approach to introduce students to the study of international relations. As outlined in the introduction, the book begins with an overview of the history of the international system (Chapters Two through Four), then offers a discussion of regionalism (in Chapter Five). Next, with this historical foundation in place, it describes the operation of key aspects of the international system, including the world economy (Chapters Six, Seven, and Eight), international law and organizations (Chapter Nine), and global issues (Chapter Ten).

The text then examines the overarching concept of security in more detail (in Chapter Eleven) before presenting contending theories of international relations, grouped according to levels of analysis, in Chapter Twelve. The concluding chapter (Thirteen) draws upon all the events, concepts, and theoretical approaches discussed in previous chapters to construct scenarios for the future of world politics. While each chapter of *World Politics in a New Era* is thus designed to build upon and reinforce material presented in previous chapters, instructors should not feel bound to present the conceptual units of the book in this exact sequence. In a course emphasizing current events, for example, the global issues chapter (Ten) could be presented right after the introduction, while a course focusing on international relations theory might begin with the chapter on levels of analysis (Twelve), then use the theories outlined in those chapters to interpret the historical record (in Chapters Two through Four).

The purpose of this manual is to help instructors get maximum value out of the text and to suggest how to integrate the text with lectures, class activities, and enrichment material. The chapters of the manual correspond to like-numbered chapters of the text and are divided into nine sections: *Scope, Objectives, and Approach; What Students Should Learn from This Chapter; Outline of the Chapter; How the Chapter Relates to Central Themes of the Text; Suggested Lecture Topics; Study and Exam Questions;* and finally *Recommended Enrichment Readings.* The material in these sections, as described below, is intended to help instructors prepare and conduct a unit of a course based on each text chapter.

Scope, Objectives, and Approach. These sections briefly summarize the chapter's topics, themes, and organizational plan. The first section of each chapter of this manual therefore describes how the text chapter fits into this building-block approach and indicates how the chapter builds upon and reinforces material presented in previous chapters.

What Students Should Learn from This Chapter. These sections summarize the learning objectives for each text chapter and are graduated into three levels: *foundation, enrichment,* and *mastery.* The foundation level identifies the fundamental facts and concepts necessary for an elementary understanding of the material presented in the chapter. The enrichment level indicates what students should know in order to have a solid grasp on the material that extends beyond basic concepts. The mastery level suggests what students should know to demonstrate a deep understanding of the chapter and the ability to extend the themes and concepts of the chapter to other contexts.

Instructors may wish to use this section as a rough guide to evaluation or grading. Understanding of the chapter at the foundation level would indicate "average" attainment of learning objectives, the enrichment level would show an "above average" degree of success, and understanding at the mastery level should be considered "excellent." Assessment of learning is never easy, of course, and the instructor's priorities and expectations will always be the most important criteria for evaluation of students' performance.

Outline of the Chapter.   A summary of the chapter is given in outline form, concise but more comprehensive than the principal points given at the end of each text chapter.

How the Chapter Relates to Central Themes of the Text.   In each chapter, *World Politics in a New Era* attempts to show how international relations is shaped by two interrelated dialectics: globalization versus fragmentation and cooperation versus conflict. These sections of the manual will point out how these processes are illustrated in the text chapter and how examples of the central themes given in the chapter reinforce those presented in other chapters. (Of course, in order to demonstrate a mastery level of understanding, students must be able to draw their own thematic links between chapters—and point out thematic contradictions as well.)

Suggested Lecture Topics.   These sections give suggestions for lectures designed to highlight the principal events and ideas covered in the text chapter. Instructors should not feel obligated to include all of these topics in their lectures pertaining to the chapter, as lectures will be more effective if they concentrate on the aspects of the material that the instructor considers most thought provoking, puzzling, urgent, or relevant to the goals of the course. Suggested topics for class discussions and other in-class activities will also be included. Additionally, because *World Politics in a New Era* emphasizes the impact of international politics on students' own lives and interests, instructors are always encouraged to show how the material in the text chapter relates to current issues or recent events.

Study and Exam Questions.   These questions are designed to encourage students to develop their own interpretations for, and demonstrate their understanding of, the facts and concepts presented in the text chapter. These questions may be handed out as study guides before tests, employed as discussion topics for review sessions, or used as substantial essay questions (to be answered in one hour or more) on exams.

The learning objectives given in *What Students Should Learn from This Chapter* may be used as a basis for evaluating students' answers to these questions, but the questions are intended to be broad enough for instructors to employ whatever grading criteria they deem appropriate. Because introductory courses should require students to become familiar with a wide range of basic facts and ideas, it is recommended that several short-answer or identification questions (covering material outlined in the *Terms and Concepts* section) be included on exams along with these longer essay questions.

Recommended Enrichment Readings.   No attempt is made in these sections to present a comprehensive review of literature on any topic covered in the text. Instead, these brief annotated bibliographies concentrate on materials that can best guide undergraduates' further exploration of key events and ideas. Likewise, inclusion of a work in these sections does not necessarily indicate its status as a "definitive" work on any topic. These recommended readings should therefore be considered the "next step," rather than the "last word," in the investigation of their subjects. Works with topics, lengths, and approaches that make them especially appropriate for assignment as supplementary course readings are indicated with a bullet (•).

Naturally, instructors should feel free to pick and choose from the suggestions and recommendations in each chapter of this manual. Taken separately or as a whole, they can be used to tailor courses utilizing *World Politics in a New Era* according to institutional requirements, varying levels of students' background knowledge, and instructors' interests and priorities.

This brings up an important point. An introductory course must be basic, in that it must present the fundamental principles of an area of knowledge, but it does not have to be either simple or easy. Grasping the basic elements of any field can be quite challenging, and describing these elements and evaluating students on their knowledge of them is often an even greater challenge. The authors hope that this manual will encourage instructors to make their introductory courses in international relations challenging and rewarding experience for both teacher and students.

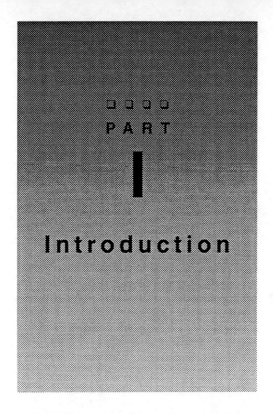

□ □ □ □
PART

I

Introduction

CHAPTER 1
World Affairs in Our Lives

World Affairs in Our Lives

SCOPE, OBJECTIVES, AND APPROACH

This chapter tells students why they should take an active interest in global politics and introduces some of the basic concepts they will need to begin their study of global affairs. Its premise is that world politics is a dynamic process that affects us every day and will have an even greater impact on our lives and careers in the future. The chapter is designed to bring the complex and often abstract "high politics" of international relations "down to earth."

The chapter uses examples from popular culture (music, films, etc.) to illustrate the generalizations and assumptions that many people use to form their views on international issues. It then gives students a first glance at the conceptual tools required for serious study of global politics, including anarchy, the nation-state, the security dilemma, and levels of analysis. These concepts are not explained in detail, but presented briefly so that students will be more familiar with them when they are examined in depth in later chapters. Next, it outlines some controversies that frequently recur in debates over global issues and foreign policy, including the conflicts between realism and idealism and between internationalism and isolationism. Finally, in outlining the organizational plan of the book, it describes the two dialectic processes that serve as the underlying themes of the text: cooperation versus conflict and globalization versus fragmentation.

WHAT STUDENTS SHOULD LEARN FROM THIS CHAPTER

N.B.: Because Chapter One introduces many concepts that will be discussed in detail later, many of the learning objectives for this chapter are necessarily less specific than those of subsequent chapters. In general, students should be able to identify the basic themes and concepts presented briefly in the chapter and relate them to contemporary international events and trends.

Foundation Level

1. Identify ways in which international events, trade, issues, trends, and problems affect the student's own life.
2. Explain the contrasts between the "It's a Small World after All" and "Star Wars" views of world politics and identify examples of each from speeches or writings of contemporary public figures.
3. Explain the fundamental differences between an anarchic political system (such as the international system) and one governed by a legitimate authority (as in most domestic political systems).
4. Define nation-states, intergovernmental organizations (IGOs), and nongovernmental organizations (NGOs) and give examples of each.
5. Outline the basic controversies between these sets of contending perspectives on international affairs:
   a. idealism versus realism
   b. internationalism versus isolationism
   c. free trade versus protectionism
   d. capitalism versus socialism
6. Identify and give contemporary examples of these opposing trends in international relations:
   a. globalization versus fragmentation
   b. cooperation versus conflict

Enrichment Level

1. Identify global political, economic, or environmental trends that are likely to have increasing effects on the student's life in the foreseeable future.
2. Explain how either popular images of world politics—"It's a Small World after All" and "Star Wars"—could promote both cooperation and conflict among states and give examples. Give historical examples of leaders who appear to have held one of these images.
3. Explain ways in which the international system is not entirely anarchic, and ways in which domestic politics is not always governed by law and authority.
4. Give concrete examples of actions by international organizations and nongovernmental organizations on specific issues. Identify ways in which some of these groups have attempted to influence state policy.
5. Give historical examples of how each of the four major controversies outlined in the chapter have influenced foreign policy debates in the United States or other states.
6. Using historical or contemporary examples, explain how a state or region could simultaneously experience either globalization and fragmentation or cooperation and conflict.

Mastery Level

1. Explain why the lives of people living in different parts of the world may experience varying degrees of "internationalization." Identify trends that (a) primarily affect residents of industrialized countries, (b) have a stronger impact on people in developing states, and (c) affect everyone more or less equally.
2. Explain how popular images of world politics are formed and perpetuated. Identify other images that have been expressed in culture or held by individual leaders.
3. Identify both regional subsystems of the international system that are less anarchic than the system as a whole and the institutions that maintain order in these regional subsystems.

4. Identify types of governmental and non-state actors that might be expected to play a greater role in the international system in the future, as well as types whose role and influence could be expected to decline.

5. Outline issues that typically prompt conflict among developed states, among developing countries, and between the industrialized states and the developing world.

6. Using recent events, conflicts, treaties, or debates as examples, identify which positions on the four major controversies appear to be gaining strength in contemporary international politics and which seem to be declining.

7. Identify social, political, economic, or technological developments that are likely to accelerate or slow the processes of globalization, fragmentation, cooperation, and conflict.

OUTLINE OF THE CHAPTER

0. Introduction

   Our individual lives are becoming increasingly "internationalized" due to global trade, communications, and cultural exchange.

I. Popular Images of World Politics

   A. Two basic views of the nature of international relations are prevalent in popular culture: the *"It's a Small World after All"* view and the *"Star Wars"* perspective.

   B. "It's a Small World after All" is one view.

      1. The "normal" condition of the world is one of harmony and accord.

      2. The primary cause of conflict is misunderstanding.

      3. Conflicts and disputes are superficial anomalies that can be resolved amicably if the parties become able to communicate effectively.

      4. Humanitarian organizations typically espouse this view when they act to relieve suffering.

   C. "Star Wars" is another view.

      1. World politics is fundamentally a struggle between good and evil.

      2. Conflicts are created when evil states or leaders attempt aggression against weaker nations.

      3. Good states must oppose evil states and regimes in order to survive and preserve their values.

      4. President Ronald Reagan espoused this view when he called the Soviet Union the "Evil Empire."

II. Anarchy versus Authority

   A. International politics takes place in an environment of *anarchy*.

      1. There is no higher authority that governs the behavior of states.

      2. States make their own rules of behavior and are responsible for their own security—"every state for itself."

      3. This anarchic environment corresponds to that of the jungle, where the strong prey upon the weak—"kill or be killed."

   B. World politics thus fundamentally differs from domestic politics, which takes place in an environment of *authority*.

      1. In national political systems, order is created by laws and authorities who enforce those laws.

      2. This environment resembles that of the football field, where competition between teams is regulated by rules enforced by referees.

   C. Even in the anarchic international system, however, rules and norms of behavior exist.

      1. For example, most states consider aggression against other nations to be "against the rules" of world politics.

      2. Nations, groups of nations, or organizations such as the United Nations may attempt to enforce these rules.

      3. Enforcement, though it can be effective (as was the U.S.-led coalition's reaction against Iraq's invasion of Kuwait in 1990–91), is usually ad hoc, and violations are often subjective (aggression is in the eye of the beholder).

      4. Thus, international action against aggression often resembles "vigilante justice"—reactive, unreliable, and often hurting the innocent in attempts to punish the guilty.

   D. States have a security dilemma.

      1. The *security dilemma*, a major factor in international relations, is a consequence of the anarchy of the international system.

2. The security dilemma arises when one state, responding to demonstrated, perceived, or potential threats, decides to increase its military strength to safeguard its own security.
3. This action, however, typically makes neighboring states feel less secure and prompts them to respond in kind, creating an upward spiral of military preparations or arms race.
4. The security dilemma can, and frequently does, occur even if none of the involved states actually intends to threaten its neighbors; thus, it explains how conflicts can arise even in the absence of hostile intent.
   a. Commonly cited examples include the Cold War between the United States and the Soviet Union, 1945–90, and the Arab–Israeli disputes after World War II.
   b. Of course, in these and other conflicts, many (especially those with a "Star Wars" orientation who view world politics as a struggle between good and evil) believed that one or both parties caught in the security dilemma actually harbored aggressive intentions toward its adversaries.
5. The security dilemma helps explain why "good" states often believe that they must resort to intrigue, deceit, and force in order to survive or prevail against evil.

E. Cooperation under Anarchy
   1. Even in an anarchic world, there is far more cooperation than conflict among nations.
   2. States pursue their common interests through trade, diplomatic contact, and *reciprocity* ("Do unto others as you would have them do unto you").
   3. States can also cooperate to solve common problems, such as environmental degradation.
   4. Thus, though the anarchic nature of world politics encourages conflict, common interests and problems facilitate cooperation enforced by reciprocal compliance.

III. Cooperation versus Conflict
   A. Cooperation and conflict in the international system are frequently intertwined; states often cooperate in one area while conflicting in others.
   B. *Interdependence* arises out of the increasing level of interaction between states.
      1. States depend upon one another for goods, resources, services, investment, and markets; no state produces everything it needs.
      2. Problems that affect neighboring states or the entire international community, such as pollution, migration, terrorism, and global climate change, also increase states' dependence upon one another.

IV. Domestic Factors in International Relations
   A. States' actions toward other states are frequently constrained by domestic concerns, including internal politics and public opinion. Examples include pacifism in Britain and France prior to WWII and opposition to the Vietnam War in the United States.
   B. These constraints may increase as telecommunications make it easier for citizens to obtain information on their governments' policies (even in authoritarian states) and on events and conditions in other countries. Examples include television coverage of the Vietnam and Persian Gulf Wars and the Tiananmen Square protests and massacre in China.

V. Who Participates in International Politics?
   A. The primary type of actor in contemporary world politics is the *nation-state*.
      1. The nation-state is a comparatively recent (rooted in the American and French Revolutions of the late eighteenth century) fusion of the concepts of nation and state.
         a. A *state* is an independent political entity with governing institutions and authority over a specific territory.
         b. A *nation* is a group of people who have a sense of mutual identification based on language, history, and culture and who believe they possess a common heritage and destiny.
         c. Ideally, a nation-state is a state structure that exists to protect and promote the interests of a single nation; among existing states, in 1994, France, Germany, Turkey, and Japan approach this ideal.
      2. *Nationalism* is the belief that each nation should have its own state.
      3. Historically, nationalism has given rise to many conflicts when nations (such as Greece, Poland, and Croatia) attempted to obtain their own states and when states such as Germany, North Korea, and Serbia sought to unify all members of a nation.
   B. Nevertheless, various types of *non-state actors* are becoming increasingly important in world politics.
      1. *Intergovernmental organizations* (IGOs) are groups of states or government agencies organized for a common purpose.

a. International organizations are IGOs that provide a diplomatic and legal framework for interaction between member states (examples: the United Nations [UN] and the Organization of Petroleum Exporting Countries [OPEC]).
b. Other IGOs facilitate cooperation among governments on specific issues (examples: the World Health Organization [WHO] and the International Atomic Energy Agency [IAEA]).
2. *Nongovernmental organizations* (NGOs) are groups independent of or organized outside of governments.
a. *Multinational corporations* (MNCs) are companies with offices, assets, and production and sales facilities in several states (examples: IBM, Exxon, Volkswagen, the Mitsubishi Group).
b. *Humanitarian and special-interest groups* seek to promote some common good in many states (examples: Greenpeace, Amnesty International, the Red Cross).
c. *Media organizations* report on issues, events, and problems worldwide (examples: Cable News Network [CNN] and Independent Television News [ITN]).
d. *Terrorist groups* use violence and terror (often against civilians) to achieve political objectives.
   i. Some political organizations include elements or member groups that use terror (example: the Irish Republican Army [IRA]).
   ii. Others depend primarily or exclusively on terrorist action (example: the Popular Front for the Liberation of Palestine–General Command).
   iii. The difference between terrorism and heroic resistance to a foreign occupier, however, is often a matter of perspective, as one side's "terrorists" may be another's "freedom fighters" (example: the Contras, who fought against the Sandinista regime in Nicaragua in the 1980s).

VI. Levels of Analysis in International Relations
  A. The multitude of factors influencing world politics may be grouped into *levels of analysis*.
    1. These levels may be thought of as categories of variables or theories attempting to explain actions and conflicts.
    2. Different sources use different levels of analysis, but this book finds it most useful to consider three: the systemic, domestic, and individual levels (see "At a Glance" box, p. 19)
  B. The *international systemic* (or just *systemic*) level examines factors related to the interactions and relationships among states.
    1. Explanations from the systemic level contend that all states are essentially similar, are motivated by the situations in which they find themselves, and react to similar situations in similar ways.
    2. This level considers factors such as relative military strength, GNP, and the number of major powers in the international system as the main influences on state behavior.
    3. Systemic level explanations that will be discussed in Chapter Twelve include balance of power theory, the security dilemma, and theories of hegemonic stability.
  C. The *domestic* level of analysis examines factors that operate within states.
    1. This level considers each state as unique, with its own distinctive history, culture, interests, and political system.
    2. Factors considered at this level include a state's form of government, political institutions, ideology, economic structure, and public opinion.
    3. Domestic level explanations summarized in Chapter Twelve include theories of peace among democratic states, bureaucratic politics, and product cycles.
  D. The *individual* level considers people and the decisions they make as the most important explanations for international events.
    1. Factors considered at the individual level include personal experience and belief systems, gender, generational experience, leadership style, interpersonal relationships, and individual goals and values.
    2. Theories of state action from the individual level, examined in Chapter Twelve, include attribution theory, the operational code, crisis decision making, and coalition building.
  E. The three levels of analysis provide an organizational scheme for theories of international relations; they help analysts formulate and test explanations for the behavior of states, non-state actors, and individuals.

VII. Themes and Controversies
  A. History of Controversy
    1. The history of world politics shows that several major controversies seem to recur.
    2. These controversies reflect important debates about the nature of the international system and how states should act within it.

B. Realism versus Idealism
    1. *Realists* believe that in the anarchic international system, states have no choice but to "look out for number one" and increase their power in order to protect their own independence, security, and vital interests; courses of action advocated from this position are often referred to as *realpolitik* (literally "policy of realism").
    2. *Idealists* believe that the security dilemma may be overcome, that interdependence makes it necessary and possible for states to cooperate, and that even if human nature and the structure of the international system lead to recurrent conflict, it may be possible to reform either or both to decrease conflict and promote cooperation.

C. Internationalism versus Isolationism
    1. *Internationalists* contend that states have no choice but actively to participate in world politics to pursue their vital interests; problems in one part of the globe, if left unchecked, will spread to other regions.
    2. *Isolationists* counter that because the world is complex and unpredictable, taking action within the international system is inherently risky; states are thus better advised to follow a policy of "live and let live," concentrating on solving their own problems and improving the welfare of their own citizens.

D. Free Trade versus Protectionism
    1. Advocates of *free trade* contend that free flow of goods, services, labor, and resources allows all states to maximize their economic efficiency through the free market and makes everyone better off.
    2. Supporters of *protectionism* or *managed trade* argue that unrestricted trade allows predatory states or companies to drive competitors out of business and thus dominate the market; thus, trade barriers are necessary to protect domestic industries and jobs.

E. Capitalism versus Socialism
    1. *Capitalists* argue that means of production of goods and services should be owned privately, because private enterprise maximizes productivity; the free market will let more efficient producers earn greater profits by minimizing prices and maximizing quality to the benefit of producers and consumers alike.
    2. *Socialists* contend that productive assets should be owned collectively (usually by the state) in order to maximize the social benefits of production; a more equal distribution of wealth should be sought, and economic rewards should be allocated according to "human need, not corporate greed."

VIII. The Contemporary International Arena: Globalization and Fragmentation
A. Many economic, political, and technological developments are drawing distant parts of the world closer together and increasing the interdependence of states; this trend may be termed *globalization*.
    1. Direct-dial telephones, satellite television, and global computer networks make international communication direct and practically instantaneous.
    2. The volume of trade and financial flows is increasing at a rapid rate.
    3. Political, economic, and environmental problems spread across borders easier than ever before (examples: acid rain, terrorism, narcotics traffic).
    4. International organizations such as the UN and the European Union are increasing their activities and influence.

B. At the same time, however, state structures of authority are collapsing or being eroded in many parts of the world, and groups are asserting their identity and autonomy; this creates a process of *fragmentation*.
    1. States such as Yugoslavia and the Soviet Union have collapsed entirely, and other states (including Canada and India) are becoming increasingly vulnerable to peaceful or violent divisions.
    2. Demands for regional and cultural autonomy are increasing (examples: Scotland, Catalonia [in Spain], federalist movements in Italy, many regions within Russia).
    3. To some degree, these demands for autonomy and assertions of identity may be reactions against globalization; individuals and groups resist the possibility of homogenization.

C. Globalization and fragmentation are thus concurrent, opposing processes likely to characterize world politics in the new era; likewise, cooperation and conflict will continue to coexist.

HOW THE CHAPTER RELATES TO CENTRAL THEMES OF THE TEXT

Chapter One introduces students to the themes of globalization versus fragmentation and cooperation versus conflict and explains how these processes can occur simultaneously. In its conclusion, it lays out the organizational plan of the text and describes how the "building-block" approach is designed to help students see how the central themes recur both historically and in many aspects of international relations. It also outlines some key concepts in international relations theory—anarchy, the security dilemma, and levels of analysis—that will be discussed in detail in later chapters. The introductory chapter gives students a brief "first glance" at the main themes of the text, so that students can be "on the lookout" for them in the coming chapters and will be more familiar with them when they are considered in depth.

SUGGESTED LECTURE TOPICS

1. Summarize the direct and indirect repercussions of a recent major international event to show how global affairs affect students' lives in ways they might not realize; then use a familiar object whose design, marketing, and manufacture involves several different countries—a compact disk or item of fashionable clothing, for example—to illustrate cultural and economic globalization.
2. Quote from historical figures (Woodrow Wilson, Bertrand Russell, Lenin, Churchill, Gandhi, Truman, etc.) to show how popular images of world politics are reflected in political rhetoric; then compare leaders' rhetoric to the policies they actually carried out to assess how strongly belief systems or worldviews are connected with foreign policy.
3. Compare how a specific problem (such as toxic chemical or sewage spills, gang violence, or inflation) is handled in domestic and international contexts to highlight the differences between anarchy and authority. (For example, compare how governments and police deal with gang violence in American inner cities with the policy responses considered and applied to the Bosnian civil war. This comparison, in particular, may show that the presence of authority does not ensure that a problem will be solved and that tradeoffs between independence and security exist at both the national and international levels.)
4. Use a daily newspaper to show how some small states receive substantial media attention, while events in larger states are comparatively ignored. (For example, count the number of stories or column-inches devoted to events in Israel and compare this with a similar count for India, or compare Britain and Brazil in the same manner.) Solicit explanations for this disparity from students to begin a discussion of how economic power and cultural affinity affect media attention or public opinion.
5. Use quotations from noted leaders to illustrate how the controversies in world affairs have raged for centuries. Possible exemplars of each position might include the following:

Realism:	Theodore Roosevelt
Idealism:	Woodrow Wilson
Internationalism:	John F. Kennedy
Isolationism:	George Washington
Free Trade:	Grover Cleveland
	Ronald Reagan
	Bill Clinton
Protectionism:	Alexander Hamilton
	William McKinley
	Richard Gephardt
Capitalism:	Margaret Thatcher
Socialism:	Tony Benn

6. Use the examples of UN action in Cambodia, Bosnia, and Somalia in the early 1990s to show how globalization and fragmentation can occur simultaneously and how the end of the Cold War has accelerated both processes.

STUDY AND EXAM QUESTIONS

1. Which perspective on world politics has had more influence on U.S. foreign policy since 1990, the "It's a Small World after All" view or the "Star Wars" view? Use three events or policies as examples in support of your answer.
2. Identify a contemporary political, economic, technological, or social development that heightens *both* cooperation and conflict in the international system. Show how this development has simultaneously promoted cooperation and conflict in two separate instances.

3. Which trend in world politics is likely to gain strength in the near future—globalization or fragmentation? Give three examples of events or processes that show why one trend or the other is more likely to prevail.
4. Identify three positive and three negative aspects of the internationalization of your own life. Would you prefer your life to become more globalized in the future, or less so? Why?

RECOMMENDED ENRICHMENT READINGS

- Barber, Benjamin R. "Jihad vs. McWorld." *Atlantic Monthly,* March 1992, 53–62. A good survey of the contending processes of globalization and fragmentation.

Brown, Seyom. *New Forces, Old Forces, and the Future of World Politics.* Glenview, Ill.: Scott, Foresman, 1988. A somewhat dated but still valuable examination of the changing nature of world politics.

Bull, Hedley. *The Anarchical Society.* New York: Columbia University Press, 1977. Examines how the "rules of the game" of world politics developed.

Herz, John H. *Political Realism and Political Idealism.* Chicago: University of Chicago Press, 1951. Classic study of the realism versus idealism debate and of the role of morality in world affairs.

- Kaplan, Robert D. "The Coming Anarchy," *Atlantic Monthly*, February 1994, 44–76. Thought-provoking and sometimes shocking (though not sensationalistic) description of fragmentation in the developing world. Contains graphic illustrations.

Keohane, Robert O., and Joseph Nye. *Power and Interdependence.* 2nd ed. Glenview, Ill.: Scott, Foresman, 1988. Considers the complex relationship between power politics and globalization.

- Ohmae, Kenichi. "Rise of the Region State." *Foreign Affairs* 72, no. 2 (spring 1993): 78–87. Interesting essay on economic globalization.

Osgood, Robert E. *Ideals and Self-Interest in America's Foreign Relations.* Chicago: University of Chicago Press, 1953. Another classic exploration of the tensions between idealism and realism.

Oye, Kenneth A., ed. *Cooperation under Anarchy.* Princeton: Princeton University Press, 1986. A collection of essays that address how cooperation between states can occur in the anarchic environment of the international system.

Snyder, Jack. "Averting Anarchy in the New Europe." *International Security* 14, no. 4 (spring 1990): 5–41. Suggests that Europe may have to move further in the direction of globalization in order to avert dangerous forms of fragmentation.

Waltz, Kenneth N. *Man, the State, and War: A Theoretical Analysis.* New York: Columbia University Press, 1959. Masterful, pioneering use of levels of analysis to examine the causes of conflict and cooperation. Very readable and highly recommended.

□ □ □ □
PART

II

The History of World Politics

Origins of the Modern International System

SCOPE, OBJECTIVES, AND APPROACH

This chapter begins a three-part survey of the history of world politics by tracing the beginnings and early development of the modern international system. It covers the period from 1648, when the idea of the sovereign state gained recognition in international law, to 1890, when Bismarck's system of strategic alliances between the European powers was on the verge of breaking down. Because the text uses history as a "building block" for the study of contemporary international relations, the chapter pays more attention to developments that set the stage for present-day conflicts; therefore, a good deal of the chapter is devoted to the rise of nationalism in the nineteenth century.

Chapter Two does not pretend to be a comprehensive history of world politics during the 250-plus years it covers. Instead, it traces the historical roots of important legal, political, and cultural concepts shaping modern world politics, including the sovereign state, nationalism, collective security, and international organizations. It also outlines the impact of major historical events and processes, such as the French Revolution and the Industrial Revolution, which dramatically changed the nature of world politics and continue to have repercussions to this day.

WHAT STUDENTS SHOULD LEARN FROM THIS CHAPTER

Foundation Level

1. Define the concept of state sovereignty and explain its codification in the Peace of Westphalia.
2. Identify the European Great Powers of the eighteenth century and list the defining characteristics of international politics in that era (diplomacy among monarchies, frequent but limited wars, action by the European great powers to prevent French hegemony).
3. Outline the major changes in world politics resulting from the French Revolution and Napoleonic Wars (spread of liberalism and nationalism, establishment of the Concert of Europe).
4. List the major developments in international relations during the "long peace" of the ninetheenth century (absence of major wars between the great powers, breakdown of the Ottoman Empire and weakening of the Russian and Austrian Empires, unification of Italy and Germany) and identify the major powers of that period.
5. Outline the major changes wrought on world politics by the Industrial Revolution (mass production and economic globalization, growth of cities, dramatic improvement of communication and transportation, increases in the mobility of military forces and lethality of weaponry).
6. Explain the strategic concepts underlying Bismarck's system of alliances and identify the major reasons for the system's decline (opposition between monarchy and liberalism; nationalist conflicts in Central, Eastern, and Southern Europe; increasing competition among the Great Powers; domestic politics in Germany).

Enrichment Level

1. Explain the major differences between the sovereign state and pre-Westphalian forms of political authority.
2. Describe how similarities in the domestic political and social structures of the Great Powers contributed to the exercise of diplomacy and the limitation of conflict in the eighteenth century.
3. Explain why the French Revolution was so threatening to the conservative monarchies at the end of the eighteenth century and beginning of the nineteenth.
4. Identify the membership and goals of the Concert of Europe and describe how it attempted to limit conflict in the nineteenth century.
5. Explain how the Industrial Revolution accelerated economic globalization and how nationalism heightened political fragmentation.
6. Describe how Bismarck's alliance system attempted to maintain the balance of power in Europe.

Mastery Level

1. Explain how state sovereignty and collective security affect conflict and cooperation in contemporary world politics.
2. Identify the impact of the "world wars" of the eighteenth century and the American Revolution on the balance of power in Europe.
3. Identify the main reasons for France's early successes and ultimate defeat in the Napoleonic Wars.
4. List the main institutional weaknesses of the Concert of Europe and give examples of how these weaknesses prevented the concert from acting effectively to prevent conflicts.
5. Explain how the industrial revolution heightened the security dilemma for many of the European Great Powers.
6. Describe the successes and failures of the revolutions of 1848.
7. Explain the political and military strategies used to accomplish the unification of Germany (harnessing of nationalism in support of traditional *realpolitik* goals, exclusion of Austria, isolation of France, use of industrial-age military technology to achieve rapid victories).

OUTLINE OF THE CHAPTER

0. Introduction
   A. Chapter Two traces the origins and development of the modern international system and its major elements:
      1. The sovereign nation-state
      2. The Great Powers
      3. The balance of power
      4. Collective security
      5. Nationalism
   B. Because these elements originated in Europe and later spread throughout the world, the chapter concentrates on Europe. This is not to suggest that European institutions and ideas were inherently superior, but does recognize their historical importance and lasting influence.

I. Politics before Nations
   A. Before the seventeenth century, political entities were defined by ruling elites and/or religion.
      1. Political units were either city-states, feudal lordships, dynastic kingdoms, or religious empires (including the Muslim Caliphate and the Holy Roman Empire).
      2. Leaders usually based their authority on tradition, force, or religious sanction (cf. Macchiavelli).
      3. As the concept of state sovereignty (q.v.) was not yet established, rulers had to constantly defend their authority from dynastic rivals and domestic and foreign challengers (as Shakespeare depicted in *Richard III* and *Henry V*).
      4. Trade was important, but risky; commerce was often subject to piracy, blockade, or capricious tariffs and taxation.
   B. In the absence of enforceable international law or treaties, trade and relations among rulers were generally unpredictable and fragmented.

II. Thirty Years' War and Peace of Westphalia
   A. After the Reformation challenged papal authority over Western Christianity (beginning in the fifteenth century), many European rulers (such as Henry VIII) broke away from the political and religious authority of the Holy Roman Empire.
   B. These challenges to the Empire culminated in the Thirty Years' War (1618–48), a complex and wide-ranging conflict devastating Europe.
   C. The Thirty Years' War ended with the *Peace of Westphalia* (1648), which established the principles of *sovereignty* and *collective security* in international law.
      1. *Sovereignty* means political independence and ultimate legal authority over internal affairs; Westphalia recognized that this rested with secular rulers rather than with the Pope, the Church, or the Holy Roman Empire.
      2. *Collective security* is the principle that states should unite in opposition to blatant aggression by one state against another.
      3. These principles remain key features of the contemporary international system.
         a. Collective security and the restoration of Kuwait's sovereignty were used to justify the U.S.-led coalition's military operations against Iraq in the Persian Gulf War in 1990–91.
         b. However, while the UN authorized the use of force to oppose Iraq's aggression against Kuwait, it refused to violate Iraq's sovereignty by sanctioning intervention into Iraq's domestic affairs.
   D. The contradictions between sovereignty and collective security became immediately apparent, however.
      1. In an anarchic system of sovereign states, conflicts of interest and shifts of alliances are practically inevitable.
      2. Objective determination of aggression and achievement of consensus to enforce collective security are inherently difficult in such a system.

III. Origins of European Imperialism
   A. *Imperialism* is a process of extending a nation's authority by territorial acquisition or by the establishment of political and economic hegemony over other nations.
   B. Although empires had risen and fallen since ancient times, the various regions of the world were relatively isolated from one another by vast mountain ranges, oceans, and deserts; European expansion started the globalization of the modern world.

C. Spanish and Portuguese colonial expansion began in the late fifteenth century, as Portuguese rulers strove to establish trade routes to Asia that circumvented the Ottoman Empire.

1. Portuguese technological advances and European military power provided the means of transportation, defense, and conquest.

2. Spanish and Portuguese explorers developed new trade routes to Asia and Africa.

D. Spain and Portugal agree to the Treaty of Tordesillas in 1494, which purported to divide up the world; this established Spanish authority in the New World except for what is now Brazil and for Portuguese control of Africa and the Indian Ocean.

E. Spanish conquest of the Aztec and Inca Empires in the early sixteenth century provided massive riches for the Spanish crown, but also resulted in the subjugation and near extinction of indigenous peoples.

F. Spain was the most powerful state in sixteenth-century Europe, but after a failed attempt to conquer England in 1588 it began a rapid decline; Portugal and Holland could not defend their colonial outposts; by 1700, Britain and France emerged as the leading colonial powers.

G. Britain possessed domestic and geographic advantages over France in their colonial competition, which became a driving force in world politics in the eighteenth century.

IV. Eighteenth-Century Europe

A. Characteristics of International Politics in the Eighteenth Century

1. *Multipolarity* is a condition where many *Great Powers* contended for leadership (for more on this subject, see Chapter Twelve).

2. Monarchies existed.

a. Social stratification heightened the distance between rulers (kings, landed aristocracy, and upper levels of the religious establishment) and ruled; world politics was the province of the ruling class.

b. Rulers had a great deal in common with one another (all spoke French, and many were related), which facilitated diplomacy.

c. The lack of centralized, efficient institutions for assessing and levying taxes, the weakness or absence of democratic institutions, and the fact that in many cases taxes on peasant farmers could be paid only in kind (i.e., in grain or livestock) rather than money, severely limited states' abilities to raise revenues.

3. There were limitations on war making.

a. Armies were expensive to raise, equip, and supply, so most states could not carry out protracted wars.

b. Rulers relied heavily on *mercenaries* (hired professional soldiers, usually foreign), often of dubious reliability.

4. As a result, states fought often, but wars were usually limited in duration, geographic scope, and objectives; similar cultural backgrounds of rules and a common interest in preserving the institution of the monarchy facilitated peacemaking once the limited objectives of war were achieved.

B. The Great Powers

1. The requirements for Great Power status have always been imprecisely defined, but in general *great powers* are economically and militarily strong states that do not depend on other states for their security; they are the major "players" in the "game" of international politics.

2. The ranks of the European Great Powers changed over time (Sweden dropped out in the early eighteenth century, for example, while Russia achieved Great Power status in the same period), but throughout the eighteenth century France, England, Austria, Russia, Prussia, and the Ottoman Empire were recognized as Great Powers.

3. The interests of the Great Powers frequently conflicted, but most sought to prevent any single power (usually France, which was the strongest Great Power for most of the century) from dominating the European system.

4. Therefore, the Great Powers entered into many shifting alliances to preserve the *balance of power*—that is, to prevent one state from becoming dominant.

C. "World Wars" of the Eighteenth Century

1. While most wars of this period were limited in scope (see above), three major conflicts in the eighteenth century included significant fighting within Europe and combat in the European powers colonial empires (see Chapter Five) in Asia, Africa, and North and South America.

2. In the War of the Spanish Succession (1702–13), the "Grand Alliance" of Austria, England, and the Netherlands prevented an attempt by France's King Louis XIV to establish French domination over Spain.

3. The War of the Austrian Succession (1740–48) saw France and Spain support a successful attempt by King Frederick II ("the Great") of Prussia to take Silesia from Austria, which was backed by England.

4. In the Seven Years' War (1756–63), Austria, France, and Russia opposed England and Prussia.
   a. Though surrounded by enemies in continental Europe, superior military organization and Frederick the Great's leadership allowed Prussia to fight its adversaries to a standstill.
   b. Meanwhile, England and France fought for each other's colonies in North America, the West Indies, and India.
   c. England gained vast territories in North America (including Canada) and established its domination of India as a result of the war, but both England and France ran up huge war debts in the process.
D. Aftermath of War and Prelude to Revolution
   1. Both England and France had to raise taxes dramatically and look for new revenues to finance the massive debts accumulated during the Seven Years' War.
   2. Attempts to raise extra revenues prompted Britain's American colonies to revolt over "taxation without representation"; in the American Revolution (1776–83), the colonies won their independence as the United States of America with French support.
   3. France, however, continued to face a political and financial crisis as a result of its war debts.

V. French Revolution and Napoleonic Wars
A. The French Revolution
   1. The *French Revolution* (1789–93) toppled the French monarchy and struck terror in the crowned heads of Europe.
   2. The revolution, inspired in large part by the philosophies of the Enlightenment, promoted two ideologies:
      a. *Nationalism* held that each nation (see Chapter One) should have its own independent state; it focused popular loyalty on the nation rather than the monarch.
      b. *Liberalism* argued that the power of government should be vested in citizens, not monarchs, and that government should allow individuals more freedom and responsibility over their own thoughts and actions.
   3. The French Revolution created a new security dilemma in Europe: The success of the Revolution, with its slogan of *liberté, égalité, fraternité* (liberty, equality, brotherhood), and the ideologies it promoted threatened European monarchs; France feared that the monarchs would attempt counterrevolutionary intervention.
   4. To defend France and spread revolution throughout Europe, the radical French regime raised an army of conscripts owing loyalty to the nation rather to a king (the *levée en masse*).
   5. Revolutionary turmoil in France allowed the capable and ambitious Napoleon Bonaparte to seize dictatorial power in 1799 and have himself crowned Emperor of the French in 1804.
B. The Napoleonic Era
   1. Under Napoleon's rule, France attained temporary domination of Europe with a series of stunning military victories, establishing liberal institutions in the countries it controlled.
   2. By 1810, France controlled Spain, the Netherlands, Switzerland, Poland, and most of Germany and Italy and was allied with Austria, Prussia, and Denmark, but was opposed by Britain, which established control of the seas after the naval battle of Trafalgar (1805).
   3. The Napoleonic social and political institutions established in French satellites greatly increased the efficiency of government and government's responsiveness to broader segments of society; Napoleon was revered by many, and reviled by many others, throughout Europe.
   4. Napoleonic warfare, fought to establish nations and topple monarchies, was far more costly and destructive than the limited warfare of the eighteenth century; huge armies of millions of soldiers were mobilized, and decisive battles of 500,000 or more troops caused casualties and devastation on a scale unseen since the Thirty Years' War.
C. Napoleon's Downfall
   1. Three factors led to the breakdown of the French Empire and Napoleon's eventual defeat:
      a. The Continental System (Napoleon's embargo on trade with Britain) alienated many French-controlled and allied states that profited from trade with England and its colonies.
      b. The Peninsular War (1808–14), which resulted from Napoleon's attempt to control Spain, drained French manpower and material resources in a protracted struggle with popular resistance fighters *(guerrillas)*.
      c. Napoleon's ill-advised invasion of Russia (1812) overextended French forces in a disastrous campaign.
   2. Britain, Austria, Prussia, and Russia united to defeat France and force Napoleon to abdicate in 1814; Napoleon returned from exile to lead France once again in 1815, but was defeated by British, Prussian, and Dutch forces at the battle of Waterloo.

D. Napoleon's Legacy
  1. Napoleon inspired works by creative geniuses for generations to come (including Beethoven and Tolstoy), as well as influencing legal and governing systems all over the world.
  2. During the Napoleonic Era much of Latin America achieved independence.

VI. The Concert of Europe
  A. The Congress of Vienna
    1. After Napoleon's defeat in 1814, representatives of the Great Powers (Castlereagh of Britain, Tsar Alexander I of Russia, King Frederick William III of Prussia, France's Talleyrand, and Austria's Prince Metternich, who was the most active and influential negotiator) gathered in Vienna to restore Europe to "normalcy" (i.e., to reestablish the monarchical system existing before the French Revolution).
    2. The Congress adopted the following provisions in an attempt to preserve peace and the balance of power in Europe:
      a. The French monarchy was restored, and France was forced to pay indemnities to the victors.
      b. Neutral buffer states (especially Switzerland) were established to contain future French expansion.
      c. Territorial changes were made throughout Europe, mostly in favor of Prussia and Russia.
      d. The *Concert of Europe* (see below) was established to promote cooperation between the Great Powers against future threats.
  B. The Concert of Europe
    1. France, Britain, Austria, Russia, and Prussia agreed to meet periodically to review European affairs and hold special consultations to manage crises.
    2. The Concert was based on the principle of collective security—that is, the Great Powers were formally committed to unite against aggression.
    3. The main goals of the congress were to maintain the political status quo against the threat of revolution and nationalism and preserve the strategic balance of power in Europe.
    4. From the outset, however, the Congress was shackled with inherent weaknesses:
      a. *Realpolitik* conflicts among the Great Powers continued, undermining the principle of collective security.
      b. Britain, with its strong democratic institutions and emerging liberal views on trade and human rights, disagreed with the goal of the conservative powers (Austria, Prussia, and Russia) to suppress liberalism and nationalism.
      c. The Concert had no effective means of enforcing cooperation among the Great Powers.

VII. Stability and Change in the Nineteenth Century
  A. Nationalism in New Europe
    1. Nationalism posed a threat to the stability of Europe throughout the nineteenth century; the belief that each nation should have its own state threatened the multinational empires (Austria, Russia, and the Ottoman Empire) most acutely.
    2. Some nationalist issues were resolved peacefully (examples: Belgian independence from the Netherlands in 1830, Norwegian independence from Sweden in 1905); other nationalist movements, however, threatened the territorial integrity of the multinational Great Powers.
    3. Nationalism could be a force for unification (as in Germany and Italy) as well as separatism and fragmentation, but both forms threatened the security of the continental Great Powers.
  B. Disharmony in the Concert
    1. The years 1815–1914 were an unprecedented era of peace in European history; wars continued to be fought, but they were limited both in duration and geographic scope.
    2. The conflict management system of the Concert of Europe thus enjoyed some success, but the inherent tension between the principle of collective security and the self-interests of the Great Powers remained.
    3. Ideological differences between the Liberal Two (France and Britain) and the Conservative Three (Austria, Prussia, and Russia) persisted, but all Great Powers gave *realpolitik* precedence over ideology.
      a. Examples include the French intervention into Spain, Russian support for it, Britain's reluctance to support, and Greek nationalism.
      b. The alliance between Britain, France, and Russia, which backed Greece's independence in 1830, illustrates cooperation among the Great Powers for strategic reasons despite their ideological differences.
    4. Liberal revolutions in France, Belgium, and Poland in 1830 alarmed the conservative powers; the French monarchy continued under Louis Philippe, Belgium became independent, and the Polish revolt was crushed by Russian forces.

C. The Industrial Revolution
  1. The Industrial Revolution, which first began in Britain the late eighteenth century, changed the organization of industrial production and harnessed new sources of energy, especially steam power.
  2. The social, economic, and strategic impact of the Industrial Revolution was tremendous:
     a. Factories produced more new products faster than ever before, and manufacturing, transportation, and communication became mechanized.
     b. International trade and investment skyrocketed, and competition among industrialized states for markets and raw materials heightened.
     c. Cities grew rapidly, swelled by workers seeking jobs in the new industries.
     d. Successful industrialists made huge fortunes (exceeding those of the traditional landowning aristocracy) and the middle classes prospered, but the living conditions of the working poor were slow to improve.
     e. Women entered the industrial labor force in significant numbers, and traditional extended family structures in farming villages were increasingly replaced by the "nuclear family."
     f. Capitalist "captains of industry," labor unions, and the mass media became important political forces.
     g. The telegraph, steel cannon, iron warships, and the railroad revolutionized military affairs; armies and navies could move dramatically faster, and possessed much more destructive power, than before.
  3. The spread of industrialization gradually but profoundly changed the European system.
     a. The spread of industrialization was uneven; Britain industrialized first, followed later by Germany and France, still later by Austria, much later by Russia; Britain's early lead gave it significant strategic and economic advantages, until it was eclipsed by Germany (see Chapter Three).
     b. Britain began to champion free trade with its increased industrial, financial, and naval strength (see Chapter Seven), while in other countries (especially Germany) demands for protection against imported goods won out.
     c. The growing political and economic strength of the middle and working classes threatened authoritarian regimes in Central and Eastern Europe and Russia.

D. Revolutions of 1848
  1. Waves of popular discontent, energized by the economic and social changes wrought by the industrial revolution, broke across Europe in 1848 and threatened the established monarchies.
     a. The French king fled to England, and a short-lived republic was proclaimed (President Louis Napoleon Bonaparte, Napoleon Bonaparte's nephew, was crowned Emperor Napoleon III in 1852).
     b. Promised reforms in Prussia were withdrawn after violent clashes between soldiers and protesters.
     c. Reforms in Austria led to the emancipation of peasants, but rural and urban uprisings continued until they were violently suppressed, with Russian assistance, by 1849.
  2. The revolutions showed that the Concert of Europe was incapable of controlling internal change.
     a. The excesses of capitalism and inequalities of wealth that appeared during the Industrial Revolution resulted in an upwelling of socialism and the rise of communism.
     b. Social divisions and the spread of liberal ideas increased nationalist sentiments and demands for democratic reforms.
     c. Monarchists and the landed aristocracy generally carried the day in 1848, as liberal regimes were crushed with the aid of the conservative powers, especially Russia, the "Gendarme of Europe."

VIII. A Perspective at Mid-Century
  A. By 1850, Europe appeared stable on the surface, but the European system was about to be convulsed by the growing impact of nationalism.
  B. The Crimean War (1853–56) was the first war between Great Powers since 1815; Russia's defeat by Britain, France, and the Ottoman Empire resulted in some liberalizing reforms in that country, but demonstrated that the Concert of Europe could not maintain collective security when the interests of the Great Powers conflicted.

IX. Unification of Italy and Germany
  A. Italian Unification
    1. Italian nationalism was led by the Count di Cavour of Piedmont-Sardinia (which dominated northern Italy) and Giuseppe Garibaldi (whose nationalist troops won control of Sicily and Naples by 1860).
    2. The Great Powers' positions on Italian unification were determined by *realpolitik* concerns; France under Napoleon III supported it, but Austria opposed it.
    3. Piedmont, Sicily, and Naples united with other Italian states to form the Kingdom of Italy in 1861.

    4. At first, the new Italian state acted as a useful buffer state between France and Austria; its political divisions and economic weakness prevented it from attaining the Great Power status its leaders envisioned.

B. German Unification

    1. German unification was masterminded by Otto von Bismarck, the "Iron Chancellor" of Prussia.

       a. Bismarck's foreign policy was determined almost exclusively by *realpolitik*.

       b. A conservative junker (aristocratic landowner), he had little interest in liberal ideas initially, but realized that nationalism could be used as a means to increase Prussia's power, enlist the aid of the middle classes, and address the concerns of the masses.

    2. Bismarck pursued a step-by-step strategy of unifying Germany under Prussian domination.

       a. Realizing that a union of Prussia and Austria would alarm the other Great Powers, Bismarck rejected the nationalist ideal of a "greater Germany" and opted for the "small Germany" solution of a Germany without Austria.

       b. In 1864, taking advantage of a blunder by the Danish king, Prussia seized the northern German duchies of Schleswig and Holstein with Austrian support.

       c. When Berlin and Vienna fell out in 1866, Prussia defeated Austria in only two months (using superior military organization and leadership and modern technology, including railroads and the telegraph); Austria gave up its authority over northern Germany and the northern German states were incorporated into a Prussian-dominated North German Confederation.

       d. Relations between Prussia and France, alarmed at Prussia's growing strength, deteriorated rapidly; after hidden diplomatic manipulation by Bismarck, Napoleon III declared war on Prussia in 1870.

       e. Again using superior military organization, rapid mobilization, and modern technology, Prussia smashed France's armies within weeks, captured Napoleon III, and took Paris after a siege.

       f. In January 1871, the formation of a German Empire was declared in the Palace of Versailles (Louis XIV's palace outside of Paris); the empire included two provinces seized from France, Alsace and Lorraine, even though the population of Lorraine was largely French.

    3. German unification radically altered the European system and balance of power.

       a. Germany became the strongest power in continental Europe.

       b. The proclamation of the German Empire in a French cultural monument and the seizure of French territory humiliated France and resulted in the rise of French revanchism (desire to avenge a defeat).

       c. The rapid success of Prussian armies against Austria and France led European military planners to believe that future wars would be decided quickly; thus, rapid mobilization was essential (Chapter Three explores the tragic consequences of this belief).

X. Imperialism in the Industrial Era

A. The demand for raw materials from the Industrial Revolution made imperialism even more beneficial for industrializing nations.

B. Industrialization and technological advances gave European powers decisive strategic advantages over traditional African and Asian states; maintenance of military power also created its own incentives for imperial expansion.

C. The Pax Britannica thrived.

    1. Britain's naval and economic power allowed it to impose a pax Britannica ("British peace"), discouraging major war by threatening aggressors with embargoes and other economic sanctions.

    2. Assisted by English chauvinist and white supremacist Cecil Rhodes, Britain secured a major expanse of African territory.

    3. The Boer War (1899–1902) between Dutch Africaners and the Brtish in South Africa was the most important and costly colonial war for the British.

    4. By 1897, the "sun never set" on the British empire and Britain's primacy in the colonial world was indisputable, but its ability to maintain this vast empire was open to question.

D. Imperial rivals sought power.

    1. Following the Napoleonic Wars, France built an extensive empire, especially in Africa and Indochina; the French saw their goal as bringing culture and civilization to backward peoples, thus they attempted to assimilate and colonize them to the French way of life.

    2. Germany, Italy, and Russia attempted to expand their colonial influences further—the Germans and Italians in Africa and the Russians in South Asia.

    3. The decline of the Ottoman Empire (also known as the "sick man of Europe") accelerated and the other European powers tended to counterbalance each other out of a need to protect their interests in Ottoman-controlled areas.

XI. Bismarckian System
    A. In the last decade of the nineteenth century, Bismarck used a series of defensive alliances (known as the *Bismarckian system*) to protect German security, ameliorate the security concerns of Germany's neighbors, and forestall war between the Great Powers.
        1. The objectives of the system were to keep Germany, Austria-Hungary (as Austria was known from 1867, after making concessions to Hungarian nationalists after its defeat in 1866), and Russia together, while keeping France isolated.
        2. Germany allied with Austria-Hungary in the Dual Alliance (1879).
        3. Russia was added to the system with the Three Emperors' Alliance in 1881, but Austria-Hungary and Russia continued to conflict over their support of various Balkan nationalist movements in the disintegrating Ottoman Empire.
        4. Italy was brought into the system in 1882 with the Triple Alliance among Germany, Austria-Hungary, and Italy.
    B. Bismarck's system helped moderate conflicts between the Great Powers, but by 1888 the system was on the verge of breaking down.
        1. Russia was becoming increasingly distrustful of Germany.
        2. Britain and France had settled most of their differences.
        3. Conflict between Russia and Austria-Hungary increased as Balkan nationalist movements succeeded in winning independence from the Ottomans.
        4. German expansionists pressed for the acquisition of overseas colonies to guarantee Germany's "place in the sun" and political equality with Britain and France.
        5. German domestic politics resulted in Bismarck's dismissal in 1890.

XII. International System on the Eve of the Twentieth Century
    A. By 1890, the stability Europe had enjoyed under the Concert of Europe was rapidly collapsing.
    B. In retrospect, the Concert's and Bismarck's systems of alliances had been able to resolve the conflicts between the Great Powers that arose from the security dilemma (i.e., conflicts between *states*), but were incapable of dealing with conflicts between nations, which often defied solution through *realpolitik* or rational compromise.
    C. In general, the Concert and other European institutions were able to cope well with the economic globalization caused by the Industrial Revolution, but could not handle the increasing political fragmentation brought about by social changes and nationalism.
    D. The extent of European power and influence throughout the world by the end of the century meant that in all likelihood any major conflict between the Great Powers would become a global war.

HOW THE CHAPTER RELATES TO CENTRAL THEMES OF THE TEXT

The historical material in Chapter Two supports the book's central themes in three important ways. First, it describes the early development of basic structural elements of the international system—the sovereign nation-state, alliances, the balance of power, and international organizations—that students must be familiar with in order to understand the processes of cooperation and conflict. Second, the chapter points out that cooperation and conflict, and globalization and fragmentation, are not unique features of the contemporary world, but dynamics that can be observed throughout history.

Third, Chapter Two provides "raw data" for the book's conceptual and theoretical chapters, giving historical examples of events, conflicts, agreements, and decisions that may be used to illustrate analytical constructs such as the security dilemma, collective security, and bandwagoning and balancing (see Chapters Eleven and Twelve). In keeping with the "building-block" approach, after students become familiar with the events, movements, and personalities described in Chapters Two through Four, they will be better able to use the concepts and analytical frameworks outlined in later chapters to form their own interpretations of history.

SUGGESTED LECTURE TOPICS

    1. Compare the conduct of international relations in the eighteenth century (the "golden age of diplomacy," when aristocratic rulers negotiated *realpolitik* treaties, paying scant attention to the interests of the masses) with international politics in the nineteenth century (when leaders had to take

ideologies such as nationalism, liberalism, and socialism into account and required more popular support to raise revenues and implement policies).

2. Illustrate how the European powers entered into numerous short-lived, ad hoc alliances to preserve the balance of power; contrast these alliances with Cold War era groupings such as NATO and the Warsaw Pact.
3. Compare the Concert of Europe to contemporary councils of Great Powers, such as the UN Security Council (see Chapter Nine) or the OECD's G-7 (see Chapter Seven). Point out areas in which the modern institutions are more effective in securing cooperation among the powers (exchange rate stability, assembly of the coalition to oppose Iraq's 1990 invasion of Kuwait) and areas in which policy coordination is still difficult to achieve (trade and tariffs, nuclear proliferation, intervention into civil wars and internal conflicts).
4. Use the partition and reestablishment of Poland (eighteenth century), the Greek war of independence (nineteenth century), and the Bosnian civil war (twentieth century) to show how *realpolitik* shapes the Great Powers' policies toward nationalist conflicts.
5. Describe how the Industrial Revolution made trade more lucrative and warfare more destructive. Compare the "tools of the trade" of pre-industrial and industrial-era merchants, sailors, and soldiers (horse-drawn wagons versus railroads, the telegraph versus the Pony Express, the sailing ship versus the steam-powered ironclad, and the muzzle-loading musket versus the repeating cartridge rifle) to show how economic cooperation among states became more profitable, and the security dilemma more acute, in the industrial age.

STUDY AND EXAM QUESTIONS

1. Was the Concert of Europe a success? Why or why not? In your answer, explain the Concert's main goals and show how the Concert achieved or failed to attain these goals in three European conflicts that it attempted to manage.
2. Which "revolution" had the most impact on world politics: the American Revolution, the French Revolution, the Industrial Revolution, or the Revolutions of 1848? In your answer, explain how the revolution of your choice changed the international system, using historical events to support your argument.
3. Choose one of the individuals listed below and explain his impact on world politics:
   a. Frederick the Great
   b. Napoleon Bonaparte
   c. Prince Metternich
   d. Simon Bolivar
   e. Napoleon III (Louis Napoleon)
   f. Otto von Bismarck
4. Both nationalism and *realpolitik* played major roles in the unification of Italy and Germany. Which was more important in each case and why?
5. Which system of conflict resolution was more successful in maintaining peace in Europe: the eighteenth-century system of diplomacy among monarchs or the Concert of Europe? What factors best explain the success of this system, and which events best illustrate it?

RECOMMENDED ENRICHMENT READINGS

Bergeron, Louis. *France under Napoleon.* Translated by R. R. Palmer. Princeton: Princeton University Press, 1981. Outstanding concise survey of the Napoleonic era, including an interesting assessment of the character and career of the Emperor of the French.
• Elrod, Richard B. "The Concert of Europe: A Fresh Look at an International System." *World Politics* 28, no. 2 (January 1976): 159–74. Very useful analysis and description of the concert system.
Diamond, Jared. *Guns, Germs, and Steel: The Fates of Human Societies.* New York: W. W. Norton, 1997. A biologist's explanation of the origins and progress of European domination of the international system.
Doyle, William. *Origins of the French Revolution.* Oxford: Oxford University Press, 1980. Very readable account and analysis of the fall of the *ancien regime* and rise of the Republic.

Fox, Edward Whiting. *The Emergence of the Modern European World*. Cambridge, Mass.: Blackwell, 1991. Probably the best one-volume review of modern European history for lower-division undergraduates; good choice for instructors looking for a historical companion volume to Spiegel's text.

Greenfeld, Liah. *Nationalism: Five Roads to Modernity*. Cambridge, Mass.: Harvard University Press, 1992. Highly original comparison of British, French, Russian, German, and American nationalism.

Hobsbawm, E. J. *Nations and Nationalism since 1780: Programme, Myth, Reality*. Cambridge: Cambridge University Press, 1990. Thought-provoking long essay on the changing nature of nationalism and its role in history.

Holsti, Kalevi J. *Peace and War: Armed Conflicts and International Order 1648–1989*. Cambridge: Cambridge University Press, 1991. Interesting discussion of the causes and character of wars.

Howard, Michael. *War in European History*. New York: Oxford University Press, 1976. Classic volume on the causes and courses of armed conflict among the European powers.

Keegan, John. *A History of Warfare*. New York: Knopf, 1993. Not a book of campaigns, battles, and generals, but an innovative study of war as a human social activity. Highly recommended for strategists and pacifists alike.

Kennedy, Paul. *The Rise and Fall of the Great Powers*. New York: Random House, 1987. Destined to become a classic, this comprehensive study contains a wealth of data on the strengths, weaknesses, and strategies of the Great Powers from the sixteenth century to the end of the Cold War. Chapters Three and Four are most relevant to the period covered in Chapter Two of the text.

Kissinger, Henry M. *Diplomacy*. New York: Simon and Schuster, 1994. An interesting exploration of a topic the author knows well from personal experience—and one that reveals much about the author as well as the subject.

Landes, David. *The Unbound Prometheus*. Cambridge: Cambridge University Press, 1969. Masterful economic history of the Industrial Revolution and its continuation to the present day.

McDougall, Walter A. *Promised Land, Crusader State: The American Encounter with the World since 1776*. Boston: Houghton Mifflin, 1997. Insightful, lively overview of the conflict between realism and idealism in U.S. foreign policy. (Also useful for Chapters Three and Four).

Pflanze, Otto. *Bismarck and the Development of Germany: The Period of Unification, 1815–1871*. Princeton: Princeton University Press, 1973. A balanced assessment of the Iron Chancellor's policies.

• Rosecrance, Richard. *International Relations: Peace or War?* New York: McGraw-Hill, 1973. (Recommend assignment of pp. 25–39.) This short excerpt from Rosecrance's book offers a good comparison of the "golden age of diplomacy" in the eighteenth century with international politics in the period of the Concert of Europe.

Taylor, A. J. P. *The Struggle for Mastery in Europe 1848–1918*. Oxford: Oxford University Press, 1964. Classic analysis of the powers' attempts to preserve and manipulate the balance of power from the Revolution of 1848 to World War I.

The World Wars

SCOPE, OBJECTIVES, AND APPROACH

Chapter Three discusses the origins, course, and aftermath of World Wars I and II. It concentrates on the events leading up to and following these conflicts rather than on the battles, campaigns, and strategies of the wars themselves. While primarily a historical chapter, it does not take the primarily narrative approach used in Chapter Two. Rather, it concentrates on presenting alternative explanations for the origins of most devastating and momentous conflicts of the twentieth century, encouraging students to decide for themselves which explanations best fit the historical facts. The chapter thereby begins to encourage students to think in terms of theories, hypotheses, and alternative explanations as it outlines the historical record.

WHAT STUDENTS SHOULD LEARN FROM THIS CHAPTER

Foundation Level

1. Identify the six major contending explanations for the outbreak of World War I.
2. Describe the crises and conflicts among the European Great Powers preceding the war.

3. Identify the Central and Entente powers involved in WWI and describe the general course of the war.
4. List the principal provisions of the Versailles settlement.
5. Describe the organization of the League of Nations.
6. Identify the major contending explanations for the outbreak of World War II.
7. Outline the events and conflicts in Europe and Asia that preceded the war.
8. Identify the Axis and Allied powers in WWII and describe the general course of the war.
9. Describe the conflicts between the Western Allies and the USSR that came to the forefront after the war.

Enrichment Level

1. Identify the strengths and shortcomings of the contending explanations for WWI.
2. Describe the affect of the Russian Revolution and U.S. entry on the course of the war.
3. Outline the institutional strengths and weaknesses of the League of Nations and identify its principal successes and failures.
4. Describe the rise of Adolf Hitler.
5. Explain the significance of the Munich Agreement and the Nazi–Soviet Pact.
6. Outline the main reasons why the United States remained neutral until 1941 and why Japan brought the United States into the war by attacking Pearl Harbor.
7. Describe the reasoning behind U.S. development and employment of the atomic bomb.

Mastery Level

1. Outline how the Great Powers attempted to maintain the balance of power in Europe before WWI and explain why their efforts failed to maintain the peace.
2. Trace the links between the Versailles settlement, the Great Depression, and the establishment of Nazi rule in Germany.
3. Explain why the Western powers failed to stop German and Japanese expansion in the years prior to WWII.
4. Describe why German forces achieved success in the early stages of the war, but were ultimately defeated by the Allies.
5. Outline the conflicts between the Western Allies and the USSR that arose during the war.
6. Explain the strategic and political significance of the atomic bombing of Hiroshima and Nagasaki.

OUTLINE OF THE CHAPTER

0. Introduction
   A. The World Wars were conflicts of unprecedented scope and destructiveness that had tremendous political, economic, strategic, technological, and social consequences.
   B. This chapter describes the origins, conduct, and aftermath of the wars and presents contending explanations for why they occurred; the reader must decide which explanations are best and whether or not these catastrophic conflicts could have been avoided.

I. Causes of World War I
   A. Six major factors are advanced as primary causes of WWI; debate continues over which was most important.
   B. Rise of Germany
      1. Germany's unification and growing power worried its neighbors, especially France and Russia.
      2. At the same time, Germany felt encircled by potential enemies.
      3. Germany's ambitious naval construction program alarmed Britain and precipitated a naval arms race.
   C. Alliance System
      1. After 1890, Bismarck's system of flexible alliances began to be replaced by rigid strategic alignments.
         a. Russo–French alliance, 1894
         b. Anglo–Japanese alliance, 1902
         c. Anglo–French entente, 1904

2. These alliance were designed to prevent a major war, but their net affect was that if two of the Great Powers went to war, the rest would quickly follow.

D. Economic Change and Competition
   1. Population and industrial capacity grew throughout Europe in the late nineteenth and early twentieth centuries, but some states grew much faster than others.
   2. Germany and the United States, in particular, grew rapidly, and outdistanced Britain as the world's leading economic power.
   3. Germany's economic growth enabled it to challenge Britain for political influence and caused British grand strategy to shift from containment of Russia and France to containment of Germany.

E. Nationalism
   1. The continued appeal of nationalist political doctrine threatened the security, and the very existence, of Europe's multinational empires (Russia, Austria-Hungary, and the Ottoman Empire).
   2. The Great Powers continued, however, to play *realpolitik* with nationalism; they suppressed nationalist movements within their own borders, but encouraged them in their neighbors and rivals.

F. Imperialism
   1. The empires of the Great Powers were not confined to Europe; by 1900, most of the world outside Europe (except the Western Hemisphere) was under European control or domination.
   2. The Great Powers felt that resources from their colonial empires were vital to their security.
   3. Conflicts over colonial interests, particularly in Asia and Africa, heightened tensions in Europe as the imperial powers clashed over their *spheres of influence*.

G. "Cult of the Offensive"
   1. Germany's rapid victories in the wars of German unification led strategists to believe that future wars would be very short, and that speed of mobilization would determine victory or defeat; this belief is now known as the *cult of the offensive*.
   2. This belief in the superiority of the offensive ignored technological developments (such as the machine gun) and evidence from recent wars (such as the American Civil War and the Boer War), which were protracted struggles of attrition.
   3. As a result, by 1914, the European powers prepared grandiose offensive plans (especially the *Schlieffen Plan,* which was seen as Germany's only chance to avoid defeat in a two-front war with France and Russia) and European armies were on a "hair trigger."

II. Path to War
A. Moroccan Crises
   1. In 1905–1906, German challenges to France's sphere of influence in Morocco led to a diplomatic crisis.
   2. In 1911, Germany and France conflicted again over France's attempt to establish a protectorate over all of Morocco; the crisis was resolved by a diplomatic compromise, but tensions and mutual resentment remained high.

B. Balkan Powder Keg Leads to July Crisis
   1. In 1908, 1912, and 1913, crises and wars in the Balkans escalated the conflict between Russia and Austria-Hungary, which were competing for the spoils of the declining Ottoman Empire.
   2. At the same time, Austria increasingly clashed with Russian-backed Serbia; Serbia claimed Austrian-controlled Bosnia as its own national territory.
   3. The heir to the Austro-Hungarian throne, Archduke Franz Ferdinand, was assassinated in Sarajevo on June 28, 1914; Austria held Serbia responsible for the assassination.
   4. In response, Austria delivered an ultimatum to Serbia, but Russia felt it had to back Serbia if Austria attacked; war between Russia and Austria, however, was bound to bring in Germany, and war between Germany and Russia was bound to provoke French intervention.
   5. At the same time, the "cult of the offensive" created pressure on decision makers to mobilize early and attack first.
   6. The resulting chain of mobilizations and alliances led to war between Germany and Austria-Hungary (the Central Powers) on one side and Russia, France, and Serbia (the Entente Powers or the Allies) on the other by August 3; because Germany invaded Belgium to attack France, Britain declared war on Germany the next day.

III. The Great War
A. Stalemate on All Fronts
   1. In 1914, the Great Powers expected a short and relatively bloodless war, but the initial offensives all failed, and by 1915 all fronts had bogged down into static trench warfare.

2. The scale of the war and new military technology (machine guns, barbed wire, improved artillery, flamethrowers, poison gas, aircraft, submarines, and so on resulted in horrific casualties. (In 1916, Britain lost more men killed in one day than the United States lost during the entire Vietnam War.)
3. Both sides gained allies during the war; Italy and Japan joined the Allies while the Ottoman Empire joined the Central Powers, but the entry of these and smaller states had little effect on the fighting, which spread to the Middle East, Africa, and the Pacific.

B. Russian Revolution
1. In November 1917, continued political and economic crisis in Russia, combined with Russian defeats in the war and huge casualties, precipitated the Bolshevik Revolution.
2. The new Communist government (under Vladimir Lenin) signed a peace treaty with Germany in 1918; German forces occupied much of the former Russian Empire.

C. United States Enters the War
1. While the United States had been neutral since the start of the war (though U.S. banks heavily financed the British and French war effort), the German strategy of unrestricted submarine warfare after 1917 (attacking ships without warning, regardless of nationality) increasingly angered the United States.
2. Germany took the calculated risk that submarine warfare would force Britain to surrender before the United States entered the war, but the gamble didn't pay off; the United States entered the war on the Allied side in April 1917.

D. Armistice
1. U.S. entry into the war gave the Allies a decisive advantage in industrial capability and boosted Allied morale; meanwhile, German and Austrian will to fight began to collapse.
2. On November 11, 1918, Germany and the Allies signed an armistice, ending the fighting.
3. The war devastated Europe; more than 13 million people were killed, more than in any previous conflict.

IV. Versailles Settlement
A. In January 1919, leaders of France, Britain, Italy, and the United States convened a conference at Versailles to prepare a peace settlement that would restore stability to Europe and prevent another major war.
B. The European powers generally pursued traditional *realpolitik* goals (punish and weaken Germany, divide the fallen Russian and Austro-Hungarian empires), but U.S. President Woodrow Wilson sought to create a "new world order" based on international law and collective security.
C. The final document (the Treaty of Versailles) was a compromise containing the worst elements of idealism and realism.
1. A League of Nations was established to provide for collective security, but it had many institutional weaknesses (see below).
2. Germany was forced to cede Alsace-Lorraine to France, give up territory to the re-created state of Poland, and demilitarize the Rhineland area of Germany; the size and armament of Germany's army and navy were strictly limited, and it was forbidden to have an air force.
3. The Austro-Hungarian Empire was divided into the successor states of Austria, Hungary, Czechoslovakia, and Yugoslavia (which included Serbia); Austria was forbidden to unite with Germany, and the Sudetendland (a territory with a large German population) was incorporated into Czechoslovakia.
4. The Ottoman Empire lost vast territories in the Middle East to British and French colonial control (although the Allies had promised to create independent Arab states and a Jewish homeland in these territories).
5. Germany was forced to accept primary responsibility for the war and pay massive reparations to the Allies.
D. The Versailles settlement angered many and satisfied no one.
1. Some nationalities were given self-determination (Czechs, Serbs, Poles) but others were not (Arabs, Germans).
2. The new government of Germany, the Weimar Republic, was forced to sign the humiliating treaty (the United States refused to sign, later signing a separate peace treaty).

V. The False Peace of the 1920s
A. A Weak League
1. The U.S. Senate would not ratify the Treaty of Versailles, and the United States did not join the League of Nations; the absence of the world's largest industrial power ensured that Wilson's vision of a collective security system would be stillborn.
2. Another major power, the USSR, was never invited to join the League.

    3. The League's Security Council lacked effective provisions to enforce collective security.

    4. The European powers responded to American isolationism and instability in Europe (unstable new states in Eastern Europe, civil war in the USSR) with *realpolitik* security measures.

      a. France established a network of defense pacts with Central and East European states.

      b. France also built an extensive system of fortifications, the Maginot Line, on its border with Germany.

      c. The Locarno Treaties of 1925 allayed some Western security concerns, and Germany was admitted to the League of Nations in 1926.

    5. Domestic developments in Europe, however, soon undermined these measures.

      a. The desire to avoid another destructive war increased antiwar sentiments, which led the Great Powers to respond to aggression with *appeasement* (making partial concessions to aggressors to persuade them to moderate their demands).

      b. Economic problems in Germany and reparations payments led to *hyperinflation* and economic collapse.

      c. Discontent with the terms of the Versailles settlement, social upheaval, and economic crises fueled *fascism,* or radical authoritarian nationalism in Italy and Germany (Mussolini became Prime Minister of Italy in 1922).

  B. The Great Depression

    1. The crash of the U.S. stock market in 1929 and the spasmodic contraction of world trade following the Smoot–Hawley Tariff of 1930 precipitated financial crisis and depression throughout the world.

    2. Germany's political and economic system was paralyzed, and many Germans began to look toward the "strong hand" of Adolf Hitler, leader of the fascist National Socialist (Nazi) Party, who became Chancellor in 1933.

VI. What Caused World War II?

  A. The reasons for the outbreak of WWII are less disputed than the primary explanations for WWI, because it is almost universally accepted that if Germany, Italy, and Japan had not pursued expansionist policies in the 1930s, a global war would probably have never occurred; nevertheless, several factors contributed to the war.

  B. The terms of the Versailles Treaty were harsh and regarded as humiliating by many Germans.

  C. At the same time, the provisions were poorly enforced by the feeble League of Nations.

  D. Growing military and economic strength of Germany, Japan, and the USSR altered the global balance of power.

  E. Germany, Italy, and Japan pursued expansionist policies to resolve or avoid domestic political problems.

  F. The rise of fascism in many European states and militarism in Japan contributed to aggressive policies and destroyed many fledgling democracies.

VII. Rise of the Third Reich

  A. Hitler's Two Phases of Rule over Nazi Germany before WWII

    1. From 1933 to 1935, Hitler avoided provoking the Western powers directly (though Nazi domestic policies were brutally repressive) and concentrated on building Germany's economic strength.

    2. After 1935, however, Hitler began to openly defy the Versailles Treaty.

      a. Remilitarization of the Rhineland, 1936

      b. Massive German military buildup

      c. Articulation of demands for union of Germany with Austria

    3. Hoping to avoid a major war, Britain and France acceded to Hitler's initial demands.

  B. China, Ethiopia, and Spain

    1. Japan seized Manchuria in 1931 and invaded China in 1937; the League of Nations imposed limited, ineffective economic sanctions.

    2. Italian forces invaded Ethiopia in 1935; again, the League imposed limited economic sanctions.

    3. Spanish Nationalists led by Francisco Franco gained control of Spain in the Spanish Civil War (1936–39); Germany and Italy supported the Nationalists, while the USSR sent aid to the opposing Republicans.

  C. *Anschluss*

    1. In 1938, Germany annexed Austria.

    2. The *anschluss* was in open violation of the Versailles Treaty.

  D. Czech Crisis and Munich Conference

    1. After the *anschluss*, Germany pressed for the annexation of the Sudetenland from Czechoslovakia; Hitler wanted to force a confrontation over the issue, but Britain and France hoped to avoid one.

2. In September 1938, Hitler, Mussolini, British Prime Minister Neville Chamberlain, and French Prime Minister Edouard Daladier met at a conference in Munich.
    a. The Western powers agreed that the Sudetenland would be turned over to German control.
    b. The Czech government was not invited to the conference.
    c. Chamberlain declared that the Munich Agreement meant "peace for our time," but opposition leader Winston Churchill disagreed.
3. Britain and France hoped that Germany would be satisfied with the incorporation of nearly all German-populated territories into the *Third Reich,* but in March 1939 Germany invaded the remainder of Czechoslovakia.

VIII. The Approach of War
   A. The Nazis and Soviets struck a deal.
      1. After France and Britain balked at signing an alliance with the USSR to defend Poland, Germany and the USSR signed the Nazi–Soviet Pact (August 1939).
      2. This agreement stunned the world—Hitler and Stalin had been bitter ideological enemies, but signed the pact to further their *realpolitik* interests; the agreement contained secret protocols allowing the USSR to take over eastern Poland and the Baltic states (Latvia, Lithuania, and Estonia).
   B. After the signing of the Pact, Hitler no longer needed to fear war with the USSR over Poland, and the failure of Britain and France to support Czechoslovakia suggested that they might abandon Poland as well.

IX. Second World War
   A. The *Blitzkrieg*
      1. WWII began with the German invasion of Poland on September 1, 1939.
      2. The allies expected a protracted war of attrition as in WWI, but the German *blitzkrieg* strategy quickly defeated Poland.
      3. After invading Norway, Denmark, and the Low Countries, Germany stunned the world again by defeating France in another *blitzkrieg* in May–June 1940.
      4. Also in June 1940, Italy declared war on the Allies.
      5. When Churchill replaced Chamberlain as British Prime Minister and refused to sue for peace, Hitler contemplated an invasion of Britain, but decided on massive air attacks instead.
      6. Even though President Roosevelt wanted the United States to come to Britain's aid, the United States remained neutral as public and congressional opinion remained isolationist.
      7. In 1941, the defeat of an Italian invasion of Greece prompted Germany to invade Yugoslavia and Greece; in occupied Yugoslavia, Croatian units aided German troops in persecuting Serbs who resisted the Axis forces.
   B. Barbarossa
      1. Believing that war with the USSR was inevitable, Germany invaded Russia in June 1941 (German forces were aided by Hungary, Romania, and Finland, which had resisted a Soviet attack in 1939).
      2. Axis forces achieved dramatic initial success, but the USSR's strategic depth and growing military–industrial capacity blunted the *blitzkrieg*.
      3. By 1943, the war on the eastern front became a struggle of attrition, in which Soviet forces had the advantage.
   C. The Pacific War
      1. Japan entered the war on the Axis side and brought the United States in on the Allied side with an attack on the U.S. naval base at Pearl Harbor on December 7, 1941.
      2. Why would Japan attack the much stronger United States?
         a. The United States had replied to Japanese aggression in 1937–40 with economic sanctions.
         b. Trying to persuade Japan to cease its war in China, the United States imposed an oil embargo on Japan in July 1941.
         c. Unwilling to withdraw from China, Japan's leadership felt war with the United States had become inevitable and that their only chance to avoid defeat was to strike a strong initial blow against the United States.
   D. Arsenal of Democracy
      1. U.S. entry into the war gave the Allies a decisive advantage in military and industrial strength, but Axis forces would still have to be driven from the territories they had conquered.
      2. The United States gave billions of dollars in lend-lease aid to Britain and Russia; amassed huge land, naval, and air forces; and fought Axis forces on all fronts.

3. Allied forces defeated the Axis in North Africa, Italy (which surrendered in 1943) and Russia, and the United States and Britain carried out a prolonged campaign of strategic bombing against Germany.

E. Second Front
    1. The USSR, whose forces and civilian population had borne the brunt of the fighting in Europe, continued to pressure the Western allies to strike at Germany more directly.
    2. On June 6, 1944 (D-Day), U.S., British, Canadian, and Free French and Polish troops landed in Normandy.
    3. Allied forces inexorably pushed through France into Germany, while Soviet troops closed in on Berlin from the east; Hitler committed suicide on May 1, 1945, and Germany surrendered unconditionally on May 8.

F. Uneasy Alliance
    1. The Allies, united to defeat Germany, developed differences of opinion over the future of postwar Europe.
    2. Churchill, Roosevelt, and Stalin (the "Big Three" Allied leaders) met several times during the war; at their final meeting, at Yalta in February 1945, Stalin agreed to elections in the liberated nations of Eastern Europe, but did not take the issue seriously.
    3. In July 1945, after Germany's defeat, Harry Truman (who became President upon Roosevelt's death in April), Churchill (whose party was voted out of power during the conference and who was replaced in mid-meeting by Clement Atlee) and Stalin met at Postdam, near Berlin; Germany was divided into four Allied occupation zones, and Truman informed Stalin that the United States had developed an atomic bomb.

G. Atomic Bomb
    1. The United States feared that an invasion of Japan would result in more than a million U.S. casualties (and many more Japanese lives lost); the Western Allies also feared that the USSR would try to establish lasting control over any territories it might liberate from Japan.
    2. Fearing that German scientists would try to build an atomic weapon, the United States launched the *Manhattan Project* (see Chapter Eleven) in 1942; in July 1945, the project finally succeeded in developing an atomic bomb.
    3. Truman decided to use the new weapon in an attempt to persuade Japan to surrender without an Allied invasion of the home islands.
        a. An atomic bomb was dropped on Hiroshima on August 6, 1945; a second bomb was dropped on Nagasaki on August 9 (the USSR declared war on Japan and attacked Japanese forces in Manchuria on August 8).
        b. Japan decided to sue for peace on August 10, formally surrendering on September 2.

X. The End of the War—And the Beginning of Another?
A. World War II was the most destructive war in history; at least 40 million people were killed.
B. The war ended the era of European domination, but what would come next was not immediately clear.
    1. The European powers and Japan were devastated, but the United States had suffered little damage and far fewer casualties.
    2. After the war, only the United States and the Soviet Union possessed the resources necessary to compete for global leadership; the USSR fielded huge ground forces, while the United States had a large army and navy—and the atomic bomb.
    3. A new collective security organization—the United Nations—was created; the United States, USSR, Britain, France, and China were made permanent members of its Security Council (see Chapter Nine).
    4. It was not certain that the United States and the USSR would be adversaries; they had cooperated during the war, but they possessed radically different political and economic systems and distrusted each other deeply.

HOW THE CHAPTER RELATES TO CENTRAL THEMES OF THE TEXT

The World Wars and the events surrounding them offer history's most dramatic illustration of the continuous processes of globalization versus fragmentation and cooperation versus conflict. The fragmentation resulting from the disintegration of Europe's multinational empires in the early years of the twentieth century resulted in a catastrophic conflict that quickly became globalized, as fighting spread to the powers' colonial empires and the United States was pulled toward intervention.

The League of Nations established by the Versailles settlement attempted to globalize conflict resolution, but in reality the treaty only served to increase fragmentation by creating new national states. The Great Depression shows the risks involved in economic globalization and interdependence, while the failure of the League to facilitate cooperation among the powers for collective security contributed to the outbreak of a truly global war. Instructors can therefore find a wealth of material in this chapter that exemplifies the text's central themes and, in particular, points out the positive and negative aspects of globalization.

SUGGESTED LECTURE TOPICS

1. Describe how each of the contending explanations for the outbreak of WWI heightened tensions among the European powers.
2. Examine the interests and risks involved in the July 1914 crisis from the vantage points of Vienna, St. Petersburg, Berlin, Paris, and London.
3. Play the role of "defense attorney" for the League of Nations in the interwar period; argue why it would have been impossible for the League to act more resolutely to oppose German, Italian, and Japanese aggression.
4. Present the interests, capabilities, and vulnerabilities that Germany, Italy, France, and Britain took to the table at the Munich Conference; do the same for Germany and the USSR at the signing of the Nazi–Soviet Pact.
5. Explain the factors and calculations involved in the Italian and Japanese decisions to enter WWII and America's policy of neutrality from September 1939 to December 1941. Invite students to assess whether the United States was really "neutral" during this period and whether Roosevelt's actions were legal.
6. Outline the objectives, strategies, and accomplishments of each of the "Big Three" at the Yalta conference.

STUDY AND EXAM QUESTIONS

1. What factor was primarily responsible for the outbreak of World War I? In your answer, use historical examples illustrating this factor in operation and explain why it was more important than other possible causes of the war.
2. Was the Treaty of Versailles a victory for realism over idealism or of idealism over realism? In your answer, identify the main proponents of each view among the leading Allied negotiators and use four provisions of the treaty to support your contention.
3. The League of Nations achieved little success in containing aggression and providing for collective security between WWI and WWII. Was its failure due to its inherent flaws or were the instruments available to it used poorly? Examine three instances of League action, or inaction, in your answer.
4. Which contributed more to the outbreak of WWII: the terms of the Treaty of Versailles or poor enforcement of those terms? Use at least one event in the period 1919–32 and at least one event from 1933–39 to illustrate and support your answer.
5. Choose one of the individuals listed below and explain his impact on world politics:
   a. Woodrow Wilson
   b. Tsar Nicholas II
   c. Benito Mussolini
   d. Neville Chamberlain
6. Choose one of the actions listed below, identify the main reasons why the action was taken, briefly summarize the consequences of the action, and, in terms of the interests and objectives of the leaders who made it, explain why the decision to take the action was or was not correct:
   a. British entry into WWI, 1914
   b. U.S. entry into WWI, 1917
   c. U.S. refusal to join the League of Nations, 1919
   d. British appeasement of Germany at the Munich Conference, 1938
   e. Soviet signing of the Molotov–Ribentropp Pact, 1939
   f. German invasion of the USSR, 1941
   g. Japanese attack on Pearl Harbor, 1941
   h. U.S. use of the atomic bomb on Hiroshima, 1945

RECOMMENDED ENRICHMENT READINGS

Bell, P. M. H. *The Origins of the Second World War in Europe*. London: Longman, 1986. Fresh, balanced analysis of the causes of the war.

Fromkin, David. *A Peace to End All Peace*. New York: Holt, 1989. Outstanding story of the machinations of the Great Powers in the Middle East, showing how the struggle between imperialism and nationalism planted the seeds of contemporary regional conflicts.

Hogg, James F., ed. *The American Encounter: The United States and the Making of the Modern World*. New York: Basic Books, 1997. Collection of articles from *Foreign Affairs* magazine, many of which have influenced or reflected American thinking on world politics.

Keegan, John. *The Face of Battle*. New York: Viking, 1976. Gripping front-line depiction of ancient and modern combat; the story of the first day's fighting at the Somme in 1916 drives home the tragic futility of trench warfare.

• Kennedy, Paul. *The Rise and Fall of the Great Powers*. New York: Random House, 1987. (Recommend assignment of pp. 194–255.) Brilliant analysis of how changes in the balance of economic and military power shaped the origins and strategies of WWI.

Kindleberger, Charles P. *The World in Depression, 1929–1939*. Berkeley: University of California Press, 1986. Probably the best account of the Great Depression's impact on the world economy.

Lafore, Laurence. *The Long Fuse: An Interpretation of the Origins of World War I*. 2nd ed. New York: Lippincott, 1971. Well-presented, thorough, and balanced examination of the factors that put out the lights of Europe.

Lederer, Ivo J. *The Versailles Settlement: Was It Foredoomed to Failure?* Boston: Heath, 1960. Good presentation of several interpretations of the Treaty of Versailles.

Liddell Hart, B. H. *History of the First World War, 1914–1918*. London: Faber and Faber, 1938. Classic military history of the Great War.

———. *History of the Second World War*. New York: Putnam, 1971. Equally classic history of an even greater war.

Massie, Robert K. *Dreadnought: Britain, Germany, and the Coming of the Great War*. New York: Random House, 1991. Very thorough and engaging narrative of how the Anglo–German naval arms race led to enmity and war, concentrating on the colorful personalities involved.

Rhodes, Richard. *The Making of the Atomic Bomb*. New York: Simon and Schuster, 1986. A rewarding history of the Manhattan Project, regardless of whether one regards the development of the bomb as a strategic necessity, a remarkable scientific and technical achievement, or an grievous sin.

Shirer, William L. *The Rise and Fall of the Third Reich*. New York: Simon and Schuster, 1960. The classic history of Nazi Germany.

Taylor, A. J. P. *The Origins of the Second World War*. New York: Atheneum, 1965. A discussion of the Munich agreement and its implications.

Tuchman, Barbara. *The Guns of August*. New York: Macmillan, 1962. Masterful story of the first disastrous month of World War I, which shattered so many of Europe's political, strategic, and cultural illusions.

• Van Evera, Stephen. "The Cult of the Offensive and the Origins of the First World War." *International Security* 9, no. 1 (summer 1984): 58–107. The original presentation of the "cult of the offensive" thesis and its implications for modern policy and strategy.

The Cold War

SCOPE, OBJECTIVES, AND APPROACH

This chapter outlines the period of Soviet–American rivalry from the mid-1940s to the early 1990s and explains why the superpowers' political and strategic interaction became the defining characteristic of the international system of that era. It discusses key events in much more detail than the preceding historical chapters, in keeping with the books' "sharpening of focus" as the historical narrative moves closer to the present. The chapter concentrates on the waxing and waning of U.S.–Soviet tensions during the Cold War, describing how the "mood swings" in the Soviet–American relationship affected the probabilities for cooperation and conflict. It reviews some contending explanations for the beginning and the ending of the Cold War in some detail, again encouraging students to use the various analytical frameworks to form their own interpretations of the origins and conclusion of the conflict dominating world politics in the second half of the twentieth century.

WHAT STUDENTS SHOULD LEARN FROM THIS CHAPTER

Foundation Level

1. Identify the six principal explanations for the "outbreak" of the Cold War.

2. Identify the main periods of increase and relaxation in Cold War tensions.
3. Describe the precipitating events and consequences of the Korean War.
4. Describe the basic concept of nuclear deterrence.
5. Explain the conflicts underlying the Cuban Missile Crisis and the risks involved in that confrontation.
6. Identify U.S. objectives in the Vietnam War.
7. Explain the significance of the era of détente.
8. Outline the philosophy and objectives of Gorbachev's policies of perestroika.
9. Identify the four major explanations advanced for the end of the Cold War.

Enrichment Level

1. Outline the goals of the U.S. strategy of containment.
2. Describe the goals and methods of Soviet foreign policy under Nikita Khrushchev.
3. Outline how the Kennedy administration's policy toward regional conflicts differed from the Eisenhower administration's policies.
4. Explain the significance of the Sino–Soviet dispute.
5. Explain why the Johnson and Nixon administrations found it difficult to disengage the United States from the war in Vietnam.
6. List the goals of both parties in the SALT process.
7. Identify the USSR's objectives in the invasion of Afghanistan and describe the Carter administration's reaction to it.
8. Explain the objectives and significance of the Reagan Doctrine.
9. List the main reasons for the collapse of the communist regimes in Eastern Europe and the USSR.

Mastery Level

1. Identify the strengths and weaknesses of the contending explanations for the start of the Cold War.
2. Describe the Truman Doctrine and identify the events that led to its adoption.
3. Explain why the formation of NATO represented a historic shift in the orientation of U.S. foreign policy.
4. Explain the political and social impact of McCarthyism.
5. Identify the view of U.S.–Soviet relations underlying the Eisenhower administration's policy of "roll-back" and describe how this policy was put into practice.
6. Explain the significance of Nixon's visit to China.
7. Identify the view of U.S.–Soviet relations underlying the Nixon administration's policy of "linkage" and describe how this policy was put into practice.
8. Outline the main reasons why the United States and USSR became dissatisfied with détente.
9. Assess the strengths and shortcomings of the contending explanations for the Cold War's end.

OUTLINE OF THE CHAPTER

0. Introduction
   A. The bipolar conflict between the United States and the USSR dominated world politics between the end of WWII (1945) and the collapse of the USSR (1991).
   B. This chapter outlines the major explanations advanced for the onset and end of the Cold War and discusses how and why it brought the frightening spectre of nuclear war—but also a kind of comforting stability—to international relations in the mid to late twentieth century.

I. Who or What Caused the Cold War?
   A. Various explanations
      1. Six basic explanations for the "outbreak" of the Cold War are commonly advanced.
      2. All three levels of analysis are represented among them, and they are likely to continue to be debated in the future.
   B. It Was Moscow's Fault

1. Conventional American view: the Cold War was caused by Soviet aggression and expansionism.
2. This view hold that the USSR was an "evil empire," which the United States was correct in containing at all costs.
3. The personality and policies of Soviet leader Josef Stalin deserve special blame under this explanation.
4. Example of a domestic-level argument, though emphasizing Stalin, adds an element of the individual level (see Chapter Twelve).

C. No, It Was Washington's Fault
1. Alternative view: The United States is to blame, because it tried to expand its overseas influence and markets after WWII and failed to comprehend the USSR's severe security problems after the war.
2. Variant: U.S. development and use of the atomic bomb at the end of WWII was intended as a political warning to the USSR and caused the Soviet Union to be even more concerned for its own security.
3. This is a domestic-level argument.

D. Ideological Conflict
1. U.S. and Soviet political and economic systems (capitalism and communism) were incompatible; conflict between the two systems was inevitable.
2. Variant: Either capitalism or communism (choose one) is inherently evil and aggressive.
3. This is a domestic-level argument.

E. Leadership or the Lack Thereof
1. U.S. and Soviet leaders and their policies drew their countries into the Cold War.
   a. Truman had little experience in foreign policy and was more suspicious of Soviet intentions than Roosevelt had been.
   b. Stalin's suspicious nature led him to magnify his perceptions of the threat posed by the United States to the USSR after the war, carrying out brutally oppressive policies in Russia and the territories liberated by Soviet forces, which appalled and alarmed the West.
2. This explanation is an individual-level argument, though it does not necessarily paint U.S. and/or Soviet leaders as heroes and villains—only fallible human beings.

F. One World Divided by Two Superpowers Equals Conflict
1. The international system became *bipolar* (dominated by only two "superpowers" capable of challenging each other and exercising global influence; see Chapter Thirteen); therefore, conflict of some kind between the two was inevitable.
2. A systemic-level argument stresses *realpolitik* and the security dilemma (see Chapter Eleven).
3. Under this explanation, there is no point in assigning blame, as the two major states in any bipolar system are bound to conflict.

G. It Was All a Misunderstanding
1. Neither the United States nor the USSR harbored hostile intentions toward each other after WWII, but both misinterpreted the other's actions, creating a spiral of mistrust and tension.
2. Another systemic-level explanation; conflict may not have been inevitable, but considering the limited information available to the leaders of both superpowers, breaking the cycle of misperception would have been very difficult.

II. Heating Up the Cold War, 1945–53
A. Initial Confrontations: Iran, Greece, Turkey
1. The first international crisis post–WWII occurred in 1946 when the USSR refused to withdraw its troops from Iran as provided for in a Soviet–British agreement.
2. Moscow backed down, which may have led the United States and United Kingdom to believe that pressure on Moscow could convince the USSR to stop supplying communist partisans in Greece (through the newly established communist governments in Eastern Europe) and cease pressuring Turkey for territorial concessions and access to the Mediterranean.

B. The Iron Curtain Descends
1. By 1946, the West began to perceive a growing Soviet threat to Europe; Churchill warned that an "Iron Curtain" was descending across the continent, dividing the West from the Soviet-controlled East.
2. In 1947, Britain, weakened and devastated by the war, informed the United States that it could no longer afford to counter Soviet advances in Greece and Turkey; withdrawing from its empire, Britain thus effectively conceded its leading role in world affairs to the United States.

C. Truman Doctrine
1. In 1947, to overcome isolationist sentiments in the United States in order to persuade Congress to authorize aid to Greece and Turkey, Truman portrayed the conflict between Western democracy and communism as a struggle between freedom and oppression, good and evil.

    2. The policy of U.S. aid to states attempting to resist communist insurgencies or takeovers became known as the *Truman Doctrine*.

  D. Marshall Plan

    1. Also in 1947, the United States offered a massive program of economic aid (known as the Marshall Plan after U.S. Secretary of State George Marshall) to the war-demolished nations of Europe (including the USSR).

    2. The USSR rejected Marshall Plan aid in 1948, however, and forbade the communist Eastern European governments to accept it, claiming that it was an attempt to establish U.S. economic domination of Europe.

    3. The Marshall Plan was a huge success and had three lasting effects:

      a. It revitalized Western European economies.

      b. It thwarted communist influence in Western Europe by easing the economic hardship that served as a breeding ground for discontent and communist agitation (particularly in France and Italy).

      c. It facilitated European economic and political integration, a process that would culminate in the European Union decades later (see Chapter Seven).

  E. Stalin and Tito

    1. Initially, the USSR allowed the communist regimes in Eastern Europe considerable latitude in their policies; elections (though biased) were held in which noncommunist parties could compete.

    2. After friction developed between Stalin and Josef Broz Tito, popular communist and nationalist leader of Yugoslavia, Stalin began to crack down on the Eastern European states to prevent any other independent communist leaders from emerging.

  F. Czech Coup

    1. In 1948, Soviet-backed communist forces seized power in Czechoslovakia (which had been considering whether to accept Marshall Plan aid) in a heavy-handed coup.

    2. The coup convinced the West that Stalin had never intended to keep his promise, made at Yalta, of open elections in Eastern Europe and precipitated an open break between Stalin and Tito.

  G. Berlin Blockade

    1. In June 1948, Soviet forces closed all land access routes to the Western-occupied sectors of Berlin (which, like Germany, had been divided into four Allied occupation zones) and refused to allow food, fuel, or other supplies to enter the Western zones.

    2. The United States responded by organizing a massive airlift of basic necessities to West Berlin, which the USSR could not stop without going to war with the Western Allies.

    3. The blockade was halted in May 1949, but the crude attempt to take control of all of Berlin reinforced the USSR's aggressive reputation in the West.

    4. During the blockade, the USSR and the Western Allies took independent steps to set up governments in their occupied zones of Germany (the Federal Republic of Germany in the West and the German Democratic Republic in the East); both sides wanted unification of Germany under their own terms and could not tolerate a unified German state under the other's terms, so the division of Germany resulted by default.

  H. NATO Alliance

    1. The Berlin Blockade convinced the Western Allies that a new alliance was necessary to resist possible future Soviet aggression in Europe.

    2. In April 1949, the nations of Western Europe joined with the United States and Canada to form the North Atlantic Treaty Organization (NATO).

    3. NATO was the first alliance the United States had entered into in peacetime; entry into a permanent alliance was a rejection of the historic U.S. policy of isolationism.

III. The Cold War in Asia

  A. Chinese Revolution

    1. Communists and Nationalists had been struggling for control of China since the 1920s; after WWII, the Nationalist Kuomintang, led by Chiang Kai-shek, was rapidly weakening in strength and declining in popularity due to rampant corruption and undemocratic policies.

    2. The United States was thus caught in the quintessential Cold War dilemma: support a repressive regime or allow potentially pro-Soviet communist forces to win control of a strategically important country; a compromise U.S. aid policy alienated the Chinese Communists, but didn't provide enough aid to their opponents to prevent a communist victory.

    3. In 1949, Chinese Communists led by Mao Zedong won the civil war and established the People's Republic of China; the Nationalists retreated to Taiwan; Stalin and Mao signed an alliance, but inherent Sino–Soviet tensions were apparent from the start.

B. NSC-68
  1. The communist victory in China in 1949 and the USSR's test of an atomic bomb that same year convinced many in the United States that military measures, as well as political and economic ones, would be necessary to carry out the U.S. strategic objective of *containment* of the USSR (preventing further expansion of Soviet control or influence).
  2. The National Security Council prepared a controversial plan, *NSC-68*, for the increase of U.S. armed forces to levels unprecedented in peacetime; Truman, and many congressional leaders, did not accept the plan at first, fearing that the high military spending called for in the plan would ruin the U.S. economy.
C. Korea: The Turning Point
  1. After WWII, Korea, like Germany, had been divided into Soviet and U.S. occupation zones; the USSR arranged a rigged election in the North, and a communist government under Kim Il Sung (the same Kim in office in 1994) took over.
  2. Both the USSR and the United States withdrew their occupation forces by 1950; U.S. Secretary of State Dean Acheson may have appeared to "write off" South Korea by proposing a U.S. defense perimeter in Asia that seemed to exclude that country.
  3. In June 1950, North Korean forces attacked the South, attempting to unify the country by force; the USSR refused to participate in a UN Security Council debate on the crisis (boycotting the assignment of China's seat on the council to the Nationalists), and the Security Council authorized intervention into the war by a U.S.-led coalition (much as it did in the Iraqi invasion of Kuwait in 1991).
  4. The U.S.-led UN intervention saved South Korea, but talk of "unleashing" Nationalist forces against the PRC and a UN offensive into North Korea resulted in Chinese intervention on the Northern side.
  5. The Korean War became stalemated near the original border along the 38th parallel; in 1953, newly elected U.S. President Eisenhower warned that if the war was not halted, the United States might use nuclear weapons, and a cease-fire was negotiated in July 1953. (North and South Korea remain officially in a state of war.)
  6. The Korean War was a turning point in the Cold War.
     a. The war prompted the adoption of NSC-68 and a large buildup of U.S. and NATO military forces.
     b. U.S. involvement in Asia was increased, and the U.S.–Soviet and U.S.–Chinese conflict was heightened.
     c. The global U.S.–Soviet conflict worsened, as many Americans began to view communist action anywhere in the world as a threat to U.S. vital interests.
     d. The war set a precedent for *limited war,* in which nuclear weapons were not used and U.S. and Soviet troops avoided direct combat with each other (though there were some dogfights between U.S. aircraft and Soviet pilots flying North Korean or Chinese planes).

IV. Relaxation and a Renewal of Tensions, 1953–57
  A. New Leaders, New Challenges
    1. The death of Josef Stalin in 1953 precipitated a power struggle among his potential successors, who faced difficult domestic challenges.
    2. Changes in Soviet policy were reflected in the 1955 agreement between the major powers for the neutralization of Austria.
  B. Spirit of Geneva
    1. A summit meeting in Geneva in 1955 between Soviet leaders and Eisenhower resulted in no concrete agreements, but helped reduce tensions.
    2. Nikita Khrushchev's 1956 "Secret Speech" indicated that sweeping changes in Soviet domestic and foreign policies might be forthcoming.
  C. Regional Tensions Return
    1. In 1953 and 1956, domestic unrest posed serious challenges to communist rule in East Germany, Poland, and Hungary; the new Hungarian regime was crushed by a Soviet invasion when it announced its intention to leave the *Warsaw Pact* (the Soviet led Eastern-bloc counterpart of NATO).
    2. In Asia, military incidents between the PRC and the nationalist Republic of China led to two Taiwan Straits crises in 1954 and 1958.
  D. Third World
    1. In the 1950s, the USSR began to establish ties with newly independent nations in Asia and Africa that had previously been under European colonial control.
    2. The United States sought to limit Soviet influence in these developing "Third World" countries, leading to an further globalization of the Cold War.
       a. A U.S.-engineered coup overthrew the Iranian government in 1953.

b. In 1954, another CIA-backed coup ousted the president of Guatemala, whom the United States believed to be influenced and supported by communists.

c. Suez Crisis: Egyptian President Gamel Abdel Nasser's nationalization of the Suez Canal in 1956 led to a British, French, and Israeli invasion of Egypt; Eisenhower, infuriated by their pretense and collusion, exerted diplomatic and economic pressure to force a halt to the action, but the debacle increased the U.S. and Soviet role in the Middle East.

d. The defeat of French forces in Vietnam in 1954 resulted in the division of the country into communist North and U.S.-backed South, initially intended as a transitional stage until nationwide elections.

E. The Nonaligned Movement

1. Beginning in the mid-1950s, Third World nations attempted to assert their independence from both the USSR and the United States and to play the superpowers off against each other in order to gain aid.

2. The USSR established close relations with a number of nonaligned countries (especially India and Egypt), which led to U.S. distrust of the movement and an increase in aid to anticommunist U.S. allies (including Iran and South Vietnam).

V. To the Brink and Back, 1957–64

A. Sputnik

1. After the Suez crisis, recent Soviet economic success, and the USSR's launching of the first artificial satellite in 1957, the communist East appeared to some to be gaining political, technological, and economic advantages over the West.

2. Khrushchev's rhetoric, which stressed the superiority of Soviet rocket technology, acted to increase this perception, but the United States responded by instituting a massive space program and programs to develop strategic missiles.

3. The "Missile Gap": Eisenhower's opponents claimed that his administration had allowed the USSR to gain superiority in strategic weapons, though this was not actually the case; nevertheless; as missile arsenals increased, the fear of nuclear war and pressure for disarmament became widespread.

B. Quemoy and Matsu

1. In 1958, Chinese Communists resumed shelling Quemoy and Matsu, two islands off the coast of Taiwan.

2. Although the United States threatened war, the Soviets withheld strong support for their allies, and the Chinese eventually ceased the shelling.

C. New Tensions: Berlin and Cuba

1. In 1958, a crisis erupted over Soviet demands for the Western Allies' withdrawal from Berlin.

2. In 1959, Fidel Castro overthrew a corrupt and repressive pro–U.S. regime in Cuba (see box); after the United States imposed economic sanctions, Castro turned to the USSR for aid and developed close relations with Moscow.

D. Summitry

1. A series of meetings between U.S. and Soviet leaders in 1958–59 helped reduce Cold War tensions.

2. Khrushchev visited the United States in 1959 and received a warm welcome, and a reciprocal visit by Eisenhower to the USSR was planned.

E. U-2 Incident

1. Plans for Eisenhower's visit were canceled, however, after an American U-2 reconnaissance plane was shot down over the USSR in 1960.

2. The incident resulted in a return to tension and mutual suspicion.

F. JFK, Cold Warrior

1. John F. Kennedy's administration took office in 1961 with promises to strengthen America's hand in the Cold War with a stronger defense and more active foreign policy.

2. Kennedy's strategic programs included adoption of the doctrine of *flexible response,* under which U.S. forces would respond to Soviet actions in kind at any level of conflict (from guerrilla warfare to nuclear war) and the rapid building of ICBMs, bombers, and submarine-launched missiles to redress the purported "missile gap."

3. An abortive U.S.-backed invasion by Cuban exiles at the Bay of Pigs in 1961 humiliated the United States and alarmed Castro.

4. U.S. aid programs such as the Peace Corps tried to bolster U.S. influence and reputation in the Third World.

G. Berlin Wall

1. A crisis erupted when East German authorities sealed off West Berlin with barbed wire and concrete barricades in August 1961 in an effort to stop the flow of refugees.

2. The outcome allowed both sides to claim victory, but U.S.–Soviet tensions escalated further.

H. Cuban Missile Crisis

1. Sometime in 1962, Soviet medium-range nuclear missiles were secretly placed in Cuba; in October 1962, however, before they could become operational, they were detected by U.S. intelligence.

2. The resulting crisis was the most acute of the Cold War.

a. The United States demanded the withdrawal of the missiles and threatened military action if they were not removed.

b. The United States instituted a blockade ("quarantine") of Cuba to prevent any further Soviet weapons from entering the island.

c. Fears of nuclear war peaked, but the USSR agreed to withdraw the missiles (the United States had indisputable conventional military superiority in the Caribbean and a strong lead in strategic forces); war was averted, but the USSR was humiliated.

3. The immediate result of the crisis was a relaxation of Cold War tensions and establishment of the Moscow–Washington "hot line" to improve communication.

4. The USSR, however, became determined to achieve strategic parity with the United States and began building up its nuclear forces at tremendous cost.

5. Americans became overconfident about the ability of the United States to accomplish its foreign policy tasks; the United States now underestimated the difficulties of containing communism in the Third World.

VI. Intensified Competition, 1964–68

A. Leadership Changes

1. The early 1960s saw changes in leadership styles in the United States and USSR.

2. JFK was assassinated in 1963 and Khrushchev was ousted in 1964.

B. Dominican Republic

1. The new U.S. President, Lyndon Johnson, had little experience or interest in foreign policy, but was determined to maintain a strong posture against communism.

2. U.S. Marines intervened in the Dominican Republic to back an authoritarian anticommunist regime in 1965.

C. Vietnam

1. By 1963, the United States had more than 16,000 military advisors in South Vietnam; that country's president Diem was overthrown and killed in a coup (to which the United States acquiesced) that same year, but North Vietnamese and communist Vietcong forces continued to gain the upper hand.

2. In 1965, Johnson sent U.S. combat forces into Vietnam to forestall a communist victory; though the United States tried to keep the war limited (to avoid provoking intervention by China, as in the Korean War), more and more troops were progressively sent, until by 1968 the United States had more than 500,000 soldiers fighting in Vietnam.

3. U.S. troops, military aid, and bombing campaigns failed to defeat the Vietcong or strengthen the corrupt South Vietnamese regime; the fruitless conflict became increasingly unpopular with the U.S. public, and protests erupted all over the United States.

D. The Six-Day War

1. In an attempt to unite their Arab allies, Moscow spread false reports about a purported Israeli invasion of Syria in May 1967; the strategy backfired as Israel launched a preemptive attack and quickly defeated the Arab armies.

2. Israel's occupation of territories captured during the conflict led both superpowers to increase their involvement in the region.

E. The Prague Spring

1. Pro-reform communist leaders in Czechoslovakia, led by Alexander Dubcek, adopted liberalizing policies, but in 1968 Warsaw Pact forces invaded and restored a government more subservient to Moscow.

2. Soviet leader Leonid Brezhnev justified the invasion by asserting the USSR's right to ensure the survival of any neighboring socialist regime, which came to be known as the "Brezhnev Doctrine."

F. Strategic Parity and the Nonproliferation Treaty

1. Following the Soviet Union's build-up of nuclear weapons and missiles in the 1960s, neither superpower could claim military superiority over the other and both were left vulnerable to attack.

2. American strategists were guided by the belief in mutual assured destruction (MAD), while Soviet leaders believed that strategic parity would finally force the U.S. to accept it as an equal.

3. In 1968, Britain, the U.S., and the USSR signed the Nuclear Nonproliferation Treaty, in which they pledged not to employ nuclear weapons against or share nuclear weapons technology with non-nuclear states that signed the treaty.

VII. Era of Détente, 1969–79

    A. The Sino–Soviet Split

        1. The Cultural Revolution in China intensified Sino–Soviet differences in the mid to late 1960s, and border troops of the two communist giants clashed in 1969.

        2. Taking advantage of the opportunity presented by the dispute, the Nixon administration sought to open a dialogue with China in hopes of gaining leverage over Russia and facilitating U.S. exit from the Vietnam War.

        3. In February 1972, U.S. President Nixon (who had been an ardent anticommunist in Congress and as vice-president) visited China, signaling new flexibility in U.S. policy.

        4. The new American policy toward China did facilitate U.S. withdrawal from Vietnam, helped China's communist government assume a permanent UN seat, and also transformed the U.S. image of China.

    B. Linkage

        1. Nixon and Kissinger sought to improve U.S.–Soviet relations by gradually making the USSR more comfortable with the international status quo.

        2. The United States acknowledged the USSR's superpower status and attainment of strategic parity with the United States, signaling that the United States would deal with the USSR on an equal basis.

        3. The United States also tried to gain acceptance of a set of rules or "code of conduct" in the international arena to try to moderate the security dilemma.

        4. Kissinger, especially, sought to explicitly link economic and political incentives to Soviet behavior on a *quid pro quo* basis, attempting to use "carrots and sticks" to moderate Soviet actions.

    C. The Moscow Summit and SALT

        1. In May 1972, at a summit in Moscow, Nixon and Brezhnev signed the first *Strategic Arms Limitation Treaty* (SALT I).

        2. The treaty, designed to stabilize the arms race, included limits on offensive missiles and restrictions on antiballistic missiles (ABM; see Chapter Eleven).

        3. Economic and trade agreements and an agreement on "basic principles of mutual relations" were also signed at the Moscow Summit.

        4. The new phase of the Cold War, which seemed to promise a less hostile relationship between the superpowers, became known as the era of détente (French for "relaxation of tensions").

        5. U.S. moves to establish détente followed steps taken in Europe to reduce East–West tensions.

            a. German Chancellor Brandt's *ostpolitik* sought to improve relations between the two Germanies and between Bonn and Moscow.

            b. France had attempted to warm relations with the USSR also.

    D. Tensions in Détente

        1. As the 1970s progressed, it became apparent that the United States and USSR had different goals and expectations for détente.

            a. The United States, by giving the USSR a "stake in the system," hoped to avoid confrontations and challenges to each others' vital interests.

            b. The USSR regarded détente as a recognition of political equivalence with the United States, expected that the Cold War competition would continue, and saw no contradiction between détente and support for "national liberation movements" in the Third World.

        2. Many Americans opposed closer engagement with the USSR while ignoring human rights abuses; U.S. economic aid was linked to allowance of Jewish emigration from the USSR in the Jackson–Vanik Amendment of 1975, which Moscow viewed as an interference in Soviet internal affairs.

        3. After the United States withdrew from Vietnam in 1973, many Americans wanted to avoid further involvement in Third World conflicts; while the United States attempted to recover from the political and social turmoil caused by the war and the Watergate scandal, Vietnam fell to communists in 1975.

        4. Other Third World conflicts exacerbated U.S.–Soviet tensions:

            a. The Arab–Israeli War of 1973 resulted in an alert of U.S. nuclear forces and an Arab oil embargo against the United States.

            b. Throughout the 1970s, tensions rose as Soviet and Cuban aid flowed to socialist forces fighting U.S.-backed factions in civil wars in Angola, Ethiopia, Mozambique, and elsewhere.

            c. The USSR increased its military presence at bases in Third World states in Asia and Africa, further alarming the United States.

d. The CIA was involved in the overthrow of the Marxist-leaning president of Chile, Salvador Allende, in 1973.

E. From Dialogue to Discord: The Carter Administration

1. In 1977, new U.S. President Jimmy Carter emphasized interdependence, economic factors, and human rights in his foreign policy.

2. The Conference on Security and Cooperation in Europe (CSCE) accepted Soviet positions on political issues (especially borders) in return for guarantees of human rights; the USSR did not take these guarantees seriously at first, but "Helsinki Watch" committees in Eastern Bloc states organized to monitor compliance.

3. Carter and Brezhnev signed SALT II in 1979, though the U.S. Senate never ratified the treaty (see Chapter Eleven).

4. Conflicts in the Third World continued to undermine détente.

   a. The pro–United States Shah of Iran was overthrown in 1979 and replaced with a fanatically anti–United States regime.

   b. A U.S.-leaning dictatorship in Nicaragua was overthrown in 1979 and succeeded by the socialist-oriented Sandinista Front, which quickly fell out with the United States and accepted Soviet and Cuban military aid.

VIII. The Cold War Returns, 1979–85

A. Invasion of Afghanistan

1. In 1979, the USSR sent troops into Afghanistan to install a more strongly pro-Soviet regime.

2. The invasion was widely denounced in the West and Third World as an act of aggression, while the invasion itself became bogged down in guerrilla warfare against U.S.-backed resistance fighters.

3. The Carter administration applied economic sanctions and withdrew the U.S. team from the Moscow Olympics in 1980, but the Soviet intervention continued, and many in the United States viewed these responses a pusillanimous.

B. Reagan and the Reagan Doctrine

1. Ronald Reagan became U.S. President in 1981, pledging to return to a more assertive form of containment of the USSR.

2. Reagan labeled the USSR the "evil empire" and increased U.S. support for anticommunist insurgencies in the Third World, a policy that became known as the "Reagan Doctrine."

3. The Reagan Doctrine was accompanied by large, controversial, and expensive improvements in U.S. military forces.

4. U.S. forces intervened unsuccessfully in Lebanon to attempt to halt an ongoing civil war in 1982 and successfully to defeat a newly installed Marxist government in Grenada in 1983.

5. By 1985, arms control came to a temporary halt as the United States went ahead with plans to deploy missiles in Europe to counter recently deployed Soviet intermediate range missiles, and the USSR walked out of nuclear arms control negotiations in Geneva.

IX. The Cold War Ends, 1985–91

A. Death of Brezhnev

1. After Brezhnev's death in 1982, the USSR began to experience domestic political upheavals.

2. The economic stagnation, bureaucratic inefficiency, corruption, and blatant disregard for human rights inherent in the Soviet system became increasingly apparent.

B. The Gorbachev Era

1. In 1985, Mikhail Gorbachev became head of the Soviet Communist Party and instituted policies of *glasnost* (openness) and *perestroika* (economic restructuring).

2. The reforms did not go far enough to reinvigorate the Soviet economy, however, but went too far to be tolerated by the communist establishment.

3. In the late 1980s, the USSR refused to prop up communist regimes in Eastern Europe with military support or economic aid; this revocation of the Brezhnev doctrine was followed by mass uprisings in the communist states; liberalizing reforms and/or new repression failed to quiet public discontent, and communist regimes in Poland, Hungary, East Germany, Czechoslovakia, and Romania fell in 1989.

C. The Cold War Ends

1. The Berlin Wall was dismantled in 1989, and Germany was unified under the Federal Republic in 1991.

2. After an abortive coup by hard-line communists failed in 1991, the Soviet regime was completely discredited, and the Soviet Union broke up into an independent Russia and other republics at the end of the year.

3. The Cold War thus ended with a whimper, rather than a nuclear bang.

X. Why Did the Cold War End?
   A. Explanations
      1. As with the beginning of the Cold War, there are a number of contending explanations for the Cold War's end.
      2. Each explanation corresponds to an image of world politics and level of analysis.
   B. The Gorbachev Factor
      1. Mikhail Gorbachev's leadership and policies were instrumental in the end of the Cold War; had leaders with attitudes similar to Brezhnev or Stalin been in power in the late 1980s, the Cold War might still be going on.
      2. This explanation fits with the individual level of analysis and the "great man" theory of world politics.
   C. The End of History
      1. According to this explanation, internal changes in Soviet policy and society made the United States and USSR more compatible.
      2. The demonstrable failure of the Soviet system signaled the triumph of capitalism over communism and thus an end to global ideological conflict (though it might continue in some areas of the Third World) (see Fukuyama article in recommended readings).
      3. This view offers a domestic-level explanation—conflict ended as systems of government became similar.
   D. End of the Evil Empire
      1. In this view, the Cold War ended because the Soviet Union became too weak to challenge the United States and ultimately collapsed; Kennan's doctrine of containment, using "counterforce" to stop Soviet expansion, prevailed without the need for direct military confrontation.
      2. A variant of this argument holds that economic and military competition with the West was the deciding factor in the collapse of the Soviet system; therefore, the United States was right to pursue its military buildup and assertive policies of the late 1980s.
      3. This is essentially a systemic-level, *realpolitik* explanation for the end of the Cold War.
   E. A New World Order
      1. The Cold War ended from this perspective because of the decline in bipolarity; the USSR ceased to be strong enough to challenge the United States globally, and other states gained in economic and political strength.
      2. In this view, the real "winners" of the Cold War are Europe and Germany, which relied on the United States for military security while they invested in their own economies; the world is heading either towards unipolarity (with the United States as the only superpower, facing no real challengers) or multipolarity (see Chapter Twelve), as new "economic superpowers" challenge the United States for global economic leadership.
      3. This view is another systemic-level explanation.

XI. Conclusion
   A. In comparison with the history presented in the previous two chapters, the Cold War was really the Long Peace—more than 40 years with no wars between major powers, despite (or perhaps because of) the presence of huge nuclear arsenals on both sides.
   B. This chapter has attempted to present contending perspectives on the beginning, perpetuation, and end of the Cold War so that readers may decide for themselves whether personalities, global power politics, economic competition, or ideology best explains the conflict; the debate is likely to continue for years to come.

HOW THE CHAPTER RELATES TO CENTRAL THEMES OF THE TEXT

Like the text's other historical chapters, Chapter Four provides examples of events, policies, and personalities that will be used to illustrate concepts and theories presented in later chapters. The contending explanations for the start and end of the Cold War are examples of theories grounded in specific levels of analysis, further familiarizing students with those key concepts. More generally, the chapter traces the waxing and waning of cooperation and conflict between the superpowers during the Cold War, showing how both can occur simultaneously. (In the era of détente, for example, arms control and trade negotiations progressed while disputes over human rights continued.)

The Cold War era saw the ultimate globalization of politics—any conflict, no matter how local, could become an East–West issue if either superpower became involved, and the global U.S.–Soviet confrontation affected local and regional conflicts throughout the world. It will come as no surprise, however, that fragmentation was also a major factor during this period; ethnic and national conflicts in the Third World frustrated efforts by the superpowers to establish a mutually acceptable "code of conduct" during détente, for example. The end of the Cold War also saw an upsurge in fragmentation, as the political unity imposed on members of the Warsaw Pact collapsed and the USSR itself disintegrated.

The tensions between isolationism and internationalism, and idealism versus realism, are palpable during this period. U.S. leaders such as Truman, Dulles, and Kissinger had to use American values and ideals to justify policies designed to pursue *realpolitik* objectives, and proponents of disarmament constantly questioned the morality of nuclear deterrence. During the Vietnam War, the principles of *realpolitik*, anticommunism, liberal internationalism, and noninterference in other states' affairs all collided, and the crash shook the foundations of American society.

SUGGESTED LECTURE TOPICS

1. Illustrate the policy options available to Truman when Britain notified the United States that it could no longer support anticommunist forces in Greece and Turkey, noting how each option would signal the primary course of postwar U.S. foreign policy (return to isolationism, reliance on multilateralism, or active containment of the USSR). Point out the domestic constraints that had to be overcome in pursuing each policy.
2. Survey the postwar world from the Soviet perspective; point out Moscow's security concerns in Europe (especially Germany) and interests in South and East Asia.
3. Discuss the various instances in the 1950s when greater U.S.–Soviet cooperation seemed possible, only to be frustrated by events such as the Suez Crisis and the U-2 incident. Did these chances represent missed opportunities, or was the whole idea of improving superpower relations futile at that time?
4. Compare the strategy of containment as articulated by Kennan with the policy courses adopted by the Eisenhower, Kennedy, Nixon, Carter, and Reagan administrations. Which came closest to Kennan's idea of containment? Was the basic concept of containment sound or flawed?
5. Discuss the superpowers' expectations for the era of détente and the events that brought that era to a close. Were the expectations of Moscow or Washington, or both, unreasonable?
6. Explain the start and the end of the Cold War from the three levels of analysis, using the contending theories presented in this chapter. Encourage students to independently evaluate the possible causes.

STUDY AND EXAM QUESTIONS

1. Which of the contending causes for the Cold War discussed in this chapter best explains the onset of superpower conflict after WWII? Use three events from the years 1945–50 as evidence in support of your answer.
2. Was the Cold War inevitable? Why or why not? Discuss two events from the period 1945–53 to show why the global conflict between the United States and the USSR could or could not have been avoided.
3. Was the United States correct in adopting the strategy of containment? Be sure to define containment in your answer, give two historical examples of its application, and discuss the major costs and benefits of the strategy.
4. Was the Kennedy administration's policy toward the USSR guided primarily by idealism or by realism? Use three events or policy programs (the Peace Corps, flexible response, foreign aid, etc.) from the period 1961–63 to support your answer.
5. Which side deserves more blame for the failure of détente—the United States, the USSR, or were both equally at fault? Discuss how two regional conflicts during the period 1973–79 show where primary responsibility for the failure of détente resides.
6. "The assertive foreign policy and strong defense posture of the United States during the Reagan administration were major causes of the end of the Cold War." Do you agree with this statement? Use three events from the years 1981–90 to show why it is correct or incorrect.
7. Choose one of the individuals listed below and explain his impact on world politics:
   a. Josef Stalin
   b. Harry Truman
   c. Nikita Khrushchev
   d. Richard Nixon
   e. Jimmy Carter
   f. Mikhail Gorbachev

RECOMMENDED ENRICHMENT READINGS

Blight, James G., and David A. Welch. *On the Brink: Americans and Soviets Reexamine the Cuban Missile Crisis.* New York: Hill and Wang, 1989. Many of the decision makers involved discuss one of the most frightening (or reassuring, depending on one's viewpoint) episodes of the Cold War.

• Fukuyama, Francis. "The End of History?" *The National Interest,* summer 1989, 3–18. Concise, intriguing presentation of his "End of History" thesis.

Gaddis, John Lewis. *Strategies of Containment.* New York: Oxford University Press, 1982. Very well done examination of containment, and especially its military aspects, from the Truman through Carter administrations.

• ———. "The Long Peace: Elements of Stability in the Postwar International System." *International Security* 10, no. 4 (spring 1986): 99–142. Outstanding examination of why the Cold War stayed cold, discussing influences operating on all three levels of analysis.

Garthoff, Raymond L. *Détente and Confrontation.* Washington: Brookings, 1985. Thorough, detailed study of the rise and fall of détente.

———. *The Great Transition: American–Soviet Relations and the End of the Cold War.* Washington: Brookings, 1994. Comprehensive account of the waning of U.S.–Soviet conflict and transition to a new and uncertain relationship between Washington and Moscow.

Goncharov, Sergei N., John W. Lewis, and Xue Litai. *Uncertain Partners: Stalin, Mao, and the Korean War.* Stanford, Calif.: Stanford University Press, 1993. Fascinating analysis of Soviet and Chinese decisions leading up to the war and of the roots of the Sino–Soviet conflict.

Hyland, William. *The Cold War: Fifty Years of Conflict.* Rev. ed. New York: Times Books, 1991. Good one-volume history of the period.

Khrushchev, Nikita S. *Khrushchev Remembers: The Last Testament.* Translated and edited Strobe Talbott. Boston: Little, Brown, 1974. The Soviet leader reflects on his years in power; somewhat more self-serving than most memoirs, but intriguing and informative nonetheless.

Kissinger, Henry. *White House Years.* Boston: Little, Brown, 1979. A classic insider account of foreign policy making in Washington. Highly recommended, especially for its unabashed tone of self importance.

LaFeber, Walter. *America, Russia, and the Cold War 1945–1990.* 6th ed. New York: McGraw-Hill, 1991. Useful revisionist history of the U.S.–Soviet conflict, often critical of American policy.

Larson, Deborah Welch. *Origins of Containment: A Psychological Explanation.* Princeton, N.J.: Princeton University Press, 1985. Expert individual-level analysis of U.S. entry into the Cold War.

Lebow, Richard Ned, and Janice Gross Stein. *We All Lost the Cold War.* Princeton, N.J.: Princeton University Press, 1994. Provides a detailed explanation of Soviet and U.S. decisions in the Cuban Missile Crisis and in the 1973 Arab–Israeli War, while addressing the question of whether nuclear deterrence and compellence preserve or endanger peace. Also useful in Chapters Five and Eleven.

• "X" [George Kennan]. "The Sources of Soviet Conduct." *Foreign Affairs* 25, no. 4 (July 1947): 556–582. The original, highly influential articulation of the assumptions, objectives, and basic strategy of containment.

Globalism and Regionalism in a New Era

SCOPE, OBJECTIVES, AND APPROACH

Chapter Five examines regional relations in the Third World since 1945. While issues and conflicts in the developed world (especially the Cold War) and among the developed and developing states appear frequently in this chapter, it focuses on conflicts among and within Third World nations. The chapter opens with a discussion of two major trends in the New Era: the United States as unchallenged in global military capability and the rise of Europe and Asia to new economic prominence. It then addresses the role of interdependence in conflict and cooperation and the prospects for collective security. The chapter then continues with a conceptual section listing the major internal and external sources of conflict. It then adopts a historical approach, presenting fairly detailed surveys of interstate conflict in the Middle East, South Asia, and East Asia. By emphasizing the dynamics of regional systems, the chapter demonstrates how the trends we observe in the New Era are linked together.

The chapter discusses the reasons why regional and global institutions have helped to moderate conflicts in some areas and failed to do so in others. In so doing, it attempts to illustrate how the processes of globalization, fragmentation, cooperation, and conflict are taking place in the contemporary South.

WHAT STUDENTS SHOULD LEARN FROM THIS CHAPTER

Foundation Level

1. List the main internal and external sources of conflict in the contemporary developing world.
2. Identify the regions where interstate conflict has been frequent and the major reason why this has been the case for each region.
3. Define the concept of regional balances of power and explain how the security dilemma operates at the regional level.
4. List the main issues in the Arab–Israeli conflict and describe the immediate consequences of the creation of the state of Israel, the Suez Crisis, the 1967 Arab–Israeli War, and the Camp David Accords.
5. List the main issues in the India–Pakistan conflict and describe the chain of events that led to the independence of Bangladesh.
6. Describe the immediate consequences of the Sino–Soviet split, the Vietnam War, and the Sino–American rapprochement.

Enrichment Level

1. Explain how the U.S.'s position as the sole global military superpower has changed the dynamics of the international system and relations among states.
2. Define interdependence and discuss its prospects for fostering cooperation or conflict.
3. Define pan-Arabism and Zionism and identify their major historical proponents.
4. Describe the origins of the Yom Kippur War, the Iran–Iraq War, and the Persian Gulf War.
5. Describe the philosophy and impact of the Nonaligned Movement.
6. Explain the consequences of the Soviet invasion of Afghanistan on regional relations in South and East Asia.
7. Explain the origins and consequences of the Tiananmen Square Massacre.

Mastery Level

1. Define the different types of ethnic conflict, giving examples of each, and explain how these types of conflict affect international relations.
2. Explain how nationalism has led to interstate conflict in the Middle East.
3. Describe the causes and consequences of the *intifada*.
4. Explain how the security dilemma contributed to nuclear proliferation in South Asia.
5. Explain the causes and consequences of the Vietnamese invasion of Cambodia (1979).
6. List and evaluate the reasons why many Southern states attempted to develop nuclear weapons after 1967.
7. Explain why East Asia changed from a multipolar regional system in 1945 to a bipolar system by 1980, but returned to multipolarity after 1990.

OUTLINE OF THE CHAPTER

0. Introduction
   A. Chapter Five discusses the emerging structure of world politics, showing how international institutions reflect the simultaneous progress of globalization and fragmentation, as seen in renewed efforts towards collective security and the reemergent trend toward ethnic conflict.
   B. This chapter will survey the Middle East, South Asia, and East Asia to demonstrate areas of potential conflict as a well as possible cooperation.

I. A New World Order?
   A. Although global political confrontation and rivalry have receded since the end of the Cold War, how long they will remain in the background is far from clear.
   B. The structure of world politics in the New Era has two clear trends.
      1. The era of bipolar military competition has been replaced by a system in which the United States is unchallenged in military capability.

      a. The United States is the only nation capable of intervening in any conflict anywhere in the world.

      b. Despite these capabilities, the United States must join with regional allies to conduct sustained, large-scale military operations (for example, the Persian Gulf and Bosnia).

  2. The rise of Europe and Asia to new economic prominence has led to competition for export markets and investment opportunities.

      a. The United States maintains advantages in some economic sectors, such as agriculture and aircraft, while other states match or exceed the United States in productivity in consumer electronics and automobiles.

      b. Some forecast that it is only a matter of time before China overtakes both Japan and the United States in overall economic output.

C. As demonstrated in the Gulf War, the information revolution is transforming the links between material abundance and military might; there is a premium on precision and quality (rather than quantity) in military hardware as well as manufacturing and agriculture.

II. Interdependence and Globalization

A. Interdependence links together the fate of states, through economic, political, and environmental conditions; the result is a "global village" where states must work together to achieve common goals.

B. Interdependence can be defined as "a relationship of interests such that if one nation's position changes, other states will be affected by that change."

C. Interdependence has two dimensions.

  1. Sensitivity refers to the speed and extent with which changes in one country bring about changes in another.

  2. Vulnerability measures the degree to which a state can suffer costs imposed by external events even after policies have been altered in response.

D. Interdependence does not necessarily foster cooperation.

  1. Interdependence can leave states vulnerable to economic blackmail.

  2. It also means less government control over domestic affairs, and less flexibility in addressing domestic problems (see Chapter Seven and the European Union).

  3. When interdependence leads to conflict, other nations can also be affected (for example, the deterioration of American–Japanese relations in the 1980s and early 1990s sent chills through the world economy).

E. Interdependence seems to lead to cooperation more often than it generates conflict once fundamental disagreements (such as disputes over territory) are resolved, as seen with the European Union (see Chapter Seven).

F. Although interdependence requires negotiations among nation-states, they will always retain responsibility for the welfare and security of their citizens, and political and cultural values will still define national identity.

III. Collective Security

A. Every major war has been seen by statesmen as an opportunity to establish a system of *collective security* where there would be a "one for all and all for one" system of unified response to aggression (example: the United Nations was founded on the principle of collective response to aggression and breaches of the peace).

B. While the New Era has highlighted the prospects for collective security, it also demonstrates its limitations.

  1. Nations have acted as "free riders," thus using the expectation of international action as an excuse to avoid acting themselves (example: the former Yugoslavia in 1992–94).

  2. The problem of command and coordination can lead to costly delays and provide states with an additional means of avoiding commitment and responsibility (example: the confusing relationship between the UN and NATO in Bosnia reinforced the impression that participation in international peacekeeping operations contravened U.S. sovereignty).

C. Collective international actions were proven to be successful in many areas.

  1. The Gulf War demonstrated that concerted international action against aggression is possible, although difficult to arrange and coordinate.

  2. Missions to provide food, medicine, and other basic needs to refugees in Iraq, Bosnia, Somalia, and Rwanda have shown that the international community can carry out humanitarian intervention.

  3. The United Nations' efforts to manage peaceful transitions to democracy in Namibia and Cambodia have achieved marked success.

IV. Ethnic Conflict
   A. Many efforts toward collective security were prompted by ethnic conflict, as no states is ethnically homogeneous.
      1. Minority groups can seek secession and independence, either peacefully (Canada, Czech Republic, and Slovakia) or violently (India, Nigeria, former Yugoslavia).
      2. Ethnic tensions and conflict can spill over across national boundaries (as with Credit separatism in Iraq and Turkey).
      3. States may intervene in ethnic conflicts for strategic or humanitarian reasons (Indian intervention into Sri Lanka, late 1980s–early 1990s; U.S. intervention into Somalia, 1992; French intervention in Rwanda, 1994).
      4. The arbitrary drawing of boundaries by colonial and imperial powers often contributes to ethnic strife after independence.
      5. The decline or collapse of empires and multinational states has historically led to significant ethnic conflict, illustrated by the breakup of the Ottoman Empire (see Chapter Three) and the dissolution of the USSR and Yugoslavia at the end of the Cold War (see Chapter Four).
   B. There are four types of violent ethnic conflict in the post–WWII era.
      1. *Civil wars* occur when two or more groups fight for control of a state (Lebanon, 1975–91; Angola, 1974–present; Bosnia, 1992–present); these conflicts often provoke foreign intervention, either unilateral (Israeli and Syrian action in Lebanon) or multilateral (UN intervention in Bosnia).
      2. *Wars of secession* result when one ethnic group attempts to break away and form its own state (Congo [Zaire], 1960–65; Nigeria, 1967–70; Bangladesh, 1971; Georgia, 1991–present).
      3. *Irredentism* leads to conflict when one state lays claim, on historical or ethnic grounds, to territory controlled by another (Israel, Egypt, Jordan, and Syria, 1948, 1967, 1973; India and Pakistan, 1965, 1971; Armenia and Azerbaijan, 1991–present).
      4. *Wars of unification* occur when leaders of one state or group attempt to create a single nation-state for members of an ethnic group divided among several states (Korea, 1950–53; Kurds, 1960–present).
   C. Ethnic divisions do not inevitably lead to violence, however.
      1. Democratic constitutional arrangements have enabled some multiethnic European states (Belgium, Switzerland, Finland) to experience little or no ethnic fighting despite long histories of conflict.
      2. Deep ethnic divisions and long-standing conflicts in some Asian states (India, Malaysia, Indonesia) might prompt one to expect much more ethnic violence than has actually occurred.
      3. Nationalism based on civic institutions rather than ethnic identity can be a force for uniting rather than dividing groups (Canada, Switzerland).

V. Regional Conflict
   A. Domestic Sources of Conflict
      1. Ethnic conflict
      2. Religion
      3. Economic, especially where a pronounced gap between rich and poor exists (compare poor Egypt with the rich United Arab Emirates)
   B. Imported Sources of Conflict
      1. The legacy of imperialism—arbitrarily drawn borders, colonial policies of divide and rule
      2. Nationalism—a European idea imported to the South (examples: Pan-Arabism, Zionism)
      3. The Cold War (1945–90)
   C. External versus Indigenous Sources of Conflict
      1. In general, external sources of conflict derive from political and economic globalization.
      2. Indigenous sources usually result from fragmentation within Southern states.
   D. Contemporary Regional Dynamics
      1. The external sources of conflict generally derive from political and economic globalization, while the indigenous sources typically result from fragmentation.
      2. Almost every region has been affected by intrastate conflict; wars between states have been concentrated in the Middle East, South Asia, and East Asia.

VI. The Middle East
   A. Three Balances of Power
      1. Three balances of power coexist in the Middle East, complicating regional relations enormously.
        a. Arab–Arab
        b. Arab–Israeli

        c. Arab–Iranian

    2. These balances are founded on conflicting nationalist aspirations.

        a. Pan-Arabism versus statist Arab nationalisms

        b. Jewish Nationalism (Zionism) versus Palestinian nationalism

        c. Arab versus Persian nationalism, exacerbated by religious conflicts between Shi'a and Sunni Islam

    3. Superpower involvement in the region during the Cold War helped to restrain some conflicts, but also fueled regional arms races.

B. End of the Ottoman Empire

    1. Nationalism began to emerge in the Ottoman Empire in the late nineteenth century; when the Empire was destroyed by WWI, nationalist ambitions collided with imperial designs.

    2. The Balfour Declaration of 1917 stated that Britain supported the establishment of a Jewish national home in Palestine; however, this appeared to conflict with British promises of Arab independence in return for Arab support against the Ottomans.

    3. After the war, the Middle East was divided into mandated territories (a transitional stage between imperial control and self-government) controlled by Britain and France; national aspirations were only partially satisfied and sometimes suppressed violently.

C. Arab–Israeli Conflict Begins

    1. By the end of WWII, several Arab states had become independent.

    2. Pressure for Jewish emigration to Palestine increased after the Holocaust (see Chapter Three), but this led to increased Arab–Jewish conflict in the territory.

    3. The UN devised a plan for the partition of Palestine into separate Arab and Jewish states; the Jews accepted the plan, but Arab Palestinians and Arab states did not.

    4. As a result, when Britain withdrew from the territory and Israel declared its independence in 1948, an Arab–Israeli war broke out; Israeli forces fought off Arab armies, and Israeli, Egyptian, and Jordanian forces took over territory that had been allocated to an Arab state of Palestine under the UN plan.

    5. After the war, authoritarian nationalist regimes came to power in Egypt and Syria; these regimes sought and received economic and military aid from the USSR.

D. Conflicts of 1950s and 1960s

    1. Suez Crisis

        a. Egyptian President Nasser, angered by America's refusal to finance construction of the Aswan Dam, nationalized the Suez Canal (which had been controlled by an Anglo–French company) in 1956.

        b. In response, Britain, France, and Israel devised a secret plan to attack Egypt; the plan succeeded militarily, but failed politically when the United States forced Britain and France to back down; Nasser remained in power, and the USSR's reputation as a friend of the Arabs increased.

    2. Nasser

        a. Nasser's ideology of Pan-Arabism gained great strength in Arab countries in the 1950s and 1960s; Syria and Egypt were briefly united in a single republic, and Pan-Arabist forces put pressure on many ruling Arab regimes.

        b. Egypt; supported the losing side in a civil war in North Yemen, frightening conservative Arab monarchies.

    3. Increased Hostility

        a. Hostility between Israel and its Arab neighbors increased, as a radical regime in Syria supported military and terrorist attacks against Israel.

        b. The Palestinian refugee problem remained unsolved.

E. Six-Day War (1967) and Its Aftermath

    1. An Israeli–Egyptian crisis in 1967 led Israel to believe its Arab neighbors were preparing a unified attack; Israel launched a preemptive strike in June 1967 and routed Egyptian, Jordanian, and Syrian forces in only six days.

    2. The war resulted in Israeli control of all of Jerusalem, the West Bank, the Golan Heights, and Gaza, but Arab states demanded the return of these occupied territories.

    3. The superpowers tried to achieve a negotiated settlement, but their positions tended to support their allies (Israel for the United States, Arab states for the USSR) fairly closely; UN Resolution 242, though deliberately ambiguous, called for an exchange of "land for peace."

    4. The Arab–Israeli conflict continued, and Israel and Egypt fought a War of Attrition in 1969–70; Arabs resented Israeli occupation of the West Bank and other territories.

    5. The 1967 war also led to the Palestine Liberation Organization (PLO) to become an independent Arab force under Yassir Arafat.

F. Petroleum, Power, and Politics

1. In the 1950s and 1960s, the North's dependence on Arab oil steadily increased; this led many Arabs to believe that the "oil weapon" could be wielded to pressure Europe and the United States to restrain Israel and adopt more pro-Arab policies.
2. In the 1973 Yom Kippur War, Egypt and Syria attacked Israel by surprise in an attempt to recapture the territories lost in 1967; the plan failed, but a concurrent Arab oil embargo dealt a great economic shock to the United States, Europe, and Japan.

G. Land for Peace
1. Instability increased in many Middle Eastern states in the 1970s; a civil war broke out in Lebanon in 1975.
2. Persistent diplomatic efforts by the Nixon, Ford, and Carter administrations brought Israel and Egypt closer to the negotiating table.
3. In 1977, Egyptian President Sadat astounded the world by visiting Jerusalem and calling for Arab–Israeli peace.
4. Israel and Egypt signed the U.S.-brokered Camp David Accords, which outlined a framework for a peace settlement in 1978 and concluded a peace treaty in 1979; Egypt was expelled from the Arab League and denied economic aid for concluding the treaty.

H. Conflicts of the 1980s
1. The Shah of Iran was overthrown by a radical Islamic revolution in 1979; this worried many Gulf Arab monarchies and dealt a severe blow to U.S. influence in the Gulf.
2. Iraq invaded Iran in 1980; despite covert support from both superpowers, Iraq failed to capture the territory it claimed, and the war dragged on until ending in stalemate in 1988.
3. Israel invaded Lebanon in order to destroy PLO bases there in 1982; the invasion became "Israel's Vietnam," and after Israeli forces were withdrawn Syria consolidated its dominance over most of the country.

I. New World Order, Old Regional Conflicts
1. Three trends in the late 1980s and 1990s had a major impact on the balances of power in the Middle East.
    a. The decline and demise of the USSR deprived many Arab states of a major source of economic and military aid.
    b. The *intifada*, the Palestinian uprising in the occupied territories, strained relations between the United States and Israel and increased the economic and political cost to Israel of controlling the territories.
    c. Iraq became a major military power in the region, unchecked by a weakened Iran.
2. Conflict resulted in the Persian Gulf War.
    a. Experiencing serious economic problems after the war with Iran and possessing a huge military machine (including a program to develop nuclear weapons), Iraq invaded and quickly overran Kuwait in 1990.
    b. This first attempt by one Arab state to conquer another shocked the world; the United States formed an international coalition under U.S. auspices to pressure Iraq to withdraw its forces.
    c. When Iraq failed to withdraw, the U.S.-led coalition launched an offensive in 1991 that quickly evicted Iraqi forces for Kuwait and severely damaged Iraq's military capability.
3. The new regional order is hopeful, but unsettled.
    a. The end of the Cold War and Israeli–Palestinian agreements in 1993–94 bode well for peace.
    b. However, many Arab regimes remain unstable, and economic disparities and Islamic radicalism threaten to generate new conflicts.

VII. South Asia
A. The Legacy of the Raj
1. The Indian subcontinent was under British control or domination prior to WWII.
2. As nationalist movements in British India gained strength, religious and ethnic differences came to the fore; Muslim nationalists pressed for independence in areas of Muslim majority.
3. British India was partitioned into the states of India and Pakistan (the Muslim state) in 1947; a massive refugee problem resulted, and migrations of refugees were accompanied by widespread violence.
4. The territory of Kashmir was disputed between the two states, and Indian and Pakistani troops fought over the area from 1947–49.

B. Era of Nonalignment
1. Under Jawaharlal Nehru, India pursued policies of *nonalignment* (neutrality in the Cold War, noninterference into internal affairs, limitation of the superpowers influence in the region, and playing the superpowers off against each other to obtain aid).
2. Nonalignment became a popular and influential movement in the developing world, but the United States was suspicious of it, as was Pakistan, which feared Indian domination of the subcontinent; both India and Pakistan received aid from both superpowers.
3. Territorial disputes between India and China led to a border war in 1962.

C. Indian–Pakistani Hostilities

1. Religious rioting and Pakistani perceptions of Indian weakness (after the fighting with China and Nehru's death in 1964) prompted Pakistan to attack in 1965; U.S. and Soviet mediation secured a cease-fire after an indecisive conflict.

2. Political conflicts between east and west Pakistan led the eastern half of the country to declare its independence (as Bangladesh) in 1971.

3. Believing that war was inevitable and that the balance of power was moving in India's favor, Pakistan attacked again in 1971 hoping to gain a victory like Israel's in 1967; this strategy failed, and India won the resulting war.

4. The conflict over Kashmir remained unresolved despite India's de facto control of the territory.

5. Becoming increasingly concerned by U.S., Soviet, and Chinese nuclear weapons, India initiated a nuclear program in 1972 and conducted a "peaceful nuclear explosion" in 1974; Pakistan began its own program out of fear that India would use its capability to blackmail it.

D. Global Tensions and Internal Conflicts

1. After the USSR invaded Afghanistan in 1979, substantial U.S. aid poured into Pakistan, and the United States restrained its criticism of Pakistan's nuclear program until 1989.

2. India's international strength grew in the 1970s and 1980s, but so did its internal ethnic and religious divisions; India's president Indira Gandhi declared a state in 1975–77, and conflicts between Hindus, Muslims, and Sikhs continued (Gandhi was assassinated by her own Sikh guards in 1984).

3. Ethnic conflict in Sri Lanka erupted into civil war in the 1980s, into which India intervened at the Sri Lankan government's request; the intervention was not successful, however, and Indian troops were withdrawn in 1990 (the same year Indian Prime Minister Rajiv Gandhi, Indira's son, was assassinated).

4. The end of the Cold War has left India as South Asia's strongest power, but ethnic and religious conflicts continue.

5. The potential nuclear threat to the region intensified in 1998 when India's new nationalist government openly tested five nuclear weapons and Pakistan responded with its own series of tests, raising the specter of an arms race in the region.

VIII. East Asia

A. The East Asian System

1. East Asia after WWII is a complex system containing three types of actors.

   a. Global powers (the United States and the USSR before its collapse)

   b. Major regional powers with global aspirations (China, Japan, and Russia after 1991)

   c. Smaller but nonetheless economically and/or militarily capable regional powers (North and South Korea, Taiwan, Vietnam, etc.)

2. Thus, East Asia resembled a classic multipolar system, similar to Europe in the eighteenth and nineteenth centuries.

3. Three main features characterized international politics in East Asia in the years immediately following WWII.

   a. The global rivalry between the superpowers

   b. The emergence of Communist China (PRC)

   c. The independence of formerly colonized Asian countries

B. Early Cold War Tensions

1. After the establishment of the PRC in 1949, the United States adopted containment of China as part of its global strategy.

2. The Korean War (see Chapter Four) poisoned U.S.–Chinese relations for almost two decades; East Asia became the military focal point of the Cold War.

3. During or after the war, the United States signed security treaties with South Korea, Taiwan, the Philippines (a former American colony) and Japan.

C. The Sino–Soviet Split

1. A rift developed between Moscow in Beijing in the 1950s over the USSR's lukewarm support for the capture of Taiwan and retraction of promises to help China develop nuclear weapons.

2. In the 1960s, the split deepened as China exploded a nuclear weapon (1964), isolated itself and criticized Moscow during the Cultural Revolution (1966–69), and supported revolutionary "people's wars" in the Third World, competing for influence with both the United States and the USSR.

3. By 1965, U.S. troops were fighting in the Vietnam War (see Chapter Four), while China supported the communist North Vietnamese and Vietcong.

    D. Chinese–American Rapprochement
       1. Three events changed international politics in the region in the late 1960s.
         a. China ended its self-imposed diplomatic and economic isolation.
         b. The Sino–Soviet dispute grew beyond a war of words to armed border clashes in 1969 (Moscow hinted that it could employ its nuclear weapons if the fighting escalated).
         c. Nixon and Kissinger saw in China an opportunity to put pressure on the USSR and ease an American exit from Vietnam.
       2. Cautious signaling of willingness to talk (including travel by a Chinese table-tennis team to the United States) culminated in a dramatic visit by Nixon to China in 1972; Japan, Australia, and New Zealand restored diplomatic ties with China soon after.
       3. After the rapprochement between Washington and Beijing, Vietnam became the USSR's only reliable ally in East Asia; after the fall of South Vietnam in 1975, the USSR and Vietnam began military cooperation, which further alienated China.
    E. The New Asian Cold War
       1. By 1978, antagonism between the USSR and China took on the dimensions of a regional cold war.
       2. In 1979, Vietnam's invasion of Cambodia further angered China and alarmed the Association of South-East Asian nations (ASEAN); a Chinese "punitive" incursion into Vietnam in 1979 led to greater Vietnamese dependence on the USSR for military and economic aid.
       3. The Soviet invasion of Afghanistan in 1979 dashed hopes for normalization of Sino–Soviet relations; the move also worsened Soviet–Japanese relations and prompted China and the United States to begin tacit military and intelligence cooperation.
       4. Continued actions by Vietnamese forces in Southeast Asia led to improvement of relations between China and ASEAN.
       5. By the early 1980s, the balance of power in East Asia became essentially bipolar, with the United States, China, Japan, and ASEAN cooperating to contain expansion by the USSR and Vietnam.
    F. Global Confrontation Recedes, Regional Powers Emerge
       1. The new strategic alignment soon changed, but the changes were caused by domestic developments rather than geopolitical maneuvering.
         a. Gorbachev's policies of perestroika included a new opening to China; the USSR began to withdraw its forces from Afghanistan in 1989, and Soviet relations with ASEAN and the United States improved as well (see Chapter Four).
         b. China's policies of economic and political liberalization were reversed after protests in Beijing's Tiananmen Square were brutally crushed (on live television) in 1989; China's relations with the United States took a downward turn.
       2. The end of the Cold War created favorable conditions for resolving regional conflicts; a UN plan to end fighting in Cambodia and nurture a democratic government began in 1991.
       3. In the early 1990s, the United States gradually reduced its military commitments in East Asia, but trade among the United States, Japan, and ASEAN ensured that the United States would remain active in the region.
       4. China's economy grew rapidly in the early 1990s, and with the cutback in U.S. military presence in the region, China and Japan began to view each other as potential security threats.
       5. East Asia now resembles a classic multipolar system once again, with alignments likely to continue to shift in the future; since the end of Vietnam's war in Cambodia, interstate conflict has played less of a role in the region, though the possibility of development of nuclear weapons by North Korea remains a major point of tension and danger.

IX. Conclusions: Coming Together or Falling Apart
    A. There are two images of the world in the New Era.
       1. Many states have sought to cooperate with their regional neighbors (for example, the European Union, regional free trade agreements in North and South America, and APEC and ASEAN in Asia and the Pacific).
       2. The use of famine, genocide, terrorism, and the threat of weapons of mass destruction by warring groups suggests that political, economic, ecological, and social fragmentation is becoming an even greater trend in the New Era.
    B. Both visions have components of truth, as interdependence has accelerated both cooperation and conflict, and as old institutions fail new ones are created.
    C. Many developments in the New Era are not new (for example, ethnic conflict and shifting alliances have been a part of history for thousands of years), and, while some technological developments

are new (for example, computers and nuclear weapons), the need for political, economic, and social structures to adapt to new elements is not.

HOW THE CHAPTER RELATES TO CENTRAL THEMES OF THE TEXT

Chapter Five demonstrates conflict, explaining how local conflicts become globalized and vice versa. Yet cooperation also runs through the surveys of regional relations—alliances, international and regional organizations, and the asymmetric interdependence of North and South (which will be discussed in more detail in Chapter Eight). As the chapter's historical narratives show, decolonization and retreat from empire have typically resulted in political fragmentation, while superpower rivalries during the Cold War contributed to the globalization of long-standing ethnic and religious conflicts (especially in the Middle East).

As the book's final historical chapter, Chapter Five outlines more events that will be used as examples and supporting evidence for concepts and theories presented in later chapters. As in Chapters Three and Four, which outlined contending explanations for the World Wars and the Cold War, the chapter offers several reasons for the outbreak and persistence of Third World conflicts, leaving it to the reader to decide which causes of conflict have been more important.

Finally, Chapter Five draws implicit and explicit parallels between regional systems and the relations between the Great Powers in the global system as described in Chapters Two through Four, showing how concepts such as the balance of power and the security dilemma operate at the regional level. The chapter thus emphasizes that many of the theories and concepts introduced in Chapter One and elaborated in later chapters, including anarchy, polarity, collective security, and the tension between idealism and realism, are just as applicable to North Africa or Southeast Asia as they are to Western Europe.

SUGGESTED LECTURE TOPICS

1. Compare the "domestic" causes of conflict in the developing world with the "imported" causes; discuss which causes are likely to become less important, and which more important, now that the Cold War has ended.
2. Draw parallels between the conflicts in the Middle East after WWII and the conflicts in the Balkans before WWI; ask students to suggest why the Balkan Powder Keg led to WWI, but Middle Eastern conflicts did not lead to war between the superpowers.
3. Compare the regional systems of the Middle East and East Asia; encourage students to discuss why interstate war has been far more frequent in the Middle East, even though the two regions share many similarities (multipolarity, superpower involvement, regional arms races, nuclear proliferation, etc.).
4. Discuss the security role of the "regional superpowers"—China, India, Brazil, and South Africa. Have these states acted effectively to preserve or enforce peace in their respective regions? Why or why not? Would the Middle East be more stable and/or peaceful if it were dominated by a "regional superpower"?
5. Discuss the impact of nuclear proliferation in each of the regions considered in this chapter. (See Chapter Eleven for more information on this issue.) Why has India *not* built a substantial nuclear arsenal even though its neighbor and potential adversary China has a large number of nuclear weapons and Pakistan has developed some? Why is Iraq's potential development of weapons of mass destruction an important regional concern for the Middle East?

STUDY AND EXAM QUESTIONS

1. Chose one of the regions listed below and discuss whether conflicts in this region after 1945 have been primarily internal or external in origin, using at least three specific examples of regional conflict to support your answer:
   a. The Middle East
   b. South Asia
   c. East Asia
2. Were regional conflicts a *cause* of superpower involvement in the developing world during the Cold War or were they an *effect* of the global rivalry between the United States and the USSR? Refer to three

or more examples of conflicts, chosen from at least two different regions of the Third World, to support your answer.

3. "The major powers in the developed world have a responsibility to provide the leadership and resources necessary for the resolution of regional conflicts in the developing world." Do you agree with this statement? Use three examples of conflicts in the Third World after 1945, successfully resolved or not, to show why it is correct or incorrect.

4. Choose one of the actions listed below, identify the main reasons why the action was taken, briefly summarize the consequences of the action, and, in terms of the interests and objectives of the leaders who made it, explain why the decision to take the action was or was not correct:
   a. Chinese intervention into the Korean War, 1950
   b. Israeli preemptive strike against Egypt, Jordan, and Syria, 1967
   c. Indian development of nuclear weapons, 1974
   d. Vietnamese invasion of Cambodia, 1978
   e. Egyptian signing of the Camp David Accords, 1978

5. Choose one of the individuals listed below and explain his impact on world politics:
   a. Mohandas Karamchand Gandhi
   b. Ho Chi Minh
   c. Gamal Abdel Nasser
   d. Jawaharlal Nehru
   e. Aung San Suu Kyi

RECOMMENDED ENRICHMENT READINGS

Borthwick, Mark. *Pacific Century: The Emergence of Modern Pacific Asia.* Boulder, Colo.: Westview, 1992. Good overview of the evolution of the East Asian system.

Brown, L. Carl. *International Politics and the Middle East.* Princeton: Princeton University Press, 1984. Noteworthy survey of globalization and fragmentation in that famously fractious region.

Brown, Michael, ed. *The International Dimensions of Internal Conflict.* Cambridge: MIT Press, 1996. Examines both "domestic" and "imported" sources of regional conflict from a variety of viewpoints.

Brzezinski, Zbigniew K. *The Grand Chessboard: American Primacy and Its Geostrategic Imperatives.* New York: Basic Books, 1997. A practitioner of *realpolitik* makes his case for how the United States should exercise its responsibilities as the world's sole remaining superpower.

• Freedman, Lawrence. "The Gulf War and the New World Order." *Survival* 33, no. 3 (May/June 1991): 195–210. Excellent analysis of the political and strategic impact of the Gulf conflict.

• Gilpin, Robert. "International Politics in the Pacific Rim Era." *Annals AAPSS* 505 (September 1989): 56–67. Interesting discussion of the changes in world politics that may be brought about by developments in East Asia.

Haass, Richard N. *The Reluctant Sheriff: The United States After the Cold War.* Washington: Brookings, 1997. Examines how the United States could lead global responses to threats to international peace without trying to become the world's policeman.

Horowitz, Donald L. *Ethnic Groups in Conflict.* Berkeley: University of California Press, 1985. Excellent work on ethnic conflict and its resolution in an international context.

Karnow, Stanley. *Vietnam: A History.* Rev. ed. New York: Viking, 1991. Not the best scholarly work on the Vietnam War, but a comprehensive, readable history of the roots and course of the conflict for the general reader.

Lewis, Bernard. *The Middle East: A Brief History of the Last 2,000 Years.* New York: Scribner, 1995. A masterful, scholarly exegesis of the deep roots of conflict and cooperation in the region.

• Lewis, Jason D. "Southeast Asia—Preparing for a New World Order." *Washington Quarterly* 16, no. 1 (winter 1993): 187–200. Very useful essay on regional relations in the New Era.

Malik, Hafeez, ed. *Dilemmas of National Security and Cooperation in India and Pakistan.* New York: St. Martin's Press, 1993. Noteworthy collection of articles on conflict and cooperation in South Asia.

Mazarr, Michael J. *North Korea and the Bomb.* New York: St. Martin's Press, 1995. The story of North Korea's nuclear program and the tensions created by it.

McMahon, Robert J. *The Cold War on the Periphery: The United States, India, and Pakistan.* New York: Columbia University Press, 1994. Good look at the global dimension of the India–Pakistan conflict.

Quandt, William B. *Camp David: Peacemaking and Politics.* Washington: Brookings, 1986. Excellent insider's look at the negotiations at Camp David.

Roberts, Brad, ed. *Order and Disorder after the Cold War.* Cambridge: MIT Press, 1995. Useful collection of articles on various aspects of globalization and fragmentation.

Shipler, David K. *Arab and Jew: Wounded Spirits in a Promised Land.* New York: Times Books, 1986. Moving look at the Palestinian–Israeli conflict at the personal level; puts a sometimes depressing, sometimes inspiring human face on the regional conflict.

Tessler, Mark A. *A History of the Israeli–Palestinian Conflict.* Bloomington: Indiana University Press, 1994. Balanced, scholarly account of the irrepressible conflict from its early origins to the eve of the Oslo accords.

PART

III

The Economic
Dimension in
World Politics

CHAPTER

6

□ □ □ □

Introduction to International Economics

SCOPE, OBJECTIVES, AND APPROACH

Chapter Six presents an overview of the operation of the global economy, involving both conflict and cooperation. It offers students a "crash course" in international economics, including trade, finance, and theories of political economy. The chapter thus reverses the approach to presenting history and theory used in the book as a whole—here, theory is presented first, then illustrated with historical facts in Chapter Seven. This was done because the author felt that students needed at least passing familiarity with fundamental principles of international economics in order to grasp the evolution of the global economic system.

The chapter also discusses important aspects of economic power to demonstrate some of the means of conflict and cooperation used by states. Finally, to demonstrate the potential for cooperation, the chapter presents barriers to cooperation and means of overcoming those barriers.

WHAT STUDENTS SHOULD LEARN FROM THIS CHAPTER

Foundation Level

1. Explain how comparative advantage can make trade mutually beneficial even if one trading partner has an absolute advantage in the production of all goods.
2. Identify the assumptions and objectives of free trade and protection.
3. Describe the difference between fixed and floating exchange rate systems.
4. Define trade surplus and trade deficit.
5. List the assumptions and priorities of the three basic schools of thought on the international political economy (liberalism, realism, and Marxism).
6. Identify the components of economic power.
7. Explain how reciprocity can increase the probability of cooperation among states.

Enrichment Level

1. Identify the major types of trade barriers and give contemporary examples.
2. List the main components of a state's balance of payments.
3. Describe the basic principles of theories of hegemonic stability.
4. Explain how geography and natural resources can increase or decrease a state's power.
5. Describe the most commonly used indices of economic power.
6. Define an international regime and list its essential components.

Mastery Level

1. Explain the advantages and disadvantages of fixed and floating exchange rate systems.
2. Explain the factor and sector approaches to analyzing domestic influences on trade policy.
3. Explain how the size and characteristics of a state's population can increase or decrease its economic power.
4. Describe how industrial competitiveness impacts upon economic power.
5. Define the tit-for-tat strategy and explain how it may be applied in attempts to overcome the Prisoners' Dilemma.
6. Outline the goals, and institutional strengths and weaknesses, of GATT.

OUTLINE OF THE CHAPTER

0. Introduction
   A. Trade and economic exchange have gone hand and hand with the struggle for national power and security.
   B. The first three sections of this chapter introduce the basic economic concepts required for an understanding of the global economy.
   C. The next sections define economic power, discuss the means of measurement, and the ways in which economic power is obtained.
   D. The final sections examine the problems and prospects for economic cooperation.

I. To Trade or Not to Trade
   A. Trade and Resource Allocation
      1. No state produces all the goods or services it needs; therefore, almost all states engage in trade.
      2. Even when countries produce the same things, trade may occur due to different allocation of resources.
         a. States may be land, labor, or capital abundant, depending on the resources they possess.
         b. Because resources differ among states, a state enjoys a *comparative advantage* in producing goods that utilize its abundant factor (example: states rich in arable land, like the United States, have a comparative advantage in agriculture).

     c. A state possesses an *absolute advantage* in the production of a specific good if it produces that good more efficiently than other states (example: Switzerland, because of its abundance of capital and large skilled-labor force, may have an absolute advantage in making high-quality watches).

B. Ricardo's Model of Trade

    1. David Ricardo's model of trade shows why trade may be mutually beneficial even if one trading partner has an absolute advantage in production of all goods (see diagram).

    2. Even if one state produces all goods more efficiently, the less efficient state may still gain from trade if it has a comparative advantage in one good over another; each country gains by exporting goods in which it has a comparative advantage and importing goods in which it has a comparative disadvantage.

    3. Mutual gains from trade will lead to specialization within each country, increasing efficiency and making goods less expensive for both.

C. Trade Barriers

    1. Why, if states would be better off by trading with countries that produce specific goods more efficiently, do governments often erect *trade barriers* (restrictions, taxes, or prohibitions on trade)?

      a. Foreign competition may force domestic producers out of business, and other states may "corner the market" on vital goods.

      b. More efficient foreign competition may also result in lost jobs or bankruptcies; governments may be pressured to stop this if the industries involved are politically influential and/or employ many workers (example: the U.S. auto industry).

    2. The setting up of trade barriers is known as *trade protection* or *protectionism;* its opposite, the removal or absence of barriers, is *free trade.*

    3. Trade barriers result from a conflict of two interests: consumers who want inexpensive products versus industries who want to stay in business and make profits.

    4. Since protection typically benefits a concentrated group of industrialists and workers, and hurts a large group of unorganized consumers, political support for protection can influence governments ostensibly committed to free trade.

D. Types of Trade Barriers

    1. *Tariffs* are taxes on imported goods.

      a. Tariffs make foreign goods more expensive, aiding local producers at the cost of higher prices for consumers and decreased incentives for efficiency.

      b. Tariffs can increase domestic production and strengthen developing industries, albeit at the cost of higher consumer prices and less efficient production and allocation of resources.

      c. An infamous example of tariffs: The *Smoot–Hawley Tariff* of 1930, which provoked retaliatory tariffs on U.S. goods around the world, led to a collapse of global trade and contributed to the Great Depression (discussed later in this chapter).

    2. States sometimes employ non-tariff barriers.

      a. *Import quotas* are quantitative limitations on imports; if a trading partner is pressured to "voluntarily" limit its exports, a *voluntary export restraint (VER)* results (example: limits on Japanese auto exports to the United States after 1980).

      b. *Subsidies* are government payments to producers allowing them to price their goods competitively (example: agricultural price supports in the United States); *internal subsidies* allow producers to compete against imports in the home market and *external subsidies* allow producers to compete in the international market.

      c. Export subsidies, which allow goods to be sold for less than their cost of production, are difficult to distinguish from *dumping* (deliberately selling goods at a loss in order to force producers in a target market to go out of business).

II. Money Makes the World Go Around

A. Trade before Money

    1. Prior to the development of money, domestic and foreign trade were conducted by *barter* (direct exchange of goods for goods).

    2. Money simplifies and increases the efficiency of trade, but since each state has its own currency, a system of *exchange rates* is necessary for international trade.

B. Exchange Rate Systems

    1. *Fixed* exchange rate systems set all currencies at defined relative values.

      a. Examples include the *gold standard* (1870–1914) and the *Bretton Woods system* (1945–73), both discussed later.

    b. Advantages: Prices will not change due to currency fluctuations, eliminating this element of risk from trade.

    c. Disadvantages: When recessions occur, states must either preserve or "defend" the value of their currency (which can further weaken their economies) or renege on agreements made with other states in the fixed system.

  2. *Floating* exchange rate systems allow currencies to fluctuate.

    a. Example includes the world monetary system after 1973 (discussed in part II).

    b. Advantages: Floating rates accurately reflect a country's economic health; allow manipulation of exchange rate to improve balance of trade (see below); and allow states more freedom to use monetary policy in attempts to alleviate inflation, unemployment, etc. (though some would argue that this is actually a disadvantage).

    c. Disadvantages: Floating introduces an element of risk and uncertainty into trade; exchange rate maneuverings can create international tensions, as between the United States and Japan in the 1980s and 1990s.

C. Balance of Payments

  1. States, like companies, keep "balance sheets" of their transactions with the rest of the world; accounting procedures guarantee that this *balance of payments* always equals zero, just like a firm's books must always balance.

  2. *Current account balance* equals the sum of a state's imports, exports, official transfers (such as foreign aid payments or receipts), and investment income and payments.

    a. This balance is often referred to (in news reports, etc.) as a country's "balance of trade."

    b. A positive current account balance equals a *trade surplus,* or "net profit" from trade.

    c. A negative current account balance equals a *trade deficit,* or "net loss" from trade; this does not mean that a nation is worse off because of trade, however, as consumers may have access to cheaper and/or better goods and overall national welfare may have been improved.

D. Exchange Rates and Trade Deficits

  1. If the value of a state's currency increases, imports become cheaper and exports become more expensive; this may decrease the country's current account balance.

  2. Conversely, if the value of a state's currency decreases, imports become more expensive and exports become cheaper; this may increase a country's current account balance.

  3. This relationship is not perfect, however, as importers may sacrifice profits to retain market share, consumer behavior may lag as buyers stick with familiar imported products, or demand for foreign goods may have become *price inelastic* (unchanging regardless of price; example: oil, which buyers may still need even if prices go up dramatically—see discussion of oil crisis below).

III. Economics and Politics

A. The discipline of international political economy studies the interaction of politics and economics at the national and global level; the three major schools of thought within this discipline are *liberalism, realism, and Marxism.*

B. *Liberalism* theorizes that states should allow the free market to function unhindered by trade barriers.

  1. Assumptions of economic liberals:

    a. *Individuals* are the principal actors within an economic system.

    b. Individuals are *rational.*

    c. Individuals *maximize utility*—that is, make tradeoffs between costs and benefits.

  2. Liberals argue that the free market allocates resources in the most efficient manner possible, thus maximizing global welfare.

    a. Trade is viewed as a *positive-sum game*—both trading partners benefit from it.

    b. Government interference with the market only frustrates efficiency.

  3. Liberals thus usually argue that states should follow policies of *laissez-faire*—that is, should interfere in the economy as little as possible.

C. *Realism* contends that power relations determine economic outcomes; economics should therefore follow politics.

  1. Assumptions of economic realists:

    a. *Nation-states,* not individuals, are the principal actors in the world economy.

    b. Nation-states are *rational.*

    c. Nation-states seek to maximize *power.*

2. For realists, therefore, states must pursue power and security first and foremost; they may have no choice but to sacrifice wealth for power and security, and trade barriers must be used to protect domestic producers (while, conversely, exporters should seek to capture markets abroad).

3. This perspective dominated international trade policies before the late eighteenth century; states generally pursued policies of *mercantilism,* which regards trade as an instrument of power politics.

4. *Hegemonic stability theory* attempts to answer this question: If trade barriers help states maximize their power, why has trade been relatively free in various periods?

   a. An economically and militarily powerful state may become the dominant power in the international system.

   b. This *hegemon* sets and enforces the rules of the global economy; it promotes trade because increased trade and economic stability are in its own interest (examples: Britain in the mid-nineteenth century, the United States 1945–73).

   c. Hegemony is ultimately self-defeating, however; as the cost of keeping trade and markets open grows, other states may become richer and challenge the hegemon; the hegemon may demand that its allies "share the burden" of enforcing security and stability, as the United States began to do in the 1970s.

5. If there is no hegemon, states may still cooperate, but major trade powers may form trade blocs to protect their markets and industries (example: trade blocs between WWI and WWII; possibly, the European Union and NAFTA, discussed below).

D. Marxism views trade as one element of the class struggle, contending that trade policy is primarily determined by class interests.

   1. In capitalist states, the capitalist class or *bourgeoisie* tends to set trade policies that favor capital and "big business."

   2. The working class, or *proletariat,* may be able to force trade adoption of policies that favor labor, or fight or overthrow the bourgeoisie, through unified action.

   3. The Marxist perspective is useful for analyzing the role of labor in the global economy.

   4. *Dependency theory,* a branch of Marxist thought, looks at economic conflicts among developed and developing states (see Chapter Eight).

E. International conditions interact with the domestic political economy.

   1. Economics and politics interact in the making of trade policy at the domestic as well as the international level; there are two broad approaches to analyzing this interaction.

   2. The *factor approach* looks at conflict and commonality of interest between three basic interest groups: landowners, capital owners (shareholders and investors), and workers (example: U.S. corporations supported NAFTA, because the United States has an advantage in the export of capital and capital intensive industries, while labor groups opposed it, because Mexico has a comparative advantage in labor).

   3. The *sector approach* looks at the political influence of groups of related industries (examples: the "energy sector" or the "high-tech sector").

      a. Conflicts develop between sectors that enjoy comparative advantage and those that do not.

      b. Sectors at a comparative disadvantage (example: the U.S. auto industry) seek protectionist policies, while those with comparative advantages (example: the aircraft industry in the United States) advocate free trade.

F. Domestic politics affect the international arena.

   1. Interest groups, not surprisingly, advocate trade policies that favor their interests.

   2. International cooperation can arise when domestic coalitions within several states agree on specific policy goals.

   3. Conversely, conflict can occur when domestic groups influence trade policies that harm the interests of groups in other countries (example: conflicts between U.S. and French farmers in the early 1990s).

   4. According to this approach, trade policy is determined by the struggle for power between competing interest groups; states' preferences for free trade or protection to not arise because of the relationships among states, but instead because of the domestic clout of interest groups.

IV. Economic Power

A. Basic Elements

   1. Elements of economic power include those that are relatively easy to quantify, such as gross national product, oil reserves, and balance of trade.

   2. Those that are more difficult to quantify include skills of a nation's labor force and the creative potential of its research and development establishment.

B. Territory: Geography and Natural Resources
   1. Geography
      a. A state's size, location, climate, and physiography are important territorial assets (or liabilities).
      b. Location is particularly important, as it determines access to and ability to control trade routes (historically, Britain's access to trade routes has been superior, while Russia's has been poor) and harbors.
      c. Territory also determines a state's defensibility in wartime (Russia's long borders and vast territory make it easy to invade, but very difficult to conquer; Israel, by contrast, has no strategic depth and thus must put its armed forces on a "hair trigger").
   2. Natural Resources
      a. Production and accessibility determine the importance of natural resources in the short run; in the long term, reserves and sustainability are more important.
      b. Since the Industrial Revolution, metals and *fossil fuels* (particularly oil) have been the most important natural resources; many wars have been fought over them.
      c. Oil is the lifeblood of an industrial economy; at present, however, many heavy oil users (especially Japan) have few oil reserves, making them vulnerable to supply interruption (see Table 6.3).
      d. Agricultural land and food supply are critical resources as well; states having little *arable land* (Britain, Japan) or insufficient water (Saudi Arabia) must typically import food, and food supplies may be threatened or interdicted in wartime (as Britain's and Japan's were).
C. Population
   1. Population Size
      a. A large population allows a state to have sizable labor and military forces.
      b. Bigger is not always better, however; poor populous states (India, Pakistan, Bangladesh, Nigeria) must spend large portions of scarce capital and resources to provide their people's basic needs, which can severely hamper economic growth.
   2. Demographic Structure
      a. States with high birth rates and large proportions of children and teenagers must devote more resources to child education, health, and welfare; this makes development of a skilled labor force difficult and exacerbates unemployment (example: Egypt).
      b. States with low birth rates and long life expectancies can develop a "baby bust" shortage of young workers, as well as problems with caring for so many senior citizens.
   3. Labor Force
      a. A large, skilled labor force is a vital component of economic power.
      b. The overall skill level of a nation's workers is hard to measure, but education, literacy, and percentage of labor force involved in agriculture are useful indicators.
D. Trade and Industry
   1. Gross national product (GNP) is a crude but useful measure of economic strength.
      a. GNP measures the market value of goods and services produced in a given period (usually annually).
      b. Since power in world politics is relative, GNP is a good indicator of rankings and changes in overall economic strength (see Table 6.4).
      c. Rate of growth of GNP is an important indicator of economic dynamism; during the Cold War, Germany and Japan grew faster than the United States and USSR, and in the early 1990s China's economy grew much faster than the established industrial countries.
   2. Per capita income indicates the prosperity of a state's population and the amount of capital available for investment or spending to increase military and political influence (see Table 6.5).
   3. Rates of growth show how states are rising and declining in terms of economic power and therefore reveal potential for influence in world politics.
   4. Balance of trade indicates a state's productivity and competitiveness in world markets.
      a. In 1990, most G-7 countries experienced a trade deficit, while Germany and Japan enjoyed a trade surplus.
      b. Persistent trade surpluses can lead to conflict if trading partners blame the surplus on protectionism (see Chapter Seven) and call for a "level playing field" or raise trade barriers of their own.
E. Research, Development, and Technology
   1. Technology plays a major role in the development and use of economic power, but overall levels of technology are difficult to quantify.
   2. Measuring spending on research and development (R&D) will not indicate success at technological advancement, but it will at least indicate efforts in this direction.

F. Managing Conflict
1. There is considerable need to manage conflict among international economic actors in the New Era.
2. Coordination will be difficult due do the incentives to compete and seek unilateral advantages.

V. Barriers to Cooperation
A. Although the global market is highly competitive, there are significant rewards for cooperation.
B. Realists and liberals have differing perspectives on the possibility on states overcoming incentives for conflict and realizing the mutual benefits of cooperation.
   1. Realist Perspective
      a. States cannot overcome the concern for loss in relative ranking in the international system (in a zero-sum game); states fear that others will disproportionately benefit from cooperation.
      b. The reluctance to cooperate is further enhanced by states having a natural distrust of one another and the lack of a world government or supranational body to enforce agreements.
      c. National security is more important than trade, thus states should be reluctant to trade with other states because profits from the transactions might be used to gain advantages over them.
   2. Liberal Perspective
      a. Cooperation is both possible and beneficial, but difficult to arrange.
      b. Trade is a variable-sum game, where all states simultaneously and mutually benefit through cooperation.
      c. International institutions can act as mediators when disputes occur.

VI. Overcoming Barriers
A. Reciprocity
   1. If the game of Prisoners' Dilemma is played for only one round, it is rational for both players to defect.
   2. However, if the game is played repeatedly with the same players, mutual gains may be achieved through the use of a *tit-for-tat* (TFT) strategy.
      a. In the first round, "lead" by cooperating.
      b. In subsequent rounds, do whatever the other player did on the previous round.
      c. This strategy demonstrates both willingness to cooperate and determination not to be taken for a "sucker."
   3. TFT can thus be used to enforce cooperation agreements through *reciprocity* ("do onto others as you would have them do unto you").
B. International Regimes
   1. International institutions or *regimes* can help states to cooperate in an anarchic world by creating incentives for cooperation and sanctions for defection.
   2. Regimes establish rules, principles, and *norms* of state behavior that facilitate cooperation.
      a. These rules are usually formalized in treaties.
      b. International organizations may be established to enforce rules or facilitate communication and resolution of disputes.
      c. Regimes may also be informal, tacit, or customary.
C. International Law
   1. As discussed in Chapter Nine, international law sets forth rules for states' and other actors' relations with one another.
      a. In general, international law encourages states to concentrate on the long-term benefits of cooperation and forsake the short-term advantages of cheating.
      b. Example: During WWII, all parties generally complied with the Geneva Protocol of 1925, which forbade the use of chemical weapons (though gas was used against civilians in the Holocaust).
   2. In general, international law has most of the same advantages and disadvantages as international regimes.
      a. Both establish rules and norms for cooperative behavior.
      b. However, in the absence of an international sovereign, both lack adequate enforcement mechanisms.
D. Hegemonic Stability
   1. Realists contend that economic cooperation can be established only when one major state becomes the dominant military and economic power, or hegemon.
      a. The regimes function because the hegemonic power sets and enforces the rules to make them work (example: the gold standard before WWI).
      b. Regimes may nevertheless continue to function even after a hegemon has declined (example: the Bretton Woods international monetary system; see Chapter Seven).

2. Hegemony is, however, ultimately self-defeating.
   a. As the hegemon's trading partners become more competitive relative to the hegemon, the hegemon becomes less capable of enforcing the rules without help from its partners and it becomes more willing to attempt to coerce its growing partners to pay for the benefits they receive.
   b. Hegemonic-stability theory also contends that the hegemon provides public goods or "services"; failure to do so, coupled with free-riding by other states, can cause the international system to decline into disorder.
3. Periods of free trade tend to correspond with periods of hegemony, and economic protectionism and chaos often correspond with periods of hegemonic decline.

VII. Conclusion: A World Thriving on Chaos?
   A. Despite the barriers to cooperation, the world economy is thriving (for example, international trade continues to grow annually).
   B. As economic interdependence continues to increase, so will the incentives and risks of cooperation among states.

HOW THE CHAPTER RELATES TO CENTRAL THEMES OF THE TEXT

As demonstrated throughout this chapter, the economic aspects of international relations offer an excellent illustration of the simultaneous operation of conflict and cooperation. Examples of the processes are evident in the tensions between defending a currency and stimulating the national economy. The discussion of the components of economic power acquaints students with some of the instruments of cooperation and conflict used by states in the actions detailed in the historical chapters. The chapter also introduces students to the discussion of whether conflict can be overcome and by what means. The discussion of hegemonic stability theory, in particular, provides an opportunity for students to consider whether concentration of power promotes cooperation or leads to increased conflict in the long run. Each level of analysis is also represented in the chapter, and the discussion of the liberal, realist, and Marxist views of trade and domestic effects on the international political economy should encourage students to ponder whether individuals, interest groups, states, or multinational blocs are the primary actors in the global trading system.

SUGGESTED LECTURE TOPICS

1. If most students are unfamiliar with economic theory, explain the basic principles of comparative advantage to show why trade can be a positive-sum game; so that students will understand what conflicts over trade deficits, currency devaluations, and so on are all about, go over the essential elements of exchange rates and balance of payments.
2. Solicit opinions from students as to whether trade with Japan, Mexico, and Europe benefits or harms the United States and why; then discuss the three perspectives on the international political economy to show how each of these views affect debate over trade policy.
3. Discuss the significance of economic power in the post–Cold War world, noting which actors in the international system are strong and weak in economic power and what steps have been taken by the major states since 1990 to maintain "balances" of economic power.
4. Using examples from history, demonstrate the effectiveness of cooperation through international law (for example, WWII), international regimes (for example, GATT), hegemonic-stability theory (for example, the Bretton Woods system), and tit-for-tat (for example OPEC).

STUDY AND EXAM QUESTIONS

1. Should the world's major trading states adopt a fixed exchange rate system? In your answer, discuss the costs and benefits of such a system, using historical examples to support your argument.
2. Which perspective on the international political economy—liberal, realist, or Marxist—offers the best guide to trade policy?
3. Does hegemony maximize cooperation in the global economic system or does it ultimately lead to increased conflict? Use historical examples from the hegemonic careers of Britain and/or the United States to illustrate your argument.

4. Which strategy is most effective in overcoming barriers to international cooperation: reciprocity, international law, or international regimes? Use examples of successful and/or unsuccessful cooperation in the twentieth century to support your answer.

RECOMMENDED ENRICHMENT READINGS

Alexandersson, Gunnar. *World Resources: Energy and Minerals: Studies in Economics and Political Geography.* New York: W. de Gryter, 1978. Explains natural resources and their effect on economic power in the world economy.

Frieden, Jeffry A., and David A. Lake, eds. *International Political Economy: Perspectives on Global Power and Wealth,* 3rd ed. New York: St. Martin's, 1995. A collection of works that provide a good survey of the free trade versus protectionism debate.

Grieco, Joseph. *Cooperation among Nations: Europe, America, and Non-tariff Barriers to Trade.* Ithaca, N.Y.: Cornell University Press, 1990. Investigation of non-tariff barriers between the United States and European Community countries and the GATT.

Isard, Peter. *Exchange Rate Economics.* New York: Cambridge University Press, 1995. Expands on central issues in contemporary economic theory and policy.

Keohane, Robert O. "Institutional Theory and the Realist Challenge after the Cold War." *Neorealism and Neoliberalism: The Contemporary Debate.* Edited by David Baldwin. New York: Columbia University Press, 1993, 269–300. Good discussion of the continuing dialectic between realism and liberalism.

———. *After Hegemony: Cooperation and Discord in the World Political Economy.* Princeton: Princeton University Press, 1984. Highly influential statement and examination of the neoliberal perspective.

Melsinnon, Ronald I. *The Rules of the Game: International Money and Exchange Rates.* Cambridge, Mass.: MIT Press, 1995. Provides a detailed history of international finance in the nineteenth and twentieth centuries.

Morishima, Michio. *Ricardo's Economic: A General Equilibrium Theory of Distribution and Growth.* New York: Cambridge University Press, 1989. Gives reader insights into Ricardo's "equilibrium economics."

Semmel, Bernard. *The Liberal Ideal and the Demons of Empire: Theories of Imperialism from Adam Smith to Lenin.* Baltimore: Johns Hopkins University Press, 1993. Will help reader gain a further understanding of imperialism, liberalism, and free trade.

Snidal, Duncan, "The Limits of Hegemonic Stability Theory," *International Organization* 39 (autumn 1985): 579–614. Discussion of the utility of hegemonic stability theory.

Zarkovic, Milica. *The Demographic Struggle for Power: The Political Economy of Demographic Engineering in the Modern World.* Portland, Ore.: Frank Cass, 1997. Study of the effects of population and demographic influences on economies.

Evolution of the World Economy

SCOPE, OBJECTIVES, AND APPROACH

This chapter introduces students to the history of the economic aspects of international relations. This chapter provides an historical overview of the effects of the theories learned in Chapter Six. The knowledge attained from reading Chapter Six will allow students to better understand the history introduced in this chapter. Chapter Seven, combined with Chapter Six, does not pretend to tell students all they need to know about global economics, even at the foundation level, but it is designed to impart a basic understanding of the political and economic aspects of international trade to students who may be unfamiliar with world economic history or international political economy.

WHAT STUDENTS SHOULD LEARN FROM THIS CHAPTER

Foundation Level

1. Explain why Britain established hegemony over world trade in the mid-nineteenth century.
2. Identify the major institutions of the Bretton Woods system.
3. Explain how and why the United States established hegemony over the world in the mid-1940s.

4. List the members of the G-7 and describe the purpose of G-7 summits.
5. Identify the major free trade areas of the late twentieth century.

Enrichment Level

1. Describe the challenges to British trade hegemony between 1871 and 1914.
2. Describe the causes and explain the consequences of the Great Depression.
3. Describe the goals and operation of the Bretton Woods system.
4. Describe the political and economic effects of the "oil crisis" of 1973.
5. Describe the effects of trade blocs on the world economy.

Mastery Level

1. Explain the efforts made to support the gold standard before WWI.
2. Explain the effects of WWI and postwar reparations on the world economy.
3. Explain why the United States moved towards multilateral management of the global monetary system after 1960.
4. Describe the factors contributing to the decline of the Bretton Woods system.
5. Explain the purpose and methods of policy coordination in the G-7.
6. Explain how the world economy is moving toward globalization and fragmentation at the same time.

OUTLINE OF THE CHAPTER

0. Introduction
   A. This chapter outlines the history of global economic relations.
   B. It outlines how the global trading system has evolved from a poorly regulated hegemonic system in the early tenth century to a multilateral system of global and regional institutions at the dawn of the twenty-first century.

I. The Origins of the World Economy
   A. The Industrial Revolution
      1. Nations have traded since ancient times, but the Industrial Revolution resulted in a massive expansion of production, international trade, and capital flows.
      2, The Industrial Revolution made the development of a truly international economy possible.
   B. The Rise of Britain
      1. From 1780 to 1820, Britain was able to use its advantages as the first industrialized nation to achieve economic and technological leadership.
      2. British trade boomed, led at first by exports of textiles, and trade with other states quickly outstripped trade within the British Empire, encouraging policies of free trade.
      3. By the mid-1800s, Britain's economic, financial, and political strength made it the first global superpower.

II. British Hegemony
   A. Free Trade
      1. After the Napoleonic Wars, Britain progressively adopted free trade policies advocated by economists David Ricardo and Adam Smith.
      2. Proponents of free trade secured the repeal of the *Corn Laws* (system of grain tariffs) by 1846, which prompted a boom in global trade.
      3. The Cobden–Chevalier trade treaty with France in 1860 introduced the concept of *most-favored-nation (MFN) status;* nations with this status trade with the granting nation on terms "no less favorable"—that is, with barriers no higher—than those given to any other nation (p. 308).
      4. World trade and production grew tremendously under these liberal trade policies.
   B. Challenges to British Hegemony
      1. As other nations industrialized, their growth outstripped that of Britain.

2. Germany, in particular, became a major political and economic rival; the *Zollverein* (customs union) created a German "common market" even before the unification of Germany.

3. In the late nineteenth and early twentieth centuries, Britain's economic power was eclipsed by that of the United States (Figure 7.1).

C. Protectionism and Discord

1. Growing trade in the nineteenth century was not free from problems.

    a. Industries suffered from foreign competition where they did not enjoy comparative advantages.

    b. Competition for international markets intensified.

    c. The rise of nationalism encouraged promotion of domestic industries as a matter of national pride.

    d. The changing balance of power in Europe, affected by changes in economic strength, heightened security concerns.

2. The influx of American and Russian grain into European markets and a depression in 1873–79 prompted intense lobbying for protection, especially in France and Germany (where the "marriage of Iron and Rye," a protectionist coalition of agricultural and industrial interests, formed).

D. The Calm before the Storm

1. By the end of the 1880s, free trade began to collapse, but trends toward economic conflict moved slowly at first.

2. The *gold standard* promoted economic stability with its system of exchange rates fixed to the value of gold, but the need to transfer gold reserves in order to maintain currency values caused some friction; most countries thought the tradeoff between currency stability and moderate tariff protection was worthwhile.

3. Britain remained committed to free trade as WWI approached, but protectionism gained strength in France and Germany and anti-gold standard pressure increased in the United States; the rising tide of protectionism helped to create a spiral of insecurity that led to WWI (see Chapter Three).

III. World War and Global Depression

A. World War I and Massive Economic Disruption

1. World trade contracted; many European states found themselves at war with their major trading partners.

2. European states ran up huge war debts; Germany, in addition, was saddled with demands for punitive reparations.

3. The war gave economic benefits to some states, however; the United States supplied war materials to the Allies and became the world's largest creditor, and Japan experienced growth in trade and industry.

4. Reparations and hyperinflation occurred.

    a. After WWI, the United States insisted upon payment of its war loans to the Allies, and Britain and France insisted on German reparations payments.

    b. Germany was forced to print money to service its debts, resulting in hyperinflation (see Chapter Three) of 500% or more per month; the U.S.–Germany exchange rate exceeded 1 million marks to the dollar.

    c. In 1924, the *Dawes Plan* provided private U.S. loans to Germany to pay reparations to the Allies; the Allies would then use these payments to repay loans from the United States; this system stabilized international finance for a few years, but linked the United States and Europe in a vulnerable cycle.

B. Boom and Bust

1. The U.S. economic boom in the 1920s was accompanied by high levels of speculation (in stocks and other investments); to curb this, the Federal Reserve raised U.S. interest rates; higher interest rates in the United States encouraged private capital to flow to the United States from Germany, breaking the cycle of the Dawes Plan.

2. Inability to cooperate on debt and reparations led to increased tensions; the reinstated gold standard fell apart, and protectionist trade policies began to increase.

3. The crash of the U.S. stock market (1929) and the surge of protectionism fueled by the Smoot–Hawley tariff (1930) precipitated a global Great Depression.

4. The interwar period thus serves as an example of the difficulty of cooperation without a hegemon, as the isolationist United States refused to play this role before WWII.

IV. Transformation of the World Economy

A. WWII altered the distribution of power in the international system, set the stage for the Cold War, and fundamentally changed the international political economy.

    B. The United States emerged as hegemon, dominating the world in terms of production and leading to a massive increase in U.S. GNP.

        1. International trade and investment grew during the period of U.S. hegemony.

        2. Living standards throughout much of the industrialized world increased rapidly during the 1950s and 1960s.

    C. The Bretton Woods System was influential.

        1. This system of international institutions designed to facilitate economic cooperation was established in 1945 with three main components.

        2. *The International Monetary Fund (IMF)* managed a fixed exchange rate system (pegging world currencies to the value of the dollar) and provided short-term loans to rectify balance-of-payments deficits.

        3. The *International Bank for Reconstruction and Development (IBRD,* or *World Bank)* was created to finance the rebuilding of war-torn nations, but found a larger role in providing capital for development in newly independent Third World countries.

        4. The proposed International trade organization faced U.S. congressional opposition and never got off the ground; in 1947, the *General Agreement on Tariffs and Trade (GATT)* sought to open world markets and increase trade, while allowing protection for "infant industries" in developing countries.

V. American Hegemony

    A. The Bretton Woods system managed the world economy relatively smoothly throughout the 1950s, and U.S. support for open trade encouraged dramatic growth in most economies.

        1. Some problems became apparent in the system, however; the large outflow of dollars, the key international currency, created balance-of-payments problems in the United States.

        2. Cooperation to maintain economic stability began with cooperation between central banks (the Federal Reserve, the Bank of England, and the Bundesbank) and was institutionalized through ministerial and summit meetings of the *Group of Seven (G-7)* the leading member nations of the *Organization for Economic Cooperation and Development (OECD).*

    B. The difficulties of multilateral management and huge financial flows through multinational corporations (MNCs) put further strains on the system.

    C. The decline of U.S. hegemony resulted.

        1. As the economies of Europe and Japan grew, along with their share of world trade (Table 7.4) unilateral U.S. leadership of the world economy became politically and economically unsustainable.

        2. The United States developed a chronic current-account deficit after 1971, and social programs and the Vietnam War increased strains on the U.S. budget.

        3. The "Nixon Shock": In 1971, U.S. President Nixon announced that the United States could no longer bear the whole burden of international monetary stabilization; the United States ended its commitment to convert dollars to gold, raised tariffs, and devalued the dollar.

        4. The G-7 failed to agree on how to fix the Bretton Woods system, and in 1973 the fixed-exchange rate system was ended.

    D. OPEC and the oil crisis arose.

        1. As economies in the developed world grew, their dependence on imported oil (especially from the Middle East) increased.

        2. When the United States did not withdraw its support for Israel in the Yom Kippur War (see Chapter Six), Arab members of the *Organization of Petroleum Exporting Countries (OPEC)* imposed an oil embargo and raised prices to other countries dramatically; the fourfold increase in oil prices from 1973 to 1974 created a major shift in economic power.

VI. From Hegemony to Multilateralism

    A. "Petrodollars" and International Finance

        1. Trade did not collapse with the demise of the Bretton Woods system; instead, trade continued to grow, and export-led growth fueled economic booms in Japan and Southeast Asia.

        2. OPEC states developed huge surpluses of "petrodollars" which were "recycled" as international loans, many to developing countries (see Chapter Eight).

        3. Cooperative efforts to manage the monetary system continued, spurred on by expansion of trade and financial flows; major states began to coordinate their macroeconomic policies (taxation, spending, and money supply) to manage exchange and interest rates.

    B. From Shock to Recovery

        1. Increases in oil prices led to serious economic disruption and stagflation (low growth plus high inflation) in many developed countries in the mid-1970s; another round of stagflation and recession occurred after the Iranian revolution threatened oil supplies in 1979 (see Chapter Five).

2. U.S. efforts to curb inflation resulted in a severe recession in 1981–82; tax cuts, deregulation, and high defense spending fueled U.S. growth thereafter, but budget deficits increased.

3. The United States continued to run trade and budget deficits during the 1980s and 1990s, prompting attempts to devalue the dollar.

C. Consequences of Increased Interdependence after 1973
  1. Multilateralism in economic management has increased, as the G-7 states became forced to coordinate their policies in order to maintain economic growth.
  2. The number of economically powerful states has increased, heightening competition for markets and raising the chances of economic and trade conflicts.

D. Eastern Europe and Russia: From Communism to the Free Market?
  1. The collapse of communism in Eastern Europe and the USSR (see Chapter Four) has profoundly affected European economies, and its potential impact on the world economy is much greater.
  2. The former communist states continue to face daunting challenges in reforming their economies—reforms that will take place at different rates.
  3. The states that have pursued economic liberalization, including freeing of prices and privatization, most diligently (Poland, the Czech Republic, Hungary) have been most successful, despite temporary setbacks; those that have not removed the control of former communist bureaucracies (Romania, Bulgaria, and to a lesser extent Russia) have been less successful.
  4. The West has promised the former communist states massive aid, but has been slow to deliver it; many members of the European Union have been reluctant to admit or cooperate with the post-communist states, fearing an influx of less expensive goods and labor.

E. The Need for Cooperation
  1. Interdependence has shown the major trading states that cooperation pays, but conflicts of interest continue.
  2. G-7 summits have had some success in multilateral economic management, but their ad hoc nature makes cooperation difficult to predict reliably.
  3. Though the G-7 states favor increased cooperation, domestic considerations can derail international cooperation all too easily.

VII. Economic Blocs: The Shape of the Future?
  A. Economic Blocs
    1. An economic bloc is a political or economic organization designed to promote internal cooperation and enhance competitiveness with the rest of the world.
    2. Two most common types of blocs:
      a. *Common markets* combine common external trade areas with uniform internal trade barriers.
      b. *Free-trade areas* feature uniform or absent internal trade barriers without standardizing external barriers.
    3. The rise of trade blocs has increased fears that these blocs will become protectionist "fortresses" closed to imports from the outside; at the same time, negotiations between blocs may be easier to manage than large multilateral treaties such as GATT.
    4. It is too early to tell what impacts trade blocs will have.
      a. Some predict easier negotiations of international economic agreements as there would be fewer independent actors.
      b. Others argue that the self-sufficiency of regions is impossible and interregional trade will continue to increase.
  B. European Union
    1. The ECUEU is the world's largest and most highly integrated economic bloc.
    2. The development of the EU shows progressively increasing integration among Western European economies.
      a. *European Coal and Steel Community* was formed in 1951 (France, West Germany, Italy, Benelux countries).
      b. Treaty of Rome in 1957 created *European Economic Community (EEC)*.
      c. The United Kingdom, Ireland, and Denmark join in 1973; Greece, Spain, and Portugal join by 1986; other countries, including former communist states, have subsequently applied.
      d. Single European Act, 1985, commits EC members to further policy coordination and lowered trade barriers.
      e. Maastricht Treaty, 1991, gives more power to supranational coordinating institutions and creates the *European Union;* the member countries also agreed to establish an economic and monetary union

(EMU), with a single currency, the euro (which banks and stock exchanges in eleven EU countries will begin using in 1999) and to provide for an independent European central bank.

3. Progress toward European Union has not been easy, however, as domestic interests opposed various aspects of policy coordination and some members have been loath to surrender some of their sovereignty to European institutions.

C. North American Free Trade Agreement (NAFTA)

1. NAFTA, which went into effect in 1994, is designed to eliminate trade barriers between the United States, Mexico, and Canada, but does not create supranational economic or political institutions.

2. Formation of NAFTA was accompanied by bitter debate in the United States and Canada.

   a. Supporters argued that freer trade would lower prices, improve productivity, create jobs, and increase demand for goods and environmental protection in Mexico as that country became more prosperous.

   b. Opponents feared the loss of U.S. and Canadian jobs to less expensive Mexican labor, increased drug smuggling and illegal immigration, and the transfer of production to Mexican factories with lower environmental standards (including *maquiladoras,* factories assembling U.S.-produced components and reexporting finished products to the United States).

D. MERCOSUR

1. Prompted by the movement toward free trade to their north, Brazil, Argentina, and Uruguay formed the Southern Cone Common Market (MERCOSUR).

2. These countries, along with Paraguay and Chile, have lowered tariff barriers among themselves.

3. Integration to a common market has proved to be difficult, though there has been progress on external trade barriers.

4. Controversial questions remain about the possibility of MERCOSUR countries joining NAFTA (as a bloc or individually) and about the proposed Free Trade Area of the Americas.

E. Free-Trade Areas of the Pacific Rim

1. ASEAN states, concerned that EU and NAFTA would divert trade and investment, formed the *ASEAN Free Trade Area (AFTA)* in 1993.

2. Some Asian states later advocated formation of an East Asian Economic Caucus (EAEC), including ASEAN, Japan, and China.

3. U.S. and Australian concern over being left out of Asian economic blocs prompted convening of the *Asia-Pacific Economic Cooperation Organization (APEC),* including more than a dozen Pacific Rim states, in 1993.

4. Through APEC, the export-oriented Pacific Rim nations seek to prevent exclusion from American markets as a result of NAFTA.

F. Are Trade Blocs Cooperation or Conflict?

1. In general, regional integration and trade blocs have arisen in response to the decline of U.S. hegemony; each contains elements of both cooperation (with bloc members) and conflict (with outside states).

2. There are two major issues in international economics since 1973.

   a. Major industrialized states have attempted to cooperate since the demise of the Bretton Woods system and have avoided a major economic collapse in the absence of a hegemon.

   b. Economic conflict and uncertainty have remained prevalent, however, and regional blocs have arisen to deal with global competition.

3. It is far from clear whether regional cooperation will increase global tension; likewise, whether blocs will heighten conflict, or cooperation, at the global level remains uncertain.

VIII. Conclusion: The Global Economy in the New Era

A. Economic globalization and fragmentation have also simultaneously increased.

1. Trade and financial flows increase constantly, and markets for goods, services, labor, and capital are continually globalized.

2. At the same time, increased global competition has led to more conflict over markets for goods and labor, and demands for protection parallel the increase in trade; political conflicts will continue to be played out in the economic sphere, and vice versa.

B. The world economy is becoming more globalized and fragmented simultaneously.

1. Technology has allowed small firms and individuals to have routine access to global markets.

2. Some economists fear that the world is dividing into antagonistic trading blocs, as Europe, the United States, and Japan decrease barriers to regional trade while creating barriers to international trade.

3. The sovereignty of the nation-state is weakening as power is being transferred to supranational institutions and subnational groups.

HOW THE CHAPTER RELATES TO CENTRAL THEMES OF THE TEXT

As pointed out in the chapter's conclusion, the economic aspects of international relations offer an excellent illustration of the simultaneous operation of conflict and cooperation. Examples of these processes are presented by the difficulties of policy coordination in the G-7 despite explosive growth in world trade.

While the history of the modern world economy is generally a story of increasing globalization, fragmentation is in evidence as well, in the division of the global economy into trade blocs and the devolution of economic power from national governments and central banks to multinational corporations and small businesses trading in global markets. Naturally, the opposition between free trade and protectionism is a major theme of the chapter. The economic history in Chapter Seven also offers examples of actions and policies, not involving military security or war, which can later be used to construct theoretical arguments from each level of analysis.

SUGGESTED LECTURE TOPICS

1. Enumerate the costs and benefits of free trade and protection and show how states have followed these opposing policies—sometimes simultaneously—at various times since 1870.
2. Compare the overall level of international economic cooperation and conflict in the periods 1919–45, 1945–73, and 1973 to the present to show how global trade operates under no hegemon, a strong hegemon, and a declining hegemon; discuss the costs and benefits of hegemony for the hegemon and the other states in the system.
3. Trace the history of the European Union, ASEAN, and NAFTA to illustrate the trend towards trade blocs and economic policy coordination; discuss whether this trend is likely to lead to global integration (through the WTO, for example) or to a world of regional trade "fortresses."

STUDY AND EXAM QUESTIONS

1. Discuss the role of the G-7 in the international political economy. In addition, explain the benefits of membership (*hint:* Why has membership been important to Russia following the collapse of the Soviet Union?).
2. Should the United States have signed the North American Free Trade Agreement? Why or why not? Be sure to discuss both general and specific costs and benefits of free trade and protectionism in your answer.
3. Does the rise of trade blocs indicate a trend towards greater cooperation in the world economy or a trend toward increased conflict? Use examples of trade policies in Europe, East Asia, and North America to support your answer.
4. Explain how globalization and fragmentation are occurring simultaneously in the current world economy.

RECOMMENDED ENRICHMENT READINGS

Bhagwati, Jagdish. *The World Trading System at Risk*. Princeton: Princeton University Press, 1991. Strong presentation of the case for free trade in the contemporary global system.

Bhagwati, Jagdish, and Anne Krueger. *The Dangerous Drift to Preferential Trade Agreements*. Washington D.C.: AEI Press, 1995. This will help the reader understand the new trade agreements such as NAFTA, the EU, ASEAN, and MERCOSUR and their effects on world trade.

Cameron, Rondo. *A Concise Economic History of the World from Paleolithic Times to the Present*. 2nd ed. Oxford: Oxford University Press, 1993. Unlike most books, this one lives up to its title; an excellent one-volume survey of the evolution of the world economy.

Gourevitch, Peter. *Politics in Hard Times: Comparative Responses to International Economic Crises*. Ithaca, N.Y.: Cornell University Press, 1987. Classic study of the success and failure of international economic cooperation.

Hersh, Jacques. *The USA and the Rise of East Asia since 1945*. New York: St. Martin's, 1993. Interesting look at the growth of economic power along the Pacific Rim.

- Inoguchi, Takashi. "Four Japanese Scenarios for the Future." *International Political Economy: Perspectives on Global Power and Wealth.* Edited by Jeffry A. Frieden and David A. Lake. New York: St. Martin's, 1991. 411–22. Thought-provoking, speculative essay on the changing structure of the world economy. The Frieden and Lake volume is highly recommended as a supplementary text for courses on international economic issues.

  Keohane, Robert O. *After Hegemony: Co-operation and Discord in the World Political Economy.* Princeton, N.J.: Princeton University Press, 1984. Good examination of trends toward conflict and cooperation in the post–Bretton Woods era of multilateralism.

- Kindleberger, Charles P. "The Rise of Free Trade in Western Europe." *International Political Economy.* Edited by Jeffry A. Frieden and David A. Lake. 72–88. New York: St. Martin's, 1991. Concise yet surprisingly detailed examination of the transition from mercantilism to liberalism.

  ———. *The World In Depression, 1929–1939.* Berkeley, Calif.: University of California Press, 1973. Superior study of the greatest world economic crisis in modern times.

  Krugman, Paul. *Rethinking International Trade.* Cambridge, Mass.: MIT Press, 1990. Useful, well thought-out presentation of the case for protectionism.

  Lairson, Thomas D., and David Skidmore. *International Political Economy: The Struggle for Power and Wealth.* 2nd ed. Fort Worth, Tex.: Harcourt Brace, 1997. Very good introductory text on the world economy for lower-division students; includes painless explanations of basic concepts in trade and finance.

  Lake, David A. *Power, Protection and Free Trade.* Ithaca, N.Y.: Cornell University Press, 1987. Outstanding study of the making of U.S. trade policy from the decline of British hegemony to the end of the Great Depression.

  Rosecrance, Richard. *The Rise of the Trading State: Commerce and Conquest in the Modern World.* New York: Basic Books, 1986. Highly recommended comparison of the military and economic paths to political power in the international system and of the reasons why states choose one or the other.

  Spero, Joan Edelman. *The Politics of International Economic Relations.* 5th ed. New York: Routledge, 1997. Another good text on the international political economy, falling roughly midway between Lairson and Skidmore and Gilpin in difficulty and accessibility.

  Yergin, Daniel. *The Prize: The Quest for Oil, Money, and Power.* New York: Simon and Schuster, 1991. Thorough, engaging account of how industrialists and politicians throughout the world have been prepared, willingly or reluctantly, to shed blood for oil.

North–South Economic Relations: The Challenge of Development

SCOPE, OBJECTIVES, AND APPROACH

As its title indicates, this chapter covers the economic relationships between the industrialized North and the developing South. The major theme of the chapter is the asymmetric interdependence between the First and Third Worlds, which underlies the chapter's discussions of theories, strategies, and problems of economic development. The chapter takes an issue-oriented approach to the overall North–South relationship and focuses on the ongoing challenges faced by developing nations, though some historical material and theoretical perspectives (particularly dependency theory) are presented as well. While the chapter naturally focuses on economics, political, environmental, and social issues also receive substantial attention.

WHAT STUDENTS SHOULD LEARN FROM THIS CHAPTER

Foundation Level

1. Describe in general terms why developed and developing countries are interdependent.

2. Describe the basic economic characteristics of the industrialized countries, newly industrialized countries (NICs), middle-income developing countries, oil-exporting countries, and least developed countries (LDC), giving examples of each.
3. List the basic premises and conclusions of modernization theory and dependency theory.
4. Define demographic transition and summarize the economic and social effects of urbanization.
5. Identify the three types of development aid.
6. Describe in general terms the development strategies of import-substitution industrialization (ISI), collective bargaining, and export-led industrialization (ELI).

Enrichment Level

1. Outline the difficulties faced by primary product exporters in the world economy.
2. Describe the advantages and disadvantages of each type of development aid.
3. Define the New International Economic Order (NIEO) and describe the objectives of the Group of 77.
4. Explain the role of the IMF and World Bank in financing development in the South.
5. Identify cases of success and failure of each basic development strategy.
6. Describe the origins of the debt crisis of the 1970s and 1980s.
7. Describe the contentions made by both sides in the U.S. debates over NAFTA and continued MFN status for China.

Mastery Level

1. Assess the strengths and weaknesses of modernization theory and dependency theory.
2. Explain the political strategy followed by the Group of 77 and point out the main reasons for its successes and failures.
3. Define structural adjustment and explain why it has led to political problems in some developing countries.
4. Explain why OPEC rose to and fell from global political and economic prominence.
5. Assess the strengths and weaknesses of the three basic development strategies.
6. Explain the major economic and environmental problems associated with increased economic integration of developed and developing countries.

OUTLINE OF THE CHAPTER

0. Introduction: The Contemporary South
   A. Differences between the North and South
      1. While it is difficult to define development precisely, and development goals vary among states, the economic gap between Northern and Southern states remains pronounced.
      2. Demands for improvement of living standards in the South are certain to continue.
   B. Development in Theory and Practice
      1. While developmental goals differ, the experience of development is similar in most countries.
         a. All countries started with most of their populations engaged in subsistence agriculture.
         b. Development in whatever form encourages growth in manufacturing and services.
         c. Rural residents typically flood into cities to obtain manufacturing and service jobs; rapid growth of cities can lead to social and political problems (see under urbanization, below).
      2. Under any definition of development, increases in agricultural and industrial *productivity* are vital.

Part I: Contending Theories of Development
   I. Modernization Theory
      A. Causes of Underdevelopment
         1. Modernization theory contends that the main causes, and solutions, to underdevelopment may be found in developing countries themselves.
         2. Modernization theorists study the experience of developed and developing states, but focus on the development path taken by established industrialized states.

3. Distinctions are drawn between "traditional" (agrarian, village societies based on traditional practice and ritual) and "modern" (urban, innovative, and adaptable) societies.

4. From the modernization perspective, traditional culture, which blocks the societal transformations necessary for rapid economic growth, is the fundamental obstacle to development.

B. Necessity of Change

1. From this perspective, states will develop economically only if they adapt or change traditional social, political, and economic institutions.

2. Individuals must gain freedom to attain status through merit or success rather than birth.

3. Political institutions such as rule of law, democracy, freedom of speech, and property ownership must be encouraged.

4. A market-based economy is most conducive to economic growth, though some level of intervention by the state for social reasons is possible and desirable.

5. Economic, political, and social aspects of development reinforce and stimulate each other—for example, increased incomes lead to education and strengthening of democracy, which in turn protect the free market economy.

6. Because trade is the engine of economic growth, free trade and open markets are encouraged; though aid plays an important role, states can "pull themselves up by their own bootstraps" through trade and investment in physical, financial, and human capital.

C. The Social Impact of Modernization

1. Resulting Problems
   a. Though the changes wrought by modernization are beneficial in the long term, they typically cause short- or medium-term problems that must be addressed.
   b. These problems occur in all developing societies, but modernization theory regards them as inevitable "growing pains" that can and must be overcome.

2. Demographic Transition
   a. Traditional societies generally have very high birth and death rates, but improvements in medical care and standard of living associated with industrialization raise life expectancy and lower infant mortality.
   b. Thus, populations explode in countries in the initial to middle stages of development; this causes social problems, increases the need for education and other social programs, and requires changes in traditional attitudes (such as giving women access to jobs and education) to lower birth rates and curb population growth.

3. Urbanization
   a. Population increase and the creation of better-paying jobs in cities typically lead to rapid urbanization.
   b. Urbanization in turn often leads to social and political problems, such as increased crime, disruption of traditional family and social structures, increased need for infrastructure and social services, and demands for subsidized food prices by urbanites.

D. Critiques of Modernization Theory

1. Some critics question whether the Northern path to development can be followed in the South.
   a. Modernizing countries now face environmental obstacles and resource shortages.
   b. While Britain, the United States, Japan, and so on were able to develop autonomously, Third World states now depend on the First World for markets and capital.
   c. Southern countries face stiffer competition from states with strong manufacturing sectors.

2. Other critics contend that traditional social and political institutions are very difficult to change.

3. Still others charge the modernization theory is culturally biased, Eurocentric, and reflects a Cold War mentality (trying to keep the Third World out of the Soviet sphere by locking developing nations into a capitalist development pattern).

4. Finally, some contend that the structure of the world economy is biased against the South, first through colonialism and later through multinational corporations and aid and credit policies; these criticisms spawned an alternate school of thought known as *dependency theory*.

II. Dependency Theory

A. Inequality of the North and South

1. Dependency theorists contend that the main reasons for development and underdevelopment may be found in the structure of the world economy, which is biased against the Third World.

2. According to this perspective, developed states and multinational corporations have kept the Third World dependent on the First.

3. Northern states export manufactured goods to the South, while Southern states generally export lower-valued raw materials to the North; this *international division of labor* is enforced by the North.

    4. This unequal relationship between developed *core* and developing *periphery* began in the age of European expansion and continues today.

  B. Primary Product Exports

    1. The disadvantaged position of the South stems from its dependence on export of *primary products* (raw materials and agricultural produce; see Table 8.2).

    2. The exports of many Southern countries are also dominated by a *single commodity*, such as coffee, cocoa, copper, or oil; thus, their economies are highly vulnerable to *price fluctuations* (if world prices for this commodity decline, the impact on the developing state can be severe, though profits can be great when prices are high).

  C. Unequal Terms of Trade

    1. Dependency theorists argue that developing countries' ratio of export prices to import prices—their terms of trade—tend to decline over time (as improved productivity tends to lower the relative prices of raw materials).

    2. Furthermore, collusion among developed states and MNCs keep terms of trade artificially low.

  D. Multinational Corporations

    1. Many productive assets in Third World states are controlled by MNCs based in the First World.

    2. According to dependency theory, MNCs exploit Southern states and hinder their development; they have become the chief means for maintaining the colonial system in the developing world.

    3. Various MNC practices hamper Third World development.

      a. *Transfer pricing mechanisms* are used to evade taxes and increase profits (though MNCs do this in the developed world as well).

      b. The technology MNCs transfer to the South is typically *capital intensive,* requiring sophisticated equipment and skilled labor, and is thus not appropriate for Southern economies.

      c. MNCs do not bring capital into the Third World, according to dependency theory, but suck up the limited supply of local capital and crowd out local entrepreneurs.

  E. Critiques of Dependency Theory

    1. Critics of dependency theory reply that the structure of the world economy has not prevented many Southern states from industrializing; a number of Southern states have achieved great economic success, with the help of Northern trade and investment, by actively participating in the world economy.

    2. Fluctuations in terms of trade hit developed as well as developing economies; the best way to become less vulnerable to fluctuations is economic diversification, which should be an integral part of development.

    3. Finally, dependency theory ignores factors in the developing world, such as unconstrained population growth, corruption, and lack of democracy, which contribute to underdevelopment.

    4. In general, critics of dependency theory do not seek to "blame the victims" for underdevelopment, but they contend that industrialization will alleviate many of the problems (such as dependency on a single primary product), which dependency theorists see as systemic obstacles to development.

Part II: Development Strategies

  I. Alternative Strategies

    A. Import-Substitution Industrialization (ISI)

      1. Import-substitution industrialization (ISI) attempts to promote production of domestic goods to replace products that had been imported.

      2. A number of means are used to implement this strategy.

        a. High tariff barriers

        b. Undervalued exchange rates, to make imports expensive and domestic products relatively cheaper (see Chapter Seven)

        c. Subsidies for domestic producers

      3. Many Latin American countries attempted ISI following the Great Depression.

        a. The first stages of ISI in the region were fairly successful, as domestic producers developed products to replace imported consumer goods (many of which became unavailable after WWII).

        b. The later stages of ISI ("deepening") were less successful, however, as investments in these industries required more capital and Northern technology; ISI in practice thus led to massive borrowing from foreign banks and growing external debts.

      4. On balance, ISI has not been very successful and has resulted in many cases in greater dependence on the North without raising living standards in the Southern countries attempting it.

    B. Export-Led Growth

      1. The strategy of growth through export-led industrialization (ELI) attempts to work with, rather than against, the structure of the world economy.

2. The ELI strategy involves undervaluing exchange rates (to make exports cheap and imports expensive), deregulation of and investment in export industries, borrowing technology from the North, research and development, and state intervention to focus the economy on profitable export sectors.
3. From the 1960s onward, many countries that promoted export industries have achieved high rates of growth in NICs; the most spectacularly successful are the East Asian "tigers" (Hong Kong, Singapore, South Korea, and Taiwan; see Figure 8.2).
4. Export-led growth is not free of problems, however.
   a. Some critics have argued that existing NICs have saturated trading opportunities with the North, making the rise of future NICs unlikely.
   b. Industrial development has had significant environmental and social costs in the NICs (as it has everywhere else).
5. Nevertheless, as long as world markets remain open, opportunities for export-led growth are likely to continue.

C. New International Economic Order (NIEO)
1. In the 1970s, many Southern countries joined together to attempt to change the structure of the world economic system.
   a. Guided by dependency theory, these countries called for a *New International Economic Order* (NIEO) more favorable to Southern states.
   b. The Group of 77, an alliance of developing states, was formed to press for NIEO and exploit the North's dependence on primary goods from the South.
2. During the 1960s and 1970s, mineral and agricultural commodity cartels were formed to push up world commodity prices and reduce the control of Southern resources by MNCs; the most successful of these was OPEC (see box).
3. Cartelization did not work for most non-oil primary products, however, as coordinating policy among many producers was difficult and substitutes were more easily found.
4. By the end of the 1980s, repeated failures to improve primary product exporters' terms of trade convinced most countries that collective bargaining was no substitute for diversified growth.

II. Aid and Development
A. Desire for Aid
1. The success of the Marshall Plan after WWII (see Chapter Four) led many to believe that aid from Northern countries could initiate or accelerate development in the South.
2. From the 1950s onward, three types of aid evolved.
B. Bilateral Aid
1. Bilateral aid—direct aid from a single developed country to a single developing state (commonly referred to as "foreign aid")—has not duplicated the success of the Marshall Plan.
2. Many in the North criticize bilateral aid as an international welfare system that encourages corruption and stifles initiative in the South.
3. Aid has become a significant percentage of the GNP of many LDCs; in the long run, high aid dependence is very unhealthy for a nation's economy.
4. Bilateral aid is criticized in many developed countries as a waste of tax money.
5. Bilateral aid often comes with political or economic "strings" attached; recipients may be strongly persuaded or required to purchase equipment or align politically with the donor country.
C. Multilateral Aid
1. Multilateral aid is official development assistance channeled through international institutions; two UN agencies, the World Bank and IMF (see Chapter Seven) are the most important multilateral aid agencies; they have also become important negotiating channels between the First and Third Worlds.
2. The IMF and World Bank provide grants and loans to developing states; unlike bilateral aid, the multilateral aid they extend is relatively free of political "strings."
D. The Debt Crisis
1. The IMF and World Bank played a crucial role in managing the *debt crisis*.
   a. During the 1970s, when huge sums of "petrodollars" were "recycled" as loans to developing states, many Third World countries ran up huge debts.
   b. In the global recession of the late 1970s and early 1980s, however, many states that had overborrowed found it impossible to pay back their loans on the original terms; defaults on these loans would have caused major international banks huge losses, threatening a serious world financial crisis.
   c. The IMF and World Bank helped ease the crisis by renegotiating loans and providing new loans, but much of this new aid was made contingent on structural adjustment (see below).

      d. Though a new debt crisis seems unlikely, many Third World states remain severely indebted, and a large portion of their export earnings goes to repay foreign debt, leaving little left over to invest in the debtor country.

  2. Controversy exists over structural adjustment.

      a. Beginning in the 1980s, the IMF and World Bank began insisting on policies of *structural adjustment*—usually market-oriented economic reforms, such as opening of markets to imports and reduction of price controls and subsidies—as a condition for receiving multilateral aid.

      b. Most debtor governments resist these conditions, which are frequently viewed as foreign meddling and often entail unpopular cuts in subsidies or increases in consumer prices, but most have little choice but to accept the IMF/World Bank conditions.

E. Private Aid

  1. Nongovernmental organizations (NGOs) and other private groups also extend development assistance to the South (examples: CARE, Save the Children, Oxfam).

  2. NGOs typically give aid for specific purposes or projects, emphasizing humanitarian concerns.

  3. Private aid has the advantage of bypassing official channels in both donor and recipient states, but the funds of private organizations are limited, and private aid can rarely provide enough capital for major infrastructural or investment projects.

F. Evaluating Aid

  1. Developing countries often complain that bilateral aid is usually driven by political concerns rather than economic or humanitarian needs; many big U.S.-aid recipients, for example, have been "front-line states in the Cold War" (Pakistan, Turkey), and other donors use similar political objectives.

  2. Tying of bilateral aid to the purchase of products from the donor country is also criticized.

  3. Northern donors have tended to favor big, visible projects (factories, ports, dams) over smaller or less tangible ones (like clinics and schools); this has sometimes resulted in the construction of grandiose "white elephants" (example: the Aswan Dam).

Part III: The Development Debates of the 1990s and Beyond

I. Contemporary Development Dilemmas

A. Open Markets

  1. Continued growth of exports from NICs and other developing countries depends on open markets in the North.

  2. However, pressure for protecting Northern markets from developing-country exports can arise out of political or domestic economic concerns (see Chapter Seven).

B. China: Should Free Trade Require Freedom?

  1. China's economic growth from the mid-1980s to the early 1990s has been very strong, but many exported goods were produced by prison labor, and the Tiananmen Square Massacre (see Chapter Five) marked a turn away from democratization and back toward repression of dissidents.

  2. Many in the United States thus argued that China's most-favored-nation (MFN) trading status should be revoked or made contingent upon progress in human rights, but others contended that trade and economic development would promote democracy in the long run.

  3. The Clinton and Bush administrations have refused to revoke China's MFN status, but pressure to do so in Congress continues.

C. Controversy over NAFTA

  1. The United States, Canada, and Mexico negotiated as sweeping lowering of trade barriers known as the North American Free Trade Act (NAFTA) by the early 1990s.

  2. Opposition to NAFTA in the U.S. Congress was very strong, however, and the question of ratification of NAFTA provoked an acrimonious debate.

      a. Proponents argued that free trade would create more U.S. jobs in the long run, lower prices for consumers, open up export opportunities, and improve democracy and prosperity in Mexico over time.

      b. Opponents argued that NAFTA would result in the "export of jobs" to Mexico, as Mexican unskilled labor was much less expensive, and in increased pollution, as Mexican environmental standards were poorly enforced.

  3. Despite strong objections from labor and environmental groups, NAFTA passed in November 1993 after intense lobbying and logrolling.

D. The Political Aspects of Economic Interdependence

  1. As trade between North and South continues to grow, the NAFTA and MFN debates are likely to be repeated and North–South interdependence will increase.

2. The question of which rules should govern trade and production in an interdependent world—the stringent labor and environmental standards of the North or the lenient ones of the South—grows increasingly acute.

II. Conclusion: The Development Imperative
   A. This chapter has spoken of the First and Third Worlds, but of course developed and developing countries share the same planet, and as interdependence increases each will be increasingly affected by the other's problems.
   B. Advocates of *sustainable development* warn that environmental concerns and constraints on resources must be taken into account, but they still call for development, if only to fulfill basic human needs.
   C. Sharp disagreement over the causes of underdevelopment and development strategies remain; each development strategy has succeeded in some cases and failed in others.
   D. Nevertheless, there is widespread agreement that diversified economic development (with all its faults and costs) is the only cure for poverty in developing nations; for the Third World, development is not an option, but an imperative.

HOW THE CHAPTER RELATES TO CENTRAL THEMES OF THE TEXT

By discussing the interdependent relationship between the North and South, this chapter shows how interdependence simultaneously increases conflict and promotes cooperation; like it or not, North and South need each other and must find some means of getting along. Though it does cover some successes of international cooperation (such as management of the debt crisis), the unstated theme of the chapter is the failure of cooperation—the collapse of commodity cartels, the failure of the collective bargaining strategy, the drawbacks of and disillusionment with development aid. Perhaps the "moral" of the chapter's story, however, is that cooperation in pursuit of selfish motives (driving up prices, donation of aid for political reasons) is ultimately self-defeating, even when a cartel temporarily dominates or "corners" a market (as OPEC's rise and fall illustrates).

The processes of globalization and fragmentation are visible in Chapter Eight as well, as the global economy ties North and South together through increasing interdependence while the developing world fragments into successful NICs and impoverished, aid-dependent LDCs. The reasons advanced for success and failure of development reinforce the economic philosophies discussed in Chapter Seven (liberal modernization theory versus Marxist dependency theory) and further exemplify analytical perspectives based on specific levels of analysis (domestic for modernization versus systemic for dependency).

The three development strategies also show how the choice of level of analysis can lead to widely differing conclusions and policy prescriptions. Systemic-level dependency theory suggests that reforming the international system through collective bargaining offers the best path to development, while domestic-level explanations contend that political and economic choices made within states (ISI versus export promotion, market reforms versus state-directed production) determine whether a developing state will succeed as an NIC or languish as an LDC.

SUGGESTED LECTURE TOPICS

1. Compare the prescriptions for development offered by modernization theory and dependency theory, critically assessing each school of thought and linking each to its related perspective on international political economy (presented in Chapter Six).
2. Compare the economic status and policies of pairs of neighboring states in the South (Singapore and Indonesia, for example, or Colombia and Mexico) and invite students to suggest reasons for their differing levels of development.
3. Discuss the three trading strategies adopted by Southern states (ISI, ELI, and collective bargaining), pointing out their strengths and weaknesses and giving examples of states that have followed each strategy.
4. Discuss the international debt crisis from Northern and Southern perspectives; show how the crisis illustrates the asymmetric interdependence between North and South.

5. Show how the conflict between protection and free trade plays out in debates over trading strategies for development (ISI versus ELI; the NAFTA debate in the United States, Mexico, and Canada). Do the same for the conflict between idealism and realism (multilateral versus bilateral aid, controversy over renewing China's MFN status).

STUDY AND EXAM QUESTIONS

1. Does modernization theory offer useful guidelines for the development strategies of Southern nations at present? Why or why not? Use examples from at least three developing states to argue why the Northern development experience is, or is not, reproducible in the contemporary South.
2. "The failure of collective bargaining to achieve the New International Economic Order shows that dependency theory is fundamentally correct; Northern states and MNCs colluded to break the bargaining power of the Southern cartels." Do you agree with this statement? Why or why not? Discuss the experience of both OPEC and non-oil commodity cartels in your answer.
3. Which factor has contributed more to the economic success of the East Asian NICs: their inherent advantages or the policies they adopted? Be sure to discuss both economic and political aspects of development in your answer.
4. Should the IMF and World Bank require recipients of their loans to adopt policies of structural adjustment? In your answer, discuss the costs and benefits of structural adjustment from the viewpoints of both Northern lenders and Southern borrowers.
5. Has the provision of development aid contributed more to international cooperation or to conflict? Discuss both multilateral and bilateral aid in your answer.
6. Do developing countries have a viable alternative to the trading strategy of export-led industrialization? Why or why not? Discuss the positive and negative aspects of export-led growth and at least one alternative strategy in your answer, then discuss the experiences of developing states that have followed each strategy.

RECOMMENDED ENRICHMENT READINGS

Almond, Gabriel, and James Coleman, eds. *The Politics of the Developing Areas*. Princeton: Princeton University Press, 1960. A classic work on modernization theory.

Billet, Bret L. *Modernization Theory and Economic Development: Discontent in the Developing World*. Westport, Conn.: Praeger, 1993. Will provide reader with a more in-depth understanding of modernization theory by presenting cases demonstrating the weaknesses of development theory.

• Broad, Robin, John Cavanagh, and Walder Bello. "Development: The Market Is Not Enough," in Jeffry A. Frieder and David A. Lake, *International Political Economy*, 3rd ed. (New York: St. Martin's, 1995): 434–446. Provocative essay arguing that the success of the East Asian Tigers cannot be repeated; also offers an alternative Southern development model.

Cardoso, Fernando Enrique, and Enzo Falleto. *Dependency and Development in Latin America*. Berkeley, Calif.: University of California Press, 1979. Noteworthy study of development and the lack thereof from a dependency perspective.

Cassen, Robert, et. al. *Does Aid Work?* Oxford: Clarendon, 1988. Comprehensive, thorough, and balanced assessment of development aid.

Haggard, Stephan. *Pathways from the Periphery: The Politics of Growth in the Newly Industrializing Countries*. Ithaca, N.Y.: Cornell University Press, 1990. Outstanding study of development strategies in the NICs, examining the role of factors operating at all three levels of analysis.

• Hollings, Ernst F., "Reform Mexico First," and G. C. Hufbauer and J. J. Schott, Prescription for Growth," in *Foreign Policy* 93 (winter 1993): 94–114. Concise presentations of the arguments for and against NAFTA.

International Bank for Reconstruction and Development (World Bank). *World Development Report*, current issue. Authoritative source for statistics on development, including trade, finance, and social indicators. Each issue features a detailed examination of one aspect of development—health, environmental concerns, food, etc.

Kahler, Miles, ed. *The Politics of International Debt.* Ithaca, N.Y.: Cornell University Press, 1985. A very useful collection of essays on the debt crisis, including good presentations of key concepts and contending theoretical perspectives.

Mortimer, Robert, ed. *The Third World Coalition in International Politics.* Boulder, Colo.: Westview, 1984. Detailed examination of the strategy of collective bargaining and the history of the NIEO movement.

Prebisch, Raul. "Commercial Policy in the Underdeveloped Countries." *American Economic Review* 49 (May 1959): 251–73. Classic, concise critique of modernization theory and presentation of the dependency perspective.

• Valenzuela, J. Samuel, and Arturo Valenzuela. "Modernization and Dependency: Alternative Perspectives in the Study of Latin American Underdevelopment." *From Dependency to Development: Strategies to Overcome Underdevelopment and Inequality.* Edited by Heraldo Munoz. Boulder, Colo.: Westview, 1981. Outstanding concise, balanced comparison of the modernization and dependency perspectives on development.

Weintraub, Sidney, and Julius L. Katz. *NAFTA at Three: A Progress Report.* Washington, D.C.: Center for Strategic and International Studies, 1997. A balanced assessment of the economic effects of NAFTA.

□□□□
PART
IV

Issues and Institutions in World Politics

CHAPTER

9

International Law and Organizations

SCOPE, OBJECTIVES, AND APPROACH

Chapter Nine discusses the ways in which states and other actors in the international system have attempted to make the system less anarchic. Its first part covers basic concepts of international law, including sovereignty and human rights, and explains how the law of nations is codified and enforced in the absence of an international sovereign. The second part examines the history, structure, and functioning of the United Nations and other major international organizations. Both parts of the chapter also offer evaluations of these efforts to reduce international anarchy, discussing the strengths, limitations, successes, and failures of international institutions. Overall, the chapter is designed to introduce students to concepts and structures within the international system that have had limited influence in the past but may be expected to grow in importance in an increasingly interdependent world.

WHAT STUDENTS SHOULD LEARN FROM THIS CHAPTER

Foundation Level

1. List the major means for establishment and enforcement of international law.
2. Explain how principles of human rights have become recognized under international law.
3. Explain the difference between intergovernmental organizations (IGOs) and nongovernmental organizations (NGOs).
4. List the UN's six primary organs and describe the organization of each.
5. Describe the objectives of FAO, WHO, the IAEA, and UNICEF.
6. Define and give examples of special-purpose global IGOs, general-purpose regional organizations, and special-purpose regional organizations.
7. Define and give examples of multinational corporations and terrorist organizations.

Enrichment Level

1. Give examples of the use of reciprocity, sanctions, and reprisals to enforce international law.
2. Describe the objectives and major provisions of the Geneva Protocol, the Montreal Protocol, UNCLOS, and the Antarctic Treaty.
3. Explain how the UN's activities are financed.
4. Define the three types of UN peace operations (peace observation, peacekeeping, and peace enforcement) and give examples of each.
5. Describe the objectives and list the leading members of the CSCE and OECD.

Mastery Level

1. Explain how the principles of territorial and personal sovereignty can hinder the enforcement of international law.
2. Explain how the doctrine of positive law challenged the establishment of principles of human rights in theory and in practice.
3. Identify the main reasons for the failure of the League of Nations to maintain collective security in the interwar period.
4. Explain how the major organs of the UN were designed to address the institutional weaknesses of the League of Nations.
5. Describe the controversy over UNESCO that led to U.S. withdrawal from that organization.
6. Explain the differences between the scope, objectives, and functions of UN peace operations in Cambodia and the former Yugoslavia.

OUTLINE OF THE CHAPTER

0. Introduction
   A. Though the international system is an anarchic environment (see Chapter One), attempts to reduce its inherent anarchy have been made since the seventeenth century.
   B. This chapter examines and evaluates the two main means that have been employed to reduce international anarchy: international law and organizations, both of which are forces for globalization in the contemporary world.

I. International Law
   A. Differences between Domestic and International Law
      1. *International law* is the body of rules that bind states and other actors in world politics in their relations with one another.
      2. Unlike domestic law, international law reflects the lack of an international sovereign (institution possessing ultimate legal authority and monopoly on coercive force); thus, international law can be enforced only through *reciprocity, sanctions,* or *reprisals* (see below).

3. There is no international legislature to set laws for all nations; thus, international law is ultimately based on explicit or implicit consent to its provisions.

B. Sources of International Law
   1. Customary Practices
      a. Customary practice represents established and consistent practices of states in international relations (examples: diplomatic immunity, prohibition of slavery and genocide before these were codified under League of Nations or UN conventions).
      b. Customary practice as a means for establishing law has its origins in Roman law (the *jus gentium*, "law of the tribes" observed by Roman jurists among all subject peoples of the Roman Empire).
      c. When states' adherence to written or unwritten rules becomes widespread and commonplace, they may be regarded as binding on all states, *even those that do not explicitly consent to them.*
   2. Treaties
      a. Treaties are "contracts" between states or formal agreements to accept a set of obligations.
         i. Consent is explicit, unlike with customary practice—but if a treaty's provisions are widely observed by most states, it can be argued that those provisions have become customary law.
         ii. International law declares that agreements must be kept *(pacta sunt servanda)* and performed in good faith *(bona fide).*
         iii. A state's internal laws cannot exempt it from compliance with international law; this has caused many problems with the expansion of free trade areas (examples: health and safety standards, United States prohibition of tuna caught in dolphin-mangling drift nets).
      b. Forums for negotiation of treaties exist.
         i. International organizations such as the UN (example: UN convention on chemical weapons, GATT)
         ii. Multilateral forums (example: Helsinki Final Act [see Chapter Four], NAFTA)
   3. Bilateral Negotiations (example: SALT and START)

C. Violation and Compliance
   1. Like domestic law, international law is frequently violated (examples: U.S. mining of Nicaraguan harbors in 1984, Iraqi invasion of Kuwait in 1990), but many provisions and principles are adhered to every day (example: freedom of the seas).
   2. Most governments attempt to justify their actions in terms of international law, even when their legality is questionable (example: U.S. military action in Panama, 1989); because there is no international sovereign, the legality of an action often depends on one's point of view.
   3. Why then do states obey international law?
      a. International law provides a framework for the orderly conduct of international affairs (example: diplomatic immunity).
      b. States may obey the law out of fear of sanction or reprisal (example: Germany and Britain refrained from using chemical weapons against each other in WWII, even though Hitler used poison gas to exterminate defenseless concentration camp inmates).
      c. International law may be enforced by *reciprocity*—"tit-for-tat" behavior or "do unto others as you would have them do unto you" (example: GATT).
      d. States that routinely flout international law may gain a reputation as untrustworthy and may become "pariah states," ostracized from the international community.

II. Areas of International Law
A. The Principle of Sovereignty
   1. Formally established in the Peace of Westphalia (see Chapter Two), this principle holds that individual states have ultimate legal authority within their own borders.
   2. States have freedom to govern their own nationals (personal sovereignty) and their own territory (territorial sovereignty), to make use of the public domain (high seas, outer space), to make legal agreements with other states, and to fight wars in self-defense.
   3. Sovereignty also implies that interference with domestic affairs is outside the scope of international law; this causes many problems in the area of human rights (see below).
   4. There are problems with sovereignty.
      a. Actions taken on another state's territory in response to threats to sovereignty can be seen by others as armed aggression (example: U.S. intervention in Lebanon, 1956 and 1983, Soviet and Vietnamese invasions of Afghanistan and Cambodia).
      b. Some countries declare that sovereignty allows them to violate international commitments (examples: North Korea's refusal to allow IAEA inspection of its nuclear facilities, the frequent defiance of GATT).

    c. According to the principle of personal sovereignty, individuals cannot be subjected to international law nor claim any rights under it; this may be interpreted to allow governments to treat their citizens brutally, making it difficult to "bring to justice" leaders who perpetrate egregious violations of human rights.

B. Human Rights under International Law

1. The idea that humans have inalienable rights is ancient (occurring in Greek and Christian philosophy, for example), but guarantees of human rights under international law is a relatively new concept (originating with the Enlightenment—see Chapter Two).

2. Conceptions of human rights are grounded in the doctrine of *natural law*—certain human rights derive from a "higher law" rather than from actions of rulers or governments.

3. In the nineteenth century, international law developed a doctrine of humanitarian intervention to stop shocking atrocities.

4. In the late nineteenth and early twentieth centuries, international conventions on human rights were signed (Slavery Convention, Hague and Geneva Conventions on laws of war).

5. Efforts to develop a universal law on human rights were hindered by the doctrine of positive law, which claimed that there can be no law in the absence of sovereignty and that international law did not apply to sovereign states; this doctrine was put into practice in Nazi Germany's Nuremberg Laws, which legalized persecution of Jews.

6. After WWII, with the Holocaust in recent memory, the UN codified principles of human rights into international law (Universal Declaration of Human Rights, 1948; Accord on Women's Rights, 1981).

7. Attempts to codify human rights law have spurred conflicts, however, between democratic Western states (which stress individual freedoms and civil rights) and states that stress collective economic rights (consistent with Marxism and other forms of socialist thought).

8. In recent decades, the rights of women have acquired a special place in international human rights law.

    a. Although they are frequently violated, women's rights that have become international norms include gender equity in civil and political rights; equal access to education, economic opportunities, and health care; and prevention of violence against women.

    b. The abolishment of abuses of women's human rights is made difficult due to cultural ignorance, indifference to women's concerns, and strong political resistance in many countries.

C. Can Human Rights Decrees Be Enforced?

1. When human rights have clashed with sovereignty, sovereignty has usually won out; torture, political imprisonment, and the like are still widespread.

2. During the Cold War, human rights questions became entangled with East–West conflict; both sides publicized abuses in the opposite camp and tolerated them in their own camp.

3. After the Cold War, countries have been more willing to consider enforcing human rights in principle, but states and the UN have been very reluctant to commit troops to enforce human rights laws in practice (example: reluctance to send forces to stop "ethnic cleansing" in Bosnia).

D. Warfare and Aggression

1. The conduct of war has been another major area of international law, though as with human rights these attempts have been only partially successful.

2. Some international conventions cover the rights of *belligerents* (countries fighting in war) and *neutrals* (countries supporting neither side) during wars and permit self-defense against aggression.

3. Other conventions seek to limit the means of warfare (Hague Convention of 1899 and Geneva Protocol of 1925 prohibit poison gas; others prohibit biological weapons).

4. A third set of agreements attempts to protect human rights during war (1864 Geneva Convention covered sick and wounded combatants; agreements of rights of POWs were refined most recently in 1977 to cover guerrilla warfare).

E. The Environment

1. International environmental law has been an area of great cooperation *and* conflict, especially between Northern and Southern states.

2. The 1972 Declaration of the Human Environment and Agenda 21, adopted at the 1992 Earth Summit (see box) set forth an international program of environmental action but reflect environmental disputes between developed and developing nations.

3. The 1994 UN Framework Convention on Climate Change was designed to achieve stabilization of atmospheric greenhouse gases so as to limit the impact of human activity on climate change, but it remains controversial in many signatory states; the revised Convention, signed in 1997 in Kyoto, also faces serious domestic opposition in many signatory states.

4. Specific environmental treaties attempt to limit acid rain (Convention on Long-Range Transboundary Air Pollution, 1979), preserve the ozone layer (Montreal Protocol, 1987), or address other environmental problems.

F. Antarctica

1. The 1959 Antarctic treaty prohibited new territorial claims on that continent and declared that it shall only be used for peaceful purposes.

2. Current negotiations focus on banning mining and establishing a nature preserve in the South Polar region.

G. Law of the Sea

1. The UN Convention on the Law of the Sea (UNCLOS), which governs the use of the world's oceans, was adopted in 1982 after protracted negotiations.

2. UNCLOS established a 12-mile limit for territorial waters and a 200-mile exclusive economic zone (though the Reagan administration refused to recognize the latter provision, fearing that U.S. companies would be excluded from many ocean resources); the Clinton Administration, favoring most of the convention's provisions, signed the treaty in 1994 and it went into effect that same year.

3. UNCLOS illustrates that if the interest of most nations runs counter to those of a powerful few, the few may carry the day; to reach and implement international agreements, perception of shared interests is almost always necessary.

H. The Verdict on International Law

1. International law's success and failure suggests that the same attitudes toward law that prevail among individuals exist among states; laws states are willing to enforce (example: GATT) are obeyed far more often than laws states are unable or unwilling to enforce (example: human rights provisions).

2. The existence of international law shows that the international system is not a completely anarchic environment, but attempts to enforce international law resemble frontier "vigilante justice"—the "sheriff" is weak, all the citizens are armed, and "posses" must be formed to bring criminals to justice.

III. International Organizations

A. *International organizations* of various types are called upon to deal with an increasing array of political, social, and economic issues that states are unwilling or incapable of managing by themselves (see "At a Glance," p. 394).

1. *Intergovernmental Organizations* (IGOs) are associations of sovereign states with a common purpose, established through formal agreement.

a. Some IGOs have a global membership (example: the UN) while others are regional (example: CSCE, ASEAN, ECOWAS).

b. Likewise, some IGOs are general-purpose forums while others concentrate on specific issues (OECD, NATO).

2. *Nongovernmental Organizations* (NGOs) unite groups and individuals, usually for action on specific issues (Greenpeace, Amnesty International); these groups lie outside the traditional structure of international politics, but many have a significant impact on world affairs.

B. IOs have taken on increasingly important roles in the nineteenth and twentieth centuries as states have become more interdependent; almost all seek to promote international cooperation.

IV. The Genealogy of the United Nations

A. The Concert of Europe (see also Chapter Two)

1. The Concert of Europe was established after the Napoleonic Wars to resolve European conflicts and provide collective security.

2. The Concert did not always operate in an impartial manner, however, but reflected political relationships among the Great Powers.

3. The elitism of the Concert proved its undoing; it was incapable of responding to the rise of nationalism among many subject peoples in Europe, which contributed greatly to WWI.

B. The League of Nations (see also Chapter Three)

1. The League of Nations was created by the Treaty of Versailles in 1919 and lasted formally until 1946.

2. Arguably, the League was stillborn, because the most potentially powerful state in the international system (the United States) refused to join.

3. As the European powers believed that the balance of power failed to prevent WWI, the League attempted to facilitate collective security.

4. The League proved ineffective, however, for a number of reasons.

a. The League's members continued to practice balance-of-power *realpolitik*.

b. The United States never joined the League, key states left after being censured (Japan, Italy, Germany), and the USSR was admitted only in 1934 (and expelled in 1939).

c. The League's decision-making rules, which required unanimity among all members of its Security Council and allowed vetoes by other members, hampered its ability to take action.

d. Enforcement of League-imposed sanctions was almost impossible.

5. As a result, the League's failures were many (see Chapter Three).

6. On balance, the League was an overreaction to the Great Power politics of the Concert; it demonstrated that moral force alone, without the backing of the Great Powers, could not thwart aggression.

C. The United Nations Is Born

1. The UN was established in 1945 to maintain international peace and security and promote friendly and cooperative relations among nations and peoples; almost all sovereign states belong to it.

2. The UN's six primary organs and auxiliary bodies (see below) are designed to promote cooperation, but have often served as forums for conflict as member states continue to pursue their national interests.

3. The UN's founders intended it to act as a "world policeman" to enforce collective security, but the onset of the Cold War made this practically impossible from 1950 to 1990 (see below).

4. The UN cannot raise funds on its own; it depends on dues assessed from member states, many of which (80% by 1992) are delinquent in or withhold their payments (including the United States, which owed more than $400 million in 1992).

V. The United Nations: Structure, Functions, and Politics

A. The General Assembly

1. All UN members (178 as of 1993) have one seat on the General Assembly, the UN's primary forum for discussion of global issues.

2. The United States was able to get most resolutions it supported passed until the 1960s, when many de-colonized Asian and African states joined; the GA was dominated by developing states by the 1980s.

3. The GA's agenda is usually overcrowded, and recent reforms have been proposed to give its discussions more focus (including a steering committee and rules to prohibit annual discussions of perennially in-tractable questions).

B. The Security Council

1. The Security Council has responsibility for organizing collective security operations, dispatching peace-keeping missions, and imposing sanctions to punish aggressors.

2. The Council has five permanent members (the United States, Russia, China, France, and the United King-dom) and ten other members, chosen from members of the GA.

3. The UNSC was designed to operate under the principle of Great Power unanimity; a veto by any of the permanent members kills a resolution or proposal.

a. During the Cold War, the threat of a U.S. or Soviet veto often foreclosed the possibility of Security Council action; though the USSR boycotted the Council during its vote on the Korean War (see Chap-ter Four), subsequent UN efforts to act as "world policeman" were practically impossible.

b. After the Cold War, however, diplomatic cooperation among the permanent members has allowed en-forcement of collective security measures in at least one important case (the Iraqi invasion of Kuwait in 1990).

4. The Security Council also acts as a forum for negotiations and crisis management.

C. The Secretariat and the Secretary-General

1. The Secretary-General, who serves a five-year term, is the "chief executive" of the UN but has little power to act independently.

2. The Secretariat is a large international civil service that handles administrative functions.

3. The role played by the Secretary-General in world politics has varied with the personalities and style of the person occupying the office (see pgs. 407–10); the current incumbent, Kofi Anan, a Ghanaian diplo-mat, has been the first UN bureaucrat to take on the role of secretary-general with a nonconfrontational leadership style.

D. The International Court of Justice

1. The ICJ, headquartered in the Hague, is the UN's principal judicial organ.

2. The fifteen ICJ justices are elected by the GA and Security Council; all decisions are made by majority vote, and all justices are expected act independently, rather than on the interests of their home nations (as is expected or tolerated in the GA and Security Council).

3. The ICJ's decisions are formally binding, but it has no mechanisms for enforcement of its rulings; states frequently ignore its decisions, declaring that they violate state sovereignty.

E. The Economic and Social Council
   1. ECOSOC is responsible for coordinating the "UN family" of specialized organizations.
   2. Some of these organizations undertake humanitarian efforts and are supported politically and financially by almost all member states (UNICEF, FAO, WHO).
   3. Other specialized agencies under ECOSOC concentrate on environmental issues and sustainable development (UNEP and UNDP).
   4. Others, however, have been more controversial.
      a. Inspectors from the International Atomic Energy Agency (IAEA) have often been harassed or thwarted while trying to investigate alleged attempts to build nuclear weapons; states such as Iraq and North Korea have claimed that IAEA inspections violate their sovereignty.
      b. The United States, claiming that the UN Educational, Scientific, and Cultural Organization (UNESCO) was corrupt and biased against Western nations, withdrew from that organization in 1984.

VI. UN Missions: Expectations and Experience
   A. Military Action
      1. The Security Council can authorize military actions in the interests of collective security.
      2. The UN does not maintain a standing army (though this has been suggested), but relies on troops from member states for peacekeeping forces.
      3. Since 1948, the UNSC has authorized 42 peace operations plus a number of observer missions, which have involved a total of more than 600,000 troops, 1,400 of which have died in the line of duty.
   B. Three Types of UN Peace Operations
      1. *Peace observation* missions monitor compliance with cease-fires or truce agreements, but do not attempt to enforce agreements or inhibit combatants (example: UN Truce Supervisory Organization, which monitors the cease-fire between Arab and Israeli forces).
      2. *Peacekeeping* missions act as a buffer between warring parties that have agreed to a truce; in most cases, they can use force to resist violations of the buffer zones they occupy (example: UN Protection Force [UN-PROFOR], which separates Serb and Croat forces in Croatia).
      3. *Peace enforcement* missions respond to aggression with military force in order to enforce collective security (examples: UN coalition action in the Korean War and the Persian Gulf War); unlike the other missions, these forces do not require host country permission to operate on a state's territory.
   C. Peace Operations in the New Era
      1. The end of the Cold War has removed the threat of a U.S. or Soviet veto on the employment of peacekeepers in many crises.
      2. Post–Cold War peace operations have met with mixed success.
         a. In Bosnia, peace observers have generally lacked the capability or authority to stop fighting and "ethnic cleansing," though they have escorted efforts to provide humanitarian aid.
         b. In Cambodia, peacekeepers have attempted to disarm warring insurgents and successfully supervised an election despite threats of massive violence; however, the operation has been large and expensive and will have to be maintained for some time before democracy is firmly established.
      3. Provision of funds for peace operations may become a continuing problem as UN missions take on more responsibilities.
      4. Recent suggestions for strengthening UN peace operations include establishment of a united peacekeeping budget, predesignation of member state's forces for peacekeeping duty (to make them available immediately for deployment on the Secretary-General's orders), and the establishment of a $400 million revolving fund for peacekeeping.

VII. The UN's Effectiveness
   A. The UN's founders sought to downplay expectations of the new organization; the veto power of permanent Security Council members was intended to allow the UN to take only those actions supported by all the Great Powers.
   B. The UN's effectiveness has been hampered by national sovereignty; sovereignty constrains the UN just as guarantees of civil rights constrain national governments, and for this reason many are loath to allow it to be circumvented.
   C. Like the League of Nations before it, the UN cannot force any state to comply with its resolutions unless the major powers are committed to enforcing UN decisions.
   D. Arguably, however, UN political and economic sanctions have proven effective in some cases (example: Zimbabwe and South Africa).

E. Overall, the UN's record has proven that the expectations of its founders were correct.
   1. It has acted as a world forum for discussion of issues.
   2. It has provided and coordinated humanitarian relief.
   3. It has facilitated collective security when the major powers have agreed on how to meet specific threats.
   4. It has not brought about world peace, however, and it cannot and was not designed to do so.
F. The UN's greatest challenge in the twenty-first century will be to adapt its structure and mission to the changing international system.

VIII. Other IGOs
   A. General-Purpose Regional IGOs
      1. General-purpose regional IGOs promote regional security and economic cooperation and act as forums for resolving regional disputes (examples: Arab League, European Union, ASEAN, OAU).
      2. The record of these IGOs in fostering cooperation is mixed; they have not stopped regional conflicts, but have at least served to foster communication and encourage peaceful resolution of disputes.
      3. Many regional IGOs have been quite successful at promoting regional economic cooperation (ASEAN, EU).
   B. Specialized IGOs
      1. Interpol, created in 1923, serves as an example of how IGOs can foster cooperation among states; its purpose is to promote assistance among police organizations within the limits of the law existing in the different countries and in the spirit of the Universal Declaration of Human Rights.
      2. Specialized IGOs include several groups designed to promote mutual defense (NATO, the late Warsaw Pact) or collective security (OSCE).
         a. The end of the Cold War has lead to controversy over the expansion of NATO.
         b. Poland, Hungary, and Czech Republic sought NATO membership and were invited to join in 1997.
         c. Despite the 1997 Founding Act on Mutual Relations, Cooperation, and Security between NATO and the Russian Federation, many Russian leaders continue to object to NATO expansion, fearing that it will relegate Russia to the status of a second-class power.
      3. Other IGOs focus on economic cooperation, either global (OECD) regional (ECOWAS, MERCOSUR, CARICOM), or in specific industries or commodities (OPEC).
   C. Success of IGOs
      1. IGOs have achieved some noteworthy successes (such as policy coordination in the G-7—see Chapter Seven).
      2. However, they labor under the same general constraints as the UN (sovereignty and the interests of member states).

IX. Nongovernmental Organizations
   A. NGOs operate across national boundaries independent of governments.
   B. Like IGOs, NGOs can be broadly or narrowly focused, with broad-based or restricted memberships.
   C. Because most NGOs cannot use governmental authority to command resources, they tend to focus their efforts on specific purposes or projects (many of which are discussed in Chapter Ten).
      1. Humanitarian NGOs (Red Cross/Red Crescent, Amnesty International, Oxfam, Save the Children) attempt to better the human condition by attacking specific problems.
      2. Environmental NGOs (Greenpeace, World Wide Fund for Nature) seek to improve environmental awareness and protect the "global commons."
   D. *Multinational Corporations* (MNCs) are firms based in a specific home country, but controlling assets and conducting business in several states; some of the largest MNCs (Mitsubishi Group, General Motors, Exxon) have assets greater than most sovereign states and are often (and often correctly) accused of political meddling, particularly in developing countries (see Chapter Eight).

X. Conclusion: Less Anarchy, or More?
   A. While international law and organizations are usually designed to promote cooperation and restrict conflict, many generate new controversies—just like domestic law and government.
   B. Like any other institutions, international institutions sometimes fail because they are poorly designed, sometimes because they are poorly led or supplied with resources; nonetheless, many have done much good.
   C. If nothing else, international law sets ethical standards for the conduct of international affairs.

D. As long as international relations are based on national sovereignty, international law and organizations will be inherently limited; nevertheless, they have helped advance the world slightly beyond a Hobbesian "war of every one against every one" and are likely to become more important as global interdependence increases.

E. The model for future international organizations may be the Internet, which has no central controlling authority but has rules and conventions enforced by reciprocity and common practice.

HOW THE CHAPTER RELATES TO CENTRAL THEMES OF THE TEXT

The introduction to Chapter Nine describes international law and organizations as forces for globalization, and the many attempts to deal with security, human rights, and environmental issues at the global level discussed in the chapter reflect this. At the same time, however, the examples of stonewalling, buck-passing, finger-pointing, and old-fashioned *realpolitik* in IGOs and treaty negotiations show that globalization does not necessarily lead to cooperation. In many cases examined in this chapter, establishment of an international organization or global convention merely recognizes that a problem exists; collective action to alleviate the problem still depends on the interests of sovereign states.

The conflict between sovereignty and enforcement of international law thus introduces an undercurrent of fragmentation into the chapter. States assert their sovereignty and interests in international organizations just as individuals and communities assert their rights and resist control by national governments. Chapter Nine therefore shows how the processes of globalization versus fragmentation and cooperation versus conflict interact with the inherent tension between interdependence and sovereignty—a tension that may become the defining characteristic of world politics in the New Era.

SUGGESTED LECTURE TOPICS

1. Compare and contrast domestic and international law. Note how many aspects of international law (particularly customary practice and contracts/treaties) resemble domestic civil law—both of which are designed to regulate interactions between autonomous agents with equal legal rights and responsibilities.
2. Trace the development of collective security organizations from the Concert of Europe to the UN; use the Crimean War, the First and Second Moroccan Crises, the invasions of Manchuria and Ethiopia, the Korean War, and the Bosnian civil war to discuss whether great power unanimity is a prerequisite for collective action.
3. Outline the tortured negotiating histories of UNCLOS, the Uruguay round of GATT, or the Montreal Protocol to illustrate the difficulties inherent in achieving agreement on multilateral treaties.
4. Compare the strengths and weaknesses of NGOs (Oxfam, CARE, Médecins sans Frontières, the Red Cross) in providing humanitarian aid with those of national governments and the UN family of organizations (FAO, WHO).
5. Discuss the pros and cons of NATO expansion, explaining how this enhances the organization's ability to promote collective defense and expanding on the security concerns of Russia and the former Republics of the Soviet Union.

STUDY AND EXAM QUESTIONS

1. Does the requirement for Great Power unanimity, reflected in the structure and voting rules of the UN Security Council, help the provision of collective security or hinder it? In your answer, discuss three attempts at collective response to aggression, successful or not, since 1815.
2. Has the United Nations generally achieved the objectives its founders assigned to it? Why or why not? Use at least three cases of international conflict since 1946 to support your answer.
3. "The United Nations Security Council should authorize the use of military force to enforce the Universal Declaration of Human Rights." Do you agree with this statement? Why or why not? Refer to at least two specific cases to argue that UN-sponsored military action to guarantee human rights is or is not justifiable and effective.
4. Is North Korea within its rights to refuse IAEA inspections of its nuclear facilities? In your answer, discuss both the specific issues involved and the general tension between interdependence and sovereignty.

5. You have been appointed defense attorney for one of the leaders listed below, who is being tried under international law for the action indicated. Enter a plea for your client and construct a defense or an argument for leniency.
   a. Adolf Hitler for the invasion of Czechoslovakia
   b. Kim Il Sung for the invasion of South Korea
   c. Saddam Hussein for the invasion of Kuwait

RECOMMENDED ENRICHMENT READINGS

- Blodgett, John. "The Future of UN Peacekeeping." *Washington Quarterly* 14, no. 1 (winter 1991): 207–20. Concise presentation of the capabilities, constraints, and potential of UN peace operations.

  Bozeman, Adda B. *The Future of Law in a Multicultural World.* Princeton, N.J.: Princeton University Press, 1971. Interesting discussion of how cultural diversity impacts upon international law.

  Crocker, Chester, et al., eds. *Debating the Democratic Peace.* Cambridge: MIT Press, 1996. Collection of essays considering how international institutions can respond to conflicts resulting from both globalization and fragmentation.

  Deutsch, Karl W., and Stanley Hoffman, eds. *The Relevance of International Law.* Garden City, N.Y.: Doubleday, 1971. Somewhat dated but still useful collection of articles on the topic.

  Durch, William, and Barry Blechman. *Keeping the Peace: The United Nations in the Emerging World Order.* Washington, D.C.: Henry L. Stimson Center, 1992. A discussion on the possibilities and problems with UN peacekeeping in the post–Cold War world.

  Haas, Ernst B. "Why We Still Need the United Nations." Berkeley, Calif.: Institute of International Studies, 1986. Good argument for the continued importance of the UN despite its demonstrated institutional weaknesses.

  Johansen, Robert. *The National Interest and the Human Interest.* Princeton, N.J.: Princeton University Press, 1980. Thorough discussion of the conflict between sovereignty and human rights.

  Johnson, James Turner. *Just War Tradition and the Restraint of War.* Princeton, N.J.: Princeton University Press, 1981. Good examination of one of the oldest attempts to establish "laws of war" and reconcile national self-defense with universal morality.

  Onyango, Oloka. "Women, War, and Rape." *Human Rights Quarterly* 17 (1995): 650–690. A good discussion for the special circumstances that face women in times of war.

  Roberts, Adam, and Benedict Kingsbury. *United Nations, Divided World.* Oxford: Clarendon, 1988. Good text on the objectives, structure, operation, and politics of the UN.

  Sieghart, Peter. *The Lawful Rights of Mankind.* Oxford: Oxford University Press, 1985. Thoughtful examination of the philosophical and statutory aspects of human rights under international law.

  Sorous, Marvin S. *Beyond Sovereignty.* Columbia: University of South Carolina Press, 1986. Good discussion of the case for limiting national sovereignty to protect human rights and the global commons.

  Taylor, Philip. *Nonstate Actors in International Politics.* Boulder, Colo.: Westview Press, 1982. Surveys the role and impact of IGOs and NGOs.

- Urqhardt, Brian. "Beyond the 'Sheriff's Posse'." *Survival* 32, no. 3 (May–June 1990): 196–205. Excellent discussion of the possibilities for expanded UN peace operations by a former UN Undersecretary-General for Peacekeeping.

CHAPTER

10

Global Issues

SCOPE, OBJECTIVES, AND APPROACH

While many of the text's previous chapters have discussed interdependence in general terms, Chapter Ten looks at some tangible aspects of interdependence, surveying issues and problems that concern most or all of the states in the international system. The chapter is organized topically; each section presents an overview of one set of transnational political, economic, or environmental issues. As most of these issues receive considerable media attention, Chapter Ten offers the best opportunity for students to explore how global trends can affect their daily lives and future careers.

WHAT STUDENTS SHOULD LEARN FROM THIS CHAPTER

Foundation Level

1. Describe in general terms the divergent impact of population growth and migration on the developing and industrialized nations.
2. List the main reasons why famines occur.
3. Describe how economic pressure in developing states accelerates deforestation.

4. Describe the successes and limitations of WHO immunization programs.
5. Identify the major producing areas of opiates and cocaine.
6. List and describe in general terms the categories of terrorist groups and give examples of each.
7. Identify regions of increasing and decreasing demand for oil.

Enrichment Level

1. Describe the objectives and activities of international population organizations (IPP, UNFPA) and the controversies surrounding them.
2. Explain why donation of food aid sometimes harms agricultural production in the recipient country.
3. Explain why the tension between economic development and environmental protection is particularly acute in developing countries.
4. Describe the conditions promoting the spread of malaria, and the factors making a region vulnerable to outbreaks of cholera.
5. Describe the objectives and limitations of U.S. drug interdiction and eradication programs.
6. Identify the major practitioners of agitational and enforcement terror in Europe, the Middle East, and Latin America.
7. Describe the relationship between economic development and energy consumption.

Mastery Level

1. Identify the main reasons for the resurgence of nativism in Europe and America in the late 1980s and early 1990s.
2. Describe the objectives, successes, and failures of the UN relief mission in Somalia in 1992–93.
3. Define the greenhouse effect and outline the arguments used by both sides in the debate over global warming.
4. Explain the differences between the patterns of distribution of AIDS cases in Africa and the United States.
5. Explain the advantages and disadvantages of supply- and demand-side approaches to combating drug addiction.
6. Explain why aggressive efforts to apprehend terrorists have been criticized as infringements on national sovereignty.
7. Explain how limitations on water supplies have led to conflict and cooperation among the countries of the Nile and Tigris-Euphrates basins.

OUTLINE OF THE CHAPTER

0. Introduction
   A. As this book has noted several times before, states are becoming increasingly interdependent, but increased interdependence can lead to conflict as well as cooperation.
   B. This chapter surveys eight *global issues*—transnational problems demanding international solutions.
   C. A problem that occurs everywhere is not necessarily a global problem; for a problem to qualify as a global issue, there must be *transnationality of cause and effect* (causes in one country exert effects in others).

I. Population
   A. Patterns of Population Growth
      1. The world's population is growing at an alarming rate (3 people per second, 250,000 per day) but this rate is expected to slow in coming decades; the world's current population of 5.8 billion is predicted to reach 8 million by 2020.
      2. Population increase is markedly higher in developing countries than in industrialized states; states that have not yet fully experienced demographic transition (see Chapter Eight) grow very fast, while the population of developed countries typically grows slowly and then levels off.
   B. Population Explosion

1. The population explosion has resulted in rapid urbanization.
2. The increase occurs especially in developing states where resources to provide basic services are in short supply.

C. International Responses to Overpopulation
1. International organizations such as the UNFPA and International Planned Parenthood are working to help reduce population growth.
2. Availability of contraception, education, and economic opportunities for women have proven to be effective means for reducing fertility rates.
3. Family planning programs have attained some success, but have been hampered in some areas by lack of funds and opposition to abortion.
4. Though population growth is greatest in developing states, developed countries cannot escape its effects, manifested in resource shortages, environmental degradation, and migration (see below).

II. Migration
A. Population Movements
1. Population movements have always been a major factor in history.
2. Migration usually occurs from regions poor in resources to richer areas.
3. In addition to economic factors, migration may be driven by war, ethnic conflict, environmental degradation, political repression, and/or religious persecution.

B. Economic Migration
1. With rare exceptions (such as transported slaves), economic migrants move in search of a higher standard of living.
2. As a result, millions of people migrate from developing to industrialized countries each year, and more may be expected to come as populations in Third World states increase.
3. Women face a different set of incentives for migration, often having to choose between a lack of human rights in rural areas or the disparate burdens of child care, subjection to violence, or prostitution in the cities.

C. Refugees
1. Persons who flee their home countries because of war or repression are recognized as refugees by the UN High Commissioner for Refugees (UNHCR).
2. The world's refugee population exceeded 13 million in 1995 (additionally, millions more who are not officially recognized as legitimate asylum seekers are deemed to be in "refugee-like" situations).
3. Many countries are willing to admit refugees, but limit the numbers of or refuse to accept economic migrants; determining what sort a migrant a person really is is often difficult.
4. Most refugees are displaced within their own countries or flee to neighboring states; Palestinians represented the largest refugee population in 1996.
5. Environmental refugees are forced to leave their homes because of soil exhaustion, chemical contamination, lack of clean water, or inundation of towns and farms.

D. Consequences of Migration
1. Large influxes of migrants have often provoked negative reactions from host countries; *nativism,* or discrimination against immigrants, is particularly likely when a country experiences an economic recession and high unemployment.
2. EU member states, faced with increased immigration from Eastern Europe and North Africa, have sought to tighten immigration controls, and anti-immigrant parties (such as the National Front in France) gained political strength in the early 1990s.
3. Though it strongly encouraged immigration before WWI, in the late twentieth century the United States has welcomed refugees from communist countries, but sought to restrict economic immigration; nativist sentiments rose in the early 1990s as a prolonged recession led some to believe that immigrants were "taking jobs" from citizens and consuming social services.

E. International Solutions to Problems of Migration
1. The UN and other international organizations have attempted to address the problems surrounding economic migration (convention on the rights of migrant workers, 1990).
2. The UNHCR administrates a number of programs to protect, resettle, or repatriate political refugees (example: refugee camps throughout Africa and Asia; repatriation of Iraqi Kurds after the Gulf War; and the Comprehensive Action Program for Indochinese refugees, 1989).
3. Despite international assistance, however, millions of refugees still have no place to go, and thousands of economic migrants face discrimination and anti-immigrant violence.

III. Food and Hunger
  A. Starvation amidst Plenty
    1. World food supplies, on the whole, are more than adequate—especially in developed countries; nevertheless, more than 800 million people worldwide suffer from malnutrition.
      a. The problem is not food *production*, but *distribution*—poverty, natural disasters, poor transportation systems, and war can restrict access to food supplies.
      b. Even where calorie supplies are adequate, quality of nutrition (especially protein consumption) may be less than adequate, especially in developing countries.
    2. Famine can result from natural disasters or droughts (example: the Sahel famines, late 1960s and mid-1980s) or man-made causes such as international or civil war.
    3. Some governments try to use food as a weapon, blocking food supplies and famine relief shipments to rebellious areas (example: Ethiopia in the 1980s).
    4. Somalia in 1991–92 offers an example of a natural and man-made food crisis.
      a. Severe drought caused food shortages, which were exacerbated by factional fighting after the collapse of the government.
      b. Much of the food produced was hoarded out of fear or expectation of higher prices in the future; armed gangs took what they needed by force, but those who could not steal often went hungry.
      c. Thus, while food was often available in markets, poverty or violence prevented many from buying it, and despite international relief efforts more than one-sixth of the population faced starvation at the start of 1993.
  B. International Food Aid and Famine Relief Efforts
    1. Governments, UN agencies (FAO, UNICEF), and NGOs have tried to overcome the imbalance between world food production and distribution.
    2. Some NGOs (example: Oxfam) concentrate on short-term relief of food shortages, while other groups (FAO) promote long-term solutions.
  C. Relief Programs
    1. Some agricultural development and famine relief programs have been highly controversial.
    2. UN efforts in Somalia were criticized for not creating an adequate infrastructure for food distribution.
    3. Some famine-relief efforts are criticized for having short-sighted solutions.
    4. Agricultural projects sometimes result in deforestation (see below) when land is cleared for farming.
    5. Traditional farming methods (such as swidden or "slash and burn" agriculture) can also promote deforestation or desertification.
    6. Free distribution of food by governments or aid agencies can undercut the efforts of local farmers to improve production for long-term food security; giving money, rather than food, is often more effective, but developing countries often have surpluses of food but shortages of money for foreign aid.
  D. A Solvable Problem
    1. Despite the problems associated with international relief efforts, hunger is the most soluble global problem.
    2. World capabilities for food production continue to increase and both governments and private donors are usually quick to support famine relief.

IV. The Environment
  A. A Global Problem
    1. Spectacular cases of transboundary pollution such as the nuclear accident at Chernobyl (now in Ukraine) in 1986 illustrate how environmental problems can affect all nations.
    2. Deforestation and desertification are less dramatic but equally damaging.
  B. Representative Environmental Problems: Deforestation and Pollution
    1. *Deforestation* occurs when trees are cut down and not enough seedlings are planted.
      a. Contrary to popular belief, clearing of land for housing and farming—not commercial logging—is the principal cause of deforestation.
      b. Deforestation results in loss of habitats and plant and animal species as well as trees.
      c. Burning of forests to clear land may also contribute significantly to global warming (see box).
    2. Urbanization and industrialization have led to increased *pollution*.
      a. In urban areas, pollution decreases air and water quality and can result in acute episodes of unhealthy air ("smog alerts").
      b. Pollution also causes problems far from its source; burning fossil fuels (coal, oil, etc.) creates sulfur dioxides, which can fall to earth as *acid rain* many miles away.
    3. As environmental issues become more globally problematic, conflicts arise between industrialized and developing nations.

a. Industrialized countries produce the majority of atmospheric pollutants and greenhouse gases (which contribute to global warming), but developing countries are rapidly closing the "pollution gap."

b. Industries in many developing states are often more polluting than those in developed countries (due to use of dirtier fuels, such as high-sulfur coal, and looser environmental regulations).

c. Many developing states value development and industrialization and more than preserving forests, the ozone layer, and the like.

d. Dirtier development will damage the global ecosystem in the long run, with potentially disastrous economic and political consequences.

C. International Cooperation for Saving the Environment

1. International organizations began addressing environmental problems in the mid-twentieth century; in the 1960s and 1970s, environmental issues moved up on the UN's agenda.

2. In the 1980s and 1990s, international efforts continued to link trade, economic development, and the environment, and primarily focused on sustainable development (Montreal Protocol on chloroflourocarbons, 1987; UN Conference on Environment and Development [the "Earth Summit"], 1992).

3. NGOs such as the World Wide Fund for Nature (WWF), the Sierra Club, and the Environmental Defense Fund also promote specific aspects of environmental conservation.

4. Some companies have encouraged environmentally friendly development through trade rather than aid, attempting to show that conservation pays off in the long run.

D. A Green and Pleasant Globe?

1. Economic incentives to reduce deforestation and pollution can be effective, but it is difficult to convince poorer countries to cut back on development efforts for environmental reasons.

2. Developed countries must also deal with problems of pollution and global warming.

3. The history of environmental issues shows that awareness of a global problem does not necessarily lead to global changes in behavior; environmental preservation efforts cannot succeed until developed and developing countries adopt a long-term perspective in both global vision and local action.

V. Health and Disease

A. The Global Health Picture

1. Poverty, malnutrition, and poor sanitation make populations of developing countries more susceptible to health problems.

a. Life expectancy is lower and infant mortality is higher than in developed states.

b. Many developing countries face serious problems with tropical diseases, such as malaria, cholera, and schistosomiasis.

2. AIDS has become a serious global health problem.

a. In developed countries, HIV infection is concentrated in urban areas and in high-risk groups.

b. In some developing regions, particularly central Africa, HIV is alarmingly common in both cities and countryside, and among both sexes.

c. WHO projects that up to 40 million people worldwide may be infected with HIV by 2000.

B. Responses to Global Health Problems

1. WHO has sponsored immunization programs since its foundation in 1948.

a. WHO programs were responsible for the eradication of smallpox, which had killed millions for centuries, by 1965.

b. The Expanded Program on Immunization (EPI) has achieved substantial success in immunizing children.

2. Some diseases, such as malaria and AIDS, have been resistant to immunization or eradication despite intensive research and international programs.

a. Since multi-drug treatments are prohibitively expensive for developing countries, and there is no vaccine for AIDS, programs focus on awareness and prevention of HIV transmission.

b. AIDS has exacerbated international conflict as well as cooperation; many governments refused to acknowledge the prevalence of HIV, and in many areas AIDS is still regarded as a disease of homosexuals, "foreigners," or other stigmatized groups.

VI. Drugs

A. Drug Production

1. Illegal drugs have become a major component of North–South trade; developing countries "export" drugs to industrialized states for high illicit profits.

a. Rich, drug-importing countries experience crime and health problems associated with addiction.

b. Poor, drug-producing states suffer from widespread corruption, terrorism, and economic "addiction" to the drug trade.

2. Narcotics production is concentrated in four regions, each having its own specialty product.
    a. The "Golden Triangle" region (Myanmar, Laos, and Thailand) produced more than 2.5 tons of opium in 1995.
    b. The Eastern Mediterranean is the major center for production of hashish.
    c. Mexico produces more than 42% of the world's marijuana, and Mexico and Guatemala produce opium as well.
    d. Cocaine production is concentrated in Peru, Bolivia, Colombia and Ecuador; it is estimated that cocaine accounts for 25% of Bolivia's foreign exchange earnings and employs more than 4% of its population.
3. The Growth of International Drug Trafficking
    a. Drug trafficking has become a major international criminal enterprise. Drug cartels (such as the Medellin and Cali cocaine cartels) rival major multinational corporations in scope of operations and sales volume.
    b. Criminal organizations have developed intercontinental supply and distribution networks (example: transshipment of South American cocaine through Africa has soared).
    c. Governments in many countries are heavily penetrated by narcotics cartels, and *narcoterrorism* claims thousands of lives in major producing states.
B. Bilateral and Multilateral Drug Control Efforts
    1. The United States is the world's largest consumer of illegal drugs by far; the toll taken by drugs in the United States and elsewhere has prompted international efforts to control drug traffic.
    2. Control efforts may focus on reducing demand or on restricting supply.
        a. Supply may be restricted through *interdiction* (preventing drugs from entering a country) or *eradication* (destruction of crops that are made into illegal drugs).
        b. Disappointing results with interdiction have recently prompted the United States to shift its efforts to eradication (examples: the International Drug Enforcement Program, 1988; the Andean Initiative, 1990).
    3. Efforts to reduce drug production in Latin America have been hindered by four factors.
        a. The drug trade is a major source of employment and income in many Latin American states.
        b. Eradication programs that do not provide for transitions to legal employment or balance-of-payments support for drug-producing countries encounter great resistance.
        c. Drug traffickers have exploited resistance to infringement of sovereignty and "Yankee imperialism" to undermine international anti-drug cooperation (example: the Camerana murder case, 1985).
        d. Violence and intimidation of judges, police, and political leaders have stalled drug control efforts.
C. An Expanding Global Problem, An Emerging Global Solution
    1. Drug-consuming nations have begun to realize that as long as demand remains high, traffickers will find ways to circumvent interdiction and eradication efforts.
    2. Drug addiction has also become a major problem in producing areas and often contributes to the spread of AIDS and other health problems.
    3. UN attempts to coordinate drug-control programs increased in the early 1990s; UN efforts to restrict supply have generally been ineffectual, while demand-side programs of drug treatment and education have had some success.
    4. Almost all states now regard the control of drug traffic as an important goal, but international coordination is hampered by limited funds, conflicts over aid and national sovereignty, and narcotics' continued high profitability.

VII. Terrorism
A. International Terrorism
    1. International terrorism may be defined as the use of violence across international boundaries, intended to coerce a target group into meeting political demands.
    2. Unlike war or simple murder, terrorism is directed at an audience.
        a. Terrorism is an ancient phenomenon (that can be traced back to religious zealots in first-century Judea) that creates great fear and distrust; despite this, effective international action to deal with the problem remains an elusive goal.
        b. Distinctions between terrorism and "legitimate" violence in support of a political cause are often subjective; one side's terrorist thugs are another's freedom fighters (examples: Nicaraguan *contras* in the 1980s).
B. Contemporary Terrorism around the World
    1. No region is immune to terrorism due to the regional base and political outlook of many terrorist organizations, coupled with increasing globalization and improvements in technology.

2. Advancements in transportation create new vulnerabilities and give terrorists access to new targets; improvements in communication allow terrorists to exploit their actions; and modern weapons technology allows organizations to use less conspicuous and more destructive means of terror.

3. The extent and variety of terrorism differs between regions.

   a. An estimated 40% of international terrorism occurs in, or is associated with, the Middle East.

   b. The collapse of the Soviet Union has decreased, but not eliminated, attacks by ideological terrorists (examples: Red Brigades in Italy, Red Army Faction in Germany, Action Direct in France).

   c. Ideological or separatist guerrillas are prominent in the developing South (examples: Tupac Amaru in Peru, Tamil Tigers in Sri Lanka) and they may continue their terrorist activities until they achieve their political goals or until their organizations are wiped out.

4. While terrorist groups use similar tactics, they have varying objectives and political orientations, and groups may transcend categorical boundaries (example: Hamas is a separatist group with both ideological and nationalist motivations that wages its struggle through both peaceful and violent means).

C. State-Sponsored Terrorism

1. National governments engage in terror through *enforcement terror* (subduing their own citizens by cruel and violent means) and by sponsoring non-state actors to carry out acts of violence abroad.

2. State sponsored terrorism has been seen throughout history—Ivan the Terrible in the sixteenth century, the Great Terror following the French Revolution, Nazi Germany, the United States and the USSR during the Cold War, military governments in Argentina and Brazil, the Shah's regime in Iran, and the apartheid regime in South Africa.

3. As of 1997, the U.S. State Department listed Cuba, Iran, Iraq, Libya, North Korea, Sudan, and Syria as sponsors of terrorism.

D. Nationalist Separatists

1. Terrorist groups in this category have political objectives of national liberation or self-determination and tend to have clear ethnic, cultural, or religious overtones.

   a. While separatists claim to be "freedom fighters" and typically utilize violent practices, many of these groups have elements that support nationalist causes by peaceful means.

   b. Examples of separatist terrorism can be seen in Northern Ireland (IRA/INLA), the Palestinian–Israeli conflict (PLO, PFLP), northern Spain (the Basque Fatherland and Liberty), and the separatist movements in Turkey (PKK) and India (Sikh).

2. Terrorism rooted in the desire to obtain a national homeland feed upon ethnic tensions, thus threatening the integrity and security of multinational states by rekindling old animosities.

E. Ideological Terrorism

1. Ideological terrorists are groups influenced by revolutionary doctrines that attempt to overthrow oppressive governments or express anti-imperialist sentiments through violence.

2. Examples of ideological terrorist groups include Action Direct in France, Baader Meinhof in Germany, the Red Brigades in Italy, and Sendero Luminoso in Peru.

3. Although ideological terrorism may be waning due to the collapse of the Soviet Union, the rising sense of isolation and powerlessness among disenfranchised groups discredited by the collapse of communism can provoke a new wave of ideological terrorism (example: Tupac Amaru's taking of hostages in the Japanese Ambassador's residence in 1996).

F. Religious Terrorism

1. Religious radicalism has overtaken Marxism as the prime ideological generator of international terrorism.

2. Examples of religious terrorist organizations include Hamas in the West Bank and Gaza, Hezbollah in Lebanon, Aum Shinrikyo in Japan, Sikh separatists in India, and Jewish extremists in Israel.

3. Terrorism in the name of religion is especially frightening because many organizations regard their violence as morally justified and spiritually sanctified; thus, halting religious terrorism remains particularly difficult due to the fervent commitment of its believers.

G. Combating International Terrorism

1. Coordinating an internatinoal response is difficult because states differ in their policies toward it; some actively combat it; other support it; and others do both as it serves their political objectives.

   a. Bilateral cooperation involves collaboration between two countries in terms of information exchange, police operations, and border controls; problems may arise concerning extradition or other forms of "safe haven."

   b. The Organization of American States (OAS) and the South Asian Association for Regional Cooperation (SAARC) have attempted to coordinate (largely unsuccessfully) efforts to combat violence at the regional level.

c. Modest success has been seen from the coordination of efforts from various international agencies, such as Interpol.

2. All states have an interest in combating terrorism, whether they know it or not.
   a. National, ethnic, ideological, and religious conflicts can easily spread across national boundaries.
   b. States must abandon the support of terrorism if existing or new avenues of halting terrorism are to be effective.

VIII. Energy and Natural Resources
A. Conflict and Compromise
   1. The sections on food and environment have mentioned the inherent tensions between conservation and utilization of resources.
   2. This section will consider two vital resources that have prompted both international conflict and compromise.
B. The Need for Energy
   1. All states need energy to survive; to a point, there is a close correlation between economic growth and energy consumption.
   2. In general, advanced technology allows energy to be used more efficiently (though this may encourage greater use of energy as new processes and products become feasible).
   3. For these reasons, demand for energy in developing countries has been growing at a faster rate than consumption in developed countries; half of global energy consumption now occurs outside the OECD.
C. Oil's Critical Role
   1. Oil has been the world's most important source of energy since the development of the internal-combustion engine.
   2. Dominance of world oil supplies by OPEC once gave that organization considerable political and economic power (see Chapter Eight), but this has diminished as production has increased and industrialized countries' dependence on oil has lessened.
   3. Regional differences in trends in oil use are pronounced; developed countries are gradually starting to use less oil, while developing countries are using more.
D. Energy Crises and Global Responses
   1. There have been three major oil crises (1973, 1979, 1980) and one minor crisis in 1990.
      a. In 1973, there was an approximately 7% reduction in world oil supplies following OPEC's embargoes on the United States and the Netherlands during the Arab–Israeli war (see Chapter Five); in response, the United States led an initiative to form the International Energy Agency (IEA) one year later.
      b. In 1979, the Iranian Revolution resulted in a virtual cessation of Iranian oil exports; the IEA failed to curb the crisis.
      c. In 1980, during the Iran–Iraq war, prices did not rise significantly due to the Saudis' willingness to increase production and the IEA's efforts to curb the stockpiling of oil and encourage sales.
   2. While international economic complications resulted from the minor crisis following the Iraqi invasion of Kuwait in 1990, major problems were avoided due to Saudi Arabia's desire to increase production, a reduction in global demand, and cooperation among IEA nations.
E. Coal and Natural Gas
   1. Natural gas is generally less polluting than oil or coal and widely used where available, but it is difficult to transport over long distances (especially by sea).
   2. Coal is another primary source of energy, especially for generating electricity.
      a. Many developing countries—particularly China—are becoming heavy users of coal.
      b. Coal is the dirtiest fossil fuel; the widespread use of coal to generate electricity has caused some environmentalists to question the wisdom of electric cars.
F. Renewable Energy
   1. Not all sources of energy rely on fossil fuels or result in high levels of pollution, but "alternative" energy sources account for a small fraction of world energy usage.
   2. All alternatives to fossil fuels have drawbacks.
      a. Nuclear power plants are relatively clean and safe, but they are expensive to build, and the possibility of spectacular accidents is a major concern to many (see box on Chernobyl).
      b. Hydroelectric power is available only near major rivers, and has serious environmental side effects.
      c. Solar and wind power are very expensive and unreliable.
   3. In the long run, all states will have to develop means of conserving energy to sustain economic growth without seriously depleting world energy resources.

G. Water
   1. Water is an absolutely vital resource and an ancient source of cooperation and conflict.
      a. Access to safe water supplies is a major problem in many developing areas.
      b. Conflicts over water rights, particularly for agriculture, occur even where water is plentiful; in arid regions, conflict over scare water resources is especially pronounced.
   2. The Middle East, most of which is arid, is the locus of many conflicts over water.
      a. The Tigris-Euphrates, Nile, and Jordan River basins have been the scenes of recurring conflicts over water since ancient times; as population and water usage increase, conflicts are likely to become more acute.
      b. Regional water-sharing plans have been developed in some areas (Johnston Plan for sharing the Jordan in the 1950s, Nile Consultative Group), sometimes involving cooperative hydroelectric projects as well.
      c. Dam projects in Turkey and Egypt have led to serious conflicts, bringing Iraq and Syria to the brink of war in the mid-1970s.
      d. Downstream states fear "water pressure" in the form of water embargoes by upstream countries; this has led some to oppose international funding for dam projects.
H. Conflict and Cooperation on Resource Issues
   1. As the supply of all resources is limited, all require some means for allocating them, whether through economic mechanisms (such as the free market) or political arrangements.
   2. States have gained a great deal of experience in sharing resources peacefully since WWII, but resource shortages (especially of vital energy and water resources) still have great potential to provoke conflict.

IX. Conclusion
   A. Pressing global issues are likely to remain sources of both conflict and cooperation, as all states have both common and conflicting interests involved in them.
   B. The record of international cooperation to address global issues is profoundly mixed (very good on immunizations, very poor on combating drug traffic).
   C. Many issues appear to place developed and developing countries on opposite sides (examples: rain forest preservation and banning of CFCs), but both North and South are beginning to realize that cooperation will be necessary in order to alleviate or contain transboundary problems.
   D. There is only one world, and it is getting smaller; because interdependence increases the potential for both conflict and cooperation, successful action on global issues will require states to develop and practice a code of global citizenship.

HOW THE CHAPTER RELATES TO CENTRAL THEMES OF THE TEXT

Chapter Ten helps make the process of globalization visible and concrete, offering students many specific examples of transboundary problems that require transnational solutions. It is neither sanguine nor pessimistic about the ability of states successfully to coordinate policies on drug smuggling, pollution, population movements, or other transnational problems. Instead, the chapter reinforces the point that interdependence increases both cooperation and conflict. Its conclusion does suggest, however, that in order to address global issues effectively, a more interdependent world must become less anarchic.

Besides giving more examples of conflict and cooperation to which theories from the three levels of analysis may be applied, the chapter also prepares students for the upcoming conceptual chapters by pointing out how the "low politics" of drug control, immigration, and resource management affect the "high politics" of power and security. This anticipates the argument (discussed in Chapter Eleven) that economic and environmental factors should be considered part of "national security" in the New Era.

SUGGESTED LECTURE TOPICS

1. Discuss a specific example of one of the global issues surveyed in the chapter (cocaine smuggling or acid rain, for instance) in detail to show the complex and intricate linkages involved in transboundary problems.
2. Compare issues that have been addressed relatively successfully through international cooperation (immunization, famine relief) with those that have not (drugs, AIDS, air pollution); discuss whether

the success of cooperation is determined primarily by the nature of the problem or the structure and operation of coordinating institutions (the UN, NGOs, bilateral treaties, etc.).

3. Examine the North–South disputes involved in many of the issues covered in this chapter (deforestation, CFCs, drugs, migration); assess the probability that increased interdependence will heighten conflicts between the developed and developing worlds.

4. Trace the history of terrorism from the nineteenth century to the present (or include examples of state and nationalist terror from the Roman Empire, the Crusades, the Inquisition, etc.).

5. Examine in detail the tradeoffs between economic development and environmental conservation; draw analogies between local issues that students may be familiar with (housing developments, industrial parks, wilderness areas, etc.) and international issues (dams, deforestation, global warming, acid rain, etc.) to illustrate the goals and concerns of both "developers" and "environmentalists."

STUDY AND EXAM QUESTIONS

1. Choose one of the global issues listed below and explain why international cooperation generally has, or has not, effectively addressed the issue; discuss at least two specific international examples of the problem in your answer.
   a. Drug traffic
   b. Acid rain
   c. Terrorism
   d. Refugees
   e. Hunger and malnutrition

2. Choose one of the efforts at international cooperation to resolve a specific transboundary problem listed below, state whether the effort should be regarded as a success or a failure, and explain why it did or did not succeed. Be sure to consider the goals of the program, the states or international organizations that undertook it, and the resources made available to it in your answer.
   a. The Montreal Protocol
   b. The Global Program on AIDS
   c. The UN intervention in Somalia
   d. The Andean Initiative

3. Do states have a right to go to war to ensure their access to vital resources? In your answer, discuss at least two twentieth-century crises or wars in which conflict over natural resources was a major factor.

4. Has the end of the Cold War led to a decrease in international terrorism, or an increase? Why? In your answer, consider at least two regions of the world where terrorism is or has been a persistent problem.

5. Are environmental issues likely to prompt more international cooperation in the near future, or will they intensify international conflict? Discuss three specific international environmental problems or controversies in your answer.

6. "The increasing interdependence of the world's nations and the growing salience and severity of transboundary problems demands the formation of a world government." Do you agree with this statement? Why or why not? In your answer, use at least two specific examples of transnational economic, health, environmental, or crime problems to illustrate the potential advantages or disadvantages of world government.

RECOMMENDED ENRICHMENT READINGS

Cairncross, Frances. *Costing the Earth*. London: Business Books, 1991. Outstanding examination of the manageable but unavoidable tradeoffs between conservation and development and of the concept of sustainable development.

Camp, S. L. "Population—The Critical Decade." *Foreign Policy* 90 (spring 1993): 126–44. Useful overview of population and migration issues.

• Clark, J., "Debacle in Somalia." *Foreign Affairs* 72, no. 1 (January–February 1993): 109–23, and J. Stevenson, "Hope Restored in Somalia." *Foreign Policy* 91 (summer 1993): 138–54. Contending perspectives on international relief efforts in a very troubled country.

Cooper, Richard. "Toward a Real Global Warming Treaty." *Foreign Affairs* 77, no. 2 (March/April 1998): 66–79. Discussion of why the Kyoto agreement should fail and alternatives to solving the global warming problem.

Dowty, Alan, and Gil Loescher. "Refugee Flows as Grounds for International Action." *International Security*, 21, no. 1 (summer 1996): 43–71. An interesting discussion of refugee flows as international problems that require international attention.

Ehrenfeld, Rachel. *Narco-Terrorism*. New York: Basic Books, 1990. Good description of the extent, impact, and implications of international drug traffic.

Hopkins, Raymond F., Robert L. Paarlberg, and Mitchel B. Wallerstein. *Food in the Global Arena*. New York: Holt, Rinehart and Winston, 1982. Examines the role of food and famine in world politics.

Keohane, Robert O., and Joseph S. Nye. *Power and Interdependence*. 2nd. ed. Glenview, Ill.: Scott, Forseman, 1988. Thoughtful discussion of the impact of increasing interdependence on the international system.

Pirages, Dennis. *Global Ecopolitics*. North Scituate, Mass.: Druxbury, 1978. Interesting discussion of global environmental issues, and the possibility of international cooperation to address them, from the perspective of an environmental activist.

Scott, Andrew N. *The Dynamics of Interdependence*. Chapel Hill: University of North Carolina Press, 1982. Another good study of the implications of increasing interdependence for global conflict and cooperation.

• Starr, Joyce R. "Water Wars." *Foreign Policy* 82 (spring 1991): 17–30. Excellent essay explaining how the most ancient conflicts in the Middle East, over the region's scarcest resource, still have great potential to produce international tension and war.

Stohl, Michael, ed. *The Politics of Terrorism*. New York: Dekker, 1983. Somewhat dated but still very useful collection of articles on the political use of terror.

U.S. Committee for Refugees. *World Refugee Survey,* current issue. The best source for the extent and implications of the refugee problem.

World Bank. *World Development Report 1993: Investing in Health*. New York: Oxford University Press, 1993. Authoritative examination of global health issues, focusing on developing regions.

World Commission on Environment and Development. *Our Common Future*. New York: Oxford University Press, 1987. Helpful overview of global environmental issues, leaning toward the side of conservation in the environment versus development debate.

Yergin, Daniel. *The Prize: The Epic Quest for Oil, Money, and Power*. New York: Simon and Schuster, 1991. Outstanding history of conflict and cooperation over the lifeblood of the industrialized world.

11

Security

SCOPE, OBJECTIVES, AND APPROACH

Chapter Eleven undertakes a comprehensive examination of security as an objective concept in international relations and as an objective that every state in the international system is compelled to pursue. The chapter covers both theoretical approaches to national and international security (including the security dilemma, deterrence, and crisis stability) and issues in security and defense policy (including strategic doctrine, arms control and disarmament, and alternative conceptions of national security). By drawing links between theory and practice on a pivotal component of world politics, Chapter Eleven attempts to show how theoretical analysis can structure and inform debates over vital issues of national policy and help answer questions about the causes of war and peace.

WHAT STUDENTS SHOULD LEARN FROM THIS CHAPTER

Foundation Level

1. Give the traditional definition of national security.
2. Define the security dilemma and explain how it can lead to or exacerbate conflict.

3. Describe the differences between defense and deterrence and among unilateral, multilateral, and collective security strategies.
4. Define first-strike capability, second-strike capability, and mutual assured destruction (MAD).
5. Define nuclear proliferation and list the states with declared or suspected nuclear weapons programs.
6. Describe the differences between arms control and disarmament.
7. Identify the major provisions of the Nonproliferation Treaty, SALT I and II, the INF Treaty, and START I and II.

Enrichment Level

1. Explain the differences between general deterrence and immediate deterrence and between primary deterrence and extended deterrence.
2. Describe the requirements for successful deterrence (commitment, capability, credibility, and rationality).
3. Explain how developments in military technology can alter the offense/defense balance, giving historical examples.
4. Describe the three components of the U.S. strategic triad.
5. Explain the objectives and identify the major provisions of the Partial Test-Ban, Threshold Test-Ban, and Conventional Forces in Europe Treaties.

Mastery Level

1. Explain why the traditional definition of national security is being challenged by alternative conceptions.
2. Explain the major criticisms of deterrence theory.
3. Define crisis stability and strategic stability.
4. Define ABM and MIRV and explain why deployment of these systems could decrease crisis and strategic stability.
5. Explain the U.S. strategic doctrines of massive retaliation and flexible response and describe the political and strategic contexts in which they were adopted.
6. Explain the objectives and identify the major provisions of the Chemical Weapons Convention, the Biological Weapons Convention, and the Missile Technology Control Regime.

OUTLINE OF THE CHAPTER

0. Introduction
   A. Nations have always been preoccupied with security and preserving it remains a fundamental duty of national leaders.
   B. States continue to face the dilemma of choosing between security on the one hand, and economic and social development on the other, when allocating their scarce resources.
   C. This chapters looks at unilateral strategies of self-protection, the management of arms races, and the attempts states make to protect themselves.

I. The Many Faces of Security
   A. What Is National Security?
      1. Security has many different aspects (physical, economic, environmental, cultural, etc.) that change over time and between environments.
      2. Like persons, states face different security problems and give priority to different components of security.
         a. Before and during the Cold War, the military aspects of security received the most attention in international relations.
         b. With the end of the Cold War, leaders have come under increasing pressure to address the economic, environmental, and cultural aspects of security.
   B. External and Internal Threats
      1. Most states face both internal and external threats to their security; the mix of internal and external threats determines a state's security environment.

2. Internal and external threats are often interrelated, and overreaction to one can increase risks from the other (example: The USSR spent a large percentage of its GNP on defense against external threats, but its collapse was due in large measure to economic tensions heightened by massive defense spending).

3. In the New Era, transnational threats to security are coming to the top of many states' agendas (examples: migration, drug traffic, terrorism, AIDS; see Chapter Ten).

4. However, expansion of the definition of security to include every problem a nation faces risks sweeping increases in the size and power of governments; "national security" is a favored excuse for restriction, suspension, or revocation of civil rights.

C. Subjective versus Objective Aspects of Security

1. To a great degree, security is a *subjective perception or feeling.*

   a. Historically, some states have felt threatened for reasons that other states found hard to understand (examples: USSR under Stalin, Germany under Kaiser Wilhelm).

   b. Others did not recognize threats and fell victim to surprise attack (example: the United States in 1941).

2. As with individuals, subjective perceptions of security influence a state's security precautions.

   a. States whose perceptions of threat match objective threats follow policies of pacifism (low threat/perception of security) or prudence (high threat/perception of insecurity).

   b. States facing high threats but believing themselves secure can take inadequate precautions (example: France in 1940).

   c. States facing low threats but perceiving a high level of threat can "overinsure" themselves (example: USSR during the Cold War).

3. As a nation's power increases, one might expect it to feel more secure, but history shows that the reverse (more power plus greater perception of insecurity) often occurs (example: the United States during the Cold War).

D. A Working Definition of Security

1. The definition of security used here is similar to the traditional definition: a condition in which the *sovereignty* and *territorial integrity* of a state are guaranteed.

2. In the anarchic international system, this condition has often been very difficult for states to achieve; many states face threats and have experienced military conflicts.

3. Universal security is theoretically possible, but not likely; states with growing populations and economic needs will seek more scarce resources, which creates the potential for conflict and raises the risk (and attractiveness) of armed aggression.

II. The Security Dilemma Revisited

A. The Dilemma Defined

1. The effectiveness and utility of a state's security measures are always uncertain; defensive efforts may discourage an aggressor, or they may backfire by encouraging other states to arm themselves.

2. Countries thus find it difficult to escape the vicious circle of the *security dilemma:* Measures a state takes to increase its own security are likely to decrease the security of other states; other states are then likely to respond, and the security of all is diminished.

3. This concept occurs at the personal as well as the international level (example: citizens' buying guns for self-defense increases the possibility of accidental or deliberate shootings).

B. The Security Dilemma and Arms Races

1. In the international system, the security dilemma can contribute to arms races through an action/reaction spiral of armament and counterarmament (examples: European Great Powers before WWI [see Chapter Three], United States and USSR during the Cold War [see Chapter Four]).

2. The security dilemma can apply to other actions taken to safeguard security as well, such as mobilization (example: the July Crisis precipitating WWI).

3. In an anarchic system, it is rational for states to arm themselves; the security dilemma is thus difficult to escape without a "world policeman" or world government (which would create security problems of its own; see Chapter Nine).

III. Strategies for Security: Deterrence and Defense

A. Deterrence

1. Deterrence attempts to prevent war by *discouraging a potential aggressor.*

2. This is usually accomplished by threatening retaliation or punishment, so that the likely costs of attacking will exceed any anticipated gain.

3. Three requirements must be met for the success of a deterrent strategy (all will be discussed in detail later).

   a. The defender must possess the *capability* to punish or retaliate.

b. The defender must signal its *commitment* to strike back if an opponent attacks (i.e., must warn a potential aggressor of the consequences of aggression).

c. The defender's commitment must have *credibility*—the defender must demonstrate the resolve and determination to carry out the threatened punishment if attacked.

4. Deterrence is commonly associated with nuclear weapons, but it is an ancient strategy, may be used with conventional weapons, and is used on the personal level as well (example: threatening would-be assailants with retaliation by "big brothers" or members of the victim's gang).

5. General and immediate deterrence can be contrasted.

a. *General deterrence* is a long-term strategy of discouraging serious consideration of attacks or challenges to vital interests.

b. *Immediate deterrence* is a response to a specific and explicit challenge or threat to attack.

6. Primary and extended deterrence can be contrasted.

a. *Primary deterrence* seeks to dissuade attacks on a state's own territory.

b. *Extended deterrence* seeks to dissuade attacks on a state's allies or external interests (examples: U.S. commitments to NATO, Japan, Korea, and other allies; Israel's threat to attack Syria if it had intervened in the Jordanian Civil War, 1970).

B. Defense

1. *Defense* attempts to reduce an enemy's capability to damage or take something away from the defender.

a. Defense minimizes damage from an attack and denies territory and other resources to the attacker.

b. While deterrence is primarily *psychological* (attempting to influence an opponent's decision making), defense is primarily *physical*.

2. Example of the difference between defense and deterrence: a car alarm versus a securely locked garage.

C. Deterrence and Defense Combined

1. Defense and deterrence can be combined, but states must choose the mix of strategies that meets their security needs and the resources available to them.

2. Deterrent weapons (example: ICBMs and SLBMs) may have little or no defense capability (i.e., are useless against an attacking military force), but most defensive weapons have some deterrent capability (to attack the aggressor's forces or territory).

3. Unfortunately, almost all forces usable for defense also have offensive capabilities (and even fortifications can increase suspicion and protect against retaliation); this lies at the heart of the security dilemma.

IV. The Requirements for Deterrence

A. Rationality

1. Deterrence assumes that decision makers are basically *rational*.

2. They should weigh costs and benefits of their own and other's actions before making decisions (more on this later).

B. Commitment

1. The first step in deterrence is announcing a commitment to punishing an attacker, or "drawing a line in the sand."

2. Deterrence commitments must be definite and specific, as ambiguity may encourage challenges or attack (examples: Britain's wavering commitment to support the Entente in the event of war with Germany in 1914; the omission of Korea from the U.S. defense perimeter in the Pacific, which may have contributed to the start of the Korean War in 1950).

3. Deterrence often fails when defenders do not signal commitments or fail to specify the retaliatory action that would be taken in the event of attack (examples: British nondeterrence of Argentina's attempt to occupy the Falkland Islands, 1982; U.S. failure to warn Iraq of the consequences of an invasion of Kuwait, 1990).

C. Capability

1. A state must possess the capability or means to retaliate in order to deter an attack successfully.

2. Unlike credibility, states may choose to keep their capabilities ambiguous, so that potential attackers might believe the defender's capability is stronger than it actually is (example: Israel's refusal to officially reveal its nuclear capabilities).

3. Deterrence with conventional weapons is difficult, because aggressors can estimate and perhaps counteract their ability to inflict punishment (examples: Germany initiated WWII even though Britain and France had more tanks and soldiers; Israel was not deterred from making a preemptive strike against Syria, Jordan, and Egypt in 1967).

D. Credibility

1. A state must convince the aggressor of its resolve to carry out a deterrent threat; the commitment to punish must not sound like an empty threat or bluff.

2. Credibility may depend on reputation, past behavior, and image; states may therefore risk war to defend lesser interests so that the credibility of deterrence to their vital interests is not seen as weak (example: United States fighting to defend Korea to signal willingness to defend Japan and Western Europe).

3. The destructive power of nuclear weapons creates a credibility problem: would the defender be willing to see millions of people, on both sides, die in a nuclear war? (examples: in the 1973 Arab–Israeli War and the 1982 Falklands War, nuclear-capable defenders did not deter non-nuclear challengers).

4. Crises where nuclear weapons are involved thus resemble games of "chicken": if one side backs down, the other wins, but if neither backs down, both suffer destruction.

E. Possible Failure

1. Even when the defender demonstrates commitment, capability, and credibility, deterrence can still fail.

2. The attacker may calculate that the benefits of attacking exceed the likely costs of punishment.

V. Criticisms of Deterrence

A. Rationality

1. Human beings are not always perfectly rational; states or leaders may not base their actions on accurate, rational calculations.

   a. The information available to both sides may not be accurate or reliable.

   b. Humans have a limited capacity to receive and evaluate information and options.

   c. Perceptions or biases can limit the selection of information or cause options to be discarded.

   d. Subordinates may "filter out" or hide information from decision makers.

   e. Opponents can deliberately deceive each other (example: Egypt's successful attainment of surprise in the 1973 Arab–Israeli war).

2. Psychological or bureaucratic factors, which become visible only with hindsight, can thus lead to a failure of deterrence.

B. How Do We Know When Deterrence Succeeds and Fails?

1. It is often difficult to determine and demonstrate the criteria for success of deterrence.

   a. The challenger must have intended to take the deterred action.

   b. The challenger must have backed down because of the deterrent threat.

2. Both these conditions can be ambiguous in practice; opponents may not reveal, or even know, their intentions or reasons for not acting on them.

C. Misperception

1. Opponents rarely understand each other perfectly; even if the defender does everything right, the attacker may still fail to "get the message."

   a. A defender's resolve can be misperceived if the attacker is strongly intent on taking the action.

   b. A challenger might believe the defender is bluffing (example: U.S. misperception of China's threat to intervene in the Korean War).

   c. Challengers can underestimate their adversary's capabilities and mistakenly expect an easy victory (examples: Soviet attack on Finland, 1939; Italian attack on Greece, 1941).

2. In a sense, deterrence is a form of communication; if the communication fails, deterrence fails as well.

3. Misperception does not always lead to fighting; a challenger can perceive a defender's resolve to be greater than it actually is (example: the Western Allies never considered knocking down the Berlin Wall in 1961, even though Soviet and East German forces were under orders to retreat and set up a new barricade if the Allies had tried this).

D. To Deter or Not to Deter?

1. The controversies surrounding deterrence are likely to continue long after the end of the Cold War; the real reasons why the United States and USSR never went to war during that period may never be known.

2. Proponents of deterrence will argue that it prevented war despite its flaws and contradictions (i.e., the need to threaten nuclear war to maintain peace).

3. Opponents of deterrence will argue that the strategy was based on false premises and "deterred" opponents who did not intend to attack.

4. Regardless of the final verdict on nuclear deterrence, many states will continue to rely on conventional deterrence—which has a mixed record—to discourage attacks from regional opponents (the two Koreas, Israel and Syria, India and Pakistan, etc.).

E. Strategy in the Nuclear Age

1. Nuclear weapons and missiles revolutionized strategic thinking after WWII for two main reasons.

   a. The destructive power of nuclear weapons raised the stakes of an arms race.

   b. The same destructive potential made a long, drawn-out nuclear war practically impossible; terrible destruction could be wrought in a matter of hours or minutes.

2. *First-strike capability* is the ability to launch an attack that destroys the defender's retaliatory forces, thereby preventing the defender from inflicting major damage on the attacker.
    a. A situation where any state has first-strike capability is highly unstable, because that side might feel able to do whatever it wanted without fear of nuclear retaliation.
    b. The other side would then have an incentive to launch a preemptive strike in any crisis, greatly increasing the risk of war.
3. Nuclear forces, which are vulnerable to attack, thus encourage a "use them or lose them" mentality, where both sides have an incentive to strike first (the United States worried about this possibility in the 1950s, when its strategic weapons were carried in slow, vulnerable bombers).
4. *Second-strike capability* is the ability to launch a devastating attack even if the other side strikes first.
    a. To maintain a second-strike capability, a state needs *survivable* retaliatory forces.
    b. The possession of a second-strike capability negates any advantage or incentive for attacking first, since the opponent could inflict unacceptable damage even after being attacked.
5. If both sides possess second-strike capabilities, a satiation of *mutual-assured destruction (MAD)* is said to exist.
    a. Frightening as it may seem, MAD is a stable situation, because there is no incentive or temptation for either side to strike first.
    b. The United States and USSR achieved this situation by the 1960s.
6. The United States achieved second-strike capability through the development of the nuclear triad of bombers, intercontinental ballistic missiles (ICBMs), and submarine-launched ballistic missiles (SLBMs).
    a. Bombers can carry heavy payloads and can be recalled if launched during a crisis, but are vulnerable to surface-to-air missiles (SAMs) and other air defenses.
    b. ICBMs are the most accurate, but are impossible to recall and are vulnerable before they are launched because the locations of their launchers or silos can be pinpointed.
    c. SLBMs are the least vulnerable, because submarines are difficult to detect and destroy, but they are generally less accurate (though improvements in their accuracy have been made in recent years).
7. The superpowers emphasized different "legs" of the strategic triad for their own reasons; the United States concentrated on sea- and air-based forces while the USSR concentrated on ICBMs (though both powers had all three types of forces).
8. Some types of offensive weapons can be destabilizing, especially multiple independently retargetable reentry vehicles (MIRVs), which allow several warheads to be placed on a single missile; these could allow an attacker to overwhelm and destroy most of an opponent's retaliatory arsenal with a first strike (this is why a ban on land-based MIRVs was a major goal of START II; see below).

F. Defensive Weapons Systems
    1. Paradoxically, defensive weapons systems that destroy incoming missiles are destabilizing because they reduce the effectiveness of mutual deterrence (for example, an attacker might think it could deliver a first strike and defeat the defender's surviving retaliatory weapons with defensive systems).
    2. Anti-ballistic missiles (ABMs) proposed during the Cold War are not necessarily destabilizing, if they are placed around missile sites to protect second-strike weapons.
    3. The Strategic Defense Initiative (SDI, or "Star Wars") was first intended to create a "peace shield" against incoming missiles over the United States.
    4. If any defensive system were fully effective, however, it would be destabilizing, because it would reduce the credibility of a retaliatory second strike.
    5. A limited SDI-type system known as Global Protection Against Limited Strikes (GPALS) has been proposed to defend all countries against nuclear missiles launched by terrorists or irrational leaders.

G. Nuclear Weapons and Conventional Defense
    1. Nuclear weapons are not useful for meeting all military challenges; using nuclear weapons to respond to a conventional attack might well cause more damage than the attack itself.
    2. Both theater nuclear weapons and large conventional forces played key roles in the strategies of both NATO and the Warsaw Pact throughout the Cold War.
    3. The collapse of the USSR has created a "buffer zone" between the two historical antagonists of Germany and Russia; this has created its own security roblems (especially in the former Yugoslavia), but post–Cold War conflicts have so far seemed much less threatening than the Cold War–era nuclear confrontation.

VI. Military Power
A. Aspects of Military Power
    1. Military power consists both of "hardware" (weapons and equipment) and "software" (personnel, training, and leadership); it is difficult to know beforehand which component will be decisive in a conflict.

2. Military power depends greatly on economic power; states can be stronger in one than the other, but will then face strategic vulnerabilities.

3. Military power has a number of distinct but related components; some are easier to quantify than others and not all are useful for all military purposes (particularly strategic nuclear forces).

B. Strategic Nuclear Forces

1. Nuclear weapons have dominated military affairs since 1945; *strategic nuclear forces* are designed to attack targets, including cities, at long range and *tactical nuclear weapons* are short- or medium-range weapons designed to be used primarily against military targets.

2. The United States and Russia have the largest nuclear inventories; the superpowers' nuclear balance was the key strategic balance of the Cold War era.

3. Since the end of the Cold War, the United States and Russia have undertaken to significantly reduce their nuclear forces (see Table 11.1), but remain far and away the strongest nuclear powers.

C. Other Weapons of Mass Destruction

1. In addition to the seven declared nuclear powers (India and Pakistan joined "the club" in 1998), Israel is generally believed to possess nuclear warheads, though they have not stated this openly, and other states have clandestine programs to develop nuclear weapons.

2. Other states possess different weapons of mass destruction (see Table 11.2); chemical weapons (nerve gas, poison gases like those used in WWI, or other deadly chemical) and biological weapons (weapons for germ warfare) are possessed by some states regardless of the international conventions against such horrors (see below).

D. Military Personnel

1. Overall number of military personnel indicates the strength of a nation's ground, naval, and air forces, but offers no indication of qualitative factors such as training and leadership (see Table 11.3).

2. Troop strength can be a poor predictor of a conflict's outcome; Israel was outnumbered in all four of its major wars, but prevailed in each nevertheless.

3. Numbers of personnel and equipment holdings do not tell the full military story; the relative quality and value of troops and weapons can be difficult to compare.

E. Defense Expenditures

1. Comparison of military spending makes it possible to see how much material power a state is attempting to convert into military strength (see Table 11.4).

2. Many countries with high defense burdens are poor countries that face serious regional conflicts (for example, Bosnia and Herzegovina).

3. Total military spending indicates the size of a state's military effort, but military expenditure as a percentage of GNP indicates the priority a state gives to military power (see Table 11.5); states that have major, persistent security problems (as in the Middle East) tend to spend a higher percentage of their economic output on defense.

F. Logistics and Power Projection

1. The art and science of delivering forces and supplies to the right place at the right time is known as logistics and is an important part of military power.

2. *Power projection* is the ability to apply military force beyond a state's borders (example: U.S. ability to maintain large forces in the Gulf during the Persian Gulf War) and it requires both hardware and software (see above).

3. States with large naval forces and good access to sea lanes (the United States, Britain) have an advantage in power projection; states that lack these (Russia, China) are at a disadvantage, despite their overall military power.

G. Qualitative Factors: Equipment, Training, and Morale

1. Although there are useful numerical indicators of military power, qualitative components are also important; for example, aggregate numbers fail to reveal the accuracy, lethality, or reliability of weapons.

2. The skills and motivation of soldiers and ability of their leaders have been crucial in many conflicts (example: British versus Italian forces in WWII, Coalition versus Iraqi forces in the Persian Gulf War), but are notoriously difficult to measure.

3. Small, highly trained, professional forces can be far more capable than large, poorly motivated, and incompetently officered armies.

4. Training is also vital to the proper operation of sophisticated weapons.

VII. Technology and Security

A. Advances in military technology were highlighted by the nuclear arms race in the Cold War and use of modern conventional weapons in the Persian Gulf War, but technology has always been an important component of material power.

B. Technological breakthroughs can result in the introduction of new weapons that give a state or alliance a major, though temporary, advantage.
   1. Examples include U.S. development of the atomic bomb at the end of WWII, use of the machine gun by European troops against indigenous Asian and African forces in the late nineteenth century.
   2. A breakthrough can backfire, however, if it allows an opponent to exploit its advantages better once the opponent copies the new weapon (example: Britain's introduction of the Dreadnought battleship and the Anglo–German naval arms before WWI).
   3. The effects of a technological breakthrough may be realized only after a dramatic event or military disaster (example: effect of machine guns in combat in WWI, effect of tanks in WWII).
C. *Lead time* is the time required between the decision to produce a weapon and its operational deployment; this can be substantial, allowing opponents to copy or neutralize the new weapon (example: the introduction of jet fighters in WWII failed to give Germany a significant advantage over larger Allied air forces).
D. High technology is usually costly, and it is often impossible to know whether an expensive weapons system will justify its cost (example: SDI, the U.S. B-1 and B-2 bombers).
E. The offense/defense balance can determine the outcome of the military engagement.
   1. The history of military technology can be regarded as a technological struggle between offense and defense.
   2. At certain points in history (late fifteenth century, when cannons were introduced; early stages of WWII, when tanks came into their own) prevailing military technology made offense dominant; whenever the offense is dominant, wars are more likely to occur, but can be expected to be shorter and less costly (Franco–Prussian War, *blitzkriegs* of 1939–41).
   3. At other times, technology made defense dominant (breech-loading rifles and machine guns before WWI); when defense is dominant, wars are less likely, but tend to be protracted wars of attrition with high casualties (American Civil War, WWI, Iran–Iraq War).
   4. It is often difficult to determine whether offense or defense is dominant at a particular time, especially if a new technology has just been introduced; misjudging the offense/defense balance, however, can be disastrous (example: the "Cult of the Offensive" before WWI).
F. Technology can provide the cutting edge.
   1. Three trends illustrate how technology is likely to have an even greater impact on security.
      a. The emergence of space as a theater of military operations is growing in importance due to the reliance of military forces on satellites to locate targets, track friendly and hostile forces, transmit information, and coordinate movements.
      b. The combination of advanced information systems with improved delivery systems make wars deadlier than ever (examples: satellite reconnaissance and navigation, "stealth" weapons capable of evading defenses, and "smart" weapons with uncanny accuracy).
      c. The emergence of *information warfare* (the disabling of an enemy's information system through, for example, computer viruses, terrorist attacks with "software" bombs) becomes a threat due to the high reliance on computers and instantaneous communications.
   2. While technology is an important factor of military power, highly trained, educated, and motivated personnel is needed to operate the systems.

VIII. Arms Control and Disarmament
   A. Arms Control versus Disarmament
      1. Arms control attempts to *manage* an arms race so as to minimize the danger posed by the security dilemma; this may or may not involve reducing the level of armaments deployed.
      2. Disarmament tries to reduce overall levels of arms as a goal in and of itself.
      3. Even though disarmament might seem more desirable, disarmament of a state that faces security threats could increase instability or lead to a renewed arms race later on (example: Germany after WWI).
      4. The primary goal of arms control is not a demilitarized world, but *strategic stability*—a situation where the relative levels of armament give neither side an incentive to launch an attack or to increase its arms.
   B. Early Efforts at Disarmament
      1. The horrors of WWI prompted a series of arms control and disarmament initiatives.
         a. In the Kellogg–Briand Pact of 1928, almost all nations agreed to renounce war as an instrument of national policy, but allowed self-defense and had no enforcement mechanism.
         b. The naval treaties of the 1920s and 1930s placed limitations on certain types of warships, but the Great Powers concentrated on nonregulated vessels (including aircraft carriers), Germany was left out of the negotiations, and Japan withdrew in 1934.

2. After WWII, the United States proposed that all atomic energy activities be placed under international control (the Baruch Plan), but as this would have codified the U.S. nuclear monopoly, it was rejected by the USSR.

C. Test Bans (see "At a Glance" box)

1. The Partial Test-Ban Treaty (1963) restricted the United States, United Kingdom, and USSR to underground nuclear testing.

2. The Threshold Test-Ban Treaty (1974) prohibited U.S. and Soviet tests of more than 150 kilotons in yield.

3. After two decades, the Comprehensive Test-Ban Treaty (CBT), which prohibits all testing of nuclear explosives, was signed in 1996 by more than 100 states.

D. SALT and START

1. The United States and USSR signed the first Strategic Arms Limitation Treaty (SALT I) in 1972.

   a. The Interim Agreement put ceilings on land- and sea-based nuclear missiles at existing levels (2347 for the USSR, 1710 for the United States), which were to be further reduced in subsequent treaties; this did not limit MIRVs, but provided for means of verification of this and future agreements through "national technical means" (spy satellites).

   b. The ABM Treaty limited each side to two ABM sites with not more than one hundred ABMs each (this was later reduced to one site, and the U.S. system never became operational) and prohibited space-based ABM systems (which became an important point in the debate over SDI; see Chapter Four).

2. The follow-up to SALT I, SALT II, was signed in 1979, but never ratified by the United States because of the Soviet invasion of Afghanistan (see Chapter Four); both sides nevertheless generally adhered to the guidelines of the treaty.

   a. Both sides were limited to a total of 2250 launchers (ICBMs, SLBMs, and heavy bombers).

   b. Some limits were placed on MIRVs, but they were still allowed.

   c. Overall, SALT II still allowed the superpowers to increase their nuclear arsenals, permitting both qualitative and quantitative improvements; for many, these shortcomings made the SALT process an example of the pitfalls of arms control.

3. The Strategic Arms Reduction Talks (START) began negotiations during the Reagan administration, resulting in the first arms control treaties to actually reduce levels of strategic arms.

   a. START I, signed in 1991, limited the United States and USSR to 1600 launchers each, with no more than 6000 warheads per side.

   b. START II, signed between the United States and Russia in 1993, pledged both parties to further reduce their strategic nuclear arsenals to between 3000 and 3500 warheads each and provided for total elimination of MIRVs.

   c. By 1997, START II faced serious ratification difficulties in Russia, due to Russian perceptions that the elimination of MIRVs is biased and a belief that the treaty should be rejected in protest of NATO expansion.

E. Intermediate-Range and Tactical Nuclear Weapons

1. The INF Treaty of 1987 eliminated all U.S. and Soviet nuclear missiles with ranges of between 500 and 5500 kilometers; this marked the first time that an entire class of nuclear weapons had been banned.

2. After the breakup of the Warsaw Pact and the reunification of Germany, tactical and battlefield nuclear weapons lost their military utility in Europe; between 1991 and 1993, thousands of these weapons were eliminated without formal arms control agreements.

3. Following the demise of the Soviet Union, the successor states agreed to transfer all the tactical nuclear weapons on the former Soviet territory to storage depots in Russia.

F. Nonproliferation Treaty

1. The Nonproliferation Treaty (NPT), which sought to prevent the spread of nuclear weapons, was signed in 1968.

2. NPT prohibited states that did not have nuclear weapons from acquiring them, and it banned states that possessed nuclear weapons from helping them to do so.

3. Nuclear weapons states that signed the treaty pledged to pursue disarmament and help other states develop peaceful uses of nuclear energy.

4. Many states with nuclear ambitions at the time refused to sign the NPT (India, Pakistan, South Africa, and Israel); others signed but continued nuclear weapons programs anyway (Iran, Iraq, North Korea).

5. China and France signed the NPT by 1993, but preventing determined states from developing nuclear arsenals is becoming an increasingly difficult problem.

G. Chemical Weapons, Biological Weapons, and Missiles

1. The Chemical Weapons Convention (1993) bans the possession, acquisition, stockpiling, transfer, and use of all forms of lethal chemical weapons; in 1997, the treaty was finally ratified by a sufficient number of

states, giving signatory states ten years to dispose of these weapons, but nonsignatory states (including Libya, Syria, and North Korea) continue to maintain these weapons.

2. The Biological Weapons Convention (1972) banned "germ warfare" weapons; some states nevertheless continued biological weapons programs (USSR until 1992, Iran, Iraq, Libya, Syria).

3. The Missile Technology Control Regime (MCTR) restricts the export of ballistic missile technology; while this agreement was initially negotiated by the Western powers, subsequent inclusion of other key players, including Russia, Israel, Argentina, Brazil, and China, have strengthened the MCTR.

H. Conventional Arms Control

1. Conventional arms control remained a fruitless endeavor during the Cold War; NATO and the Warsaw Pact spent thirteen years agreeing on nothing in the Mutual and Balanced Force Reduction talks (MBFR).

2. The end of the Cold War spurred change in the conventional arena as well as the nuclear.

   a. The Conventional Forces in Europe (CFE) Treaty of 1990 placed detailed limitations on NATO and former Warsaw Pact tanks, artillery, armored vehicles, aircraft, and helicopters and called for the destruction or removal of more than 125,000 of these weapons

   b. Implementation of the CFE Treaty was made difficult, as the USSR's successor states argued about the allocation of the remaining conventional weapons allowed under the agreement.

IX. Conclusion: To Arm or Not to Arm?

A. Because all nations face a security dilemma and security is a primary responsibility for all states, countries can be expected to devote a considerable portion of their resources to national security, however this is defined.

B. The proper level of "security insurance" for a state to purchase often depends on one's image of world politics.

1. Those with "Star Wars" views, worried about present and future "evil empires," will call for strong defense.

2. Those with "It's a Small World after All" perspectives will continue to argue for disarmament.

C. Armed conflict remains a possibility in the New Era, and no choice regarding national security is free of risk; states must weigh the risks and costs of armament, alliances, collective security, and disarmament, decide which costs they are willing to pay and which risks they are willing to accept, and make their security choices accordingly.

HOW THE CHAPTER RELATES TO CENTRAL THEMES OF THE TEXT

Chapter Eleven is primarily concerned with the *potential* for conflict and the *avoidance* of conflict, because these objectives drive states' security policies. While the historical chapters provide examples of conflict, and Chapter Ten (on global issues) and the upcoming theoretical chapter analyze the sources of conflict, this chapter examines states' efforts to prevent and manage conflict in the anarchic international system. At the same time, the chapter shows how conflict can necessitate cooperation, either direct and explicit (in the form of alliances and arms control) or indirect and tacit (in the superpower's security interdependence in the nuclear era).

By introducing the fundamentals of deterrence theory, developed at the height of the Cold War, Chapter Eleven provides a theoretical perspective on the globalization of superpower rivalry (discussed in historical terms in Chapter Four). The chapter's coverage of nuclear and ballistic missile proliferation further illustrates the strategic and political fragmentation that has accompanied the end of the Cold War. Overall, while the chapters on the world economy and global issues reveal how interrelated issues can intensify the contradictory trends of the New Era, Chapter Eleven shows how a single issue—the need for states to confront the security dilemma—can simultaneously increase globalization, fragmentation, cooperation, *and* conflict.

SUGGESTED LECTURE TOPICS

1. Draw parallels between the security concerns of individuals in an urban area and states in the international system to illustrate the security dilemma. Use these analogies to stimulate discussions on the advantages and disadvantages of self-help and collective security system gun ownership/armament versus gun control/disarmament, strong police forces and public order/collective security versus restricted police forces and civil rights/national sovereignty.

2. Outline the premises, conclusions, and criticisms of deterrence theory, giving examples of success and failure of deterrence at the global and regional levels.

3. Explain how the need to maintain the "Three Cs" necessary for deterrence drove U.S. foreign and defense policy during the Cold War; then discuss a) whether Soviet policies were driven by similar or different concerns and b) whether such policies are still necessary in the post–Cold War era.

4. Present the global picture of nuclear and ballistic missile proliferation and the post–WWII possession and use of chemical weapons. Discuss the NPT review process, Comprehensive Test-Ban Treaty, the Israeli raid on Iraq's Osirak reactor (1981), UN action to halt Iraq's nuclear programs during and after the Gulf War, and possible responses to proliferation in North Korea to illustrate the pros and cons of various strategies for curbing nuclear proliferation.

5. Trace the history of strategic arms control from SALT I to START II, using the Nixon administration's policies of linkage, the invasion of Afghanistan, and SDI to illustrate the interplay of strategic, international political, and domestic political factors.

STUDY AND EXAM QUESTIONS

1. Was nuclear deterrence responsible for the "long peace" of the Cold War era? Use at least three events from the period 1946–90 to show how either deterrence or some other factor served to preserve peace between the United States and the USSR.

2. Is nuclear deterrence morally justifiable? Discuss at least two positive and at least two negative aspects of deterrence to show why states do or do not have the right to threaten mass destruction in order to preserve their security.

3. Are arms races primarily a cause of international conflict or a symptom of it? Examine three twentieth-century cases of arms competition to support your answer.

4. Did mutual-assured destruction (MAD) provide strategic stability during the Cold War? In your answer, be sure to discuss the premises, requirements, and practical application of MAD.

5. Should the United States have developed and deployed the missile defense system envisioned in the Strategic Defense Initiative? Why or why not? In your answer, give at least three reasons why SDI would or would not have contributed to strategic stability.

6. Was the SALT process an example of success or failure of arms control? Be sure to discuss the objectives, achievements, limitations, and flaws of SALT I and II in your answer.

7. Choose one of the states listed below and explain why that state *should* acquire and/or maintain nuclear weapons:
   a. Iraq
   b. Japan
   c. North Korea
   d. Pakistan
   e. Ukraine

8. "The United Nations should authorize military action to prevent nuclear proliferation." Do you agree with this statement? Why or why not? Discuss three cases of proliferation to show how military force has been or would be justifiable and effective in halting the spread of nuclear weapons.

RECOMMENDED ENRICHMENT READINGS

Barash, David P. *The Arms Race and Nuclear War*. Belmont, Calif.: Wadsworth, 1987. Good, though now somewhat dated, introduction to nuclear issues, informed by a disarmament perspective but considering other viewpoints.

Blainey, Geoffrey. *The Causes of War*. 3rd ed. New York: Free Press, 1988. Thorough, accessible overview of the major theories of war and peace.

Brown, Michael, et al. *The Perils of Anarchy*. (Cambridge: MIT Press, 1995) and *Global Dangers* (Cambridge: MIT Press, 1995). Two volumes of excellent articles on contemporary international security from a variety of perspectives.

Bundy, McGeorge. *Danger and Survival: Choices about the Bomb in the First Fifty Years*. New York: Random House, 1988. Detailed study of U.S. nuclear policies, focusing on the development of norms and traditions against the use of nuclear weapons.

Drell, Sidney, Phillip Farley, and David Holloway. *The Reagan Strategic Defense Initiative.* Cambridge, Mass.: Ballinger, 1985. Well-presented technical and political critique of SDI.

Fletcher, James, et al. *The Strategic Defense Initiative: Defense Technologies Study.* Washington, D.C.: U.S. GPO, 1984. Influential government study arguing for development and deployment of ballistic missile defense.

Fosberg. Randall, et al. *Nonproliferation Primer: Preventing the Spread of Nuclear, Chemical, and Biological Weapons.* Cambridge: MIT Press, 1995. Excellent overview of a major security challenge in the New Era and possible responses to it.

Freedman, Lawrence. *The Evolution of Nuclear Strategy.* London: St. Martin's, 1983. Excellent analysis of strategic concepts and doctrine in the nuclear era.

George, Alexander L., and Richard Smoke. *Deterrence in American Foreign Policy: Theory and Practice.* New York: Columbia University Press, 1974. Outstanding study of the development and application of American strategic thought. Highly recommended.

Glaser, Charles L., and Chaim Kaufmann. "What is the Offense–Defense Balance and Can We Measure It?" *International Security* 22, no. 4 (spring 1998): 44–82. Will help reader gain a better understanding of the assessment and effect of the offense–defense balance.

International Institute for Strategic Studies (IISS). *The Military Balance,* current issue. The most authoritative source on the strength, armaments, and equipment of the world's military forces.

• Jervis, Robert. "The Political Effects of Nuclear Weapons: A Comment." *The Cold War and After: Prospects for Peace.* Edited by Sean M. Lynn-Jones. Cambridge, Mass.: MIT Press, 1991. 70–80. Argues that nuclear deterrence prevented major war during the Cold War era. Recommend assignment along with Mueller, below.

Levy, Marc A. "Is the Environment a National Security Issue?" *International Security* 20, no. 2 (fall 1995): 35–62. Good discussion of considering environmental problems as issues of national security.

Morgan, Patrick M. *Deterrence: A Conceptual Analysis.* 2nd ed. Beverly Hills, Calif.: Sage, 1983. Clear presentation and thorough discussion of deterrence theory.

• Mueller, John. "The Essential Irrelevance of Nuclear Weapons: Stability in the Postwar World." *The Cold War and After: Prospects for Peace.* Edited by Sean M. Lynn-Jones. Cambridge, Mass.: MIT Press, 1991. 45–69. Argues that nuclear deterrence was not primarily responsible for preserving the "long peace" of the Cold War.

Newhouse, John. *Cold Dawn: The Story of SALT.* New York: Holt, Rinehart and Winston, 1973. Insider's account of the SALT I negotiations.

Schelling, Thomas C. *The Strategy of Conflict.* Cambridge, Mass.: Harvard University Press, 1960. Pioneering, thought-provoking treatise on deterrence theory.

Smoke, Richard. *National Security and the Nuclear Dilemma.* 2nd ed. New York: Random House, 1987. Strongly recommended as an introduction to American security policies in the nuclear age.

Talbott, Strobe. *Endgame.* New York: Harper & Row, 1979. Inside account of the final stages of the SALT II negotiations.

Van Evera, Stephen. "Offense, Defense, and the Causes of War." *International Security* 22, no. 4 (spring, 1998): 5–43. Interesting discussion of the likelihood of war and the effects of changes in the offense–defense balance.

Waltz, Kenneth N. "The Spread of Nuclear Weapons: More May Be Better." Adelphi paper no. 171. London: International Institute for Strategic Studies, 1981. Provocative argument in favor of nuclear proliferation, at least in principle.

Wolfe, Thomas W. *The SALT Experience.* Cambridge, Mass.: Ballinger, 1979. Analytical history of the SALT process from its beginnings to the final details of SALT II (though not the U.S. debate over ratification).

Ziegler, David. *War, Peace, and International Politics.* Glenview, Ill.: Scott, Foresman, 1990. Good, very readable introductory survey of the role of security and military conflict in the international system, presenting historical cases and modern issues.

□ □ □ □
PART

V

Theory and Analysis of World Politics

CHAPTER
12

Levels of Analysis

SCOPE, OBJECTIVES, AND APPROACH

Chapter Twelve represents the main theoretical unit of the text. It outlines various theories derived from the three levels of analysis seeking to explain behavior in the international system. The discussion of systemic-level approaches includes structural realism and balance-of-power theory, collective security, power transition and long cycles, bandwagoning and balancing, polarity, and neoliberal institutionalism. The discussion of the domestic level of analysis is categorized into statist (including regime type, executive–legislative relations, political parties, and bureaucracies), societal (including interest groups, the military–industrial complex, and public opinion), and combination approaches (including ideology, political culture, and peace among democracies) to understanding a state's foreign policy. The factors presented from the individual level include leadership style and personal experience, generational experience, values and belief systems, and cognitive biases and heuristics. The chapter does not attempt to provide an exhaustive catalog of all theories and approaches grounded in each of the levels of analysis. Rather, it seeks to provide students with a representative sample of analytical frameworks in order to stimulate their own exploration of the utility and relevance of each level in the analysis of world politics.

WHAT STUDENTS SHOULD LEARN FROM THIS CHAPTER

Foundation Level

1. Identify the categories of influences on state action examined by systemic theories.
2. Identify the objectives and underlying assumptions of structural realism.
3. Give reasons why considering states as unitary rational actors is not always useful for the analysis of foreign policy.
4. Distinguish between statist and societal approaches to the study of domestic factors in international relations.
5. Give examples of how leaders' personal experiences have affected their interpretations of events and other leaders' actions.
6. Describe in general terms how stress can effect decision makers in crisis situations.

Enrichment Level

1. Describe the central differences between classical and structural realism.
2. Explain why balance-of-power theorists argue that an equal distribution of power promotes stability and why power transition theorists argue that a hegemonic distribution of power promotes stability.
3. Define the Prisoner's Dilemma and explain its application to theories of international cooperation.
4. Explain how normative influences and procedural restraints operate to maintain peace among democratic states.
5. Explain how the military–industrial complex, public opinion, and political parties can affect the attainment of foreign policy goals.
6. Characterize the leadership styles of U.S. presidents Truman and Bush.
7. Define fundamental attribution error and explain why leaders often assume their adversaries to be unitary actors when they do not hold such assumptions about their own states.

Mastery Level

1. Assess the strengths and weaknesses of structural realism's assumptions of rationality and security dominance.
2. Explain how long-cycle theory predicts the origins and approximate timing of major wars.
3. Explain how public opinion is expressed in authoritarian states.
4. Give historical examples of the impact of ideological extremism on international relations.
5. Characterize the leadership styles of Egyptian presidents Nasser and Sadat and Soviet leaders Khrushchev and Brezhnev.
6. Explain how the experience of WWI contributed to European strategies of appeasement before WWII and how those appeasement strategies affected foreign relations during the Cold War.
7. Explain WWI, WWII, and the Cold War from all three levels of analysis.

OUTLINE OF THE CHAPTER

0. Introduction
   A. The three levels of analysis (introduced in Chapter One) categorize the many factors that can influence states' behavior.
      1. The *systemic level* looks at factors arising from the nature and structure of the international system—external to states (number and strength of major powers, degree of systemic anarchy, etc.).
      2. The *domestic level* considers the unique characteristics of units within the system—that is nation-states (historical experience, political system, ideology, etc.).
      3. The *individual level* considers attributes of leaders (personality, goals, beliefs, etc.).
      4. Explanations from these three levels may appear to compete with each other, but they are ultimately complementary and aid our understanding of the "big picture" of world politics.
   B. This chapter looks at how factors operating on the systemic level affect the behavior of states within the system.

Part I: The Systemic Level

I. Realism

  A. Classical versus Structural Realism

    1. All forms of realism concentrate on the inherent *anarchy* of the international system and contend that *security* is necessarily the primary goal of all states.

    2. Classical realism influences states' behavior.

      a. Classical realists contend that the essentially evil or conflictual nature of mankind makes it a "dog-eat-dog world," and thus military power is necessary for survival (the basic logic of *realpolitik*, the "politics of realism").

      b. This school of thought on world politics goes back thousands of years (Thucydides, Sun Tzu, Machiavelli, Hobbes).

      c. More recent refinements to classical realist theory were prompted by the failure of the idealistic League of Nations to prevent a new world war (Morgenthau, Kennan, Kissinger, Dulles).

    3. Structural realists (Kaplan, Waltz, Grieco) focus on the *distribution of power in the international system*—specifically, on the number of major actors or Great Powers and their relative capabilities.

      a. *Unipolar* system = single dominant power

      b. *Bipolar* system = two "superpowers"

      c. *Multipolar* system = three or more great powers

  B. Three Central Assumptions of Structural Realism

    1. The international system is *anarchic*.

      a. There is no central authority or effective world government (the UN is too weak to impose order).

      b. Sovereign, independent states have authority and responsibility to use force to protect themselves.

      c. International relations are therefore governed by the *security dilemma* (see Chapter Eleven).

    2. All states within the system behave as *unitary rational actors*.

      a. States behave like rational individuals, making cost/benefit calculations.

      b. Domestic politics has secondary or minor influence on state behavior.

    3. The primary objective of all states is *survival*.

      a. Security takes precedence in the hierarchy of state interests.

      b. In an anarchic world, states must maximize their power to maintain their security; "if you want peace, prepare for war."

      c. Relative power, not absolute capability, is most important.

  C. Shifts in System Structure

    1. Structural realism's primary argument is that shifts in the distribution of power within the international system will lead states to respond in a uniform and predictable pattern.

      a. States will attempt to maintain their security by *balancing* against stronger powers.

      b. This may be accomplished through *internal balancing* (building up a state's own capabilities) or *external balancing* (forming alliances).

    2. Structural realism further argues that states rarely cooperate, especially on security issues.

      a. Each state fears that others may "get the better end of the deal" in a cooperation agreement.

      b. Because today's ally may be tomorrow's enemy, cooperation could therefore strengthen a potential future adversary—so its benefits must be considered carefully.

  D. Polarity and the Balance of Power

    1. Realists disagree over the type of system that best promotes stability.

      a. The parity school argues that an equal distribution of capability of balance of power creates stability; war is more likely when one state strives for or attains dominance.

      b. The preponderance school contends that an imbalance of power promotes stability; war is more likely when power is equally distributed.

      c. Within the parity school of realism, there is also debate over whether a bipolar or multipolar system is more stable.

    2. What is stability?

      a. Narrow definition is the absence of any war, continued independence of all states in the system, and maintenance of the status quo or existing order.

      b. Looser definition is the absence of major war between the Great Powers; limited wars do not necessarily indicated instability.

      c. Under any definition, a system ceases to be stable if one of the Great Powers collapses or is divided or destroyed.

      d. Proponents of different positions in the parity/preponderance and bipolarity/multipolarity debates often use different definitions of stability.

II. The Case for Parity
  A. Balance-of-Power Theory
    1. Balance-of-power theory argues that an equal distribution of power is more stable than domination by one power *(hegemony)*.
    2. Balance-of-power theory offers an equilibrium model; when an imbalance occurs, other states will form a counterbalancing alliance to restore the original balance.
    3. Power corrupts, and hegemony corrupts absolutely; even if the hegemon (dominant power) is initially benevolent, there is still a constant danger that it will impose its will on other states.
    4. States balance for self-preservation, not moral reasons; even states with histories of conflict or great ideological differences will band together against a common threat (example: Britain and the USSR allying against Nazi Germany in WWII).
  B. Internal Balancing
    1. Internal balancing converts domestic material resources into military power to meet a threat (examples: Japanese industrialization to meet Western challenges after 1983; Prussian reforms to meet threat of Napoleonic France, 1807–14).
    2. As a result, the most powerful states have often been the most developed ones.
  C. External Balancing
    1. Another balancing strategy involves formation of a counterbalancing alliance or coalition to stop one power from attaining mastery (examples: coalitions against Napoleon, 1805–15; Russo–French alliance against Germany before WWI).
    2. Historically, Britain played the role of balancer in Europe, throwing in on the side opposing attempts at hegemony by a dominant power (Spain in the sixteenth and seventeenth centuries, France in the eighteenth and nineteenth centuries, and Germany between 1900 and 1945).
    3. Balance-of-power theorists envision alliances that tend to be fluid, forming and dissolving to meet specific threats.
    4. Ideology proves not be a barrier to this process (for example, the United States allied with Syria in the 1991 Persian Gulf War).
  D. Problems with Alliances
    1. Reliability: Allies may not fulfill commitments to aid their partners (example: French failure to resist German pressure on Czechoslovakia before the Munich Conference); this may lead aggressors to attack anyway, expecting that promises of mutual defense will not be fulfilled (examples: German invasion of Belgium, 1914; North Korean invasion of South Korea, 1950).
    2. Speed: Counterbalancing alliances are often slow to form, giving aggressors a "window of opportunity" (examples: German invasion of Poland, 1939; Iraqi invasion of Kuwait, 1990—though both invaders were later expelled by counterbalancing coalitions).
    3. Buck-passing: States may expect their allies to come to the aid of an aggrieved state and delay or decline to bear the costs of resisting aggression (examples: Britain, France, and the USSR before WWII; EC and the United States after the breakup of Yugoslavia).
    4. Chain-ganging: Alliances may drag states into wars they have little or no interest in fighting (example: Germany's following Austria into war with Russia, 1914; Jordan joining Egypt in war against Israel, 1967).

III. The Case for Preponderance
  A. Domination and Stability
    1. In contrast to balance of power theory, some perspectives claim that domination by a single power is more conducive to stability (because potential challengers calculate that trying to upset the status quo would be futile).
    2. War is more likely when power is equally distributed.
  B. King of the Hill: Power Transition Theory
    1. When a strong hegemon exists, the gap between it and potential rivals is wide; therefore, few rivals attempt to challenge the hegemon and the system is stable.
    2. As states grow in power at differing rates, however, and the costs of enforcing hegemony add up, the gap between hegemon and rivals narrows, and challenges become more frequent.
    3. Finally, a hegemonic war (or series of wars) is fought in which the declining hegemon loses its position to a rising challenger, which becomes the new hegemon.
  C. Long-Cycle Theory
    1. This argument seeks to explain the surprisingly regular cycles of world leadership and global war (each lasting about one hundred years).

2. Each cycle consists of four phases (see Table 12.2).
   a. Global war: A new hegemon emerges.
   b. World power: The hegemon maintains its position through economic and naval power.
   c. Deligitimation: The hegemon's power declines.
   d. Deconcentration: Emerging rivals mount increasing challenges.
3. Periods of strong hegemony promote peace, while periods of declining hegemony are characterized by war.
4. Long-cycle theory offers a pessimistic prediction for the stability of the international system in the late twentieth and early twenty-first centuries, as America's power declines relative to that of Europe, Japan, and China.
   a. The impact of nuclear weapons on the long cycle is not clear, however.
   b. The role of regime type is also unclear; democratic states may prefer not to challenge a democratic hegemon (see below).
   c. Not all power transitions result in war: According to one argument, Britain believed the United States would continue to maintain the existing international order after WWII and that Britain would prosper under U.S. hegemony.

IV. Polarity
A. Historical Examples of System Types
   1. Multipolar (many great powers) existed from 1648 to 1945.
   2. Bipolar (two superpowers)existed from 1945 to 1991.
      a. "Tight" bipolar system (two superpowers and no independent forces) existed roughly 1945–60.
      b. "Loose" bipolar system 1960–91: two superpowers, but strong states within each camp (Europe, Japan) may act independently, and independent but weaker centers of power (China) existed.
   3. Debates rage over which type of system is more stable.
B. The Case for Bipolarity
   1. One school of thought, noting the absence of war between the superpowers during the Cold War, contends that bipolarity is more stable.
   2. There are several advantages of bipolarity.
      a. Simplicity—there are only two great powers, and smaller states cannot influence each other's policies.
      b. Bipolarity is more efficient and predictable, since the superpowers do not have to rely on their allies.
      c. Competition—through constant jockeying, imbalances of power are less likely to occur.
C. The Case for Multipolarity
   1. Another school of thought argues that a system in which more than two states, roughly equal in power, dominate is more stable.
   2. There are advantages of multipolarity.
      a. The uncertainty inherent in multipolarity is in itself stabilizing; the inability of states to monitor or control the behavior of others encourages caution and prudence.
      b. The increased number of interactions between the Great Powers creates common interests and leads to moderation of behavior; ideological antagonism is muted, and Great Powers have no incentive to destroy each other (because they might be allies at some later date).
      c. Because security in a multipolar world is not a zero-sum game, multipolarity slows arms races and restrains the security dilemma.
D. Trade-offs between Bipolarity and Multipolarity
   1. In a bipolar world, wars between the superpowers are less likely to occur, but are likely to be bigger and more destructive when they finally break out.
   2. Under multipolarity, more wars tend to occur, but they tend to be smaller in scale and shorter in duration, and defeated states are usually not destroyed or treated too harshly.
E. The Role of Nuclear Weapons
   1. One branch of realism argues that nuclear weapons make the bipolarity versus multipolarity debate moot.
      a. Because nuclear deterrence fosters stability, changes in distribution of power would probably have little if any impact on the stability of the system.
      b. The great potential for destruction in nuclear war prompts states to moderate their behavior.
   2. On the other hand, in a multipolar world, conflicts become more complicated and chances for miscalculation increase.
      a. It is difficult to determine which country is the main threat.
      b. Nuclear deterrence may work poorly under multipolarity, as several states could gang up on an adversary and nullify a second-strike capability.

V. Liberalism

   A. The world is not always consumed by warfare, relatively few Great Powers have been destroyed by war, and in the broad context of interactions between states, there has been far more cooperation than conflict.

   B. Liberalism argues that the inherent anarchy and violence of the international system can be overcome through carefully designed institutions for international cooperation.

   C. Liberals contend that the world is a variable-sum game—that is, it is possible for all states to simultaneously and mutually benefit through cooperation.

   D. The Prisoners' Dilemma (see box) reveals some of the problems.

      1. The Prisoners' Dilemma models the difficulty of cooperation in an anarchical system.

         a. Two suspects arrested for a murder are given a choice between giving evidence and remaining silent.

         b. If both remain silent, the prosecution will have insufficient evidence, and both will receive light sentences; if both talk, both will receive stiff sentences.

         c. If one talks and the other remains silent, however, the one who talks will go free, while the other will get the death penalty.

         d. In this situation, both prisoners have an incentive to "defect" and give evidence; thus, the likely outcome is that both will receive stiff sentences even though both could have gotten off lightly if both had kept silent.

      2. States are often confronted with Prisoners' Dilemma-like situations, illustrating the difficulty of organizing cooperation (example, the naval arms race between Britian and Germany between 1895 and 1914).

   E. There are several approaches to overcoming the dilemma.

      1. Liberals argue that it is possible to overcome the incentives to cheat if states can find some way to build confidence that others will not cheat.

         a. Encouraging states to focus on the long-term benefits of cooperation rather than the short-term gains of cheating can lead to increased confidence.

         b. In an iterated Prisoners' Dilemma, employing the tit-for-tat strategy (see Chapter Six) of reciprocity can lead to cooperation.

      2. *Neoliberal institutionalism* focuses on how interdependence leads to the institionalization of cooperation (example, the GATT and its successor, the WTO, have had considerable success in getting states to cooperate in the economic sphere).

      3. A new school of thought known as intergovernmentalism concentrates on the decisions of states to transfer or "pool" sovereignty over some issues from governments to specialized bodies (example, the EU's regulatory agencies).

VI. Strengths and Limits of Systemic Analysis

   A. Systemic-level explanations of state behavior have many strong points.

      1. Parsimony: Systemic theory rarely requires extensive study of every country under consideration, as the nature and structure of the international system is given primary importance.

      2. The predictions of systemic theory are often borne out in practice; many states frequently and consistently behave as realists expect them to.

   B. Nonetheless, systemic theories cannot explain everything in world politics.

      1. Systemic arguments cannot precisely predict what states will or will not do; realists, for example, can often predict the emergence of a counterbalancing coalition, but not which states will join it.

      2. The time frames of systemic predictions are usually broad and vague.

      3. Systemic theories are typically better at predicting consistency than change.

   C. Overall, systemic theories offer generalizations about how the international system creates pressures for state action, but domestic- or individual-level analyses are often more useful for explaining states' specific responses to these pressures.

Part II: The Domestic Level

   I. Introduction

      A. The previous section examined "outside-in" influences on a state's foreign policy—systemic variables.

      B. This chapter looks at foreign policy making from the inside out, considering how political institutions, cultural values, and other characteristic features of a state affect its actions in the international system.

      C. Although it is impossible to fit domestic influences on foreign policy into neat categories, dividing domestic approaches into statist, societal, and combination approaches can make it easier to grasp how both state institutions and social structures can shape a state's role in international affairs.

II. Statist Approaches
  A. Regime Types
    1. *Regime type,* or basic form of government, can exert great influence on a state's international actions.
    2. Differences exist between authoritarian and democratic foreign policy making.
      a. In authoritarian states, electoral or popular constraints on state action are weak or absent.
      b. Public opinion does not restrain aggressive intentions (example: fascist Italy and Germany in the 1930s, Iraq's 1990 invasion of Kuwait).
      c. The absence of a "deterrent effect" of public opinion can enable dictators to risk war with greater credibility, giving them more bargaining power in a crisis (example: Munich Conference, 1938).
    3. In democratic states, public opinion and interest groups constrain state action in foreign affairs.
      a. Leaders must "sell" controversial or risky policies to legislatures and the public.
      b. Public opinion often restrains aggression or military intervention (example: isolationist constraints on U.S. entry into WWII before Pearl Harbor).
      c. Interest groups lobby governments on foreign economic policies, causing domestic interests to "spill over" into foreign relations.
  B. Executive–Legislative Relations
    1. Most states have some type of legislature or parliament, but the function, power, and representativeness of legislative bodies varies considerably.
    2. In most authoritarian states, legislatures do little more than "rubber stamp" foreign policy decisions made by dictatorial leaders (example: the Reichstag under Hitler, the Supreme Soviet's subservience to the ruling Communist Party).
    3. Legislative constraints on executive authority are inherent features of most democratic societies.
      a. In most democratic states, legislatures participate in foreign policy decisions or exercise oversight over foreign relations.
      b. Many legislatures must approve or ratify treaties and can reject or demand amendments to agreements to protect or promote domestic interests (examples: GATT, NAFTA, and the Smoot–Hawley Tariff in the United States).
      c. Legislative refusal to ratify treaties can seriously weaken or undermine the agreements or institutions the treaties were intended to produce (example: the League of Nations charter).
  C. Electoral Politics and Foreign Policy
    1. Electoral systems and calendars can affect the timing and content of foreign policy initiatives.
    2. In states with fixed electoral schedules, executives typically avoid debates over risky or controversial policies in election years if at all possible, preferring to use flashy foreign trips to make themselves look like world leaders (compare Nixon's trip to China in 1972 with Carter's need to deal with the Iranian hostage crisis in 1980).
    3. In states where governments do not serve fixed terms, the governing party can call elections at opportune moments to maximize the political impact of military victories or foreign policy successes.
      a. Contrast Thatcher's call for elections shortly after Britain's victory in the Falklands War, 1982, with Bush's inability to translate the coalition victory in the Persian Gulf War into reelection in 1992).
      b. However, the threat of a vote of no confidence can constrain foreign initiatives, particularly if the governing party's majority is slim or based on a coalition (example: Israel's delicate negotiations with the PLO, 1993–94).
  D. Political Parties
    1. Parties support specific foreign policies to attract votes and sway public opinion (example: the struggle between Russian reformers arguing for cooperation and trade with Europe and the United States, and nationalists arguing for tough policies to protect Russians in the former Soviet republics).
    2. There are oft-noted similarities between supposedly competing parties in democracies (example: both Democrats and Republicans in the United States support continued defense spending—as long as the money continues to be spent in their districts and both parties get massive campaign contributions from agricultural and manufacturing interests).
    3. Other interest groups form long-term alliances with specific parties (example: most labor unions supply strong support to the Democrats).
    4. Many parties in European states have backed European union, which will strengthen multinational bureaucracies, even where public opinion has been cautious or divided.
    5. Parties reflect the institutional characteristics of a state's political system.
      a. In multiparty systems (Israel, Russia, Germany), the need to maintain a governing coalition complicates foreign policy making.

b. In states where a single party dominates (Japan), consistency in foreign policy is easier to achieve, but lack of partisan debate and oversight can strengthen unelected bureaucrats.

E. Bureaucracies

1. Ideally, bureaucracies can help leaders make decisions by obtaining and passing on information on the costs and benefits of foreign policy options.

2. In reality, bureaucracies frequently follow a set of decision-making guidelines and make routine recommendations when confronted with a foreign policy problem, rather than calculating the advantages and disadvantages of all available options.

3. Excessive reliance on standard operating procedures (SOPs) can make policies inflexible and unimaginative, can lead to delays or paralysis when unanticipated contingencies are encountered, and can seriously restrict flexibility in a crisis.

4. The *bureaucratic politics model* of decision making contends that policies are not determined by national interests, but are the result of competition between the interests of government departments or agencies (example: the Cuban Missile Crisis is often used to demonstrate the dominance of departmental interests over the national interest).

a. In this view, bureaucracies are not primarily component parts of a larger unit, but independent organizations with their own agenda and interests, competing with each other for influence and resources.

b. The model contends that "where you stand depends on where you sit"—that is, a bureaucrat's position on an issue, and recommendations to leaders, is determined by institutional rather than national interest.

5. Pursuit of different agendas by different agencies can send mixed or contradictory signals to other states (example: U.S. policy towards Iraq before the Persian Gulf War).

III. Societal Approaches

A. Statist versus Societal Approach

1. The statist approach treats the state as the dominant institution in the decision-making process.

2. The societal approach suggests that foreign policy reflects the objectives of whichever groups or forces in society exert the most influence over policy making.

B. Interest Groups

1. Many groups in society are concerned directly or indirectly with international affairs and try to influence foreign policy.

2. Examples of groups directly concerned with foreign policy include the American Israeli Public Affairs Committee (AIPAC) and the Arms Control Association.

3. Some interest groups become involved in politics for economic reasons (example: defense firms seek to promote the sales of their equipment to foreign governments; textile manufacturers often try to restrict imports of foreign-made garments; computer and software firms, aerospace manufacturers, and other high-tech companies, striving to gain market access to China, oppose efforts to impose trade and other sanctions against Beijing).

4. In most industrialized states, environmental interest groups are becoming increasingly active in foreign policy making (example: the Green Party urged Germany to initiate EU legislation to reduce vehicle and industrial plant emissions during the 1980s).

5. Separating national from individual and groups interests can be difficult (examples: Americans in general benefit from open trade in autos, which increases competition and lowers prices, but the laying off of workers from closed auto plants increases unemployment; dependence on imported oil may lead the United States to intervene militarily to protect oil supplies from nations with authoritarian governments).

C. The Military–Industrial Complex

1. The political and economic powers of defense industries and military organizations are often combined in a close alliance referred to as the military–industrial complex.

2. The military–industrial complex typically supports a strong and assertive defense policy (which requires high military spending) and has been accused of inciting aggression and even war.

a. Cobden noted how foreign policy scares exacerbated by sensational news stories prompted increases in naval spending in the nineteenth century.

b. Many in the U.S. public blamed "Merchants of Death" in military industries for garnering huge war profits and prompting U.S. entry into WWI.

c. When U.S. defense budgets grew rapidly after the Korean War, Eisenhower cautioned against the insidious effects of the growing political and economic strength of the military–industrial complex.

3. The end of the Cold War has called the continued influence of the military–industrial complex into question.
   a. The political power of defense industries did not block U.S.–Soviet arms limitations (though this is not surprising, as most defense expenditures went to conventional arms, which were not limited until shortly before the USSR broke up).
   b. The end of the U.S.–Soviet global rivalry has resulted in decreased military spending in the West and may do so in the former USSR.
   c. Nevertheless, "defense conversion" (converting defense-related factories and industries to civilian production to protect high-wage jobs) is likely to remain an important issue, and the need to design and build high-tech weapons assures that the defense industry will retain significant influence in the New Era.

D. Public Opinion
   1. Since the nineteenth century, public opinion has been an important part of the foreign-policy process in advanced industrial states.
   2. Several direct channels for the influence of public opinion exist in democracies.
      a. National leaders and many other policy makers are elected officials.
      b. Public opinion expressed through polling shapes and constrains policy options.
      c. Some major policy or constitutional changes are accomplished via referenda (example: public opinion slowed European integration when referenda on the Maastricht Treaty were held in many EU countries in 1992–93).
   3. The media—especially television—play a crucial role in shaping and mobilizing public opinion (examples: television coverage of the Tiananmen Square massacre, 1989, led to opprobrium for the Chinese government; coverage of the famine in Somalia was a major factor in U.S. intervention in Somalia in 1992).

IV. Links between State and Society
   A. Ideology
      1. Ideology refers to the central belief systems on which states and groups in society base their actions; ideology often supplies the visions, values, and ideals of a state's foreign policy.
      2. Ideological influence on foreign policy takes a number of forms.
         a. States with democratic values and traditions (Britain, Canada, the United States) often frame their international actions in terms of the need to protect democracy throughout the world (examples: U.S. interventions to "restore democracy" in Grenada and Panama in the Bush and Reagan administrations; the U.S. mission to make the world "safe for democracy" in WWII).
         b. Revolutionary France spread concepts of liberalism, egalitarianism, and nationalism throughout Europe.
      3. Ideological extremism has led to the justification of terrorism, torture, and even mass murder in states with radical regimes (Nazi Germany, Revolutionary Iran).
      4. Ideological conflict was a prominent feature of the Cold War.
         a. Soviet Russia and Communist China supported Marxist "national liberation movements" throughout the Cold War, to which the United States responded with the need to use military, economic, and political power to "contain communism."
         b. Regardless of the degree to which ideology actually influenced policy making, ideological conflict reinforced mutual threat perceptions and intensified the global political confrontation.
   B. Political Culture
      1. Political culture arises from a combination of historical experience and cultural values.
      2. Political culture often shapes a state's view of its role in the world.
         a. Spain viewed itself as champion of Catholicism in the fifteenth and sixteenth centuries, setting out to win converts in the New World.
         b. During the era of European imperialism, ideas of the "white man's burden" or *la mission civilisatrice* (civilizing mission) to bring European ideas to Africa and Asia were current in the European powers.
         c. Many Islamic fundamentalists in the Middle East have seen it as their religious duty to combat U.S. and Soviet influence or destroy the state of Israel.
         d. Some argue that Japanese traditions of deference to authority, avoidance of direct confrontation, and seeking consensus have served to make Japanese foreign policy relatively unassertive.
      3. The American style of foreign policy has been described as a conflict between crusading idealism and equally self-righteous isolationism.
         a. The concept of America's "manifest destiny" to dominate North America and transform it for the better was used to justify U.S. expansion in the nineteenth century.

    b. The tension between trying to transform international relations into a harmonious whole through intervention and then retreating into isolationism when other countries do not want to conform to the U.S. vision has made American foreign policy appear inconsistent.

C. Peace among Democracies

1. In the eighteenth century, philosopher Immanuel Kant argued that democratic states are much less likely to go to war with each other, as war making required consent of the citizens.
2. Since then, democracies have fought many wars (showing that they are no more or less inherently "peaceful" than other regime types), but have never fought wars *against each other* (or have done so only very rarely, depending on how one defines democracy).
3. Theories identify two sources of restraint on wars between democracies.
    a. *Procedural restraints* on going to war result from the influence of public opinion, legislatures, interest groups, and so on.
    b. Normative influences: Democracy includes norms of peaceful resolution of political conflict, compromise, rule of law, and the like, which democratic states may apply to each other to prevent their disputes from escalating into war.
4. The argument that democracies do not fight each other may not hold for new democracies that have weak democratic traditions, but if it does, democratization of Eastern Europe and the former USSR bodes well for peace in those regions.

V. Conclusions from the Domestic Level

A. It is far from easy to determine whether the similarities among states, or their differences, are stronger determinants of their behavior in the international system.
1. Just as with individuals, similarities among states lead to common patterns of behavior (examples: the needs for security in an anarchic international system and for markets and resources).
2. Differences in resources and objectives prompt states (again like individuals) to pursue common goals in different ways (external versus internal balancing against threats, free trade versus protectionism).
B. While state behavior is often as difficult to predict as human behavior, the existence of consistent patterns (such as the prevalence of peace among democracies, the ability of ideology to intensify disputes) shows that it is possible to identify specific attributes of states that promote cooperation or conflict.

Part III: The Individual Level

I. Introduction

A. The importance of individuals in international politics is hotly debated.
1. Leaders and other people obviously have some effect on the actions of the countries they serve.
2. However, individuals, no matter how capable, cannot overcome all the limitations imposed by systemic and domestic factors, such as massive disparities in national power and cultural norms.
B. This section of the chapter discusses how human beings and their individual and shared characteristics affect politics among nations.

II. Personal Experience and Leadership Style

A. Leadership Style
1. The beliefs and leadership styles of national leaders are strongly influenced by their perceptions of and experiences in politics, management, and personal relationships.
2. Leadership style includes conceptions of both goals (personal and national) and means (methods, approach, management style, etc.).
3. Though leadership roles are shaped by regime type and government structures, individual leadership styles vary considerably within the same political system.
B. Two American Presidents
1. Harry Truman, Pragmatist
    a. Truman had no experience in foreign affairs and assumed that world politics would resemble the operation of the Missouri political machine he was familiar with.
    b. Truman initially thought that Stalin, though corrupt, could be trusted to keep his word (much like Truman's own political mentor, "Boss" Pendergast); he quickly became disillusioned with the Soviet leader, however.
    c. Truman was a "hands-on" decision maker as well, but was confident in delegating authority and backed up his trusted subordinates.

2. George Bush, Diplomat
   a. Bush had significant diplomatic and political experience, but lacked an overall vision of America's role in a changing world.
   b. Bush relied heavily on trusted advisors and preferred to deal with foreign leaders on an informal, personal basis, often phoning them on the spur of the moment or in times of crisis.
   c. Bush acted decisively during the Persian Gulf Crisis, but was more comfortable and successful in the genteel world of diplomacy than the fractious arena of domestic politics.

C. Two Egyptian Leaders
   1. Gamal Abdel Nasser, Pan-Arabist
      a. Nasser was born into the lower middle class and appealed to the masses, but he destroyed all opposition parties and narrowly restricted the press; he ostensibly supported the idea of democracy, but contended that Egypt was still in a predemocratic stage and required authoritarian rule.
      b. Nasser symbolized Arab defiance of the West, surviving through the crises precipitated by his nationalization of the Suez Canal and Egypt's defeat in the Six-Day War.
      c. Nasser promoted the ideal of Pan-Arab unity and Arab nationalism, though his dream of a united Arab state failed; he was hailed as a hero by the Arab masses, but was resented and feared by leaders of conservative Arab monarchies.
   2. Anwar Al-Sadat, Independent Peacemaker
      a. In contrast to Nasser, Sadat believed in "Egypt for the Egyptians" and made policy with little regard for outside Arab opinion.
      b. Procrastination followed by dramatic change in policy was Sadat's typical decision-making pattern, exemplified in both the Yom Kippur War and the decision to negotiate with Israel.
      c. Sadat established the basis for a stable Egyptian–Israeli relationship and closer ties with the United States, but many in the Arab world never forgave him for either bold step; Egypt was expelled from active participation in the Arab League, and Sadat himself was assassinated.

D. Two Soviet Leaders
   1. Nikita Khrushchev, Demagogue
      a. Khrushchev was outgoing, boastful, and confrontational and not afraid of taking risks.
      b. Khrushchev loved making exaggerated claims (including the claim that communism would "bury" the West with superior production) and dramatic gestures (such as the launch of Sputnik and the first human astronauts).
      c. Khrushchev's confrontational style reflected the central ideological conflicts of the Cold War, first between the United States and USSR and later between the USSR and China.
      d. His risk taking ultimately proved his undoing; after the domestic fiasco of his Virgin Lands agricultural program and the humiliation of the Cuban Missile Crisis, Khrushchev in 1964 became the only Soviet party chief leader to be forced from office.
   2. Leonid Brezhnev, Party Hack
      a. Brezhnev's style was as dull and gray as his suits; he was deliberate, predictable, and cautious.
      b. Brezhnev typically avoided taking risks and only moved when every conceivable contingency was covered.
      c. This predictability served Soviet objectives well in the era of détente, however, when his risk aversion made the USSR seem more predictable and trustworthy to Nixon and others in the United States.
      d. The Politburo's decision to invade Afghanistan in 1979 was uncharacteristically precipitous; by the time of his death in 1982, Brezhnev embodied the stagnant, moribund Soviet communist system.

III. Generational Experience
   A. Sweeping events that have a profound impact on a generation may be reflected in the attitudes and perceptions of leaders belonging to that generation.
   B. Generational experience of war is influential.
      1. The wars of German unification (see Chapter Two) led many leaders to believe that wars would be short, constructive, and glorious, but these ideas where shattered by WWI.
      2. WWI was a traumatic tragedy that convinced a generation of leaders (and voters) that another global war must not be allowed to happen.
      3. The desire to avoid major war at almost any cost contributed to policies of appeasement of expansionist, dictatorial regimes in the 1930s, culminating in the Munich Conference.
      4. The failure of the Munich Conference to contain Hitler convinced new generations of leaders that aggression could not be appeased.

a. Eden used the Munich analogy in the Suez Crisis, 1956 (see Chapter Five).

b. Bush likened Saddam Hussein to Hitler during the Persian Gulf Crisis and War (see Chapter Five).

5. The protracted war in Vietnam made a generation of Americans wary of foreign military entanglements; this "Vietnam syndrome" contributed to American reluctance to intervene in the Bosnian Civil War in the early 1990s.

C. Different generational experiences can contribute to evolutionary policy change.

1. The experience of WWII convinced Soviet leaders of the Stalin, Khrushchev, and Brezhnev eras that the USSR needed to maintain a buffer zone of communist states around its periphery to ensure its own security.

2. Younger Soviet leaders, such as Gorbachev, remembered the horrors of WWII, but learned from the experience of the "thaw" under Khrushchev and détente under Brezhnev that Soviet security could be protected through treaties and political means as well as military force.

IV. Psychological Aspects of Decision Making

A. Various Factors

1. Most psychological approaches to the analysis of world politics focus on the inability of humans to act as ideal rational decision makers.

2. Individual traits and experiences and situational factors can lead to flawed apprehension and utilization of information.

B. Operational Codes

1. Some analysts contend that policy makers use mental "flowcharts," or *operational codes,* to translate their fundamental beliefs into decisions and actions.

2. There are several components of an operational code.

a. Beliefs about the fundamental nature of international politics

b. Beliefs about the nature of other actors in the system (allies and adversaries)

c. Perceptions of the extent to which future developments can be shaped (positively and negatively) by the actions of one's own state

d. Rules or guidelines for strategy and tactics

3. Elements of the Soviet "Bolshevik" operational code were heavily influenced by Marxism.

a. Capitalism and communism are locked in a death struggle.

b. Communism will eventually triumph, but miscalculations by Soviet leaders could lead to disaster in the short term.

c. Communist leaders are obligated to calculate risks and benefits carefully, but also to seize opportunities to "advance history in the right direction."

d. Risks derive not from the objectives of a conflict, but from the means used to pursue them; limitation of means can be used to control risks even if the objectives in a conflict are unlimited.

4. Comparisons can be made with the American operational code.

a. U.S. leaders tended to feel that limitation of *objectives,* rather than means, was the best way to limit risks; "limited war" must involve both limited objectives and limited means.

b. Thus, careful steps must be taken to show an adversary that one's objectives are limited; failure to do this led to Chinese intervention in the Korean War.

c. Consequently, in conflicts such as the Vietnam and Persian Gulf Wars, care was taken to show that U.S. and allied forces did not aim at the total destruction of the enemy (through refraining from bombing "sanctuaries" in North Vietnam and ceasing military operations before completely destroying the Iraqi army or advancing on Baghdad).

C. The Effects of Stress

1. International crises create the most stressful challenges for decision makers.

2. Stress affects individuals differently; some are overwhelmed by it, while others rise to the challenge and discover new strengths.

3. Some leaders have suffered near or total breakdowns under the intense pressures of international crisis; for example, Soviet Premier Josef Stalin broke down and became temporarily paralyzed after hearing about Germany's invasion of the Soviet Union in June 1941.

D. Cognitive Consistency and Dissonance

1. Some psychologists argue that people unconsciously try to simplify difficult decisions by seeking *cognitive consistency*—that is, people tend to see what they expect to see and change their perception of facts to fit their theories or beliefs.

2. Inconsistency between deeply held beliefs and incoming information is known as *cognitive dissonance;* decision makers may try to reduce cognitive dissonance by ignoring troubling information, reinterpreting it in a manner consistent with beliefs, or discrediting its sources.

3. Excessive attempts to maintain cognitive consistency can lead to serious miscalculations (examples: Stalin's rejection of information that Germany was about to attack the USSR in 1941; British rejection of the idea that Egypt could successfully operate the Suez Canal after it was nationalized in 1956).

4. Cold War examples of excessive consistency seeking include the U.S.'s discounting of Soviet reasons for rejecting the Baruch Plan for international control of nuclear weapons; dismissal of conciliatory Soviet gestures immediately after Stalin's death; invasion of the Dominican Republic in 1965 out of fear that it would become a "second Cuba."

5. When leaders are faced with the decision to sacrifice one goal or value for another, they may engage in *cognitive restructuring,* discounting or denying information about some of the competing objectives or ignoring advisors who advocate the sacrificed values.

6. *Cognitive biases* are psychological flaws in the reasoning processes; *motivational biases* result from the desire to attain goals and fear of failure.

E. Attribution Theory

1. *Attribution theory* considers decision makers as problem solvers attempting to understand and control events and their environments ("naive scientists").

2. Attributional biases often occur when leaders must infer or guess the motivations of others (very common in politics).

3. *Fundamental attribution error* is the application of a double standard to explain inappropriate behavior by oneself and others.

   a. One's own bad behavior is attributed to *situational variables,* circumstances or influences beyond one's control (such as previous or current actions by others, societal or structural influences, as when a defendant blames an offense on society, the circumstances of the encounter, post-traumatic stress disorder, abuse by parents, etc.).

   b. Other's bad behavior, however, is attributed to dispositional variables, that is, character and fundamental goals.

   c. Those who argue that their own good behavior is prompted by their innate moral character, while opponents act correctly only when forced to, also make fundamental attribution errors.

4. Fundamental attribution errors occur in international politics.

   a. During the Cold War, many U.S. officials viewed Soviet attempts to establish an exclusive sphere of influence in Eastern Europe as evidence of aggression while defending U.S. efforts to maintain an exclusive sphere of influence in Latin America as prompted by legitimate security concerns.

   b. Both sides in the Arab–Israeli conflict frequently defend their actions as necessary for self-defense, while opponents' actions are used as evidence of their aggressive goals.

F. Heuristics and Schemas

1. *Heuristics* are rules of thumb or mental shortcuts in information processing.

   a. The "availability" heuristic suggests that the most likely outcome of a situation is the one most easily remembered or imagined on the basis of past experience (example: U.S. policy makers' belief that the situation in the Persian Gulf in 1990 resembled that in Europe before the Munich Conference).

   b. The "representativeness" heuristic leads decision makers to expect an outcome most consistent with the salient features of the situation (example: expectation that dictator Saddam Hussein would act like dictator Adolf Hitler).

2. Generic concepts or analogies stored in an individual's mind are termed *schemas.*

   a. Schemas often reflect what an individual believes to be the "lessons of history" (example: the tendency to assume that the next war will resemble the last one).

   b. On the positive side, schemas can help a decision maker select the most relevant data and make inferences about a situation.

   c. On the negative side, schemas can lead to important information being rejected (because similar information was not important in a previous situation).

   d. Examples include the "cult of the offensive" in 1914 (see Chapter Three) assumed that the next war in Europe would be short and decided by rapid offensives, which it was not; in 1939, the "cult of the defensive" assumed that the next war would be a protracted war of attrition, which again it was not.

V. Conclusion: What Do the Levels of Analysis Explain?

A. How much impact do individuals have?

1. The real level of influence of individuals in world politics lies somewhere between the "great man" theory of history and the Tolstoyean idea that leaders are only tools of historical necessity.

2. It is often quite difficult to determine the relative importance of individuals, domestic institutions, and the structure of the international system.

3. Are individuals who take dramatic steps in foreign affairs (Nixon's trip to China, Sadat's trip to Israel, Gorbachev's policies of perestroika, etc.) unique figures whose courage and skill changed history, or did they merely recognize changes in the international system or domestic conditions that any leader of the same country would have done at about the same time?

B. Systemic and domestic factors impose major constraints on a state's international relations, but leaders almost always have some freedom of action.

1. Uncertainty or ambiguity often requires leaders to exercise their judgment or take (or avoid) risks to change policy.

2. Leaders may also make a difference through miscalculation, perceiving constraints that are not actually there or failing to recognize those that exist.

3. In any case, leaders' beliefs, goals, and personal characteristics can create new obstacles or help find ways of overcoming them.

C. There are several contending explanations for international events.

1. The Outbreak of WWI
   a. From the systemic level: WWI resulted from the security dilemma and arms races.
   b. From the domestic level: WWI resulted from the rise of nationalism and widespread adherence to the "Cult of the Offensive."
   c. From the individual level: The incompetence of many European leaders led to mismanagement of the July 1914 crisis and its development into a catastrophic war.

2. The Cold War
   a. From the systemic level: Bipolarity caused the U.S.–Soviet conflict, and the collapse of the USSR ended it.
   b. From the domestic level: Ideological conflict between capitalism and communism caused the U.S.–Soviet conflict, and the democratization of Russia and Eastern Europe ended it.
   c. From the individual level: Stalin's and Truman's mutual mistrust initiated the U.S.–Soviet conflict, and the working relationship established between Gorbachev and Reagan was required to end it.

3. The Bottom Line
   a. The "best" explanation for an event is similar to many other political and social questions.
   b. It often depends on the views and goals of the analyst.

D. The approach one takes in studying world politics also depends on the specific question one is trying to answer.

1. Systemic theories are most useful for explaining long-term trends or broad relationships.

2. Domestic theories can help explain specific policy outcomes that result from a decision-making process.

3. Individual-level explanations tell us a great deal about what happens when leaders must make quick decisions, when there is no time for substantial public or legislative debate.

E. This should not discourage the use of theory to study world politics, however; in international relations as in other fields of inquiry, it is easier to establish consistent patterns of causal relationships than to explain a single event fully.

1. Causal relationships between variables ("How does X affect Y?") lend themselves to classification and investigation according to level of analysis.

2. Questions about the origins of complex events ("Why did X happen rather than Y?") are inherently more complex and difficult to answer, as they involve counterfacutuals ("what ifs" and "might have beens") and many variables (not all of which may be recognized or even identifiable) on different levels of analysis.

3. Nevertheless, attempts to answer both types of questions are a necessary and productive part of the study of world politics.

HOW THE CHAPTER RELATES TO CENTRAL THEMES OF THE TEXT

Chapter Twelve presents an overview of some of the theories at the three levels of analysis that seek to explain behavior in world politics. Part I examines systemic explanations for cooperation and conflict, illustrating how external influences can affect states' behavior. While specific applications of systemic theory were discussed in Chapters Three and Four (as possible explanations for the World Wars and the Cold War), this chapter shows how theories intended to be broadly or universally applicable are constructed upon assumptions and central propositions. Part I points out how systemic theory may be used to analyze some of the events and issues considered in previous chapters.

While globalization and fragmentation are not explicitly mentioned in Part I, the entire text implies that changes in the international system are major factors in these processes. The breakdown of Cold War–era bipolarity has greatly contributed to political fragmentation, but efforts to establish collective security systems may open other avenues for the globalization of local and regional conflicts. The text also shows how globalization and fragmentation may be causes as well as effects of systemic change. To give one example, the increasing interdependence that has accompanied economic globalization has prompted many attempts at cooperation through international regimes and organizations.

Most of the themes and controversies described in Chapter One come into play at the domestic level and, while the historical chapters and Part I describe how the processes of globalization versus fragmentation and cooperation versus conflict operate at the systemic level, Part II considers how these dialectics take place *within* nation-states. The discussion of regime types, political parties, and political culture in Part II show how the conflicts of realism versus idealism, isolationism versus internationalism, and capitalism versus socialism take place within political systems and affect foreign policy. Turning to more material concerns, the chapter also shows how conflicts over trade and environmental policy (discussed in Chapters Six, Seven, and Ten) are fought by interest groups within a state's political institutions.

While the historical chapters discussed the policies and objectives of leaders and the impact they have exerted on the course of international events, Part III on the individual level introduces students to the systematic study of why leaders think and behave as they do. While Chapter Three reviewed the crises and miscalculations of the Cold War, this chapter describes how the psychological pressures of conflict and crisis can lead to disastrous policy mistakes, and how attempts by leaders to apply the "lessons of history" can contribute to misperceptions with serious consequences. In general, this section adds depth to the human dimension of world politics, which has lain in the background of the text's historical, conceptual, and theoretical chapters.

The chapter's concluding section addresses the crux of the level of analysis problem in international relations theory. As it has done with other controversies in the field, the text does not adopt a definitive position on the relative utility and explanatory power of theories grounded in the systemic, domestic, and individual levels, but encourages students to make this determination themselves after further study. Chapter Twelve concludes by pointing out that whatever position one takes on the level-of-analysis question, inquiry at each level is needed to advance our understanding of the complex interactions of international politics. In general, while the historical and conceptual chapters of the text show how globalization, fragmentation, cooperation, and conflict *occur* simultaneously at many levels, Chapter Twelve shows how these processes may be *explained* from many levels and how the contention of models grounded in the three levels of analysis creates productive controversy in the study of international relations.

SUGGESTED LECTURE TOPICS

1. Begin the theoretical unit of the course by introducing students to the concept of theory building in the social sciences, including the explication of assumptions and hypothesis generation and testing.
2. Use the Congress of Vienna, the Congress of Berlin (1878), the July 1914 crisis, and the Munich Agreement to illustrate the characteristic features of cooperation and conflict in a multipolar system (frequent but usually limited wars, shifting alliances, moderation and compromise, etc.) and use the Korean War, the Taiwan Straits crisis, the Cuban Missile Crisis, and the 1973 Arab–Israeli War to illustrate the characteristic features of cooperation and conflict in a bipolar system (zero-sum competition, brinkmanship, globalization of local conflict, varying independence of the superpowers' allies, etc.).
3. Using student volunteers, act out the Prisoners' Dilemma in class to show the difficulty of cooperation in an anarchic system.
4. Compare U.S. entry into World War I, the Vietnam War, and the Persian Gulf War to show a) how leaders attempt to mobilize public opinion in support of foreign policy objectives and b) how military success and casualties influence public support for war.
5. Describe the positions and tactics of key interest groups, and the progress and outcome of their competition, in the U.S. debates over NAFTA and agricultural trade under GATT.
6. Use borderline cases such as the War of 1812 and fighting among Italian republics in the fifteenth and sixteenth centuries (Genoa versus Venice, etc.) to show how different definitions of democracy yield different conclusions on the strength and scope of the "peace among democracies" thesis.
7. Compare the "normal" process of foreign policy making in Washington with decision making during the Cuban Missile Crisis, the 1973 Yom Kippur War, and the 1990 Persian Gulf Crisis to highlight the psychological effects of crisis-induced stress and its impact on strategic decisions.
8. Trace the uses of the "Munich Analogy" in the Korean War, the 1956 Suez Crisis, and the 1990 Persian Gulf Crisis to see how leaders use schemas and the "lessons of history" to inform (and misinform) decision making.

STUDY AND EXAM QUESTIONS

1. Which type of system is more conducive to international stability—bipolar or multipolar? Be sure to define stability and give historical or contemporary examples showing of the stability of one system and the instability of the other in your answer.
2. Does peace result from a balance of power and parity or from a preponderance of power and hegemony? In your answer, give historical examples that show why one relationship of power promotes peace while the other encourages conflict.
3. "The structure of a nation's political institutions determines whether the balance of power in foreign policy making favors elected officials or unelected bureaucrats." Do you agree with this statement? Why or why not? Use specific examples of policies or decisions in at least two democratic states to support your answer.
4. Which factor contributes more to the prevalence of peace among democracies: procedural restraints or normative influences? To support your answer, compare and contrast a case where two democracies might have gone to war, but did not, with one where a conflict between a democratic and an authoritarian state led to war.
5. Is public opinion primarily a *cause* of changes in foreign policy, or an *effect* of foreign policy actions? In your answer, use at least three specific decisions or foreign policies to support your argument.
6. Choose a historical or contemporary example of a bad foreign policy decision, briefly summarize why the decision was incorrect (taking the interests of the decision makers and the information available to them into account), and explain at least three ways in which psychological factors or biases contributed to the decision.
7. Accidents of fate or the results of presidential elections might have put different U.S. leaders in charge at critical times. Choose one of the counterfactual situations listed below and explain how and why U.S. actions in the situation would or would not have been substantially different if the indicated leader had been in office:
   a. Roosevelt had been president during the Czech coup and Greek Civil War, 1946–48
   b. Nixon had been president during the Cuban Missile Crisis
   c. Kennedy had been president during the Tonkin Gulf incident, 1964
   d. Johnson had been president at the start of the détente era, 1970–72
   e. Carter had been president at the start of the "new Cold War," 1981–84

RECOMMENDED ENRICHMENT READINGS

Allison, Graham T. *Essence of Decision: Explaining the Cuban Missile* Crisis. Chicago: Scott, Foresman, 1971. The original formulation of the organizational process and bureaucratic politics models; a modern classic of foreign policy analysis.

Betts, Richard K. *Nuclear Blackmail and Nuclear Balance.* Washington D.C.: Brookings, 1987. Interesting analysis of decision making in the crises of the nuclear era.

Brown, Michael E. et al., eds. *Debating the Democratic Peace.* Cambridge: MIT Press, 1996. Outstanding collection of views on the relationship between democratization and international conflict.

Booth, Ken, and Steve Smith, eds. *International Relations Theory Today.* University Park: Pennsylvania State University Press, 1995. Good collection of articles on recent developments in the theory of international relations.

Claude, Inis L., Jr. *Power and International Relations.* New York: Random House, 1962. Classic critical analysis of balance of power, collective security, and world government as alternative systems for international security.

• Doyle, Michael. "Liberalism and World Politics." *American Political Science Review* 80, no.4 (December 1986): 1151–69. Concise, thought-provoking presentation of the "peace among democracies" thesis.

Doyle, Michael, and G. John Ikenberry, eds. *New Thinking in International Relations Theory.* Boulder: Westview, 1997. Strong collection of articles written from emerging perspectives in the theoretical analysis of world politics.

Hilsman, Roger. *The Politics of Policy Making in Defense and Foreign Affairs.* 2nd. ed. Englewood Cliffs, N.J.: Prentice-Hall, 1987. Good survey of domestic influences on state action in the international arena.

- Jervis, Robert. "Hypotheses on Misperception." *World Politics* 20, no.3 (April 1968): 454–79. Excellent analysis of the impact of individual perceptions and misperceptions on foreign policy decision making.

  Jervis, Robert, Richard Ned Lebow, and Janice Gross Stein, eds. *Psychology and Deterrence*. Baltimore: Johns Hopkins University Press, 1985. Includes many incisive examinations of the psychological aspects of strategic decision making.

- Kaysen, Carl. "Is War Obsolete? A Review Essay." *The Cold War and After: Prospects for Peace*. Edited by Sean M. Lynn-Jones. Cambridge, Mass.: MIT Press, 1991. 81–103. Thorough, balanced examination of the arguments for and against the continued utility of war as "an extension of politics by other means."

  Kissinger, Henry. *White House Years*. Boston: Little, Brown, 1979. This first volume of Kissinger's memoirs is probably the most detailed, engaging, and revealing "insider" account of bureaucratic conflict and foreign policy making inside the Washington beltway.

  Larson, Deborah Welch. *Origins of Containment: A Psychological Explanation*. Princeton: Princeton University Press, 1985. Strong analysis of the impact of perceptions and belief systems of U.S. leaders in the early years of the Cold War.

  Lebow, Richard Ned. *Between Peace and War: The Nature of International Crisis*. Baltimore: Johns Hopkins University Press, 1981. Thorough study of the role of perceptual and psychological factors in crisis decision making.

- Mearsheimer, John J. "Back to the Future: Instability in Europe After the Cold War." *The Cold War and After: Prospects for Peace*. Edited by Sean M. Lynn-Jones. Cambridge, Mass.: MIT Press, 1991. 141–92. Provocative statement of the case that multipolarity will lead to conflict and war in the New Era.

  Morgenthau, Hans J. *Politics among Nations*. 6th rev. ed., Edited by Kenneth W. Thompson. New York: Knopf, 1985. The essential statement of classical realism.

  Mueller, John E. *War, Presidents, and Public Opinion*. 2nd ed. Lanham, Md.: University Press of America, 1985. Very useful examination of the impact of public opinion, and its manipulation, on decisions for and against war.

  Neustadt, Richard E., and Ernest R. May. *Thinking in Time: The Uses of History for Decision-Makers*. New York: Free Press, 1986. Considers how leaders form and apply (correctly and incorrectly) the "lessons of history."

  Rosecrance, Richard N. "Bipolarity, Multipolarity, and the Future." *Journal of Conflict Resolution* 10, no. 3 (September 1966): 314–27. Now somewhat dated, but still a very useful presentation of the polarity debate.

  Rourke, John T. *Congress and the Presidency in U.S. Foreign Policymaking*. Boulder, Colo.: Westview, 1993. Good analysis of executive–legislative relations in the foreign policy process.

  Smith, Michael Joseph. *Realist Thought from Weber to Kissinger*. Baton Rouge, La.: University of Louisiana Press, 1987. Good survey and discussion of classical realism.

- Van Evera, Stephen. "Primed for Peace: Europe after the Cold War." *The Cold War and After: Prospects for Peace*. Edited by Sean M. Lynn-Jones. Cambridge, Mass.: MIT Press, 1991. 193–243. Argues that the decline of Cold War bipolarity will not increase conflict and instability.

- Waltz, Kenneth N. *Man, the State, and War*. New York: Columbia University Press, 1959. Recommend assignment of pp. 16–79. The classic examination of the role of human nature in world politics and its implications for war and peace.

  ———. *Theory of International Politics*. Reading, Mass.: Addison-Wesley, 1979. The definitive presentation of structural realism and the stabilizing features of bipolarity. A true modern classic of international relations theory.

  Wills, Gary. *Certain Trumpets: The Call of Leaders*. New York: Simon and Schuster, 1994. Noteworthy study of the nature of leadership, examining the personal styles, beliefs, techniques, and failings of exemplary political, cultural, and spiritual leaders.

13

The Future of International Politics

SCOPE, OBJECTIVES, AND APPROACH

Chapter Twelve provided a foundation for understanding and applying the levels of analysis to trends and anomalies in world politics. Chapter Thirteen builds on this foundation by constructing scenarios for the future of world politics. First, two scenarios are derived from the systemic level, one from the liberal perspective and one from the realist perspective on international relations. Second, two scenarios will be formed on the basis that events at domestic level will be the most consequential for the future. Lastly, the role of the individual in defining new international systems will be investigated through history and with an eye to the future. The chapter challenges students to apply these scenarios to what they have learned throughout the book and to speculate on the future of international relations.

WHAT STUDENTS SHOULD LEARN FROM THIS CHAPTER

Foundation Level

1. Explain the liberal contention that interdependence makes cooperation more likely than conflict.

2. Describe the realist contention that security is the overriding dynamic of international relations.
3. List the distinguishing domestic characteristics of a "perpetual peace" system.
4. Explain the conflicts envisioned for the twenty-first century by the "Clash of Civilizations" scenario.
5. Compare and contrast the role of the individual in the systemic, domestic, and individual levels of analysis.

Enrichment Level

1. Identify the evidence that points to the realization of the "one world" scenario.
2. Describe how a "concert of powers" might moderate conflict in the realist's view of the future.
3. Explain the role of collective security in the "perpetual peace" scenario.
4. Explain the role of the individual in defining the systems following the Napoleonic Wars, WWI, WWII, and the Cold War.

Mastery Level

1. Discuss the problems associated with the realization of the "one world" scenario.
2. Identify the potential threats to U.S. hegemony in the current system.
3. Explain the problems faced by nondemocratic states in the "perpetual peace" scenario.
4. Explain the role of cultural compromise in the "perpetual peace" scenario.
5. Apply the scenarios of the future to the trends discussed in the book to gain a better understanding of the past and the future of world politics.

OUTLINE OF THE CHAPTER

0. Introduction
   A. There are several contradictory trends in the world that exist simultaneously: interdependence and cooperation versus fragmentation and conflict.
   B. This chapter will use the three levels of analysis discussed in Chapter Twelve to construct scenarios for the future of world politics.
   C. This chapter should be regarded as an exercise in speculation, designed to help clarify ideas about how the international system does, can, or should work.

I. The Big Picture: Scenarios from the Systemic Level
   A. One World, Ready or Not
      1. This scenario contends that economic interdependence has increased past the point where nation-states can control their own trade and industrial policies, and cooperation rather than conflict will be the norm in the international system.
      2. The world has become an integrated economic whole, with trade and production organized by multinational corporations and regulated by international regimes.
      3. Although it is too early to say what form a decentralized international economic regime will take, but it will probably look more like the Internet than the League of Nations.
      4. Transfer of sovereignty will occur in other areas as well.
         a. Environmental and social policies will also follow the standardization of trade regulations.
         b. A workable system of collective security will also follow, if only because states cannot afford to stay competitive while maintaining an independent defense establishment.
      5. Territorial control, large populations, and natural resources will decrease in importance and may mean only increased concerns for and costs of health care, welfare, and environmental management. (The most powerful states of the twentieth century were two giant superpowers with vast territories, but in the twenty-first century they may be "virtual states," trade and financial capitals with little territory.)
      6. Examples pointing towards the "one world" scenario: China's desire to join the WTO and reduce trade and investment barriers; the EU's move towards common environmental and safety regulations, a common currency, and a common "social charter"; NATO's deployment of IFOR and subsequently SFOR in the former Yugoslavia.

7. There are several problems with this scenario.
    a. Labor advocates claim that this scenario represents capital run wild in search of labor, resulting in decreased health and safety protection for workers and the downward standardization of wages.
        i. This trend may be balanced by the increased purchasing power due to free trade as it allows consumers access to less expensive goods and services.
        ii. This scenario could also be described as labor run wild in search of capital in that increased access to the global market creates more jobs in developing countries (example: workers in successful developing countries such as Taiwan, South Korea, and Hungary can enjoy lifestyles vastly improved over that of their grandparents).
    b. Environmental degradation may be increased as manufacturers may cut back on environmental safety to increase export profits, while governments look the other way out of fear of undermining competitiveness (example: demand for wood products may lead to accelerated deforestation).
    c. Given that domestic interest groups will have to organize at the international level to maintain effectiveness, one of the most serious questions raised about the "one world" scenario is whether environmental regulations, labor laws, and social protection will be standardized upward or downward.

B. Forward into the Past
    1. Realists' view of the future is much bleaker than that of liberals, thus they see the future as a continuation power politics and power balancing.
    2. The distribution of power is crucial, as the number of major actors and their relative strength will determine the character of the system. (The world may now be viewed as unipolar with the United States as the strongest power; the key question for realists is whether any emerging powers will become serious rivals for global power.)
    3. The world may be on a course toward a New Cold War with bipolar competition between the United States and China.
    4. A mutipolar system may arise if Japan, Europe, Russia, India, or other states mount a challenge to both U.S. hegemony and Chinese ascendancy; shifting alliances and balancing maneuvers would resemble those of the nineteenth century (see Chapter Two).
    5. A "concert of powers" that would function as a bargaining table for the Great Powers might help to moderate conflict and stabilize the system.

II. Pride and Prejudice: Scenarios from the Domestic Level
A. A Perpetual Peace
    1. The central premise of this scenario is based on the theory that the shared values, goals, procedures, and habits of democracy will cause democratic states to refrain from war against each other (see Chapter Twelve).
    2. Democratic states would not need transnational institutions to avoid war; intergovernmental institutions would exist to facilitate negotiation and help coordinate policies of mutual interest.
    3. Cultural similarities would help prevent misperceptions from aggravating disagreements, and democratic norms would prevent egregious abuses of human rights.
    4. A single global democratic alliance would provide the collective good of security by deterring or defending against undemocratic aggressors.
    5. The future of nondemocratic states in this scenario is not very bright.
        a. The possibility of violent conflict with democracies remains, especially if the democracies see no need for a global system of collective security.
        b. Civil wars that do not threaten to spread to members of the democratic club would probably be allowed to continue without intervention (much like conflicts in Liberia, Rwanda, Zaire, and Sierra Leone in the 1990s).
        c. While this scenario would likely push borderline democracies to join the democratic club, requirements for membership can be difficult to meet (see Chapters Eight and Ten).
        d. China might seem increasingly threatening to democratic states as its economic and military strength grows, thus a new bilateral cold war might emerge in which alignments would be determined by ideology and domestic political structures.
    6. Ultimately, the strength of the democratic peace would be determined by the vigor of democracy in influential and pivotal states and by the ability of democratic states to support threatened democracies.

B. A Clash of Civilizations
    1. Cultural differences and the impetus to preserve cultural autonomy will be powerful forces for fragmentation and conflict.

    2. Samuel Huntington has written that the major political conflicts of the coming century will take place along cultural fault lines.
        a. Huntington argues that the world is already dividing itself into groups of cultural nations or "civilizations" (Western, Slavic, Islamic, Confucian, Hindu, African, and Latin American) that have distinct sets of ideological, political, economic, and moral values that shape the worldview of its leaders and citizens.
        b. The ultimate result of this division is that different values, outlooks, and goals of these civilizations will inevitably lead to misunderstandings and conflict.
    3. The most enduring cultural divide is between Western culture and Islamic civilization.
        a. Islamists often perceive the social, cultural, and spiritual values of their civilization as under attack by the secularism and materialism of Western culture.
        b. Islamists are determined to prevent cultural change even at the cost of economic and political conflict with the secular West.
        c. This viewpoint is strongest in Iran and Sudan and is widely held by insurgent or opposition groups in Algeria, Egypt, Afghanistan, and elsewhere in the Middle East, Africa, and Central Asia.
    4. In addition to the struggle between Islam and the West, conflict is most likely in regions where one civilization borders another (example: African civilization clashes with the Islamic in the Sudan).
    5. Cultures must expand in scope and strength because cultural compromise always entails abandonment of fundamental values, and if these values are lost, so is the culture.
    6. The only way to deal with a rival civilization is to convert them or destroy them, because mere cultures can coexist, but civilizations must conquer or die.

III. The Defining Moment: The Future from the Individual Level
    A. The individuals who are "present at the creation" of a new system, where its structure must be clarified and its rules codified, can shape and define a new world order.
    B. The Congress of Vienna in 1815 was guided by the belief held by Metternich, Talleyrand, and Castlereagh that major wars were caused by domestic instability; thus they tried to design a system that would contain or prevent upheavals like the French Revolution (see Chapter Two).
    C. The Versailles settlement created an unstable system that lead to the rise of Hitler and blocked effective collective security due to the desire of leaders of the victorious Western Allies to punish Germany and to ensure its continued weakness.
    D. Following WWII, the leadership of the Western Allies recognized that the stability of the system would require unprecedented levels of U.S. economic aid and continued American security presence in Europe; thus the Truman Doctrine, Marshall Plan, and new institutions like NATO and the European Community helped maintain a balance of power in Europe.
    E. Post–Cold War leaders like Bush, Kohl, Thatcher, and Yeltsin were able to use the UN as an institution for containing and managing conflict.
    F. Time will tell if leaders at the start of the twenty-first century will create innovative political institutions and agree on new rules for the global economy or if they will fall back into patterns of conflict and compromise.
    G. There will be increased diversity among leaders who will build the systems of the future, which will lead to systems that are more equitable for humankind as a whole; more leaders will be women and more will be from the developing regions of the South.

IV. Conclusion: Choose Your Future
    A. In order to answer questions about the future of world politics, choose one of the scenarios for the future presented in this chapter and consider how closely this scenario resembles your apprehension of the world.
    B. Apply the chosen scenario to the periods of history presented in this book and consider how the scenario helps illuminate the events and structure of the system; this will help enhance understanding of historical events and their connections with current trends.
    C. Consider the validity, necessary conditions, and problems with the scenario to help in the consideration of the future of world politics.
    D. World affairs affect all our lives and vice versa, thus we have a responsibility to choose a vision of the future and do all we can to help achieve it.

HOW THE CHAPTER RELATES TO CENTRAL THEMES OF THE TEXT

Chapter Thirteen ties the major themes of the text together by encouraging students to extrapolate the trends and patterns discussed in previous chapters. While students may be exposed to wildly varying interpretations of historical events in their undergraduate and graduate courses, they often tend to assume that the future will be more or less similar to the past, forming their worldviews and career plans according to their perception of current conditions and trends. As a result, many students develop a view of international politics that resembles an ironic proverb frequently heard in Poland under communist rule: "The future is certain, but the past keeps changing." Chapter Thirteen is therefore designed to help students "think outside the box" by using the theoretical, historical, and economic material presented earlier to evaluate and construct scenarios for the future that differ dramatically from both historical and personal experience.

In many ways, the most important elements in these scenarios will be the strength and direction of trends toward cooperation or conflict on one hand and globalization and fragmentation on the other. Each of the five scenarios in Chapter Thirteen posits a different relationship between these trends in order to stimulate students' imagination. To review and reinforce the concept of levels of analysis explored in Chapter Twelve, each scenario is based on theories grounded in a specific level. From the systemic level, the "One World, Ready or Not" scenario postulates that increasing globalization and interdependence will lead to more cooperation and less conflict, though not everyone will regard this as a win–win situation. The "Forward into the Past" scenario, by contrast, argues that a return to multipolar patterns of conflict will accelerate fragmentation; politics may become increasingly globalized, but this scenario points out how interdependence does not necessarily lead to cooperation.

The first domestic-level scenario, "A Perpetual Peace," extrapolates the trend toward democratization and accepts that democratic regimes will tend to cooperate and to settle their differences peacefully. While this future clearly emphasizes cooperation, it is not clear whether democratization (if indeed this trend continues) will strengthen globalization as democracies unite in international institutions, or will instead result in more fragmentation as interest groups and national cultures assert themselves through the democratic process. Nationalism, of course, is the driving force behind the "Clash of Civilizations" scenario, which most authorities would consider to be dominated by fragmentation and conflict. Yet in many ways, globalization has exerted a positive impact on the strength of nationalist movements and may prove to have a moderating effect on conflict as newly independent nationalities face the same problems of interdependence as their multinational predecessors.

The final "Defining Moment" scenario, constructed from the individual level, is not so much a scenario per se as a means to prompt students to consider how leaders can shape international trends—and are in turn shaped by them. As Chapter Twelve notes and Chapter Thirteen reminds, politicians' personal and generational experiences of cooperation, conflict, globalization, and fragmentation often leave indelible marks on their styles of leadership and relationships with other world leaders. While recognizing the inevitable impact of history on belief systems and judgment, it is fair to say that the wisest leaders are those who remember that not everyone sees and experiences the world in the way they do, while being able to formulate policies and choose courses of action that take these differences in perspective into account. Capable leaders also stay focused on goals, evaluate new data, and adapt to changing conditions; by encouraging students to look at both the past and the future through different conceptual lenses, Chapter Thirteen may help students develop their own capabilities for analysis, decision making, and visionary leadership.

SUGGESTED LECTURE TOPICS

1. Briefly outline the scenarios from the systemic and domestic levels and identify prospective "winners" and "losers" in each scenario. Encourage students to present their own views on which states, organizations, interest groups, and so on are likely to come out ahead or fall behind in each scenario.
2. Highlight the most important actors in each scenario, emphasizing how each scenario assumes, or predicts, that various types of actors or organizations (states, leaders, multinational corporations, etc.) will play leading roles in each possible future.
3. In many ways, each of the scenarios is an assessment of how increased interdependence (and, in some cases, reaction to interdependence or "backlash") is likely to affect the structure and functioning of the international system. With this in mind, emphasize how interdependence shapes, and is shaped by, world politics in each scenario.

4. Identify the variables and indicators that should be monitored to determine whether each of the scenarios is moving closer to realization. Point out how correlations and oppositions between these variables (for example, the number of independent states and the frequency of war) could be used to extrapolate trends in globalization, fragmentation, cooperation, and conflict.
5. "Deconstruct" each of the scenarios in order to explicate their underlying analytical assumptions and social and cultural perspectives.

STUDY AND EXAM QUESTIONS

1. Construct an alternative explanation of one of the systemic level scenarios ("One World" or "Forward into the Past") from the domestic level of analysis or one of the domestic level scenarios ("Perpetual Peace" or "Clash of Civilizations") from the systemic level.
2. Choose one of the organizations listed below and examine each of the systemic and domestic scenarios from the perspective of the chosen actor. Be sure to identify how globalization, fragmentation, cooperation, and conflict impact upon the interests and influence of the organization.
    Microsoft Corporation
    The United Auto Workers
    Deutsche Bank
    Greenpeace
    Toyota
    NATO
    Hamas
3. You have been invited to participate in an international conference to reform the United Nations or replace it with a new organization designed to promote peace and collective security. Identify the major challenges and opportunities this organization is likely to face in the foreseeable future, and with these considerations in mind, propose an overall structure and specific functions for the organization.
4. The year is 2099, and you are a historian of international politics, writing for the twenty-seventh edition of *World Politics in a New Era*. You find that the international system at the turn of the twenty-first century closely resembles one of the scenarios identified in Chapter Thirteen of the second edition. Chose the scenario that was realized, select one event between the end of the Cold War and the date of this exam as the "defining moment" of the early twenty-first-century system, and explain the impact of that event on world politics.

RECOMMENDED ENRICHMENT READINGS

Betts, Richard K. "Systems for Peace or Causes of War? Collective Security, Arms Control, and the New Europe." *International Security* 17, no. 1 (summer 1992): 5–43. Contends that collective security organizations, multilateral alliances, and bilateral agreements are not mutually incompatible and that all of them may be needed to manage instability in a changing Europe.

Brown, Michael E., Sean M. Lynn-Jones, and Steven E. Miller, eds. *Debating the Democratic Peace*. Cambridge: MIT Press, 1996. Essays debating both sides of the argument about peace among democracies.

Fuller, Graham, and Ian Lesser. *A Sense of Siege: The Geopolitics of Islam and the West*. Boulder: Westview, 1995. An overview of the most active fronts of the "Clash of Civilizations."

Greider, William. *One World, Ready or Not: The Manic Logic of Global Capitalism*. New York: Simon and Schuster, 1997. Basis for the scenario that economic interdependence will make cooperation the norm in the international system.

Huntington, Samuel P. *The Clash of Civilizations and the Remaking of World Order*. New York: Simon and Schuster, 1996. Famous, while controversial, argument about cultural differences causing the conflicts of the twenty-first century. This version expands upon, and takes into account criticisms of, the original argument in *Foreign Affairs* in Summer 1993.

• Jervis, Robert. "The Future of World Politics: Will It Resemble the Past?" *International Security* 16, no. 3 (winter 1992): 39–73. Good speculative essay on elements of change and continuity in the international political system.

Kaplan, Robert D. *The Ends of the Earth: From Togo to Turkmenistan, from Iran to Cambodia, a Journey to the Frontiers of Anarchy*. New York: Random House, 1996. A global survey of political, economic, social, and environmental fragmentation, arguing that these trends are likely to intensify in the future, with potentially dire consequences.

Kennedy, Paul. *Preparing for the Twenty-First Century*. New York: Random House, 1993. Thoughtful, if unevenly written, extrapolation of the salient issues and key elements of power in world politics in the coming century.

Mueller, John. *Retreat from Doomsday: The Obsolescence of Major War*. New York: Basic Books, 1989. We've heard this song before, but Mueller sings it well, presenting the innovative argument that normative proscriptions will make war, like dueling or slavery, obsolete as a political and social institution in industrialized states.

Oye, Kenneth A., Robert J. Lieber, and Donald Rothchild, eds. *Eagle in a New World: American Grand Strategy in the Post–Cold War Era*. New York: HarperCollins, 1992. Strong collection of articles on what America can, cannot, and should do in the evolving international system.

Roberts, Brad, ed. *Order and Disorder after the Cold War*. Cambridge: MIT Press, 1995. Well-balanced collection of essays on globalization and fragmentation in the New Era.

Rosecrance, Richard. "A New Concert of Powers." *Foreign Affairs* 71, no. 2 (spring 1992): 64–82. Looks at how a "concert" arrangement for international security, midway between the pre-1945 balance-of-power system and a global collective security system, might function.

• Waltz, Kenneth N. "The Emerging Structure of World Politics." *International Security* 18, no. 2 (fall 1993): 44–79. Very strong and provocative presentation of the argument that power politics among nations will continue despite the spread of democracy, economic interdependence, and technological change.

Test Bank

Contents

Chapter 1

World Affairs in Our Lives

ULTIPLE CHOICE

1. Anarchy implies that

   a. There is a world government policing states.
   b. Domestic and international politics are identical.
   c. There is no world government policing states.
   d. International laws are obeyed by all.

   Answer: c Type: M   Page(s): 8

2. World politics refers to

   a. The competition for exercise of power in the international system.
   b. The totality of interactions among states and nonstate actors.
   c. Actions and positions on issues taken by an individual state.
   d. The United Nations.

   Answer: a Type: M   Page(s): 8

3. All the states of the world and international organizations comprise

   a. The United Nations.
   b. The international system.
   c. World politics.
   d. Foreign policy.

   Answer: b Type: M   Page(s): 8

1

4. The security dilemma arises because

   a. States intend to directly threaten the security of their neighbors.
   b. States act unselfishly to demonstrate their desire for friendly relations.
   c. States perceive that other nations might feel threatened by their defensive actions.
   d. States grow more and more insecure as they seek to stay militarily equal with their neighbors.

   Answer: d   Type: M   Page(s): 9

5. Those who believe in the security dilemma believe that conflict

   a. Occurs because of the relationships in which states find themselves.
   b. Occurs because states are fundamentally antagonistic.
   c. Occurs because of humankind's inherent aggressiveness.
   d. Occurs because of economic differences between nations.

   Answer: a   Type: M   Page(s): 9

6. In an anarchic world

   a. There is more conflict than cooperation.
   b. States are fundamentally aggressive because of the security dilemma.
   c. There is more cooperation than conflict.
   d. States are always peaceful.

   Answer: c   Type: M   Page(s): 10

7. Which of the following is not an example of common interest states share?

   a. Protecting diplomatic immunity.
   b. Trading to gain desired goods.
   c. Preventing international pollution.
   d. Promoting democracy.

   Answer: d   Type: M   Page(s): 10-11

8. What is the term given to the process whereby economies of different nations become linked together?

   a. The security dilemma.
   b. Interdependence.
   c. Diplomatic immunity.
   d. Exploitation.

   Answer: b   Type: M   Page(s): 11

9. Economies are connected by

   a. The dependence of many countries on foreign sources of raw materials.
   b. Foreign investment.
   c. International trade and finance.
   d. All of the above.

   Answer: d Type: M   Page(s): 11-12

10. Cooperation and order may emerge from

    a. Mutual interests.
    b. International institutions.
    c. Constraints on action.
    d. All of the above.

    Answer: d Type: M   Page(s): 13

11. The primary type of actor in international relations today is

    a. The state.
    b. The nation.
    c. The nation-state.
    d. Nationalism.

    Answer: c Type: M   Page(s): 13

12. A state is

    a. A group of people who view themselves as having a common heritage and destiny, and a
       sense of mutual identification.
    b. An independent political entity with institutions and an authority in a specific
       territory.
    c. A concept rooted in the American and French revolutions.
    d. The main motivating factor of world politics.

    Answer: b Type: M   Page(s): 13

Harcourt Brace & Company

13. A nation is

    a. A concept rooted in the American and French revolutions.
    b. An independent political entity with institutions and an authority in a specific territory.
    c. A group of people who view themselves as having a common heritage and destiny, and a sense of mutual identification.
    d. The main motivating factor of world politics.

    Answer: c Type: M   Page(s): 13

14. The concept of the nation-state

    a. Is directly related to much of the conflict in world politics over the last two hundred years.
    b. Is of ancient origins.
    c. Is irrelevant in world politics today because of interdependence.
    d. Does not influence people's political aspirations for sovereignty.

    Answer: a Type: M   Page(s): 13

15. Nationalism is

    a. The main motivating factor of world politics.
    b. The belief that a nation should have its own state.
    c. Rooted in groups claiming the right of "self determination".
    d. All of the above.

    Answer: d Type: M   Page(s): 14

16. Intergovernmental organizations

    a. Are groups of individual citizens organized for a common purpose.
    b. Can provide a diplomatic and legal framework for political interaction among nations
    c. Include such things as multinational corporations.
    d. Have little influence on world politics.

    Answer: b Type: M   Page(s): 14-15

17. Which of the following is not an example of an IGO?

    a. Organization of Petroleum Exporting Countries.
    b. North Atlantic Treaty Organization.
    c. International Business Machines.
    d. International Atomic Energy Agency.

    Answer: c Type: M   Page(s): 15

4

8. Which of the following is an example of an NGO?

    a. Organization for Economic Cooperation and Development.
    b. The United Nations.
    c. The Organization of American States.
    d. The Irish Republican Army.

Answer: d Type: M   Page(s): 15

9. The impact IGOs have on world politics depends on

    a. Their size.
    b. Their cohesion.
    c. Their popularity.
    d. Their location.

Answer: b Type: M   Page(s): 15

20. The number of multinational corporations has been increasing in the 20th century because of

    a. The liberal international economic order.
    b. Increasing world interdependence.
    c. Free trade.
    d. All of the above.

Answer: d Type: M   Page(s): 15

21. Amnesty International

    a. Seeks to improve the human condition through religious teaching.
    b. Is involved in environmental issues.
    c. Focuses publicity on individuals who are victimized by their governments.
    d. Is an extremist political faction that uses violence for political gains.

Answer: c Type: M   Page(s): 16

22. The levels of analysis include

    a. The international systemic, the domestic and the individual.
    b. The economic, the political and the military.
    c. The international systemic, the economic and the political.
    d. The individual, the nation-state and the United Nations.

Answer: a Type: M   Page(s): 17

Harcourt Brace & Company

23. The international systemic level claims that

    a. States are very different in their motivations and behaviors.
    b. States are very similar in their behaviors.
    c. Economic matters are the most important international concerns.
    d. Conflict is inevitable in international relations.

    Answer: b Type: M Page(s): 17

24. The factors that come into play in the systemic interaction between states include all except which of the following?

    a. Balance of power.
    b. Rules and norms.
    c. International Organizations.
    d. Government structure.

    Answer: d Type: M Page(s): 17

25. Systemic factors exert influence

    a. On all states.
    b. Only on major powers.
    c. Only on weaker states which cannot resist their influence.
    d. Only on individuals.

    Answer: a Type: M Page(s): 17

26. Which of the following is best characterized as a system dominated by two equally powerful states?

    a. The United Nations.
    b. A bipolar world.
    c. A multipolar world.
    d. The security dilemma.

    Answer: b Type: M Page(s): 17

27. The domestic level of analysis is concerned with

    a. Human nature.
    b. The United Nations.
    c. Influences that operate within nation-states.
    d. Influences that operate outside of nation-states.

    Answer: c Type: M Page(s): 17

Harcourt Brace & Company

28. The domestic level of analysis would examine all but which of the following factors?

    a. Government structure.
    b. Culture.
    c. History.
    d. Styles of leadership.

Answer: d Type: M   Page(s): 17

29. By using the three levels of analysis, scholars can do which of the following?

    a. Provide an organizational scheme for theories of international relations.
    b. Prove conclusively why nations go to war.
    c. Reduce the number of important factors in international relations to a bare minimum.
    d. Provide timely and accurate predictions of nation-state behavior.

Answer: a Type: M   Page(s): 18

30. The theory which asserts that all states are unique arises from which level of analysis?

    a. Systemic.
    b. Domestic.
    c. Individual.
    d. Human nature.

Answer: b Type: M   Page(s): 19

31. Which of the following types of data does the systemic level of analysis take into consideration?

    a. Ideology.
    b. Leadership style.
    c. The Number of major powers.
    d. Economic structure.

Answer: c Type: M   Page(s): 19

32. Which level of analysis is most concerned with the military-industrial complex?

    a. Domestic.
    b. Individual.
    c. Systemic.
    d. Economic.

Answer: a Type: M   Page(s): 19

33. If you were studying nuclear deterrence, you would be using which level of analysis?

    a. Domestic.
    b. Individual.
    c. Systemic.
    d. Attribution theory.

    Answer: c Type: M   Page(s): 19

34. Which of the following levels of analysis would you use with data regarding generationa experience?

    a. Domestic.
    b. Individual.
    c. Systemic.
    d. Economic.

    Answer: b Type: M   Page(s): 19

35. Which of the following examples of data would be used with the domestic level of analysis?

    a. Number of major powers.
    b. Operational code.
    c. Nuclear deterrence.
    d. Public opinion.

    Answer: d Type: M   Page(s): 19

36. Which of the following factors comes into play in the individual level of analysis?

    a. Styles of leadership.
    b. Personal goals and beliefs.
    c. A leader's experience.
    d. All of the above.

    Answer: d Type: M   Page(s): 19

37. Which of the following examples of data would be used with the systemic level of analysis?

    a. Military strength.
    b. Gross National Product.
    c. Number of major powers.
    d. All of the above.

    Answer: d Type: M   Page(s): 19

Harcourt Brace & Company

38. Scholars using the individual level of analysis would be most likely to use what kind of theory?

    a. Attribution theory.
    b. Deterrence theory.
    c. Bureaucratic politics theory.
    d. Security dilemma theory.

    Answer: a   Type: M   Page(s): 19

39. The most fundamental controversy in world affairs is the clash between

    a. The different levels of analysis.
    b. Hegemonic stability and the balance of power.
    c. Realism and idealism.
    d. The individual and the nation-state.

    Answer: c   Type: M   Page(s): 19

40. The zero-sum game is one in which

    a. Little can be gained from conflict by any nation-state.
    b. Any increase in one state's power is seen as a threat to the interests of other states.
    c. All states can maximize their self-interest.
    d. No state can ever hope to gain anything at the expense of its enemies.

    Answer: b   Type: M   Page(s): 19

41. A liberal views the international system as

    a. A zero-sum game.
    b. A "dog-eat-dog" environment.
    c. An arena where common interests can overcome anarchy.
    d. A constant struggle amongst states to protect their vital interests.

    Answer: c   Type: M   Page(s): 19

42. Realpolitik is most associated with which perspective?

    a. Idealism.
    b. The individual level of analysis.
    c. Comparative advantage.
    d. Realism.

    Answer: d   Type: M   Page(s): 19

43. Idealists tend to believe which of the following?

    a. The security dilemma is inescapable.
    b. International conflict is unavoidable.
    c. States can escape from the security dilemma.
    d. All nation-state interactions are zero-sum.

Answer: c Type: M   Page(s): 19

44. The view that interdependence may make it necessary and possible for states to collaborate is most closely identified with which of the following perspectives?

    a. Idealism.
    b. Realism.
    c. The zero-sum theory.
    d. Geopolitics.

Answer: a Type: M   Page(s): 19

45. Those who believe that engagement with other nations is an inherently risky enterprise are

    a. Realists.
    b. Internationalists.
    c. Idealists.
    d. Isolationists.

Answer: d Type: M   Page(s): 20

46. Internationalists believe that

    a. It is better for states to concentrate on their own internal problems.
    b. It is better for states to participate actively in the world.
    c. It is better for states to use force whenever possible to pursue their interests.
    d. Free trade is harmful to a nation's best interests.

Answer: b Type: M   Page(s): 20

47. Advocates of free trade argue that the removal of all trade barriers will do which of the following?

    a. Allow states to practice better managed trade.
    b. Promote isolationism.
    c. Allow states to produce goods and services more efficiently.
    d. Promote realpolitik.

Answer: c Type: M   Page(s): 20

Harcourt Brace & Company

48. Managed trade is most closely associated with which of the following theories?

   a. Comparative advantage.
   b. Realpolitik.
   c. Free trade.
   d. Protectionism.

Answer: d   Type: M   Page(s): 20

49. According to protectionists, trade barriers should be erected to

   a. Protect important industries and high-paying jobs.
   b. Get rid of zero-sum games.
   c. Diminish the influence of domestic politics on international relations.
   d. Provide for comparative advantage.

Answer: a   Type: M   Page(s): 20

50. Capitalism tends to have what effect in terms of international trade?

   a. Reduction of zero-sum conflicts.
   b. Increased wealth for industrialized nations.
   c. Increased wealth for states that export natural resources.
   d. Reduction of the influence of comparative advantage.

Answer: b   Type: M   Page(s): 21

51. Socialists advocate

   a. Private ownership of the means of production.
   b. Policies that tend to benefit nations that export natural resources and labor.
   c. The allocation of economic rewards to the corporate owners of multinational
      corporations that have helped third world economies.
   d. The idealism approach to world politics.

Answer: b   Type: M   Page(s): 21

52. Which of the following controversies is resolvable in international relations?

   a. The controversy between realists and idealists.
   b. The controversy between internationalists and isolationists.
   c. The controversy between free trade and protectionism.
   d. None of the above.
   e. All of the above.

Answer: d   Type: M   Page(s): 21

Harcourt Brace & Company

53. Progress toward increased globalization has done which of the following?

    a. Led to the creation of a central international government.
    b. Encouraged people to give up their individual identities to become a part of the world culture.
    c. Created a backlash in the form of a fragmentation process.
    d. Reduced all forms of international conflict.

    Answer: c Type: M   Page(s): 23

54. Evidence of fragmentation in world politics would include which of the following?

    a. Increased unity in Western Europe.
    b. Increased number of civil wars.
    c. Greater ease of activity by criminals.
    d. Increased international news coverage.

    Answer: b Type: M   Page(s): 23

55. Globalization has

    a. Helped Western Europe strengthen both politically and economically.
    b. Affected only industrialized nations.
    c. Made it easier for criminals to traffic drugs and arms across national boundaries.
    d. "a" and "c"
    e. "a" and "b"

    Answer: d Type: M   Page(s): 23

56. As international globalization continues

    a. Divisive tendencies will still be present.
    b. Conflict will eventually be eliminated.
    c. Interdependence will gradually diminish.
    d. Comparative advantage will be done away with.

    Answer: a Type: M   Page(s): 24

57. Which of the following forces is accelerating the rate of change in international relations?

    a. Technological developments.
    b. Political developments.
    c. "a" and "b."
    d. Neither "a" nor "b."

    Answer: c Type: M   Page(s): 25

12

58. The Star Wars approach holds that world politics is a struggle between good and evil states.

    a. True
    b. False

    Answer: A Type: T   Page(s): 7

59. Order does not exist in an anarchic world.

    a. True
    b. False

    Answer: B Type: T   Page(s): 12

60. Gross National Product is the total sum of all goods and services a nation imports.

    a. True
    b. False

    Answer: B Type: T   Page(s): 12

61. Domestic politics usually do not serve as a restraint on the actions of states.

    a. True
    b. False

    Answer: B Type: T   Page(s): 12

62. Modern communication in today's world is cheaper and easier than ever before.

    a. True
    b. False

    Answer: A Type: T   Page(s): 13

63. Nationalism is the belief that a nation should have its own state.

    a. True
    b. False

    Answer: A Type: T   Page(s): 14

Harcourt Brace & Company

64. Terrorists are extremist political factions that use violence to achieve political gains.

   a. True
   b. False

   Answer: A Type: T   Page(s): 15

65. Levels of analysis may be thought of as variables that help explain the consequences of nations' actions in world politics.

   a. True
   b. False

   Answer: B Type: T   Page(s): 17

66. An international system can be both bipolar and multipolar at the same time.

   a. True
   b. False

   Answer: B Type: T   Page(s): 17

67. Analysts of world affairs can usually find definitive explanations for historical and current events.

   a. True
   b. False

   Answer: B Type: T   Page(s): 17

68. The number of major political actors in the world and their relative strengths and weaknesses is often referred to as the balance of power.

   a. True
   b. False

   Answer: A Type: T   Page(s): 17

69. Analysis from the domestic level considers how rules and norms govern the relations between states.

   a. True
   b. False

   Answer: B Type: T   Page(s): 17

Harcourt Brace & Company

70. The individual level of analysis explores how crisis situations can affect the decision-making process.

   a. True
   b. False

   Answer: A Type: T   Page(s): 18

71. The levels of analysis can indicate what sort of data is most relevant to a particular theory.

   a. True
   b. False

   Answer: A Type: T   Page(s): 18

72. Historical cycles rarely occur.

   a. True
   b. False

   Answer: B Type: T   Page(s): 18

73. Socialists believe that the means of production should be owned privately.

   a. True
   b. False

   Answer: B Type: T   Page(s): 20

74. Capitalists believe that the means of production should be owned privately.

   a. True
   b. False

   Answer: A Type: T   Page(s): 20

75. Advanced technology makes both increased globalization and international tension possible.

   a. True
   b. False

   Answer: A Type: T   Page(s): 24

Chapter 2

Origins of the Modern International System

1. The sovereign nation-state system originated where?

   a. The United States of America.
   b. Europe.
   c. China.
   d. Latin America.

   Answer: b Type: M   Page(s): 30

2. Which of the following characteristics best describes the feudal system?

   a. Countries with precisely demarcated and recognized boundaries.
   b. Few struggles over territory because of blood-kinship ties between rulers.
   c. Authority determined by the ability of a ruler's army to keep the forces of other rulers out.
   d. Small rulers owed allegiance to only one, more powerful ruler.

   Answer: c Type: M   Page(s): 30

3. The Roman Catholic Church possessed the power to do all but which of the following during feudal times?

   a. Control a large amount of territory.
   b. Recognize one European monarch as the leader of the Holy Roman Empire.
   c. Legitimate or terminate claims to land by papal writ.
   d. Provide a central authority to adjudicate all legal disputes and enforce judgments.

   Answer: d Type: M   Page(s): 31

4. Why was it so difficult to create a sense of national identity during feudal times?

   a. The use of constitutions and rule of law benefited the rulers more than the common people.
   b. People were constantly traveling throughout Europe and developed no identification with any one nation.
   c. Individuals swore loyalty to kings, princes and God, rather than to nations.
   d. Rulers were rarely changed in many countries.

   Answer: c Type: M   Page(s): 31

5. The Reformation is best characterized as what kind of event?
   a. A Protestant revolt against the religious authority of the Roman Catholic Church.
   b. The final end of the crusades to liberate the Holy Lands in the Middle East.
   c. A Catholic revolt against the religious authority of the Protestant Church.
   d. The European discovery of the New World.

   Answer: a Type: M   Page(s): 32

6. What important principle was established by the Peace of Westphalia?

   a. Power projection.
   b. The feudal system.
   c. A just war.
   d. Sovereignty.
   e. All of the above.

   Answer: d Type: M   Page(s): 34

7. The Peace of Westphalia establishes that

   a. The Catholic Church would remain supreme in the domestic affairs of nations.
   b. States are to be sovereign in their internal affairs.
   c. Political legitimacy must originate in the democratic will of the majority.
   d. Whenever a state displays blatant aggression, other states must practice non-interference.

   Answer: b Type: M   Page(s): 34

8. The principle of sovereignty recognized in the Peace of Westphalia represents an essential element in the creation of the modern nation-state because

  a. Political legitimacy was to be derived from unified religious authority rather than secular authority.
  b. Political legitimacy was to be obtained through conquest rather than constitutionalism.
  c. Political legitimacy was to be derived from secular authority rather than divine sanction.
  d. Political legitimacy was to be derived through democratic rule of the people.
  e. All of the above.

Answer: c Type: M   Page(s): 34

9. Which of the following was not one of the effects of the high cost of waging the Thirty Years' War?

  a. It forced monarchs to loosen control over their territories to gain greater legitimacy in the eyes of the people.
  b. It encouraged the creation of centralized bureaucracies.
  c. It increased the importance of institutions outside the church and state, particularly economic ones.
  d. It helped raise taxes.

Answer: a Type: M   Page(s): 34

10. What problem(s) continued to plague Europe even after the Peace of Westphalia?

  a. Shifting alliances and ongoing conflict.
  b. States which were still apt to be most interested in their own selfish ends.
  c. A lack of world government.
  d. All of the above.
  e. None of the above.

Answer: d Type: M   Page(s): 34-35

11. The Treaty of Tordesillas was responsible for

  a. Settling a long running conflict between Britain and Spain.
  b. Setting the foundation for Portuguese colonial control of East Asia.
  c. Setting the foundation for Spanish colonial control of Latin America.
  d. Both b and c.
  e. None of the above.

Answer: c Type: M   Page(s): 37

Harcourt Brace & Company

12. The decline of Spanish colonial power was a result of

    a. The overextension of the Spanish military.
    b. Key losses at the hands of the Aztec Empire.
    c. The geographic and domestic advantages of the Portuguese over the Spanish.
    d. Domestic objections to the conflict of imperialist actions with religious ideas.

    Answer: a Type: M Page(s): 39

13. Which of the following was not a reason for Britain having a consistent advantage over France in their colonial competition?

    a. France had more need for a standing army and therefore could not compete with the British navy.
    b. France was self-sufficient in food, forcing it to concentrate more on domestic economic matters than the British.
    c. Britain had more incentive to increase trade and look for new colonies due to its population problems.
    d. None of the above.

    Answer: d Type: M Page(s): 39

14. One of the characteristics of eighteenth-century Europe that had a tremendous impact on international relations was

    a. The virtually unlimited capability of monarchs to wage war.
    b. Heated feuds between monarchs who desired to destroy each other's rule.
    c. Social stratification in society.
    d. The lack of competition among states for power and influence.

    Answer: c Type: M Page(s): 40

15. Why was the cost of war so great in eighteenth century Europe?

    a. The use of ordinary peasants to fight wars made it difficult to feed the nation.
    b. Mercenary armies required great expenditures to hire and supply.
    c. The wars were fought with unlimited means for unlimited objectives.
    d. States were often conquered, which required large armies to rule over a monarch's new subjects.

    Answer: b Type: M Page(s): 41

16. Which state actually disappeared from the map of Europe in the eighteenth century?

    a. Poland.
    b. Austria.
    c. The Netherlands.
    d. Prussia.
    e. All of the above.

Answer: a Type: M Page(s): 41

17. Which of the following statements best describes the conduct of foreign policy in eighteenth-century Europe?

    a. Rulers were often forced to respond to the wishes of the people.
    b. Rulers were constantly conquering one another's territories.
    c. Alliances were rarely used.
    d. The personalities of monarchs often figured prominently in the policies pursued by their nations.

Answer: d Type: M Page(s): 41

18. The international system during the eighteenth century is best characterized as

    a. Feudal.
    b. Multipolar.
    c. Bipolar.
    d. Unipolar.

Answer: b Type: M Page(s): 42

19. Power projection refers to the ability of states to do which of the following?

    a. Exert influence beyond their own borders.
    b. Prevent their citizens from gaining control of government.
    c. Rely on other states for their security and protection.
    d. Recognize the authority of the Roman Catholic Church.
    e. All of the above.

Answer: a Type: M Page(s): 42

Harcourt Brace & Company

20. To be a great power, a state should have which of the following?

    a. Relatively large territory.
    b. A well-organized military.
    c. A strong economy.
    d. All of the above.
    e. None of the above.

    Answer: d Type: M   Page(s): 42

21. The elimination of any one power by another

    a. Served the interests of all since it reduced the number of potential enemies.
    b. Helped preserve the balance of power because it reduced the number of unimportant states.
    c. Could threaten the interests of other states.
    d. Was commonly resorted to during the eighteenth century.

    Answer: c Type: M   Page(s): 42

22. Which of the following statements best describes the nature of alliances in eighteenth-century Europe?

    a. Alliances fluctuated constantly and unpredictably.
    b. Alliances were usually made for long periods of time.
    c. Alliances were usually formed before wars ever started.
    d. Alliances were not used to preserve the balance of power.

    Answer: a Type: M   Page(s): 42

23. Which of the following was not one of the three major wars of the eighteenth century?

    a. The War of the Spanish Succession.
    b. The War of the Austrian Succession.
    c. The Seven Years' War.
    d. The Thirty Years' War.

    Answer: d Type: M   Page(s): 43-44

Harcourt Brace & Company

24. When Frederick II of Prussia stated, "If we can gain something by being honest, we will be it, and if we have to deceive, we will be cheats," he was demonstrating what kind of view of international relations?

a. Idealism.
b. Realism.
c. Isolationism.
d. Fragmentation.

Answer: b Type: M   Page(s): 44

25. One of the things the European wars of the eighteenth century demonstrated was that

a. The major powers of Europe were not concerned with preventing any one nation from dominating the continent.
b. The question of who would rule the various states was of little importance.
c. Wars were fought exclusively in Europe.
d. Alliances could be changed rapidly.

Answer: d Type: M   Page(s): 44

26. Although the French may have helped to defeat the British in the American War of Independence, their own cause was hurt because

a. The war dramatically escalated the French government's debt.
b. The war forced the French monarch to immediately implement needed domestic reforms.
c. The war forced the king to lower taxes.
d. All of the above.
e. None of the above.

Answer: a Type: M   Page(s): 45

27. The immediate cause of the French Revolution was

a. French free trade policies.
b. France's open and democratic political system.
c. France's tremendous debt.
d. All of the above.
e. None of the above.

Answer: c Type: M   Page(s): 46

Harcourt Brace & Company

28. The French Revolution was inspired by which ideology?

    a. Monarchism.
    b. Communism.
    c. Capitalism.
    d. Nationalism.

    Answer: d Type: M   Page(s): 47

29. Liberalism is the belief that

    a. The power of government should reside in the hands of the people.
    b. Government should allow individuals as little responsibility for controlling their own actions as possible.
    c. Popular loyalty should focus on the nation rather than the monarch.
    d. All of the above.

    Answer: a Type: M   Page(s): 47

30. The French Revolution promoted all but which of the following?

    a. Liberalism.
    b. Nationalism.
    c. Monarchism.
    d. The nation in arms.

    Answer: c Type: M   Page(s): 47

31. The radical government in place during the French Revolution believed that

    a. Because of its strength at home, it could fight wars abroad better.
    b. Bringing its troops home would increase support for its foreign policies.
    c. Foreign expansion would weaken its domestic legitimacy.
    d. It could compensate for its weakness at home by waging war.

    Answer: d Type: M   Page(s): 48

32. French strength during the period of the revolution was enhanced by

    a. Its revolutionary form of mobilization.
    b. Division among its opponents.
    c. The levee en masse.
    d. All of the above.

    Answer: d Type: M   Page(s): 48

33. When waging war, Napoleon did which of the following?

    a. Practiced only limited war, as was the custom.
    b. Accepted only complete submission and occupation of a defeated country.
    c. Allowed conquered countries to remain independent to gain more allies.
    d. Increased inefficiency through the introduction of the French system of government in conquered nations.

    Answer: b Type: M Page(s): 48

34. Napoleon's "Continental System" was designed to do which of the following?

    a. Expand French economic control of Europe and weaken the British.
    b. Promote governmental efficiency in the countries he conquered.
    c. Install his relatives as monarchs in conquered nations.
    d. Increase the number of conscripts in his armies.

    Answer: a Type: M Page(s): 49

35. All except which of the following factors contributed to the undermining of Napoleon's power?

    a. The Continental System, which created considerable resentment in French colonies.
    b. France's inability to defeat Spain and Portugal.
    c. The levee en masse.
    d. The invasion of Russia.

    Answer: c Type: M Page(s): 50

36. Simon Bolivar helped liberate countries in

    a. The Middle East.
    b. Europe.
    c. Latin America.
    d. The United States.

    Answer: c Type: M Page(s): 54

37. The participants of the Vienna peace conference sought to restore normalcy, by which they meant

    a. A return to the feudal system.
    b. A return to power by Napoleon.
    c. The creation of liberal, democratic nations.
    d. The restoration of monarchical systems.

    Answer: d Type: M Page(s): 55

38. Among the consequences of the Vienna peace conference was

    a. The French loss of great power status.
    b. The beginning of the globalization of world politics.
    c. The establishment of a neutral Great Britain.
    d. The end of war in Europe in the nineteenth century.

    Answer: b   Type: M   Page(s): 57

39. The participants in the Concert of Europe agreed on which of the following ideas?

    a. Domestic developments could have international repercussions.
    b. Nations should never interfere in the affairs of other states.
    c. Democratic practices should be encouraged in all of the territories France had conquered.
    d. Self-defense was to be preferred over collective security.

    Answer: a   Type: M   Page(s): 57

40. All except which of the following were among the consequences of the Vienna settlement?

    a. Many dethroned monarchies were restored.
    b. The dispensation of territory was used to reward victors and punish losers.
    c. The institutionalization of the supremacy of particular great powers.
    d. All of the above.
    e. None of the above.

    Answer: d   Type: M   Page(s): 57

41. Advocates of national independence frequently supported

    a. Protectionism.
    b. The ancien regime.
    c. Monarchism.
    d. The free market.

    Answer: d   Type: M   Page(s): 58

42. Nationalism posed the biggest threat to what kind of political entities?

    a. The Church.
    b. Empires.
    c. Intergovernmental organizations.
    d. The nation-state.

    Answer: b   Type: M   Page(s): 58

26

43. Nationalism served as a unifying force in which European country?

    a. The Austrian Empire.
    b. The Ottoman Empire.
    c. The Netherlands.
    d. Germany.

Answer: d Type: M   Page(s): 58

44. War was largely absent from the European continent from 1815-1914 for all but which of the following reasons?

    a. The exhaustion of the great powers after the Napoleonic wars.
    b. The need of many regimes to reestablish their domestic authority.
    c. The open acceptance of nationalism and liberalism in most nations.
    d. The decline of the Anglo-French rivalry.

Answer: c Type: M   Page(s): 58

45. Tensions arose in Europe despite the Concert of Europe because

    a. France was never allowed to resume a role co-equal with that of the other great powers.
    b. Political ambitions often motivated states at the expense of ideological consistency.
    c. There was common agreement among the great powers on the need to intervene in the domestic affairs of other nations.
    d. Great Britain did not take any interest in the balance of power on the European continent.

Answer: b Type: M   Page(s): 58-59

46. Which nation was most apt to desire to intervene in the domestic affairs of other states?

    a. France.
    b. Great Britain.
    c. Prussia.
    d. The United States.

Answer: c Type: M   Page(s): 59

47. The great powers of Europe were most afraid of what kind of political development?

    a. French power.
    b. Free trade.
    c. Monarchism.
    d. The Industrial Revolution.

    Answer: a Type: M   Page(s): 59

48. The Industrial Revolution began in

    a. France.
    b. Russia.
    c. The United States.
    d. Great Britain.

    Answer: d Type: M   Page(s): 61

49. How was family life transformed by the advent of the Industrial Revolution?

    a. Families moved frequently as parents sought jobs.
    b. Women were not allowed to work.
    c. The living conditions of poor families quickly improved and brought them into the middle class.
    d. There was an increase in the number of extended-family groups.

    Answer: a Type: M   Page(s): 61

50. Which of the following developments in warfare was a result of the Industrial Revolution?

    a. Machine guns and long-range artillery.
    b. The targeting of economic and civilian targets during war.
    c. The need for public support for the success of military campaigns.
    d. All of the above.

    Answer: d Type: M   Page(s): 62

51. One of the economic effects of the Industrial Revolution was

    a. Increased British support for mercantilism and protectionism.
    b. Increased seagoing commerce.
    c. The end of colonization.
    d. The end of competition over markets and raw materials.

    Answer: b Type: M   Page(s): 62-63

Harcourt Brace & Company

52. One of the political effects of the Industrial Revolution was

   a. A decrease in domestic unrest.
   b. A decrease in demands for government involvement in the economy.
   c. An increase in the number of peasants moving to urban areas.
   d. An increase in democracy in authoritarian states such as Russia.

   Answer: c Type: M   Page(s): 63

53. The events of 1848 demonstrated that

   a. The Concert of Europe was incapable of controlling the internal threats faced by
      conservative monarchies.
   b. The public in many nations was becoming increasingly active politically.
   c. There were increased social divisions as a result of the Industrial Revolution which
      created a great deal of tension.
   d. All of the above.
   e. None of the above.

   Answer: d Type: M   Page(s): 63-64

54. One of the reasons why the monarchist regimes of central and eastern Europe regained
   control over their domains after the upheavals of 1848 was that

   a. The demands of many liberal ideologues alienated the working class.
   b. The increased radicalism of the working class scared the middle class.
   c. The middle class joined forces with the radical working class groups.
   d. The middle class was unwilling to sacrifice political freedoms for the sake of
      stability.

   Answer: b Type: M   Page(s): 64

55. Russia and Great Britain fought a war over the future of what country in the
   mid-nineteenth century?

   a. The Holy Roman Empire.
   b. The Austro-Hungarian Empire.
   c. The Ottoman Empire.
   d. France.

   Answer: c Type: M   Page(s): 65

Harcourt Brace & Company

56. Which two nations unified in the second half of the nineteenth century?

    a. Germany and Italy.
    b. The Netherlands and Belgium.
    c. The Ottoman Empire and the Austro-Hungarian Empire.
    d. Canada and the United States.

    Answer: a   Type: M   Page(s): 66

57. The unification of Italy

    a. Created a great deal of friction between France and Austria.
    b. Created a politically united and economically developed new state.
    c. Did not lead to great-power status for Italy.
    d. Did not produce a profound revision of the territorial settlement of 1815.

    Answer: c   Type: M   Page(s): 66

58. Otto von Bismarck would be best characterized as

    a. An aristocratic landlord.
    b. A foreign policy idealist.
    c. Interested in diminishing the status and importance of the monarch in Prussia.
    d. A liberal democrat.
    e. All of the above.

    Answer: a   Type: M   Page(s): 66

59. Otto von Bismarck and Prussia defeated which set of nations in the process of German
    unification?

    a. Austria, Great Britain and Russia.
    b. Austria, France and Denmark.
    c. France, Great Britain and Russia.
    d. Denmark, Russia and Great Britain.

    Answer: b   Type: M   Page(s): 68

60. While he was able to unite Germany as a result of his victory over France, Bismarck did
    which of the following after the Franco-Prussian war that later hurt German interests?

    a. Engineered a peace settlement that was far too lenient on France.
    b. Ignored the wishes of the German emperor and people in the peace settlement.
    c. Gave up the disputed provinces of Alsace and Lorraine.
    d. Allowed nationalism and chauvinism to undermine his realpolitik foreign policy.

    Answer: d   Type: M   Page(s): 70

61. Which of the following was not among the consequences German unification had on European politics?

    a. It radically shifted the balance of power in Europe.
    b. It influenced strategy and military organization.
    c. It led to repeated attempts by the powers Germany defeated to regain their territory.
    d. It created the strongest country in Europe.

    Answer: c Type: M Page(s): 70

62. The pax Brittanica was enabled and caused by

    a. An agreement by all European powers that they each had equal power.
    b. Europeans bringing foreign diseases to lands where the inhabitants lacked the proper immunities.
    c. Britain's naval power and position as the world's center of trade.
    d. The decline of British power to the point that it was vulnerable to attack.

    Answer: c Type: M Page(s): 72

63. British control of Africa was not assisted by

    a. The ambitions of diamond prospector Cecil Rhodes to create British domination of all of Africa.
    b. The establishment of Northern and Southern Rhodesia.
    c. Their victory over France for control of Egypt.
    d. The Boer War between the Dutch Afrikaners and the British in South Africa
    e. Both c and d.

    Answer: e Type: M Page(s): 72

64. Which of the following did not seek to become a colonial power in Africa?

    a. France
    b. Germany
    c. Italy
    d. Ottoman Empire

    Answer: d Type: M Page(s): 73

65. What did the French see as their role in nineteenth-century colonialism?

   a. To trade for food and other essential supplies not found in France.
   b. To get slaves to bring back to France.
   c. To bring culture and civilization to the backward people of their colonies.
   d. To encourage emigration from France to these new colonies.
   e. None of the above.

   Answer: c   Type: M   Page(s): 73

66. Which of the following was not a reason for the collapse of the Ottoman Empire?

   a. Ottoman internal attempts at reform.
   b. Attempts by the Great Powers to protect their interests in Ottoman-controlled areas.
   c. Intensified nationalism in Greece and the Balkans.
   d. Attacks from Russia and Austria to vying for control of the Empire.

   Answer: a   Type: M   Page(s): 74

67. Germany used a system of alliances to

   a. Moderate the demands of its allies.
   b. Discourage the formation of coalitions of opponents.
   c. Prevent the escalation of local conflicts into general war.
   d. All of the above.

   Answer: d   Type: M   Page(s): 75

68. Which factor played a major role in the decline of Bismarck's alliance system?

   a. German domination over the Balkans.
   b. The irreconcilable interests of Austria-Hungary and Russia.
   c. The inflexibility of Bismarck's foreign policies.
   d. Bismarck's lack of diplomatic skill.

   Answer: b   Type: M   Page(s): 75-76

69. One thing that most international relations scholars agree on is that

   a. The balance of power system is the most effective at promoting peace.
   b. The Pax Brittanica was the most violent period of the nineteenth century.
   c. War rarely occurs under balance of power and imbalance of power systems.
   d. No state will willingly allow any other to achieve domination.

   Answer: d   Type: M   Page(s): 77

Harcourt Brace & Company

70. Institutions, such as the Concert of Europe, were not successful at preventing what types of conflicts?

   a. Conflicts arising from security concerns.
   b. Conflicts arising from calculations of strategic interests.
   c. Conflicts arising from nationalism.
   d. All of the above.
   e. None of the above.

   Answer: c Type: M Page(s): 78

71. Which statement best characterizes the state of European affairs at the end of the nineteenth century?

   a. The spread of European power throughout the world ensured that democracy and capitalism would triumph.
   b. The spread of European power throughout the world ensured that conflicts in Europe might threaten the peace of the entire world.
   c. The stability of the European system would promote peace for years to come.
   d. The stability of the European system would create independence for nations in Asia and Africa.

   Answer: b Type: M Page(s): 78

72. The rapid pace of industrialization during the nineteenth century often led to

   a. Social dislocation and turmoil.
   b. Growth of cities.
   c. New and more lethal weaponry.
   d. All of the above.
   e. None of the above.

   Answer: d Type: M Page(s): 79

73. At the end of the nineteenth century, which forces helped to create a potentially explosive international political system?

   a. Industrialization.
   b. The end of the German Empire.
   c. The triumph of democracy.
   d. The decrease in nationalism.

   Answer: a Type: M Page(s): 79

TRUE/FALSE

74. Laws and treaties during the feudal times were scrupulously adhered to because of the blood-kinship ties of monarchs.

    a. True
    b. False

    Answer: B Type: T   Page(s): 30

75. Religious authorities played a very active role in politics during feudal times.

    a. True
    b. False

    Answer: A Type: T   Page(s): 30-31

76. Taxation was often a greater threat to trade during feudal times than was piracy or shipwreck.

    a. True
    b. False

    Answer: A Type: T   Page(s): 31

77. Religion provided the major motivation for the warring nations in the Thirty Years' War

    a. True
    b. False

    Answer: B Type: T   Page(s): 33

78. In the early days of Spanish expansion to America, the Spanish exchanged technology and culture in a friendly atmosphere with the indigenous peoples.

    a. True
    b. False

    Answer: B Type: T   Page(s): 37

Harcourt Brace & Company

79. In general, eighteenth century warfare was fought by limited means for limited objectives.

    a. True
    b. False

    Answer: A Type: T   Page(s): 40

80. States tried to preserve a balance of power by allying themselves with weaker nations.

    a. True
    b. False

    Answer: A Type: T   Page(s): 42

81. Throughout the eighteenth century, France was the most powerful state in Europe.

    a. True
    b. False

    Answer: A Type: T   Page(s): 46

82. Nationalism defines a country in terms of its rulers rather than in terms of its people.

    a. True
    b. False

    Answer: B Type: T   Page(s): 47

83. After the Vienna peace conference ending the Napoleonic wars, France did not lose its great power status.

    a. True
    b. False

    Answer: A Type: T   Page(s): 55

84. The years 1815-1914 were among the most violent in Europe's history.

    a. True
    b. False

    Answer: B Type: T   Page(s): 58

85. Before the 17th century, territory was not divided into states.

    a. True
    b. False

    Answer: A   Type: T   Page(s): 60

86. The increased involvement of civil society in politics as a result of the Industrial Revolution very quickly brought about greater democratization of societies.

    a. True
    b. False

    Answer: B   Type: T   Page(s): 62

87. Industrialization spread unevenly throughout Europe.

    a. True
    b. False

    Answer: A   Type: T   Page(s): 63

88. Elites in all nations consistently opposed the forces of nationalism.

    a. True
    b. False

    Answer: B   Type: T   Page(s): 64

89. After unification, Italy became one of the great powers of Europe.

    a. True
    b. False

    Answer: B   Type: T   Page(s): 66

90. After German unification, Austria merged with Turkey to form the Austro-Hungarian Empire.

    a. True
    b. False

    Answer: B   Type: T   Page(s): 68

Harcourt Brace & Company

91. Germany returned the provinces of Alsace and Lorraine to France at the conclusion of the Franco-Prussian War.

    a. True
    b. False

    Answer: B Type: T   Page(s): 68

92. The Industrial Revolution made imperialism even more beneficial for industrializing nations.

    a. True
    b. False

    Answer: A Type: T   Page(s): 70

93. The Balkans have been one of the most peaceful areas of Europe.

    a. True
    b. False

    Answer: B Type: T   Page(s): 74

94. The strategic objective of Bismarck's alliance system was to keep Germany, Austria-Hungary and Russia together and France isolated.

    a. True
    b. False

    Answer: A Type: T   Page(s): 75

95. The Three Emperors' Alliance was devised by Great Britain.

    a. True
    b. False

    Answer: B Type: T   Page(s): 75

96. Revanchism is the desire for peaceful cooperation with one's adversaries.

    a. True
    b. False

    Answer: B Type: T   Page(s): 75

97. The term "balance of power" refers to both the relative military and economic strengths of great powers.

    a. True
    b. False

    Answer: A Type: T   Page(s): 76

98. Toward the end of the nineteenth century, the stability which the Concert of Europe created was firmly established.

    a. True
    b. False

    Answer: B Type: T   Page(s): 77

99. The evidence to support the contention that a balance of power promotes peace is conclusive.

    a. True
    b. False

    Answer: B Type: T   Page(s): 76-77

100. The period of 1648-1789 was one of competition among the major monarchies of Europe.

    a. True
    b. False

    Answer: A Type: T   Page(s): 78

Harcourt Brace & Company

Chapter 3

The World Wars

1. The world wars brought which kind(s) of change(s) to international relations?

   a. Social.
   b. Political.
   c. Economic.
   d. Technological.
   e. All of the above.

   Answer: e Type: M   Page(s): 84

2. The consequences of the world wars included

   a. A weakening of the case for women's rights.
   b. The exclusion of racial and ethnic minorities from the military.
   c. The strengthening of the case for women's rights.
   d. Decreased reliance on the mobilization of men into the army.

   Answer: c Type: M   Page(s): 84

3. The Treaty of Versailles officially ended

   a. World War II.
   b. World War I.
   c. The Spanish Civil War.
   d. The Russian Revolution.

   Answer: b Type: M   Page(s): 84

Harcourt Brace & Company

4. Which of the following was not among the factors that contributed to the outbreak of World War I?

   a. The growing power of France.
   b. The changing economic balance of power.
   c. Ascendant nationalism.
   d. The cult of the offensive.
   e. None of the above.

Answer: a   Type: M   Page(s): 85

5. One of the advantages Germany enjoyed from being at the center of Europe was

   a. It had fewer points of potential conflict with other powers.
   b. It did not have to fear encirclement by its adversaries.
   c. It could concentrate its military forces to meet a threat from any direction.
   d. Its shared border with Great Britain.

Answer: c   Type: M   Page(s): 85

6. Kaiser Wilhelm made what kind of changes in German foreign policy after he dismissed Bismarck?

   a. Germany began to forge closer relations with Great Britain.
   b. Germany de-emphasized naval power.
   c. Germany developed closer ties with Austria-Hungary.
   d. Germany developed better relations with Russia.
   e. All of the above.

Answer: c   Type: M   Page(s): 86

7. The French alliance with Russia prior to World War I had which of the following consequences?

   a. It countered the increased power of Great Britain.
   b. Created an alliance system which locked the great powers into military commitments.
   c. Spain regarded it as the first step in a hostile encirclement.
   d. It represented as extension of the Triple Alliance.

Answer: b   Type: M   Page(s): 86

Harcourt Brace & Company

8. Increasing friendship between Japan and Great Britain before World War I helped lead to which of the following?

   a. The two nations agreed to go to war against Russia.
   b. It led to a worsening of relations between Great Britain and France.
   c. It helped create a flexible set of alliances.
   d. It helped create an alliance between Great Britain and France.

   Answer: d Type: M   Page(s): 87

9. Which of the following nations were on the verge of losing great power status prior to World War I?

   a. Russia.
   b. Austria-Hungary.
   c. The Ottoman Empire.
   d. All of the above.
   e. None of the above.

   Answer: d Type: M   Page(s): 87

10. The system of alliances that existed prior to World War I ensured that

    a. If two of the great powers went to war, the others would follow.
    b. Each state could remain flexible in its choice of alliance partners.
    c. Major power war could be prevented.
    d. The Triple Alliance held the balance of power in Europe.

    Answer: a Type: M   Page(s): 87

11. Prior to World War I

    a. Population growth was greater than the growth in industrial production.
    b. The growth in industrial production was spread evenly throughout Europe.
    c. The growth in industrial production outstripped the growth in population.
    d. Increased industrial growth decreased the competition for resources.

    Answer: c Type: M   Page(s): 88

12. Prior to World War I, the most powerful economic power in Europe was

    a. France.
    b. Great Britain.
    c. Russia.
    d. Germany.

    Answer: d Type: M   Page(s): 88

13. The main objective of European alliances prior to World War I was to

    a. Contain French expansionism.
    b. Prevent the spread of Russian communism.
    c. Reduce British naval supremacy.
    d. Contain German expansionism.

    Answer: d Type: M   Page(s): 88

14. The most powerful political doctrine of the nineteenth and early twentieth centuries wa

    a. Communism.
    b. Nationalism.
    c. Imperialism.
    d. Expansionism.

    Answer: b Type: M   Page(s): 89

15. The empire that felt most threatened by nationalist movements was

    a. The Ottoman Empire.
    b. The German Empire.
    c. The Austro-Hungarian Empire.
    d. The Russian Empire.

    Answer: c Type: M   Page(s): 89

16. The Austro-Hungarian Empire was afraid of

    a. Serbian nationalism.
    b. French encroachment.
    c. German revanchism.
    d. Swedish meatballs.
    e. All of the above.

    Answer: a Type: M   Page(s): 89-90

17. Which nation felt that it had been left out of the race for colonies prior to World War I?

    a. France.
    b. Germany.
    c. Great Britain.
    d. Japan.

    Answer: b Type: M   Page(s): 90

Harcourt Brace & Company

18. Colonial antagonism was especially acute between

    a. Great Britain and France.
    b. Great Britain and Germany.
    c. France and Germany.
    d. Russia and Austria-Hungary.

    Answer: b Type: M   Page(s): 90

19. German leaders were concerned about

    a. Improved relations between Russia and France.
    b. A two-front war.
    c. How quickly German armies could be mobilized.
    d. All of the above.
    e. None of the above.

    Answer: d Type: M   Page(s): 90-91

20. Which of the following helps to explain why the cult of the offensive became the primary doctrine for European military leaders?

    a. Recent experiences in the American Civil War and the Boer War.
    b. Most European leaders did not expect the next war would be like the last.
    c. The expansion of railroads.
    d. Generals were not able to oversee and control their troops.

    Answer: c Type: M   Page(s): 91

21. The cult of the offensive before World War I enhanced

    a. The security dilemma.
    b. Nationalism.
    c. The Industrial Revolution.
    d. Colonialism.

    Answer: a Type: M   Page(s): 91

22. The success of Germany's Schlieffen Plan was dependent on

    a. The defeat of Great Britain before war against Russia.
    b. Rapid mobilization of troops and equipment.
    c. The German alliance with France.
    d. All of the above.

    Answer: b Type: M   Page(s): 92

23. The crisis over Morocco in the early 1900s involved

    a. Germany and Great Britain.
    b. France and Great Britain.
    c. Germany and France.
    d. Germany and Russia.

    Answer: c Type: M Page(s): 92

24. The region of Europe which experienced a series of crises prior to World War I was

    a. Morocco.
    b. Germany.
    c. The Benelux.
    d. The Balkans.

    Answer: d Type: M Page(s): 93

25. When Archduke Franz Ferdinand was assassinated in Sarajevo, the Austro-Hungarian Empire decided to fix the blame on

    a. Germany.
    b. Serbia.
    c. The Ottoman Empire.
    d. Morocco.

    Answer: b Type: M Page(s): 93

26. Which European nation believed that it might lose its great power status if it did not stand firm against the Austro-Hungarian Empire?

    a. Russia.
    b. Germany.
    c. France.
    d. Great Britain.

    Answer: a Type: M Page(s): 93

Harcourt Brace & Company

27. All the great powers of Europe

    a. Subscribed to the cult of the offensive.
    b. Could not sustain mobilization for long without significant economic damage.
    c. Believed that whoever attacked first in a general war would gain a decisive advantage.
    d. All of the above.
    e. None of the above.

    Answer: d Type: M Page(s): 95

28. German violation of what country's neutrality brought Great Britain into World War I?

    a. France.
    b. Belgium.
    c. Spain.
    d. Serbia.

    Answer: b Type: M Page(s): 95

29. Through most of the four years of fighting during World War I, the trench lines in Western Europe never shifted by more than

    a. 10 miles.
    b. 100 miles.
    c. 500 miles.
    d. 50 miles.

    Answer: a Type: M Page(s): 95

30. Which of the following had a decisive impact on warfare during World War I?

    a. Poison gas.
    b. Tanks.
    c. Aircraft.
    d. All of the above.
    e. None of the above.

    Answer: e Type: M Page(s): 96-97

31. The Entente Powers consisted of

    a. France, Germany and Austria-Hungary.
    b. Germany, Austria-Hungary and the Ottoman Empire.
    c. France, Great Britain and Russia.
    d. France, Great Britain and Austria-Hungary.

    Answer: c Type: M   Page(s): 97

32. The Central Powers consisted of

    a. France, Germany and Austria-Hungary.
    b. Germany, Austria-Hungary and the Ottoman Empire.
    c. France, Great Britain and Russia.
    d. France, Great Britain and Austria-Hungary.

    Answer: b Type: M / Page(s): 97

33. Among the many problems Russia experienced during World I that made it ripe for
    revolution was

    a. Insufficient supplies of weapons, ammunition and food for the troops.
    b. Inflation.
    c. Increasing the draft of men into the army.
    d. All of the above.
    e. None of the above.

    Answer: d Type: M   Page(s): 97

34. When the Bolsheviks took power in Russia

    a. They continued the fight against Germany.
    b. They declared war on the United States.
    c. They made peace with Germany.
    d. They switched sides in the war.

    Answer: c Type: M   Page(s): 98

35. Which event was responsible for the United States' entry into World War I?

    a. Germany's policy of unrestricted submarine warfare.
    b. The Russian revolution.
    c. The imminent defeat of Great Britain and France.
    d. American isolationism.
    e. All of the above.

    Answer: a Type: M   Page(s): 98

36. World War I would best be characterized as a

    a. Total war.
    b. War of attrition.
    c. Defensive war.
    d. All of the above.

Answer: d Type: M   Page(s): 95-99

37. Which statement describes the effect of the United States' entry into World War I?

    a. It committed more troops to the fighting than any other nation.
    b. It boosted the morale of Allied soldiers and civilians.
    c. It helped precipitate the Russian revolution.
    d. It helped the Allies to finally invade Germany.
    e. All of the above.

Answer: b Type: M   Page(s): 98-99

38. Which of the following nations was not invited to the Paris Peace Conference in 1919?

    a. Germany.
    b. Italy.
    c. France.
    d. The United States.

Answer: a Type: M   Page(s): 99

39. The goals of the participants of the Paris Peace Conference in 1919

    a. Were radically different from the realpolitik policies of the nineteenth century.
    b. Were commensurate with Woodrow Wilson's Fourteen Points.
    c. Often involved the division of territory.
    d. Allowed for a just and fair peace for Germany.

Answer: c Type: M   Page(s): 99

40. Which of the following was not among Woodrow Wilson's Fourteen Points?

    a. Free trade.
    b. Territorial compensation.
    c. Arms reduction.
    d. Self-determination of nations.

Answer: b Type: M   Page(s): 101

Harcourt Brace & Company

41. Woodrow Wilson's Fourteen Points reflected what kind of foreign policy outlook?

    a. Idealism.
    b. Realism.
    c. Realpolitik.
    d. The cult of the offensive.

    Answer: a Type: M   Page(s): 101

42. All but which of the following were part of the Versailles Treaty that Germany was forced to accept?

    a. Germany was held responsible for the war.
    b. Germany had to give some of its territory to help create a new Polish state.
    c. Germany had to accept French and British occupation of the entire German nation.
    d. Germany was forbidden to possess submarines, tanks or an air force.

    Answer: c Type: M   Page(s): 102-103

43. The Austro-Hungarian Empire was divided into a number of new states consistent with the principle of

    a. Realism.
    b. Self-determination.
    c. The Schlieffen Plan.
    d. Comparative advantage.

    Answer: b Type: M   Page(s): 102

44. Which aspect of the Treaty of Versailles were Germans most opposed to?

    a. The reparations Germany was forced to pay France.
    b. The loss of Germany's overseas colonies.
    c. The military occupation of German territory.
    d. The blame assigned to Germany for starting World War I.

    Answer: d Type: M   Page(s): 103

45. As a consequence of the Treaty of Versailles

    a. Germany was permanently weakened.
    b. Germany was partitioned.
    c. Germany was forced to make reparation payments to the Allies.
    d. Germans were united into one state.
    e. All of the above.

    Answer: c Type: M   Page(s): 103

Harcourt Brace & Company

46. Which nation voted to stay out of the League of Nations?

    a. The United States.
    b. France.
    c. Germany.
    d. Poland.

Answer: a   Type: M   Page(s): 105

47. After World War I, the balance of power in Europe was unstable because of all but

    a. The British return to isolationism.
    b. Revolution and civil war in Russia.
    c. The potential for an upsurge in German resentment.
    d. The number of new states in Eastern Europe.

Answer: a   Type: M   Page(s): 105

48. Post-World War I public opinion in France and Great Britain was characterized by the desire to

    a. Punish Germany further for causing World War I.
    b. Increase defense spending.
    c. Blame the war on arms races.
    d. Avoid appeasement.

Answer: c   Type: M   Page(s): 105

49. Which country turned to an extremist nationalist movement to lead its government after World War I?

    a. Great Britain.
    b. Italy.
    c. France.
    d. Czechoslovakia.

Answer: b   Type: M   Page(s): 105

50. One of the effects of the Great Depression was that nations were led to

    a. Open their markets to more foreign goods.
    b. Increase the payment of war reparations.
    c. Resume the colonization of Africa.
    d. Erect trade barriers to protect domestic markets.

Answer: d   Type: M   Page(s): 106

Harcourt Brace & Company

51. Which of the following was not one of the causes of World War II?

    a. The leniency of the Versailles treaty.
    b. The rise of fascism.
    c. The changing balance of power in Europe.
    d. The lack of enforcement of the terms of the Versailles treaty.

    Answer: a Type: M   Page(s): 107

52. Adolf Hitler's ambitions for Germany included

    a. The elimination of inferior races.
    b. Rejection of the territorial settlement in the Versailles treaty.
    c. Lebensraum.
    d. All of the above.
    e. None of the above.

    Answer: d Type: M   Page(s): 108-110

53. Which action, taken by Hitler, violated the terms of the Versailles Treaty?

    a. The holding of a plebiscite in the Saar region.
    b. Compulsory conscription.
    c. The appeasement of France and Great Britain.
    d. Resolving Germany's economic problems.

    Answer: b Type: M   Page(s): 108

54. Great Britain and France were led to appease Hitler because

    a. German military spending was quite low.
    b. Both countries wished to provoke Hitler into war.
    c. Appeasement was a popular policy.
    d. Both countries' economies had recovered from the Great Depression.

    Answer: c Type: M   Page(s): 110

55. Japan undertook what action in the aftermath of World War I?

    a. Territorial expansion.
    b. Alliance with the United States.
    c. War with Germany.
    d. Acceptance of the League of Nation's condemnation of its invasion of China.

    Answer: a Type: M   Page(s): 110

Harcourt Brace & Company

56. The weakness of the League of Nations and the great powers was demonstrated in which of the following incidents?

    a. The Italian invasion of Ethiopia.
    b. The Japanese invasion of China.
    c. The Spanish Civil War.
    d. All of the above.
    e. None of the above.

Answer: d   Type: M   Page(s): 111

57. The Anschluss refers to

    a. The Spanish Civil War.
    b. The annexation of Austria by Germany.
    c. The annexation of Czechoslovakia by Germany.
    d. The Italian invasion of Ethiopia.

Answer: b   Type: M   Page(s): 112

58. Great Britain and France refused to take military action against Germany when Hitler was demanding the Czechoslovakian Sudetenland because

    a. The Soviet Union refused to come to their assistance.
    b. Hitler did not want to force a confrontation over this region of Europe.
    c. It involved a quarrel in a faraway country among people of whom the British and French supposedly knew nothing.
    d. Hitler threatened to invade Great Britain if his demands were not met.

Answer: c   Type: M   Page(s): 112-113

59. The invasion of Czechoslovakia proved to be a turning point in European acceptance of German aggression because

    a. France and Great Britain were ready and willing to help Czechoslovakia defend itself.
    b. The conquest of Czechoslovakia was justified on the basis of self-determination.
    c. Of Germany's acquisition of atomic weapons.
    d. The conquest of Czechoslovakia was not justified on the basis of self-determination.

Answer: d   Type: M   Page(s): 115

60. The non-aggression pact signed by what two nations just prior to World War II stunned the world?

    a. Great Britain and France.
    b. The Soviet Union and Germany.
    c. Great Britain and the United States.
    d. Germany and France.

    Answer: b Type: M Page(s): 115

61. After Hitler invaded Poland, the strategy of France and Great Britain was based upon

    a. Taking advantage of their superior preparation for war.
    b. Accepting Hitler's last peace initiative.
    c. Blockading Germany to prevent it from obtaining raw materials.
    d. Forming an alliance with the Soviet Union.

    Answer: c Type: M Page(s): 116

62. The term given to the German "lightning war" is

    a. Blitzkrieg.
    b. Phony war.
    c. War of attrition.
    d. Anschluss.

    Answer: a Type: M Page(s): 116

63. During the Battle of Britain in 1940

    a. The resolve of the British people was strengthened.
    b. Germany crossed the British channel with an invading army.
    c. Hitler only attacked British naval forces.
    d. The United States joined the war against Germany.

    Answer: a Type: M Page(s): 119

64. Germany's invasion of which country greatly relieved the pressure on Great Britain in 1941?

    a. The United States.
    b. Yugoslavia.
    c. Egypt.
    d. The Soviet Union.

    Answer: d Type: M Page(s): 120

Harcourt Brace & Company

55. Which country was referred to as the "sleeping giant" in the early stages of WWII?

    a. The Soviet Union.
    b. Germany.
    c. Japan.
    d. The United States.
    e. None of the above.

Answer: d Type: M   Page(s): 120

56. Which nation launched "operation Barbarossa?"

    a. Germany.
    b. The United States.
    c. France.
    d. Japan.

Answer: a Type: M   Page(s): 120

57. Which of the following helps explain why Japan decided to go to war against the United States?

    a. At that time Japan's gross domestic product was considerably larger than the United States'.
    b. American economic sanctions.
    c. The Soviet Union had promised to declare war against the United States as well.
    d. All of the above.
    e. None of the above.

Answer: b Type: M   Page(s): 121-122

58. The Allied forces wanted to be certain that the mistakes made at the end of World War I were not repeated and so they pushed for what kind of settlement?

    a. Germany's unconditional surrender.
    b. The destruction of all of Germany.
    c. A restoration of the German monarchy.
    d. Respect for Germany's territorial gains.

Answer: a Type: M   Page(s): 124

Harcourt Brace & Company

69. The "Big Three" leaders of the Allies differed on which of the following issues in 1945

    a. The self-determination of countries liberated by the Soviet Union.
    b. War reparations from Germany.
    c. Russian control over Eastern Europe.
    d. German disarmament.
    e. All of the above.

    Answer: e   Type: M   Page(s): 125

70. Who among the following was not among the Allied leaders in 1945?

    a. Joseph Stalin.
    b. Adolf Hitler.
    c. Clement Atlee.
    d. Harry Truman.

    Answer: b   Type: M   Page(s): 125

71. The "Big Three" leaders who met at Yalta in February 1945 to address important issues regarding post-war Europe were

    a. Churchill, Roosevelt, Stalin.
    b. Hitler, Mussolini, Roosevelt.
    c. Roosevelt, Churchill, Mussolini.
    d. Mussolini, Roosevelt, Stalin.

    Answer: a   Type: M   Page(s): 125

72. Which of the following factors did not influence Harry Truman as he tried to bring the war against Japan to a successful conclusion?

    a. The domestic political cost of an American invasion of Japan.
    b. The necessary participation of the Soviet Union in an invasion of Japan.
    c. The ferocious tenacity with which Japan could be expected to defend its home islands
    d. Japan's possession of atomic weapons.

    Answer: d   Type: M   Page(s): 127-130

73. The U.S. began its secret Manhattan Project in 1942 to

    a. Spy on Germany.
    b. Create an atomic bomb before Germany.
    c. Deter German expansion.
    d. Prepare to defend itself militarily from German invasion.

    Answer: b   Type: M   Page(s): 130

Harcourt Brace & Company

74. Which of the following statements most accurately describes the destruction wrought during World War II?

    a. The total of Soviet war-related deaths was the lowest among the Allied powers.
    b. World War I was more destructive.
    c. The Second World War resulted in the deaths of 40-50 million people.
    d. Civilian casualties were minimal.

Answer: c Type: M   Page(s): 130

75. At the conclusion of World War II

    a. Most of the nations of the world remained neutral.
    b. Very few nations remained neutral.
    c. Fighting had taken place only in Europe and the Pacific.
    d. The United States had suffered more damage than any other nation.

Answer: b Type: M   Page(s): 130

76. Which of the following was not among the consequences of World War II?

    a. The globalization of world politics.
    b. An increase in colonialism.
    c. An increase in nationalism.
    d. The age of European political and economic domination was over.

Answer: b Type: M   Page(s): 131

77. At the end of World War II, which two nations had the resources to contend for global leadership?

    a. Germany and the Soviet Union.
    b. Great Britain and the United States.
    c. The United States and Germany.
    d. The United States and the Soviet Union.

Answer: d Type: M   Page(s): 131

TRUE/FALSE

78. The number of people killed during the two world wars of the twentieth century exceeded 55 million.

    a. True
    b. False

Answer: A Type: T   Page(s): 83

Harcourt Brace & Company

79. Prior to the first world war, European leaders were keenly aware of the impact of political, social and technological developments on international relations.

    a. True
    b. False

    Answer: B Type: T   Page(s): 85

80. Great Britain regarded the supremacy of its ground forces as absolutely necessary to protect itself from invasion.

    a. True
    b. False

    Answer: B Type: T   Page(s): 86

81. Perceptions of political power precede changes in relative economic strength.

    a. True
    b. False

    Answer: B Type: T   Page(s): 88

82. Prior to World War I, few European leaders looked to the United States as a potential counterweight to German expansionism.

    a. True
    b. False

    Answer: A Type: T   Page(s): 88

83. Germany gave Austria-Hungary free rein to deal with Serbia after the assassination of Archduke Franz Ferdinand.

    a. True
    b. False

    Answer: A Type: T   Page(s): 93

Harcourt Brace & Company

84. Serbia accepted most of the demands of Austria-Hungary after the assassination of Archduke Franz Ferdinand.

a. True
b. False

Answer: A Type: T Page(s): 93

85. When Germany sought peace in 1918, no German territory had yet been invaded.

a. True
b. False

Answer: A Type: T Page(s): 99

86. The Treaty of Versailles granted self-determination to all nationalities.

a. True
b. False

Answer: B Type: T Page(s): 103

87. Because France was unsure of the commitment of its alliance partners after World War I, it built the Maginot Line.

a. True
b. False

Answer: A Type: T Page(s): 105

88. Appeasement is a policy aimed at discouraging aggression through the formation of alliances.

a. True
b. False

Answer: B Type: T Page(s): 105

89. Appeasement was a popular policy during the 1930s.

a. True
b. False

Answer: A Type: T Page(s): 110

90. During the Spanish Civil War, Germany and Italy gave assistance to the Nationalist forces, while the Soviet Union aided the Republican forces.

   a. True
   b. False

   Answer: A   Type: T   Page(s): 111

91. The Munich analogy has been used to justify appeasing an adversary's demands.

   a. True
   b. False

   Answer: B   Type: T   Page(s): 114

92. The Munich conference became synonymous with the discredited appeasement policy of British Prime Minister Neville Chamberlain.

   a. True
   b. False

   Answer: A   Type: T   Page(s): 114

93. There was little Great Britain and France could do prior to World War II to defend Poland.

   a. True
   b. False

   Answer: A   Type: T   Page(s): 115

94. The British prime minister who rallied his nation during World War II was Neville Chamberlain.

   a. True
   b. False

   Answer: B   Type: T   Page(s): 118

95. The initial invasion of Europe came in Italy.

   a. True
   b. False

   Answer: A   Type: T   Page(s): 124

Harcourt Brace & Company

96. The Allies spent considerable time planning the balance of power in Europe prior to the end of World War II.

    a. True
    b. False

    Answer: B Type: T   Page(s): 124-125

97. The Holocaust was the official policy of Nazi Germany which made the Jewish people responsible for Germany's post-World War I problems.

    a. True
    b. False

    Answer: A Type: T   Page(s): 127

98. Harry Truman believed that one of the benefits of using atomic weapons against Japan was that it would save Japanese lives that might have been lost in a U.S. invasion.

    a. True
    b. False

    Answer: A Type: T   Page(s): 130

99. The Soviet Union never declared war on Japan.

    a. True
    b. False

    Answer: B Type: T   Page(s): 130

100. It was not immediately clear that the United States and the Soviet Union would be adversaries after the Second World War.

    a. True
    b. False

    Answer: A Type: T   Page(s): 131

Chapter 4

The Cold War

MULTIPLE CHOICE

1. The different periods of rising and falling tensions during the Cold War

   a. Were far less stable compared to the shifting alliances and wars of earlier years.
   b. Were not shaped by the personalities and beliefs of superpower leaders.
   c. Were influenced by domestic politics.
   d. Occurred during a period of a multipolar balance of power.

   Answer: c Type: M   Page(s): 135

2. The structure of the international system during the Cold War can best be characterized as

   a. Bipolar.
   b. Multipolar.
   c. Tripolar.
   d. Imperialist.

   Answer: a Type: M   Page(s): 136

3. Those who argue the Soviet Union should be held responsible for the Cold War believe that

   a. The USSR was inherently aggressive and expansionistic.
   b. The United States should not have adopted the policy of containment.
   c. Stalin's expansionist policies were supported by many people outside the Soviet Union.
   d. The Soviets were content with their subjugation of Eastern Europe.
   e. All of the above.

   Answer: a Type: M   Page(s): 136

Harcourt Brace & Company

4. Those who believe that the United States was primarily responsible for starting the Cold War argue that

    a. The U.S. increased tensions by trying to expand its overseas export markets in Eastern Europe after World War II.
    b. The Soviet Union was forced to react to American misperceptions of an aggressive Soviet foreign policy.
    c. The American use of an atomic bomb at the end of World War II made the Soviets more aware of their own security.
    d. All of the above.
    e. None of the above.

    Answer: d Type: M   Page(s): 137

5. Those who blame the United States for the beginning of the Cold War use which level of analysis?

    a. System.
    b. Domestic.
    c. Individual.
    d. Bipolar.

    Answer: b Type: M   Page(s): 137

6. Which event occurred at the end of World War II, causing alarm for Soviet foreign policy makers?

    a. The American invasion of the Soviet Union.
    b. The German reunification.
    c. The explosion of the atomic bomb.
    d. Detente.
    e. All of the above.

    Answer: c Type: M   Page(s): 137

7. Those who believe that ideological conflict caused the Cold War use what level of analysis?

    a. System.
    b. Domestic.
    c. Individual.
    d. Bipolar.

    Answer: b Type: M   Page(s): 138

Harcourt Brace & Company

8. Which of the following characterizes capitalism?

   a. It is essentially an international system.
   b. It requires a stable international system.
   c. It relies upon the existence of a mobile labor force.
   d. All of the above.

   Answer: d Type: M   Page(s): 138

9. All but which of the following actions by the Truman administration helped create a more tense relationship between the U.S. and the Soviet Union?

   a. Marshall Plan restrictions that made it insulting for the Soviet Union to accept aid.
   b. The formation of the United Nations.
   c. The withholding of economic assistance.
   d. Truman's tough rhetoric with Soviet leaders.

   Answer: b Type: M   Page(s): 139

10. Those who argue that the Cold War was inevitable because the United States and the Soviet Union were the two dominant powers at the conclusion of World War II

   a. Use the domestic level of analysis.
   b. Believed that the two superpowers were not destined to challenge one another.
   c. Believed that if Great Britain had emerged instead of the Soviet Union as the other dominant power, the Cold War still would have occurred.
   d. All of the above.
   e. None of the above.

   Answer: c Type: M   Page(s): 142

11. Those who argue that the Cold War was inevitable because the United States and the Soviet Union were the two dominant powers at the conclusion of World War II use which level of analysis?

   a. Systemic.
   b. Domestic.
   c. Individual.
   d. Marxist.

   Answer: a Type: M   Page(s): 142

Harcourt Brace & Company

12. Those who use the systemic level of analysis to explain the origins of the Cold War point to the importance of

    a. Individual leaders.
    b. Ideological competition.
    c. The responsibility of the Soviet Union for initiating the Cold War.
    d. Zero-sum games and the security dilemma.

    Answer: d   Type: M   Page(s): 142

13. Those who believe that the Cold War was mostly a misunderstanding use which level of analysis?

    a. Domestic.
    b. Systemic.
    c. Individual.
    d. Ideological.

    Answer: b   Type: M   Page(s): 142

14. Those who emphasize the importance of misunderstanding and misperceptions in creating the Cold War argue that

    a. Once the original misperceptions occurred, a process of action-reaction between the superpowers developed.
    b. The superpowers comprehended the basic defensive nature of each other's policies.
    c. Soviet misperceptions of American interests were the cause of the Cold War.
    d. Ideological competition was primarily responsible for the Cold War.

    Answer: a   Type: M   Page(s): 142

15. Which of the following was not one of the nations that the U.S. and the Soviet Union clashed over in the early years of the Cold War?

    a. Iran.
    b. Greece.
    c. Saudi Arabia.
    d. Turkey.

    Answer: c   Type: M   Page(s): 144

16. When the Soviet union retreated from the Middle East in 1946, the Truman administration concluded

    a. That appeasement was the best policy toward the Soviet Union.
    b. That the best way to counter Soviet actions was to stand firm.
    c. That the Soviet Union would cease all its expansionist activities.
    d. That the Soviet Union could be forced out of Eastern Europe.

    Answer: b Type: M   Page(s): 145

17. The decision by which nation in 1947 to reduce its commitments in Greece and Turkey forced the United States to take a much more active international role?

    a. France.
    b. Japan.
    c. Germany.
    d. Great Britain.

    Answer: d Type: M   Page(s): 145

18. The Truman Doctrine called for the United States to

    a. Help nations throughout the world gain and keep their freedom.
    b. Support Greece and Turkey with economic and financial aid.
    c. Assume global and moral responsibility for stopping the Soviet Union.
    d. All of the above.
    e. None of the above.

    Answer: d Type: M   Page(s): 146

19. Who wrote the "Long Telegram" and developed the philosophy of containment?

    a. Harry Truman.
    b. John Foster Dulles.
    c. George Kennan.
    d. Fidel Castro.

    Answer: c Type: M   Page(s): 147

Harcourt Brace & Company

20. The Soviet Union did not accept Marshall Plan assistance because

    a. Stalin feared the revitalization of Great Britain, France and Germany.
    b. Eastern Europe has already recovered from World War II.
    c. Stalin believed an American invasion of the Soviet Union was imminent.
    d. All of the above.
    e. None of the above.

    Answer: a Type: M   Page(s): 148

21. Which of the following was not among the effects of the Marshall Plan?

    a. It restored Britain, France and eventually Germany to major-power status.
    b. It stopped the movement toward European integration.
    c. It thwarted communist control within Western European countries.
    d. It facilitated the eventual integration of West Germany into the European economy.

    Answer: b Type: M   Page(s): 148

22. Stalin became concerned about the independence of which communist regime led by Josip Tito?

    a. Italy.
    b. Czechoslovakia.
    c. Poland.
    d. Yugoslavia.

    Answer: d Type: M   Page(s): 148

23. The communist coup in Czechoslovakia had which of the following effects?

    a. If forced Germany to go to war over the Sudetenland.
    b. It demonstrated that the Soviet Union was not behind the new communist government.
    c. It forced Yugoslavia to establish good relations with the Soviet Union.
    d. It convinced the West that Stalin was not living up to the promises he made at Yalta
    e. All of the above.

    Answer: d Type: M   Page(s): 149

24. The Western powers responded to the Soviet blockade of land access to Western Berlin by

    a. Allowing the Soviets to control the entire city.
    b. Mounting a massive airlift.
    c. Going to war against the Soviet army in Eastern Europe.
    d. Reunifying all of Germany.
    e. All of the above.

Answer: b Type: M   Page(s): 151

25. By joining NATO, the U.S.

    a. Renounced isolationism.
    b. Demonstrated the will to resist Soviet aggression.
    c. Accepted membership in an entangling alliance.
    d. All of the above.

Answer: d Type: M   Page(s): 151

26. During the Chinese Civil War, U.S. foreign policy would be best characterized by which of the following statements?

    a. The United States took the side of the forces led by Mao Tse-tung.
    b. No one in the United States believed that developments in Asia would have an impact on the global balance of power.
    c. The United States' policy was caught between a repressive right-wing government and the possibility of a communist government.
    d. The United States' economic and military assistance was decisive in determining the outcome of the war.

Answer: c Type: M   Page(s): 151-152

27. Stalin believed which of the following about China?

    a. A strong, communist China might pose more of a threat than a divided China under the Nationalists.
    b. Communist strategy was more important than Soviet national interests.
    c. The United States and Communist China would work closely together.
    d. The Soviet Union should never give any assistance to the communists.

Answer: a Type: M   Page(s): 152

28. After World War II, the allies took which of the following actions in Korean?

    a. Allowed for Korean unification under Kim Il Sung.
    b. Divided Korea into U.S. and Soviet zones of occupation.
    c. Allowed for a neutral and united Korea.
    d. Permitted free and open elections in all of Korea.

    Answer: b Type: M   Page(s): 153

29. The invasion of South Korea brought to make the lessons learned

    a. At the end of World War I.
    b. At Munich.
    c. During the Concert of Europe.
    d. During Yugoslavia's break with the Soviet Union.

    Answer: b Type: M   Page(s): 153

30. The intervention of which country in the Korean War was a major blow to the UN forces?

    a. The Soviet Union.
    b. Japan.
    c. China.
    d. The United States.

    Answer: c Type: M   Page(s): 154

31. Korea was a turning point in the Cold War for all but which of the following reasons?

    a. It led to increased pressures in the United States to reduce military spending.
    b. It heightened the confrontation between the United States and the Soviet Union and China in Asia.
    c. It led the United States to believe that all communist threats were detrimental to American interests.
    d. It helped to promote a military buildup in Europe.

    Answer: a Type: M   Page(s): 154

Harcourt Brace & Company

32. Which of the following changes took place in the superpower relationship between 1953 and 1957?

    a. The Eisenhower administration began to emphasize the rollback of communist gains in Eastern Europe.
    b. The Soviet Union was preoccupied with determining who would succeed Stalin.
    c. Eisenhower promoted his "Open Skies" proposal.
    d. The United States was committed to a European-oriented version of American foreign policy.
    e. All of the above.

    Answer: e   Type: M   Page(s): 156-157

33. Nikita Khrushchev's "secret" speech before the Twentieth Congress of the Communist party of the Soviet Union in 1956

    a. Referred to the U.S. as the "evil empire".
    b. Indicated potential changes in Soviet foreign and domestic policy.
    c. Announced the existence of a Soviet nuclear weapon.
    d. Asked the U.S. for economic assistance.

    Answer: b   Type: M   Page(s): 157

34. Which of the following does not describe the situation of many Third World nations in the 1950s?

    a. They had previously been controlled by European colonial empires.
    b. They were politically unstable.
    c. They remained outside of the conflicts of the Cold War.
    d. They established a nonaligned movement.

    Answer: c   Type: M   Page(s): 158-159

35. U.S. intervention has taken place in

    a. Guatemala.
    b. Iran.
    c. South Vietnam.
    d. All of the above.
    e. None of the above.

    Answer: d   Type: M   Page(s): 159

36. Which of the following events did not characterize increasing U.S.-Soviet tension in the late 1950s?

    a. The nonaligned movement.
    b. Conflicts between Taiwan and China.
    c. The Sputnik launch.
    d. The continued division of Berlin.

    Answer: a Type: M Page(s): 160

37. The Sputnik launch had what kind of an effect on international relations?

    a. Americans no longer had to worry about the possibility they could become victims in a nuclear war.
    b. The Eisenhower administration significantly changed its defense policies.
    c. Many believed the U.S. doctrine of Massive Retaliation was no longer viable.
    d. The Soviet Union chose not to publicize its technological advantage.

    Answer: c Type: M Page(s): 161

38. In 1958, when Kruschev demanded that the United States withdraw its forces from West Berlin, the U.S. reacted by

    a. Staging a massive airlift of supplies.
    b. Launching an invasion of East Germany.
    c. Launching Sputnik.
    d. Refusing to accede to Krushchev's demands.

    Answer: d Type: M Page(s): 162

39. Flexible response is the national security policy of

    a. The Eisenhower administration.
    b. Nikita Khrushchev.
    c. Fidel Castro.
    d. The Kennedy Administration.
    e. None of the above.

    Answer: d Type: M Page(s): 165

40. The purpose of the Flexible Response policy was to

    a. Increase American credibility by providing for a wide range of options for dealing with Soviet threats.
    b. Re-emphasize the nuclear strategy of massive Retaliation.
    c. Emphasize the importance of U.S.-Soviet summits.
    d. Utilize the China card in the U.S.-Soviet relationship.

    Answer: a Type: M   Page(s): 165

41. The "missile gap" of the late 1950s

    a. Favored the Soviet Union in the number of nuclear warheads.
    b. Was a result of poor planning by the Eisenhower administration.
    c. Proved to be a hoax.
    d. Created a Soviet advantage in the strategic triad.

    Answer: c Type: M   Page(s): 165

42. The Kennedy administration tried to combat Soviet influence and project an image of American strength by

    a. orchestrating an invasion of China.
    b. Increasing military and economic assistance to the Third World.
    c. Creating a barrier around West Berlin.
    d. Placing nuclear missiles in Cuba.

    Answer: b Type: M   Page(s): 165

43. The Berlin Wall was erected by

    a. West Berlin.
    b. The United States.
    c. The Soviet Union.
    d. East Germany.

    Answer: d Type: M   Page(s): 166

44. The Berlin Wall was erected to

    a. Stem the flow of professional, intellectual, and skilled workers fleeing to the West.
    b. Punish the U.S. for its interveentionalism.
    c. Stop the "brain drain" in East Germany.
    d. Help Khrushchev take over West Germany.
    e. Both a and c.

    Answer: e Type: M   Page(s): 166

45. Which of the following is not one of the reasons Khrushchev placed missiles in Cuba?

    a. He may have been trying to exploit American political weakness.
    b. He may have been trying to redress the U.S.-Soviet strategic balance.
    c. He may have been trying to stop the "brain drain" and flow of refugees.
    d. He may have been trying to forestall another attempt to overthrow Fidel Castro.

    Answer: c Type: M   Page(s): 166

46. Which crisis was the most severe of the Cold War?

    a. The Berlin Blockade.
    b. The Nazi invasion of the Soviet Union.
    c. The U.S. invasion of the Dominican Republic.
    d. The Cuban Missile Crisis.

    Answer: d Type: M   Page(s): 166

47. The United States took what action against the Soviet Union and Cuba during the Cuban Missile Crisis?

    a. A naval blockade around Cuba.
    b. An invasion of Cuba.
    c. Surgical air strikes against Cuba.
    d. Nuclear attack against the Soviet Union.

    Answer: a Type: M   Page(s): 166

48. As a result of the Cuban Missile Crisis, the U.S. promised to

    a. Remove Fidel Castro from power.
    b. Not invade Cuba again.
    c. Remove its nuclear missiles from Cuba.
    d. Remove the Berlin Wall.

    Answer: b Type: M   Page(s): 168

49. The Cuban Missile Crisis had what effect on the Cold War?

    a. Soviet leaders set about challenging America's nuclear superiority.
    b. There was a sudden relaxation of Cold War tensions.
    c. The United States became overconfident of its abilities.
    d. All of the above.
    e. None of the above.

    Answer: d Type: M   Page(s): 168

50. President Johnson initially chose what option to prevent a Vietcong victory in the South?

    a. Withdrawal.
    b. An intermediate levy of escalation.
    c. A full-scale level of escalation.
    d. Use of nuclear weapons.

Answer: b Type: M   Page(s): 170

51. As a result of the war in Vietnam

    a. The American public's enthusiasm for the competition with the Soviet Union increased.
    b. The U.S.'s credibility with its allies was strengthened.
    c. The Soviet Union was able to increase its standing in the Third World.
    d. The U.S.-supported regime in South Vietnam stabilized.
    e. All of the above.

Answer: c Type: M   Page(s): 170

52. The Soviet Union invaded which country in 1986?

    a. Czechoslovakia.
    b. Yugoslavia.
    c. West Germany.
    d. Vietnam.

Answer: a Type: M   Page(s): 171

53. The improvement in the relationship between the U.S. and China had which of the following effects?

    a. It facilitated the American withdrawal from Vietnam.
    b. Communist China was given a permanent seat on the UN Security Council.
    c. The United States began to conduct diplomatic and commercial business with China.
    d. All of the above.
    e. None of the above.

Answer: d Type: M   Page(s): 172

54. During the Nixon administration, the United States did which of the following vis-a-vis the Soviet Union?

    a. Emphasized U.S. nuclear superiority.
    b. Employed a policy of Massive Retaliation.
    c. Pursued a policy of Flexible Response.
    d. Pursued a policy of linkage politics.
    e. All of the above.

    Answer: d   Type: M   Page(s): 173

55. During the 1972 summit, U.S. and U.S.S.R. interests were compatible in which of the following ways?

    a. The superpowers established an alliance against Communist China.
    b. The superpowers wanted to decrease the costs of the escalating arms race.
    c. The superpowers agreed to reunite Germany.
    d. The superpowers agreed to the Brezhnev Doctrine.

    Answer: b   Type: M   Page(s): 174

56. The nuclear arms agreements reached by the Nixon administration with the Soviet Union were designed to

    a. Forbid the further production of nuclear weapons.
    b. Allow for the deployment of Anti-Ballistic Missile Systems.
    c. Stabilize the arms race.
    d. Remove intermediate-range nuclear weapons in Europe.

    Answer: c   Type: M   Page(s): 175

57. For the United States, detente was intended to

    a. Give the Soviet Union a stake in the international system.
    b. Explain its intervention in the Dominican Republic.
    c. Justify the increased arms build-up of the 1980s.
    d. Allow it to establish superiority over the Soviet Union.
    e. All of the above.

    Answer: a   Type: M   Page(s): 175

Harcourt Brace & Company

58. The architect of Ostpolitik was

    a. Richard Nixon.
    b. Leonid Brezhnev.
    c. Josip Broz Tito.
    d. Willy Brandt.

Answer: d Type: M   Page(s): 175

59. For the Soviet Union, detente meant

    a. That the Soviets would make political gains without directly challenging the United States.
    b. The Soviets would promise to halt future aggressive actions.
    c. Cold War competition would continue.
    d. It would continue to support national liberation movements.
    e. All of the above.

Answer: e Type: M   Page(s): 175

60. Which of the following statements best characterized American public opinion in the 1970s?

    a. The public was comfortable dealing with the Soviet Union and ignoring its human rights abuses.
    b. Public confidence in American leaders was quite high.
    c. The Vietnam experience increased the resolve of the public to increase U.S. involvement in international conflicts.
    d. All of the above.
    e. None of the above.

Answer: e Type: M   Page(s): 176

61. During the Yom Kippur War, the United States and the Soviet Union both

    a. Pressured the oil-producing nations of the Middle East to impose an oil embargo.
    b. Engaged in massive resupply operations of their respective allies.
    c. Sent troops into Egypt, resulting in the first clash of U.S. and Soviet forces during the Cold War.
    d. All of the above.
    e. None of the above.

Answer: b Type: M   Page(s): 176

Harcourt Brace & Company

62. All but which of the following characterized Jimmy Carter's foreign policies when he took office?

  a. An increased emphasis on international economic problems.
  b. A decreased emphasis on human rights.
  c. An increased emphasis on improved relations with the Soviet Union.
  d. An increased emphasis on human rights.

  Answer: b Type: M   Page(s): 177

63. Despite Jimmy Carter's efforts, which of the following made it more difficult to establish better relations between the U.S. and the Soviet Union in the late 1970s?

  a. The Soviet invasion of Afghanistan.
  b. The Cuban Missile Crisis.
  c. The Vietnam War.
  d. Ostpolitik.

  Answer: a Type: M   Page(s): 178-179

64. Which of the following statements best characterizes the Soviet invasion of Afghanistan

  a. The Soviets realized that there would be serious international political consequence to their invasion.
  b. The invasion wad denounced by only the United States.
  c. The invasion proved disastrous for Soviet domestic politics.
  d. The invasion was not the first time the Soviets had deployed troops outside Eastern Europe.

  Answer: c Type: M   Page(s): 179

65. The Soviet invasion of Afghanistan resulted in

  a. A U.S. boycott of the 1980 Olympics.
  b. Increased Cold War tensions.
  c. The establishment of an anti-Soviet guerrilla campaign.
  d. Increased defense spending by the United States.
  e. All of the above.

  Answer: e Type: M   Page(s): 179

66. The Reagan Doctrine involved

    a. Increased support for arms control.
    b. Increasing the prominence of international economic problems in U.S. foreign policy.
    c. Abandoning the policy of containment.
    d. Supporting anti-communist insurgencies.
    e. All of the above.

Answer: d Type: M Page(s): 179-180

67. Mikhail Gorbachev's policies of glasnost and perestroika emphasized

    a. Political openness and economic restructuring.
    b. Supporting communist insurgencies.
    c. Soviet domination over Eastern Europe.
    d. The supremacy of communism.

Answer: a Type: M Page(s): 180

68. The popular movement known as Solidarity assumed power in 1989 in what country:

    a. Czechoslovakia.
    b. The Soviet Union.
    c. Poland.
    d. Yugoslavia.

Answer: c Type: M Page(s): 181

69. Which of the following statements does not characterize the collapse of communism in Eastern Europe?

    a. Established regimes took considerable time to topple.
    b. It was brought about by a deterioration in living standards.
    c. The Soviet Union did not use force to keep governments in power.
    d. The liberalization which spread to Eastern Europe originated in the Soviet Union.

Answer: a Type: M Page(s): 181

70. Which of the following is not among the explanations advanced to explain the end of the Cold War?

    a. The "great man" theory of world politics.
    b. Growing similarities in ideologies and ways of life.
    c. The collapse of the Soviet Union.
    d. An increase in bipolarity.

Answer: d Type: M Page(s): 181-184

71. Those who argue that growing ideological similarities between the superpowers helped bring about the end of the Cold War use which level of analysis?

    a. Systemic.
    b. Domestic.
    c. Individual.
    d. Capitalist.

    Answer: b Type: M   Page(s): 182

72. Those who argue that U.S.-Soviet antagonism diminished because of changes in the international balance of power argue that the real winners of the Cold War are

    a. Japan and Germany.
    b. The American people.
    c. The Third World.
    d. The Soviet Union and Eastern Europe.

    Answer: a Type: M   Page(s): 184

73. Compared with previous periods in history

    a. The Cold War era was much more violent.
    b. The Cold War era would best be characterized as multipolar.
    c. The Cold War era was relatively stable.
    d. The Cold War era was free of any international conflict.

    Answer: c Type: M   Page(s): 184

74. The Cold War period could best be characterized as

    a. A period of gradually increasing tensions that did not subside until the collapse of the Soviet Union.
    b. A period of gradually diminishing tensions that ended with the collapse of the Soviet Union.
    c. A period of little tension.
    d. A period of oscillating tension.

    Answer: d Type: M   Page(s): 184-186

Harcourt Brace & Company

75. The world is moving in what direction after the end of the Cold War?

    a. Increased globalization.
    b. Increased fragmentation.
    c. Multipolarity.
    d. All of the above.
    e. None of the above.

Answer: d   Type: M   Page(s): 186

TRUE/FALSE

76. The Soviet dictator whose post-World War II policies many believed contributed to the onset of the Cold War was Nikita Khrushchev.

    a. True
    b. False

Answer: B   Type: T   Page(s): 137

77. Those who believe that competing ideologies were responsible for the Cold War believe that it would have been impossible for the U.S. and the Soviet Union to avoid conflict.

    a. True
    b. False

Answer: A   Type: T   Page(s): 138

78. Those who believe that individual leaders played an important role in bringing about the Cold War believed that President Harry Truman took a far too conciliatory line toward the Soviet Union.

    a. True
    b. False

Answer: B   Type: T   Page(s): 139

79. The argument that the Cold War was primarily the fault of individual leaders portrays U.S. and Soviet leaders as heroes and villains in a great global drama.

    a. True
    b. False

Answer: B   Type: T   Page(s): 140

80. The end of the Cold War has bolstered the view of many that the Soviet Union was responsible for the conflict.

    a. True
    b. False

    Answer: A Type: T   Page(s): 144

81. The U.S. foreign-policy maker who developed the policy of containment was George Kennan

    a. True
    b. False

    Answer: A Type: T   Page(s): 147

82. The Soviet Union was never offered Marshall Plan assistance.

    a. True
    b. False

    Answer: B Type: T   Page(s): 148

83. The Berlin airlift defeated Stalin's attempt to gain control over the whole of Berlin.

    a. True
    b. False

    Answer: A Type: T   Page(s): 151

84. Both the United States and the Soviet Union preferred a divided Germany to a unified Germany under any circumstances.

    a. True
    b. False

    Answer: B Type: T   Page(s): 151

85. The NATO alliance was formed by the Soviet Union.

    a. True
    b. False

    Answer: B Type: T   Page(s): 151

Harcourt Brace & Company

86. NSC-68 called for a major expansion of America's armed forces.

    a. True
    b. False

    Answer: A   Type: T   Page(s): 153

87. The Korean War was an unlimited war.

    a. True
    b. False

    Answer: B   Type: T   Page(s): 154-156

88. The United States demonstrated commitment to the policy of "rolling back" communist gains in the 1950s.

    a. True
    b. False

    Answer: B   Type: T   Page(s): 157

89. The nations of the None-Aligned Movement attempted to play off the superpowers against one another.

    a. True
    b. False

    Answer: A   Type: T   Page(s): 159-160

90. The United States knew the Soviet Union was actually weaker than Soviet leaders admitted in the late 1950s.

    a. True
    b. False

    Answer: A   Type: T   Page(s): 160-161

91. The Cuban Missile Crisis ended with an embarrassing defeat for the United States.

    a. True
    b. False

    Answer: B   Type: T   Page(s): 168

Harcourt Brace & Company

92. Improving American relations with China was a major gain for the Kennedy administration.

    a. True
    b. False

    Answer: B Type: T   Page(s): 172

93. Linkage politics was intended to encourage cooperation and discourage aggression through the use of carrots and sticks.

    a. True
    b. False

    Answer: A Type: T   Page(s): 173

94. Detente means increase in diplomatic tensions.

    a. True
    b. False

    Answer: B Type: T   Page(s): 175

95. The Soviets made great gains in Southeast Asia after the end of the war in Vietnam.

    a. True
    b. False

    Answer: B Type: T   Page(s): 176

96. The Soviet invasion of Afghanistan marked the first time the USSR used its troops outside the satellite states of Eastern Europe.

    a. True
    b. False

    Answer: A Type: T   Page(s): 179

97. Ronald Reagan did not abandon the policy of detente.

    a. True
    b. False

    Answer: B Type: T   Page(s): 179

Harcourt Brace & Company

98. It took considerable time for the communist governments to fall in Eastern Europe.

    a. True
    b. False

    Answer: B Type: T   Page(s): 181

99. The U.S. and the U.S.S.R. never went to war with one another during the Cold War.

    a. True
    b. False

    Answer: A Type: T   Page(s): 186

00. More than any previous period, the Cold War saw the complete globalization of political conflict.

    a. True
    b. False

    Answer: A Type: T   Page(s): 186

Harcourt Brace & Company

Chapter 5

Globalism and Regionalism in a New Era

ULTIPLE CHOICE

1. By 1995, which four countries had the highest GNPs?

   a. U.S., Russia, China, Italy.
   b. U.S., Japan, China, Germany.
   c. Russia, China, Japan, France.
   d. France, UK, Brazil, Spain.

   Answer: b Type: M   Page(s): 191

2. Which of the following is not a trend in the emerging structure of world politics in the New Era?

   a. The U.S. is unchallenged in global military capability.
   b. The rise of Europe and Asia to economic prominence.
   c. The U.S. acting unilaterally as a "world policeman".
   d. None of the above.

   Answer: c Type: M   Page(s): 192

3. Indigenous conflicts are often a result of

   a. Ethnic conflict.
   b. Integration into the global political and economic system.
   c. The Cold War.
   d. The legacy of imperialism.

   Answer: a Type: M   Page(s): 208

Harcourt Brace & Company

4. Indigenous sources of conflict include all but

   a. Religion.
   b. Ethnicity.
   c. Economics.
   d. The Cold War.

   Answer: d   Type: M   Page(s): 208-209

5. Imported sources of conflict include all but

   a. Nationalism.
   b. Imperialism.
   c. Economics.
   d. The Cold War.

   Answer: c   Type: M   Page(s): 209-210

6. Which of the following most accurately describes the impact the U.S. and Soviet Union had on Third World conflicts during the Cold War?

   a. The superpowers caused almost all conflicts.
   b. The superpowers were active in many conflicts.
   c. The superpowers took little interest in Third World conflicts.
   d. Indigenous causes of conflict were the most important.

   Answer: b   Type: M   Page(s): 210

7. Which region of the world was the site of significant interstate conflicts?

   a. The Middle East.
   b. Africa.
   c. Oceania.
   d. Latin America.

   Answer: a   Type: M   Page(s): 211

8. Many of the interstate disputes in the Third World center on

   a. The existence of certain nations as independent states.
   b. Regional balance of power.
   c. The interrelationship between indigenous and imported sources of conflict.
   d. All of the above.
   e. None of the above.

   Answer: d   Type: M   Page(s): 211

9. Conflicts in the Middle East have involved

    a. Several regional balances of power.
    b. Little outside interference.
    c. The absence of nationalist pressures.
    d. Stable, democratic regimes.
    e. All of the above.

Answer: a Type: M   Page(s): 211-212

10. Nationalist aspirations in the Middle East have involved

    a. Zionism.
    b. Pan-Arabism.
    c. Reactions to events in Europe.
    d. All of the above.

Answer: d Type: M   Page(s): 212

11. Before World War I, the Middle East was dominated by

    a. The United States.
    b. The Ottoman Empire.
    c. The German Empire.
    d. Great Britain.

Answer: b Type: M   Page(s): 212

12. As a result of British and French influence in the Middle East in the period after World War I

    a. Independence was granted to all Arab states.
    b. An independent Jewish state was created.
    c. The British and the French drew territorial boundaries to suit their own interests.
    d. The British and the French largely remained out of political conflicts in the region.
    e. All of the above.

Answer: c Type: M   Page(s): 213

13. As a consequence of the first Arab-Israeli war in 1948

    a. Socioeconomic and political tensions within Arab regimes increased.
    b. The Soviet Union and the United States both refused to recognize the new Israeli state.
    c. A new Palestinian state was created.
    d. The Israeli forces were defeated by the combined Arab armies.

    Answer: a Type: M   Page(s): 214

14. In the 1956 crisis over the Suez Canal

    a. Egypt and its Arab allies launched a surprise attack against Israel.
    b. The United States encouraged Israel, Great Britain and France to attack Egypt.
    c. The prestige of the Egyptian leader, Gamal Nasser, was severely diminished.
    d. The United States and the Soviet Union were opposed to the actions of Israel, Great Britain and France.

    Answer: d Type: M   Page(s): 216

15. Which of the following took place during the 1950s in the Middle East?

    a. Authoritarian regimes progressed toward democracy.
    b. The U.S. launched an invasion of Lebanon.
    c. Egypt and Israel united to become one state.
    d. The Soviet Union was largely left on the sidelines with no regional friends.

    Answer: b Type: M   Page(s): 214-216

16. Which statement best describes what took place during the Six-Day War?

    a. The United States' forces defeated the combined Arab armies.
    b. The Soviet Union moved closer to the victor in that war.
    c. The Soviet Union provoked the war.
    d. The pre-war borders were left intact.

    Answer: c Type: M   Page(s): 217

17. As a result of the Six-Day War

    a. The prestige of the Arab World soared.
    b. The United Nations called for Israel to withdraw from the territory it occupied.
    c. The U.S. and the Soviet Union found it impossible to attain a negotiated settlement.
    d. The superpowers stopped arming their Middle Eastern allies.
    e. All of the above.

    Answer: b Type: M   Page(s): 217

18. Which of the following occurred after the rise to power of Anwar Sadat in Egypt?

    a. Egyptian relations with the Soviet Union grew worse.
    b. The West became increasingly dependent on Middle Eastern oil.
    c. Egypt and Syria worked together to change the balance of power in the Middle East.
    d. All of the above.
    e. None of the above.

    Answer: d   Type: M   Page(s): 218

19. During the 1973 October War, which of the following events took place?

    a. As a result of the threatened destruction of Israeli armies, the Soviet Union put its nuclear forces on alert.
    b. Saudi Arabia and other Arab oil-producing nations imposed an oil-embargo on the Soviet Union.
    c. Neither the United States nor the Soviet Union took steps to reinforce their allies.
    d. The United States gave up on trying to bring about a political settlement of the Arab-Israeli conflict.
    e. None of the above.

    Answer: e   Type: M   Page(s): 219-220

20. Gamal Nasser was known for

    a. Espousing pan-Arabism.
    b. Promoting Zionism.
    c. Supporting Apartheid.
    d. Promoting democracy.

    Answer: a   Type: M   Page(s): 215

21. The state that first made peace with Israel was

    a. Jordan.
    b. Syria.
    c. Saudi Arabia.
    d. Egypt.

    Answer: d   Type: M   Page(s): 220

22. In which country was a government led by a close American ally overthrown in 1979?

    a. Israel.
    b. Iran.
    c. Egypt.
    d. Jordan.

    Answer: b Type: M Page(s): 221

23. As a result of instability in the Middle East in the late 1970s

    a. The price of oil decreased.
    b. The balance of power finally stabilized.
    c. The industrialized economies went into recession.
    d. More Arab states made peace with Israel.

    Answer: c Type: M Page(s): 220

24. Which of the following occurred during the war between Iraq and Iran?

    a. The war was started by Iran to prevent the spread of the Iraqi revolution.
    b. The Arab world and the United States came to the aid of Iran.
    c. Iraq decisively defeated Iran.
    d. Arab states regained territory lost during the Six-Day War.
    e. None of the above.

    Answer: e Type: M Page(s): 221

25. In 1982, Israel launched an invasion of

    a. Egypt.
    b. Iran.
    c. Lebanon.
    d. Syria.

    Answer: c Type: M Page(s): 221

26. Which of the following was not one of the important trends of the 1980s that had a considerable impact on Middle Eastern politics?

    a. The decline and demise of the Soviet Union.
    b. The peace agreement between the PLO and Israel.
    c. The Palestinian intifada.
    d. The growing strength of Iraq.

    Answer: b Type: M Page(s): 222

Harcourt Brace & Company

27. Arab-Israeli peace talks were reinvigorated by

    a. The rise of oil prices.
    b. The Iran-Iraq war.
    c. Israel's invasion of Lebanon.
    d. The decline of the Soviet Union.

Answer: d Type: M   Page(s): 223

28. As a consequence of the collapse of the Soviet Union

    a. Conflicts in the Middle East have largely disappeared.
    b. The Palestinians began their intifada uprising.
    c. The United States was able to lead a coalition to reverse the Iraqi invasion of Kuwait.
    d. Iraq started its war against Iran.

Answer: c Type: M   Page(s): 222-223

29. The international relations of South Asia have been dominated by

    a. Iran and Iraq.
    b. North and South Korea.
    c. India and Pakistan.
    d. North and South Vietnam.

Answer: c Type: M   Page(s): 224

30. Which of the following does not characterize the political conflicts in South Asia?

    a. Superpower involvement.
    b. Divisions along religious lines.
    c. Several interstate wars.
    d. Little if any concern over territory.

Answer: d Type: M   Page(s): 224

31. India's foreign policy has been characterized by

    a. Non-alignment.
    b. Pan-Arabism.
    c. Alliance with the United States.
    d. Alliance with China.

Answer: a Type: M   Page(s): 228

32. Both India and Pakistan

    a. Joined into an alliance with the United States.
    b. Received assistance from both superpowers.
    c. Fought against China.
    d. Practiced non-alignment.

    Answer: b Type: M   Page(s): 228

33. India and Pakistan have quarreled over

    a. The Gaza Strip.
    b. Jerusalem.
    c. Kashmir.
    d. China.

    Answer: c Type: M   Page(s): 225-228

34. Conflicts between India and Pakistan during the 1960s were characterized by which of th following?

    a. Pakistan refrained from trying to destabilize territory whose control it disputed with India.
    b. Both superpowers introduced their own military forces into the conflicts.
    c. India and Pakistan made significant political and economic gains as a result of thes conflicts.
    d. China and Pakistan formed closer ties with one another as a result of their mutual suspicion of India.

    Answer: d Type: M   Page(s): 228

35. War erupted between India and Pakistan in 1971 over

    a. The creation of the new state of Bangladesh.
    b. India's explosion of a nuclear device.
    c. U.S. and Soviet interventionism.
    d. Chinese control of Tibet.

    Answer: a Type: M   Page(s): 229-230

Harcourt Brace & Company

36. Which nation conducted a "peaceful nuclear explosion" in 1974?

    a. Pakistan.
    b. Israel.
    c. India.
    d. North Korea.

    Answer: c Type: M   Page(s): 230

37. Which event in 1979 brought the United States and Pakistan closer together?

    a. The Persian Gulf War.
    b. The Soviet invasion of Afghanistan.
    c. The creation of the new state of Bangladesh.
    d. India's explosion of a nuclear device.

    Answer: b Type: M   Page(s): 230

38. Which of the following problems does India face as a major regional power?

    a. It faces a good deal of internal dissension.
    b. It faces the combined opposition of Pakistan and China.
    c. The collapse of the Soviet Union has deprived India of a major ally.
    d. All of the above.
    e. None of the above.

    Answer: d Type: M   Page(s): 230-231

39. India sent troops into what island nation in the 1980s?

    a. Pakistan.
    b. Japan.
    c. Sri Lanka.
    d. Bangladesh.

    Answer: c Type: M   Page(s): 231

40. Which of the following features does not characterize international relations in East Asia since World War II?

    a. The independence of formerly colonized Asian countries.
    b. The emergence of a new and powerful Communist China.
    c. The global rivalry between the superpowers.
    d. The acquisition of nuclear weapons by all major powers in the region.

    Answer: d Type: M   Page(s): 232

41. Tensions in East Asia in the period immediately following the Second World War revolved around

    a. Civil war in the Soviet Union.
    b. Conflict over the Korean peninsula.
    c. The Sino-Soviet split.
    d. U.S. avoidance of alliance with East Asian nations.

    Answer: b Type: M   Page(s): 232

42. When the Communists won the Chinese civil war, the former government escaped to what island in which it still holds power to this day?

    a. Sri Lanka.
    b. Korea.
    c. Taiwan.
    d. Vietnam.

    Answer: c Type: M   Page(s): 233

43. Relations between the Soviet Union and China worsened in the late 1950s as a result of

    a. The Korean War.
    b. Lack of Soviet assistance in China's quest to build atomic weapons.
    c. Nixon's visit to China.
    d. Detente between the United States and the Soviet Union.
    e. The USSR's weak support for China's attempt to capture Taiwan.

    Answer: both b and e Type: M   Page(s): 233

44. Which of the following best characterizes China's foreign policies during the 1960s?

    a. China supported many "peoples' wars" in East Asia.
    b. China sided with the United States during the Vietnam War.
    c. China allowed the Soviet Union to assume dominant leadership of world Communism.
    d. China invaded and gained possession of Taiwan.

    Answer: a Type: M   Page(s): 233-234

Harcourt Brace & Company

45. What event helped to contribute to the Chinese-American rapprochement?

    a. China's return from self-imposed isolation.
    b. Chinese-Soviet border clashes.
    c. Richard Nixon's commitment to improving U.S. relations with China.
    d. All of the above.
    e. None of the above.

    Answer: d Type: M Page(s): 234

46. Which of the following occurred as a result of the Chinese-American rapprochement?

    a. Border tensions escalated into war between China and the Soviet Union.
    b. The U.S. hoped both the Soviet Union and China would help it end the Vietnam War.
    c. It led to a deterioration of relations between China and many other East Asian nations.
    d. It gained the Soviet Union many new friends and allies in East Asia.

    Answer: b Type: M Page(s): 235

47. After the United States pulled its forces out of Vietnam

    a. Several nations in the region were taken over by communist forces.
    b. China became the principal ally of Vietnam.
    c. Vietnam remained a divided nation until the end of the Cold War.
    d. All of the above.
    e. None of the above.

    Answer: a Type: M Page(s): 235

48. Vietnam invaded what nation in the late 1970s and set up a puppet regime?

    a. China.
    b. India.
    c. Cambodia.
    d. Korea.

    Answer: c Type: M Page(s): 236

49. As a result of the Soviet invasion of Afghanistan

    a. Chinese relations with the USSR dramatically improved.
    b. Chinese relations with Japan and the United States were severely strained.
    c. Relations between China and Pakistan deteriorated.
    d. The United States, China and Japan moved closer together.

    Answer: d Type: M Page(s): 237

50. In the early 1980s, China's relationship with the ASEAN countries imrpoved dramatically due to

    a. The election of Ronald Reagan.
    b. The perception of a new Soviet threat.
    c. The detorioration of relations between the U.S. and the USSR.
    d. China's incasion of Vietnam.

    Answer: b   Type: M   Page(s): 237

51. When Mikhail Gorbachev came to power in the Soviet Union

    a. Relations with China worsened.
    b. The Soviet Union attempted to improve relations with both the United States and China.
    c. Relations with most South-East Asian nations deteriorated.
    d. All of the above.
    e. None of the above.

    Answer: b   Type: M   Page(s): 238

52. The normalization of relations between China and the Soviet Union under Gorbachev resulted in

    a. Soviet withdrawal of military resources from Vietnam.
    b. Escalation of Soviet involvement in Afghanistan.
    c. Increased tensions between China and Vietnam.
    d. Worsened relations with the United States.

    Answer: a   Type: M   Page(s): 238

53. Which communist nation brutally repressed a pro-democratic movement in 1989?

    a. The Soviet Union.
    b. Vietnam.
    c. China.
    d. Japan.

    Answer: c   Type: M   Page(s): 238

54. The end of the Cold War helped bring about an end to civil war in which Asian nation in the 1990s?

a. China.
b. Cambodia.
c. Vietnam.
d. Japan.

Answer: b Type: M   Page(s): 238

55. The United States has undertaken what policy in regard to Asia after the end of the Cold War?

a. Build-up of its military forces in Japan, the Philippines and South Korea.
b. Decrease of its trade with ASEAN nations.
c. Removal of its military presence in East Asia.
d. All of the above.
e. None of the above.

Answer: e Type: M   Page(s): 239

56. With the disappearance of the U.S.-Soviet rivalry, East Asia most resembles

a. A bipolar system.
b. An imperialist system.
c. A multipolar system.
d. A hegemonic system.

Answer: c Type: M   Page(s): 242

57. Interdependence has taken international cooperation to new heights in which two particular areas?

a. Trade & environment.
b. Environment & immigration.
c. Military & trade.
d. Immigration & military.
e. AIDS research & trade.

Answer: a Type: M   Page(s): 243

58. The drain of resources caused by international conflicts in the Third World may best be alleviated by

    a. Regional hegemony.
    b. Democracy.
    c. Communism.
    d. International institutions.

    Answer: d Type: M   Page(s): 243

59. The three balances of power in the Middle East have included all but which of the following?

    a. Arab-Arab.
    b. Arab-Israeli.
    c. Sub-Saharan Africa vs. Arab.
    d. Arab-Iranian.

    Answer: c Type: M   Page(s): 212

60. The Balfour Declaration concerned the establishment of

    a. A Jewish state in Palestine.
    b. The partitioning of the Korean Peninsula.
    c. A U.S. military presence in South Vietnam.
    d. A nuclear program in India.

    Answer: a Type: M   Page(s): 213

61. The dominant powers in the Middle East between the two world wars were

    a. Great Britain and France.
    b. The United States and the Soviet Union.
    c. Iran and Iraq.
    d. Israel and the Arab nations.

    Answer: a Type: M   Page(s): 213

62. Which Arab leader was widely hailed in the West for his 1977 visit to Jerusalem?

    a. Saddam Hussein.
    b. Gamal Nasser.
    c. Anwar Sadat.
    d. The Shah of Iran.

    Answer: c Type: M   Page(s): 220

63. The balance of power in which region has been the most complex?

a. The Middle East.
b. East Asia.
c. Africa.
d. Latin America.

Answer: b   Type: M   Page(s): 232

TRUE/FALSE

64. Interdependence means that what happens in one state will have a ripple effect across others.

a. True
b. False

Answer: A   Type: T   Page(s): 194

65. Conflict is particularly likely to occur when empires decline or disintegrate

a. True
b. False

Answer: A   Type: T   Page(s): 204

66. One of the effects of the Six-Day War was to increase the importance of the Palestinian national movement.

a. True
b. False

Answer: A   Type: T   Page(s): 218

67. The intifada was the name given to the Palestinian uprising in Israel.

a. True
b. False

Answer: A   Type: T   Page(s): 222

68. South Asia has been largely free of interstate conflicts.

    a. True
    b. False

    Answer: B   Type: T   Page(s): 224

69. During the Cold War, Pakistani governments, although usually run by dictators, were often favored over Indian governments by the U.S.

    a. True
    b. False

    Answer: A   Type: T   Page(s): 230

70. The principal religious division between Pakistan and India has been between the Muslims and Christians.

    a. True
    b. False

    Answer: B   Type: T   Page(s): 224

71. The colonial power whose abrupt departure set the stage for many conflicts in South Asia was the Ottoman Empire.

    a. True
    b. False

    Answer: B   Type: T   Page(s): 224

72. India saw two of its prime ministers assassinated within a seven-year period.

    a. True
    b. False

    Answer: A   Type: T   Page(s): 231

73. The end of the colonial era and the Cold War have left Pakistan as the major South Asian power.

    a. True
    b. False

    Answer: B   Type: T   Page(s): 231

Harcourt Brace & Company

74. The primary goal for most nations in maintaining the balance of power in East Asia has been to contain China.

    a. True
    b. False

    Answer: A   Type: T   Page(s): 232

75. As a result of the Chinese-American rapprochement, both countries gained powerful leverage with respect to the Soviet Union.

    a. True
    b. False

    Answer: A   Type: T   Page(s): 234

76. China invaded Vietnam in the late 1970s to "teach Vietnam a lesson".

    a. True
    b. False

    Answer: A   Type: T   Page(s): 237

77. Future U.S. involvement in East Asia will depend on ideology rather than economics.

    a. True
    b. False

    Answer: B   Type: T   Page(s): 239

78. Before the twentieth century, more blood was spilled over religious disputes than any other cause.

    a. True
    b. False

    Answer: A   Type: T   Page(s): 208

79. The United States was quick to take advantage of the Sino-Soviet split.

    a. True
    b. False

    Answer: B   Type: T   Page(s): 233

80. The Soviet invasion of Afghanistan caused Japan to move closer to the U.S.

    a. True
    b. False

    Answer: A   Type: T   Page(s): 237

Harcourt Brace & Company

Chapter 6

Introduction to International Economics

MULTIPLE CHOICE

1. Because nations have different allocations of resources, each can

   a. Be entirely self-sufficient.
   b. Enjoy a comparative advantage in producing certain products.
   c. Enjoy equality of capital abundance.
   d. Always have an absolute advantage in producing whatever it needs most.

   Answer: b Type: M   Page(s): 251

2. Nations often impose trade barriers because

   a. They wish to protect domestic industries.
   b. They wish to provide consumers with the least expensive products.
   c. Most consumers demand it.
   d. They are effective free-market economic policies.

   Answer: a Type: M   Page(s): 252-253

3. Which of the following is not a trade barrier?

   a. Tariff.
   b. Import quota.
   c. Gold standard.
   d. Internal subsidy.

   Answer: c Type: M   Page(s): 253-255

4. Tariffs have what kind of an effect on international trade?

   a. They decrease the price of imported goods.
   b. They increase the incentives for domestic producers to become more efficient.
   c. They increase consumer access to foreign goods.
   d. They decrease international competition.

   Answer: d Type: M   Page(s): 253

5. Subsidies are designed to help domestic industries by

    a. Helping domestic producers compete at home against imported products.
    b. Helping domestic producers compete abroad against foreign products.
    c. Helping producers price their goods below the cost of production without going out o business.
    d. All of the above.
    e. None of the above.

    Answer: d Type: M   Page(s): 255

6. Which of the following is an example of a fixed exchange-rate system?

    a. The Smoot-Hawley Tariff.
    b. Voluntary export restriction.
    c. The gold standard.
    d. The barter system.
    e. All of the above.

    Answer: c Type: M   Page(s): 257

7. To help protect the value of currency under a fixed exchange-rate, government officials might

    a. Raise interest rates to shore up the value of their currency.
    b. Inflate the exchange rate to maintain its fixed value.
    c. Stop defending the currency.
    d. All of the above.

    Answer: d Type: M   Page(s): 257-259

8. The advantage of a fixed exchange-rate system is

    a. It makes the international economy more stable and predictable.
    b. It accurately reflects the health of a nation's economy.
    c. It prevents states from pursuing harmful economic policies.
    d. It allows currency values to fluctuate according to their true value.

    Answer: a Type: M   Page(s): 259

Harcourt Brace & Company

9. A balance of payments sheet tells all but

    a. How much money a country's citizens earned overseas.
    b. A country's trade balance.
    c. The minimum hourly wage.
    d. The official level of foreign aid given to other countries.

Answer: c Type: M   Page(s): 259

10. If a nation's currency weakens relative to other foreign currencies

    a. Domestic goods tend to be more expensive than foreign goods.
    b. There is a decline in the consumption of domestic goods.
    c. Exported goods become more expensive in foreign countries.
    d. All of the above.
    e. None of the above.

Answer: e Type: M   Page(s): 261

11. The United States' trade deficit has worsened recently because

    a. The increased price of imported goods was passed along to the consumers.
    b. Americans' demands for foreign goods might have become price inelastic.
    c. Americans do not prefer foreign goods.
    d. The dollar has weakened considerably.

Answer: b Type: M   Page(s): 261

12. The three schools of thought on international political economy are

    a. Liberalism, Idealism and Marxism.
    b. Liberalism, Realism and Idealism.
    c. Beggar-thy-neighbor, Realism and Marxism.
    d. Liberalism, Realism and Marxism.

Answer: d Type: M   Page(s): 261

13. Liberals believe which of the following is good for international international economics?

    a. Tariffs.
    b. Voluntary export restrictions.
    c. Free markets.
    d. Government intervention.

Answer: c Type: M   Page(s): 262

14. Economic liberals believe that

    a. Individuals are irrational.
    b. States are the principal actors in economics.
    c. Government intervention is beneficial.
    d. Individuals maximize their utility.

    Answer: d Type: M   Page(s): 263

15. Belief in "laissez faire" economic is representative of which school of economic thinking?

    a. Realist.
    b. Liberal.
    c. Globalist.
    d. Marxist.

    Answer: c Type: M   Page(s): 263

16. Liberal theory is useful because it helps us understand

    a. How nation-states seek to maximize power.
    b. How economic incentives would guide states if all they were concerned about was maximizing their national incomes.
    c. Why states often have no choice but to sacrifice maximum economic growth for national security.
    d. How core countries exploit the periphery for their own ends and stunt industrialization.

    Answer: b Type: M   Page(s): 264

17. Mercantilism is associated with which school of economic thinking?

    a. Realist.
    b. Globalist.
    c. Liberal.
    d. Marxist.

    Answer: a Type: M   Page(s): 265

Harcourt Brace & Company

18. Realists believe that

    a. Nation-states are the principal actors in economics.
    b. Economic factors are more important than military power.
    c. Individuals are the principal actors in economics.
    d. Free trade is always the best policy.

Answer: a Type: M   Page(s): 265

19. That world trade may sometimes be relatively free of trade barriers is explained by realists as a function of

    a. Comparative advantage.
    b. Hegemonic stability.
    c. Laissez-faire economics.
    d. Voluntary Export Restrictions.

Answer: b Type: M   Page(s): 265

20. Marxists view international economics from which perspective?

    a. Individual.
    b. System.
    c. Class.
    d. State.

Answer: c Type: M   Page(s): 266

21. According to Marx, the main problem with capitalism is that

    a. The proletariat owns the means of production.
    b. The workers do not own the means of production.
    c. The bourgeoisie do not dominate the state.
    d. Property is distributed equitably.

Answer: b Type: M   Page(s): 266

22. Marxism most closely resembles which other theory of international economics?

    a. Realism.
    b. Idealism.
    c. Liberalism.
    d. Dependency theory.

Answer: d Type: M   Page(s): 266

23. The factor approach emphasizes the importance of

    a. Who controls the factors of production.
    b. Who controls sectors of the economy.
    c. Which types of industries are most likely to favor trade barriers.
    d. The compatibility of interests among the various factors of production.

    Answer: a Type: M   Page(s): 267

24. What might explain why American organized labor opposed the North American Free Trade Agreement while factory owners supported it?

    a. Dependency theory.
    b. The sector approach.
    c. The factor approach.
    d. The system-level.

    Answer: c Type: M   Page(s): 268

25. Which approach suggests that different types of industries will experience different effects from international economic conditions?

    a. Dependency theory.
    b. The sector approach.
    c. The factor approach.
    d. The system-level.

    Answer: b Type: M   Page(s): 268

26. The sector approach is useful for understanding

    a. Why the working classes will unite, both domestically and internationally, to revolt against capitalism.
    b. Why there have been various periods in history when world trade was relatively free from trade barriers.
    c. How states sacrifice maximum economic growth for national security.
    d. Why some industries will support free trade while others favor protectionist policies.

    Answer: d Type: M   Page(s): 270

27. When the trade policies of a state are shaped by domestic interest groups which exert pressure nationally, one effect might be

a. A decrease in international cooperation.
b. An increase in international cooperation.
c. A decrease in domestic cooperation.
d. An increase in domestic cooperation.

Answer: b Type: M   Page(s): 270

28. The largest nation in the world is

a. Russia.
b. The United States.
c. Japan.
d. Australia.

Answer: a Type: M   Page(s): 271

29. In geopolitics the most important factor is

a. Size.
b. Population.
c. Location.
d. Technology.

Answer: c Type: M   Page(s): 271

30. A key economic and strategic advantage for states is

a. Maintaining strong armed forces.
b. Controlling immigration.
c. Importing goods more than exporting goods.
d. Proximity to major trade routes.

Answer: d Type: M   Page(s): 272

31. Since the Industrial Revolution, the most important natural resources have been

a. Metals and fossil fuels.
b. Nuclear power.
c. Renewable and sustainable resources.
d. Arable land.

Answer: a Type: M   Page(s): 272

32. A consequence of Japan's dependency on imported oil would be

    a. A shift from a floating to a fixed exchange rate.
    b. An increase in stability, economically.
    c. Its economic susceptibility to any threat against its energy supply.
    d. The rise of a powerful hegemon.

    Answer: c Type: M   Page(s): 272

33. The world's leading oil producer in 1995 was

    a. Saudi Arabia.
    b. Russia.
    c. Iran.
    d. Iraq.

    Answer: a Type: M   Page(s): 273

34. Japan and the United Kingdom, both lacking in _____, have traditionally had to rely on imports of _____.

    a. skilled labor, technology
    b. arable land, food
    c. oil fields, petroleum
    d. raw materials, textiles

    Answer: b Type: M   Page(s): 273

35. The most populous country in the world is

    a. China.
    b. India.
    c. Nigeria.
    d. The European Union.

    Answer: a Type: M   Page(s): 274

36. Which of the following is not an important factor in determining the extent to which population will be a factor in material power?

    a. Size.
    b. Vulnerability.
    c. Demographic structure.
    d. Quality of the work force.

    Answer: b Type: M   Page(s): 274

Harcourt Brace & Company

37. Which of the following demographic situations is most likely to interfere with a state's power?

   a. High birth and mortality rates.
   b. A large proportion of children and teenagers.
   c. A large proportion of senior citizens.
   d. All of the above.

   Answer: d Type: M   Page(s): 275

38. The percentage of workers employed in agriculture is a useful indicator of economic advancement because

   a. The more people employed in agriculture, the more food there will be.
   b. The more people employed in agriculture, the lesser the extent of the rural/urban cleavage.
   c. As industrialization increases, there is greater availability of jobs in manufacturing and services.
   d. As industrialization increases, more people will be employed in agriculture.

   Answer: c Type: M   Page(s): 275

39. The United States employs approximately what percentage of its population in agriculture?

   a. 2%.
   b. 10%.
   c. 27%.
   d. 35%.

   Answer: a Type: M   Page(s): 275

40. Gross national product measures

   a. How much money a nation has.
   b. The market value of goods and services a nation produces.
   c. The market value of exports a nation sells.
   d. A nation's expenditures on goods and services.

   Answer: b Type: M   Page(s): 275

41. Which of the following best characterizes U.S. economic performance during the 1980s?

    a. The U.S. economy was declining in absolute terms.
    b. The relative size of the U.S. economy increased in comparison to Japan and Germany.
    c. The U.S. economy was growing in absolute terms.
    d. The U.S. share of world production was increasing both absolutely and relatively.

    Answer: c Type: M   Page(s): 276

42. The nation with the highest GNP in 1995 was

    a. Japan.
    b. The Soviet Union.
    c. China.
    d. The United States.

    Answer: d Type: M   Page(s): 276

43. Gross national product per capita takes into consideration

    a. Percentage of labor force employed in agriculture.
    b. Population.
    c. Territory.
    d. Natural resources.

    Answer: b Type: M   Page(s): 277

44. In 1995 the nation with the highest gross national product per capita was

    a. Japan.
    b. Luxembourg.
    c. Switzerland.
    d. The United States.

    Answer: b Type: M   Page(s): 279

45. Which of the following factors had a decisive impact on relative rankings based on per capita GNP in the 1980s?

    a. The price of oil.
    b. The global depression.
    c. The end of the Cold War.
    d. The rapid increase in world population.

    Answer: a Type: M   Page(s): 277

46. Which of the following economic indicators was declining for the United States during the 1980s?

a. GNP.
b. GNP per capita.
c. Trade balance.
d. Percentage of the work force employed in manufacturing and services.

Answer: c Type: M   Page(s): 279

47. In 1970, most of the leading economic powers enjoyed a _____ and in 1990 most experienced a _____.

a. trade deficit, trade surplus
b. trade deficit, trade deficit
c. trade surplus, trade surplus
d. trade surplus, trade deficit

Answer: d Type: M   Page(s): 279

48. The United States has singled out which country for criticism of its trade policies?

a. Japan.
b. Germany.
c. Russia.
d. Canada.

Answer: a Type: M   Page(s): 279

49. Which nation devoted the most money to research and development spending in the 1980s?

a. Russia.
b. West Germany.
c. Japan.
d. The United States.

Answer: d Type: M   Page(s): 280

50. The United States targets most of its research and development spending toward

a. Agriculture.
b. Computer technology.
c. The military.
d. NASA and space programs.

Answer: c Type: M   Page(s): 280

51. States may refuse to cooperate because

    a. They distrust one another.
    b. They fear other states will gain relatively more than they will.
    c. They fear other states might benefit disproportionately from cooperation.
    d. All of the above.

    Answer: d Type: M   Page(s): 281-282

52. Trade liberals argue that cooperation is both

    a. Possible and beneficial.
    b. Impossible and useless.
    c. Unfavorable and unachievable.
    d. Feasible and improbable.

    Answer: a Type: M   Page(s): 282

53. Which of the following is not a strategy designed to overcome the prisoner's dilemma?

    a. Tit for tat.
    b. International regimes.
    c. The balance of power.
    d. Economic interdependence.

    Answer: c Type: M   Page(s): 283

54. The purpose of the tit for tat strategy is to

    a. Demonstrate your willingness to cooperate with your opponent.
    b. Establish international regimes.
    c. Create prisoner's dilemmas in international relations.
    d. Provide for economic interdependence.

    Answer: a Type: M   Page(s): 284

55. Regimes do which of the following?

    a. Reduce the attractiveness of cheating.
    b. They establish norms that facilitate cooperation.
    c. They possess multiple and effective mechanisms and institutions to enforce agreements.
    d. All of the above.

    Answer: d Type: M   Page(s): 284-285

Harcourt Brace & Company

56. International law does all of the following except

    a. Encourages states to forgo the short term advantages of cheating.
    b. Encourages states to concentrate on long-term advantages of cooperation.
    c. Discourages states from unfairly maximizing their individual gains at the expense of others.
    d. Use a sovereign authority to enforce international law.

Answer: d Type: M Page(s): 285-286

57. Hegemons are often responsible for

    a. Providing loans to countries in need.
    b. Providing markets for commodities.
    c. Making the seas safe for international commerce.
    d. All of the above.

Answer: d Type: M Page(s): 286

58. Which country provided hegemonic leadership in the 19th century?

    a. The United States.
    b. France.
    c. Great Britain.
    d. Germany.

Answer: c Type: M Page(s): 287

RUE/FALSE

59. When countries produce the same goods or services, trade usually does not occur.

    a. True
    b. False

Answer: B Type: T Page(s): 251

60. Because nations have different allocations of resources, each enjoys an absolute advantage in producing those goods that utilize its abundant factor.

    a. True
    b. False

Answer: B Type: T Page(s): 251

Harcourt Brace & Company

61. Adam Smith showed that even if one nation has an absolute advantage in the production of all goods, trade can still be mutually beneficial if the less efficient nation has a comparative advantage in one good over another.

    a. True
    b. False

    Answer: B Type: T Page(s): 251

62. Mutual gains from trade will lead to specialization within each country, making goods less expensive and production more efficient for both.

    a. True
    b. False

    Answer: A Type: T Page(s): 252

63. Barriers to free trade result from the conflict of consumers who want inexpensive products versus industries who want to stay in business.

    a. True
    b. False

    Answer: A Type: T Page(s): 253

64. Tariffs aid foreign producers who compete against domestically-produced goods.

    a. True
    b. False

    Answer: B Type: T Page(s): 253

65. A "begger-thy-neighbor" policy implies decreasing trade barriers in order to import more foreign goods.

    a. True
    b. False

    Answer: B Type: T Page(s): 253

66. Dumping occurs when one country sells its products in a foreign market far in excess of the cost of production.

a. True
b. False

Answer: B Type: T Page(s): 255

57. Import quotas facilitate free trade.

a. True
b. False

Answer: B Type: T Page(s): 253

58. The periods 1870-1941, and 1945-1973 reflect the eras of a fixed exchange rate system.

a. True
b. False

Answer: A Type: T Page(s): 257

59. Artifically inflating a currency can improve a country's domestic economy.

a. True
b. False

Answer: B Type: T Page(s): 257

70. Fixed exchange rates make the international economy more stable and predictable while floating rates accurately reflect an economy's well-being and create uncertainty in the world economy.

a. True
b. False

Answer: A Type: T Page(s): 259

71. A country enjoys a trade surplus if the current account balance is positive.

a. True
b. False

Answer: A Type: T Page(s): 260

72. Accounting procedures guarantee that the balance of payments always equals zero.

    a. True
    b. False

    Answer: A Type: T   Page(s): 260

73. When the dollar weakens relative to foreign currencies, domestim goods tend to become more expensive than foreign goods.

    a. True
    b. False

    Answer: B Type: T   Page(s): 261

74. Governments were inspired to reduce their intervention in trade and other economic activity as the Industrial Revolution expanded production in Europe which increased demand for manufactured and agricultural goods.

    a. True
    b. False

    Answer: A Type: T   Page(s): 262

75. Liberals conclude that trade is a positive-sum game and that states should practice laissez-faire.

    a. True
    b. False

    Answer: A Type: T   Page(s): 263

76. Realists argue that classes will revolt and communism will prevail.

    a. True
    b. False

    Answer: B Type: T   Page(s): 265

77. Mercantilism is an economic philosophy that regards trade primarily as an instrument of power politics.

    a. True
    b. False

    Answer: A Type: T   Page(s): 265

78. A hegemon may become the leading economic and military power in the international system and it will use its power to set and enforce rules of free trade.

a. True
b. False

Answer: A Type: T Page(s): 265

79. Dependency theory is part of the Realist train of thought.

a. True
b. False

Answer: B Type: T Page(s): 266

80. The sector approach focuses on the economy rather than production.

a. True
b. False

Answer: B Type: T Page(s): 268

81. A nation's most important territorial assets include its geography and its natrual resources.

a. True
b. False

Answer: A Type: T Page(s): 271

82. When considering the short-term value of a nation's natural resources, both production and reserves must be taken into account.

a. True
b. False

Answer: A Type: T Page(s): 272

83. The United States has been called the "breadbasket" of the world because of its abundant arable land.

a. True
b. False

Answer: A Type: T Page(s): 273

84. A large population is sufficient to make a state a major power.

    a. True
    b. False

    Answer: B Type: T   Page(s): 274

85. Russia has the largest territory of any nation on earth.

    a. True
    b. False

    Answer: A Type: T   Page(s): 271

86. As industrialization increases, the percentage of the work force employed in agricultur increases.

    a. True
    b. False

    Answer: B Type: T   Page(s): 275

87. China has a population of over five billion.

    a. True
    b. False

    Answer: B Type: T   Page(s): 274

88. GNP differs from GDP in that the latter does not take into account income earned by a nation's citizens and corporations that operate outside its borders.

    a. True
    b. False

    Answer: A Type: T   Page(s): 276

89. The United States had the largest GNP in both 1974 and 1995.

    a. True
    b. False

    Answer: A Type: T   Page(s): 276

90. In the Information Age, the ability to promote cooperation and manage conflict among international economic actors will become less important due to the ease of communication.

    a. True
    b. False

    Answer: B Type: T   Page(s): 280

Harcourt Brace & Company

Chapter 7

Evolution of the World Economy

1. Which of the following made it difficult for people, goods, capital, and ideas to cross national boundaries during the era of European empires?

   a. High tariff barriers.
   b. Difficulty of moving goods over land.
   c. Underdeveloped systems of international banking and finance.
   d. All of the above.

   Answer: d Type: M   Page(s): 294

2. At what point did a true global economy begin to emerge?

   a. During the mercantilist movement in Britain.
   b. During the Seventeenth century.
   c. At the start of the Industrial Revolution.
   d. Just Prior to World War I.

   Answer: c Type: M   Page(s): 294

3. Which nation was the first to become industrialized?

   a. Germany.
   b. Britain.
   c. The United States.
   d. France.

   Answer: b Type: M   Page(s): 294

Harcourt Brace & Company

4. During the late 18th and early 19th century, British exports were dominated by what product?

    a. Coal.
    b. Wood.
    c. Textiles.
    d. None of the above.

    Answer: c Type: M   Page(s): 292-293

5. Which of the following factors facilitated the rise of British dominance in the global economy?

    a. Their long and successful experience with international trade.
    b. An emphasis on importing rather than exporting goods.
    c. Relatively late industrialization.
    d. Inadequate labor markets.

    Answer: a Type: M   Page(s): 294

6. British hegemonic leadership of the global economy involved

    a. Maintaining protectionist economic policies.
    b. Repeal of protectionist trade policies.
    c. Discouraging competition from others.
    d. Diplomatic isolationism.

    Answer: b Type: M   Page(s): 295

7. Which of the following was not an obstacle for the British free trade after the Congress of Vienna?

    a. High Tariffs.
    b. Growing urban population.
    c. Falling export prices.
    d. Uncompetitive trade abroad.

    Answer: a Type: M   Page(s): 295

8. Britain suffered a decline in exports because of its comparative disadvantage in the agricultural sector to which of the following countries?

    a. Russia and France.
    b. Belgium and Spain.
    c. The U.S. and Russia.
    d. Spain and the U.S.

Answer: c Type: M   Page(s): 295

9. Which of the following was a set of laws which imposed high tariffs and other restrictions on agricultural imports to Britain?

    a. The Wheat Laws.
    b. The Barley Laws.
    c. The Cucumber Laws.
    d. The Corn Laws.

Answer: d Type: M   Page(s): 296

10. Acting as a hegemonic power, Britain did which of the following?

    a. It engaged in a unilateral move towards openness to promote free trade abroad.
    b. It closed to trade with other nations to protect its hegemonic status.
    c. It practiced protectionism to prove that it was truly independent.
    d. It opened the doors to trade with a few select nations.

Answer: a Type: M   Page(s): 296

11. After what war did France use trade policy to improve relations with Britain?

    a. World War I.
    b. The Crimean War.
    c. The War of 1812.
    d. The French Revolution.

Answer: b Type: M   Page(s): 296

12. Most-Favored-Nation status means that

    a. One gives a trading partner better deals than one gives any other nation.
    b. One gives a trading partner the best possible price for its products.
    c. One gives a trading partner the best deal available in one's market.
    d. One drops all trade barriers to a trading partner's products.

Answer: c Type: M   Page(s): 296

Harcourt Brace & Company

13. Which of the following was not one of the developments that expedited the growth of international trade between 1850 and 1875?

    a. The rise of a number of new industrial powers.
    b. Technical innovations.
    c. Decreasing prices.
    d. Increase in trade barriers.

Answer: d   Type: M   Page(s): 297

14. Which nations emerged as significant economic and potential military rivals to Britain in the late 1800s?

    a. The United States and Germany.
    b. France and Italy.
    c. Russia and the United States.
    d. Japan and Germany.

Answer: a   Type: M   Page(s): 299

15. Which of the following was not one of the technological developments that played a vital role in the growth of the world economy?

    a. Sterm-powered industrial machinery.
    b. Railroads.
    c. Telegraph.
    d. Telephone.

Answer: d   Type: M   Page(s): 298

16. Which laws created a German "common market"?

    a. The Weimer Laws.
    b. The Vienna Laws.
    c. The Zollverein Laws.
    d. The Berlin Laws.

Answer: c   Type: M   Page(s): 298

17. Why did growing interdependence create problems for many nations in the late 1800s?

    a. It led to a decline in gross national product.
    b. It led to an increase in calls for protectionism.
    c. Comparative advantage was done away with.
    d. It led to a decline in nationalism.

Answer: b   Type: M   Page(s): 300

18. Why did free trade cause problems for many nations?

   a. Free trade pressured economies to cease producing goods for which they did not have a comparative advantage.
   b. Countries could not produce enough products to keep up with the newly created high demand.
   c. Some countries lost revenue from lower tariffs and were forced to raise domestic taxes.
   d. All of the above.

Answer: a   Type: M   Page(s): 300

19. The growing dislocation of domestic economies in the late 1800s was facilitated by

   a. Declining nationalism.
   b. Decreasing volume of world trade.
   c. Decreasing competition.
   d. All of the above.
   e. None of the above.

Answer: e   Type: M   Page(s): 300

20. The ability of the great powers to manage the world economy in the late 1800s was hindered by

   a. World War I.
   b. The decline in comparative advantage.
   c. Cheap U.S. grain exports.
   d. The Bretton Woods system.

Answer: c   Type: M   Page(s): 301

21. What kind of international monetary system existed prior to World War I?

   a. Fixed exchange-rate system.
   b. Marxist.
   c. Floating exchange-rate system.
   d. Protectionist.

Answer: a   Type: M   Page(s): 302

22. In the international monetary system prior to World War I, each nation set its currency value to

    a. The United States dollar.
    b. A floating target.
    c. Gold.
    d. Gross national product.

    Answer: c Type: M   Page(s): 302

23. Which of the following was a major reason for the success of the gold standard before World War I?

    a. The large supply of gold in the World.
    b. England's devotion to stable exchange rates.
    c. Each country pursued its own economic goals and kept its own monitoring system.
    d. None of the above.

    Answer: b Type: M   Page(s): 302

24. Prior to World War I, nations often emphasized international stability over domestic pressures because

    a. Global stability benefited them more in the long run.
    b. Domestic groups were either marginalized or placated with tariffs.
    c. They wished to encourage trade and international investment.
    d. All of the above.
    e. None of the above.

    Answer: d Type: M   Page(s): 302-303

25. The failure of which two European nations to commit to an open international economy doomed efforts to manage the effects of economic interdependence?

    a. Germany and England.
    b. Spain and France.
    c. Germany and France.
    d. England and Spain.

    Answer: c Type: M   Page(s): 303

Harcourt Brace & Company

26. Which American thinker argued that by continuing under the Gold Standard the American economy would be controled by foreign capital?

a. Benjamin Franklin.
b. Alexander Hamilton.
c. Oliver Wendell Holmes.
d. William Jennings Bryan.

Answer: d Type: M   Page(s): 303

27. The economic consequences of World War I included all but

a. The United States went into tremendous debt.
b. There was a great loss of traditional export markets.
c. Germany faced tremendous punitive reparation payments.
d. Inflation.

Answer: a Type: M   Page(s): 303

28. Germany attempted to pay its reparations by

a. Borrowing money from Great Britain and France.
b. Printing more money.
c. Increasing the value of its currency.
d. Pursuing Marxist economic policies.

Answer: b Type: M   Page(s): 304

29. In response to the booming U.S. economy in the 1920s, the U.S. Federal Reserve took what action?

a. It lowered interest rates.
b. It adopted protectionist policies.
c. It raised interest rates.
d. It adopted free trade policies.

Answer: c Type: M   Page(s): 305

30. Which of the following was not one of damaging economic policies pursued during the period between the two world wars?

a. Raising of tariffs.
b. The elimination of the gold standard.
c. Raising of interest rates.
d. Excessive hegemonic leadership by the United States.

Answer: d Type: M   Page(s): 305

31. World War II and the subsequent rise of which nation heralded a new age of global economic interdependence and growth?

    a. Japan.
    b. Britain.
    c. The United States.
    d. Russia.

    Answer: c Type: M   Page(s): 305

32. The most important change in the transformation of the world economy after World War II was

    a. The Dawes plan.
    b. U.S. hegemony.
    c. The Smoot-Hawley tariff.
    d. U.S. isolationism.

    Answer: b Type: M   Page(s): 306

33. International trade and investment grew within the American sphere because of which of the following?

    a. The outbreak of the cold war.
    b. The desire to preserve economic stability.
    c. The desire to preserve peace.
    d. All of the above.

    Answer: d Type: M   Page(s): 307-308

34. The Bretton Woods conference helped establish

    a. The International Bank for Reconstruction and Development.
    b. The International Monetary Fund.
    c. U.S. hegemony.
    d. All of the above.

    Answer: d Type: M   Page(s): 308

35. At the Bretton Woods conference, the International Monetary Fund was established to perform which of the following functions?

a. Establish fixed exchange-rates.
b. Provide short-term loans to help countries rebuild after World War II.
c. Re-establish British dominance over international finance.
d. Coordinate trading policy.

Answer: a   Type: M   Page(s): 308

36. The World Bank has been primarily used to

a. Establish exchange-rates.
b. Manage trading policy among the industrialized nations.
c. Provide loans to Third World nations.
d. Re-establish the gold standard.

Answer: c   Type: M   Page(s): 309

37. Which of the following best characterizes GATT?

a. No exceptions are allowed under its free trade policies.
b. It is fast becoming irrelevant because it has never been reviewed since its inception.
c. A liberal trading regime containing certain safeguards for disadvantaged domestic groups.
d. It is a small organization consisting only of the most industrialized nations of the world.

Answer: c   Type: M   Page(s): 309

38. The Bretton Woods system was dependent upon which of the following for its continued success?

a. The Cold War.
b. United States hegemony.
c. Protectionist trading policies.
d. Colonialism.

Answer: b   Type: M   Page(s): 309

39. The United States faced what kind of problem under the Bretton Woods system?

    a. The lack of cheap energy resources.
    b. Floating exchange-rates.
    c. Unpopularity of the dollar.
    d. Its commitment to redeem dollars with gold.

    Answer: d Type: M Page(s): 309

40. Devaluing the American dollar was a risky strategy to protect the Bretton Woods system because

    a. It might adversely affect the economies of allies.
    b. It might fuel currency speculation.
    c. It would reduce the amount of gold dollars were worth.
    d. All of the above.
    e. None of the above.

    Answer: d Type: M Page(s): 310

41. The international monetary system faced what kinds of problems in the 1960s and early 1970s?

    a. The U.S. supply of gold exceeded the amount of foreign-held dollars.
    b. The political and economic recovery of Europe and Japan.
    c. The decline of British hegemony.
    d. The lack of multilateral arrangements to manage the international monetary system.

    Answer: b Type: M Page(s): 310

42. The Bretton Woods system ultimately led to

    a. Soviet domination.
    b. The decline of Western Europe and Japan.
    c. Increasing U.S. hegemony.
    d. U.S. trade imbalances.

    Answer: d Type: M Page(s): 311

43. All of the following describe the IMF except

    a. Established at Bretton Woods.
    b. Established fixed exchange rates.
    c. Advanced credit to countries with balance-of-payment deficits.
    d. Managed international trade.

    Answer: d Type: M Page(s): 308-309

44. Among the domestic economic problems facing the United States which contributed to international economic difficulties was

    a. Excessive domestic expenditures.
    b. Increasing inflation.
    c. Budget deficits.
    d. The refusal to cut spending or raise taxes.
    e. All of the above.

    Answer: e Type: M   Page(s): 311-312

45. The "Nixon shock" of 1971 resulted in all but

    a. Fixed exchange-rates.
    b. Dollar depreciation.
    c. Wage and price controls.
    d. Increased tariffs.

    Answer: a Type: M   Page(s): 312

46. What development in the Middle East threatened the supply of cheap oil in the early 1970s?

    a. The founding of OPEC.
    b. The Yom Kippur War.
    c. U.S. support from Syna.
    d. The founding of Israel.

    Answer: b Type: M   Page(s): 313

47. The increasing dependence of the West on foreign oil resulted in

    a. Few economic dislocations.
    b. Declining oil prices.
    c. Low inflation.
    d. All of the above.
    e. None of the above.

    Answer: e Type: M   Page(s): 315

48. Which nation in the early 1970s was making particularly rapid economic progress that nearly rivaled the U.S. in terms of volume and percent of world exports?

    a. Japan.
    b. Germany.
    c. The Soviet Union.
    d. Great Britain.

    Answer: b   Type: M   Page(s): 311

49. Which event in the early 1970s resulted in a steep increase in oil prices?

    a. The end of the Bretton Woods system.
    b. The Cuban Missile Crisis.
    c. The Yom Kippur War.
    d. The Vietnam War.

    Answer: c   Type: M   Page(s): 313

50. After the oil crisis and the end of the Bretton Woods system

    a. The United States returned to isolationist policies.
    b. The world economy went into a steep decline.
    c. International economic production continued to increase.
    d. The Soviet Union assumed economic leadership.

    Answer: c   Type: M   Page(s): 313

51. Which of the following best characterizes the international economic system after the end of the Bretton Woods system?

    a. Nations developed new arrangements to manage interdependence.
    b. The importance of global economic matters has decreased.
    c. An absence of conflict over economic issues.
    d. The decline of world trade.

    Answer: a   Type: M   Page(s): 315-316

52. Which of the following has not intensified concerns about competitiveness as markets fo goods and services have become increasingly globalized?

    a. U.S. dominance in the global automobile markets.
    b. The extraordinary success of Japan.
    c. The declining dominance of the U.S.
    d. The growth of world trade.

    Answer: a   Type: M   Page(s): 316

53. Efforts to combat economic problems in the U.S. in the late 1970s and early 1980s included

    a. Decreasing interest rates.
    b. Tax increases to offset budget increases.
    c. Deregulation.
    d. Return to the gold standard.

    Answer: c Type: M   Page(s): 315

54. The increase in interest rates in the United States in the 1980s had what kind of effect on U.S. trade?

    a. It increased the trade deficit.
    b. It decreased the trade deficit.
    c. It led to more free trade.
    d. It led to more protectionism.

    Answer: a Type: M   Page(s): 316

55. Interdependence has had which of the following effects on the international economy?

    a. Multilateralism has increased.
    b. The possibility for economic conflict has increased.
    c. Nations have become increasingly reliant on one another for economic prosperity.
    d. All of the above.
    e. None of the above.

    Answer: d Type: M   Page(s): 316

56. Which of the following is most likely to characterize the transformation from communism to capitalism in Eastern Europe and the former Soviet Union?

    a. It will happen quite quickly.
    b. Change will occur at the same pace in Eastern Europe and Russia.
    c. The elimination of price controls and state industry.
    d. It will not require outside help.

    Answer: c Type: M   Page(s): 316

Harcourt Brace & Company

57. The ability of the former communist states to achieve economic reform depends most on

    a. The consent of Russia.
    b. Their willingness to accept economic hardship.
    c. Aid from the West.
    d. State ownership of industry.

    Answer: b Type: M Page(s): 318

58. Why does the West have an interest in the economic development of the former communist nations?

    a. These states constitute a great, untapped market.
    b. They want the former communist nations to be able to expand their military budgets.
    c. They want to increase economic competition.
    d. These states have expensive labor markets and strict environmental standards.

    Answer: a Type: M Page(s): 318

59. Which of the following best characterized the CMEA or Comecon?

    a. The North American version of the EU.
    b. A Soviet-led insitution which solidified trade relations in the East.
    c. A trade agreement with the USSR and Australia.
    d. An agreement between the U.S. and the USSR to begin trade just before the end of the cold war.

    Answer: b Type: M Page(s): 318

60. Which of the following best characterizes international economic cooperation?

    a. Domestic considerations have little effect on cooperation.
    b. U.S. economic policies have little direct influence on other capitalist nations.
    c. States strive to seek a balance between national autonomy and international cooperation.
    d. States have begun to scale back the formation of economic blocs.

    Answer: c Type: M Page(s): 319

61. A common market is an example of

    a. A floating exchange-rate system.
    b. Protectionism.
    c. Hegemony.
    d. An economic bloc.

    Answer: d Type: M Page(s): 319

62. Economic blocs can discriminate against other non-member nations by

a. Creating protectionist fortresses.
b. Beginning conflicts between separate blocs.
c. Undermining the accomplishments of the WTO.
d. All of the above.

Answer: d Type: M   Page(s): 320

63. The most highly integrated economic bloc is

a. The European Union.
b. The North American Free Trade Area.
c. The Association of South-East Asian Nations.
d. The Organization of Petroleum Exporting Countries.

Answer: a Type: M   Page(s): 320

64. Greater economic and political cooperation in Europe has been based on

a. Major economic powers surrendering a share of their sovereignty.
b. U.S. hegemony.
c. Fixed exchange-rates.
d. Increased protectionism.

Answer: a Type: M   Page(s): 323

65. Which of the following has not been among the problems confronting European integration?

a. Popular apprehension over integration.
b. Fears of German domination.
c. NAFTA.
d. British fears of Continental domination.

Answer: c Type: M   Page(s): 320-323

66. NAFTA was expanded to include which nation in 1994?

a. Great Britain.
b. Mexico.
c. Brazil.
d. Germany.

Answer: b Type: M   Page(s): 323

67. Opposition to the North American Free Trade Agreement in the United States has come fro

    a. Environmental groups.
    b. Low-tech and low-skill industries.
    c. Organized labor.
    d. All of the above.
    e. None of the above.

    Answer: d Type: M   Page(s): 323-325

68. MERCOSUR was orginially formed between all of the following except

    a. Brazil.
    b. Argentina.
    c. Uruguay.
    d. Chile.

    Answer: d Type: M   Page(s): 325

69. In the Pacific Rim, the free trade area is known as

    a. NAFTA.
    b. The European Union.
    c. OECD.
    d. ASEAN.

    Answer: d Type: M   Page(s): 326

70. Regional integration and trading blocs have arisen in part because of

    a. Increasing international protectionism.
    b. Increasing U.S. trade surpluses.
    c. Declining U.S. hegemony.
    d. Decreasing world economic growth.

    Answer: c Type: M   Page(s): 326

71. The global economy is becoming

    a. More independent.
    b. More protectionist.
    c. Less fragmented.
    d. All of the above.
    e. None of the above.

    Answer: e Type: M   Page(s): 327

Harcourt Brace & Company

72. Among the problems facing the world economy is

    a. The possibility that the world may be dividing up into antagonistic trading blocs.
    b. Public apathy over international economic issues.
    c. The declining value of the gold standard.
    d. Comparative advantage.

    Answer: a Type: M   Page(s): 327

73. Globalization and fragmentation are

    a. Strengthening the power of the nation-state at the expense of international institutions.
    b. Strengthening the power of subnational groups.
    c. Weakening the power of international institutions.
    d. Hindering global communication.
    e. None of the above.

    Answer: b Type: M   Page(s): 327-238

RUE/FALSE

74. The first truly industrailized nation was the United States.

    a. True.
    b. False.

    Answer: B Type: T   Page(s): 294

75. The Corn Laws were repealed in Great Britain in order to encourage free trade.

    a. True
    b. False

    Answer: A Type: T   Page(s): 296

76. Britain could not act as a hegemonic power without a free trade policy.

    a. True
    b. False

    Answer: A Type: T   Page(s): 295

Harcourt Brace & Company

77. The creation of railroads in German states during the 1800s played the key role in German unification.

    a. True
    b. False

    Answer: A   Type: T   Page(s): 298

78. Nationalism and Proctectionism are in no way related.

    a. True
    b. False

    Answer: B   Type: T   Page(s): 301

79. The pre-World War I gold standard's success was largely due to France's devotion to stable exchange rates.

    a. True
    b. False

    Answer: B   Type: T   Page(s): 302

80. It is theorized that the growth of nationalism spurred by protectionism contributed to the insecurity that led to WWI.

    a. True
    b. False

    Answer: A   Type: T   Page(s): 303

81. Japan was the main supplier of war materials to the allies.

    a. True
    b. False

    Answer: B   Type: T   Page(s): 303

82. By the end of WWI, Britain and France accumulated over $10 billion in debt to the U.S.

    a. True
    b. False

    Answer: A   Type: T   Page(s): 303

Harcourt Brace & Company

83. After World War I, the international trade and monetary systems became much more stable than in previous years.

    a. True
    b. False

    Answer: B   Type: T   Page(s): 304

84. During the 1920s, Germany borrowed money from the United States to pay reparations to Great Britain and France, who then used the money to pay back on their debts to the United States.

    a. True
    b. False

    Answer: A   Type: T   Page(s): 304

85. The gold standard, which has been reintroduced after WWI was largely successful.

    a. True
    b. False

    Answer: B Type: T   Page(s): 305

86. The Bretton Woods system was established after World War II and led by Great Britain.

    a. True
    b. False

    Answer: B   Type: T   Page(s): 308

87. The Group of Seven are the leading member nations of the Organization for Economic Cooperation and Development.

    a. True
    b. False

    Answer: A   Type: T   Page(s): 310

88. Multinational corporations have production facilities and assets in one country and headquarters in many different nations.

    a. True
    b. False

    Answer: B   Type: T   Page(s): 310

Harcourt Brace & Company

89. In the early 1970s, GATT imposed an oil embargo on the United States and the Netherlands.

    a. True
    b. False

    Answer: B   Type: T   Page(s): 313

90. Stagflation means a combination of high inflation and high unemployment.

    a. True
    b. False

    Answer: A   Type: T   Page(s): 315

91. During the 1980's the U.S. budget deficits increased and lower government spending caused economic recovery throughout the nation.

    a. True
    b. False

    Answer: B   Type: T   Page(s): 315

92. Both the U.S. budget and trade deficits grew substantially during the Reagan administration.

    a. True
    b. False

    Answer: A   Type: T   Page(s): 315

93. The West has not given a great deal of assistance to the former communist nations of Eastern Europe and the former Soviet Union.

    a. True
    b. False

    Answer: A   Type: T   Page(s): 318

94. Programs like GATT and Bretton Woods helped to integrate economies of the capitalist world.

    a. True
    b. False

    Answer: A   Type: T   Page(s): 318

95. An economic bloc is designed to discourage economic cooperation and competitiveness with the rest of the world.

    a. True
    b. False

    Answer: B   Type: T   Page(s): 320

96. The European Free Trade Area was a rival to the European Economic Community.

    a. True
    b. False

    Answer: A   Type: T   Page(s): 321

97. Great Britain is not a member of the European Community.

    a. True
    b. False

    Answer: B   Type: T   Page(s): 321

98. Maquiladoras are a type of Latin American floating exchange-rate system.

    a. True
    b. False

    Answer: B   Type: T   Page(s): 323

99. Both conflict and cooperation have characterized foreign economic relations since 1973.

    a. True
    b. False

    Answer: A   Type: T   Page(s): 327

00. International political economy is the study of links between domestic and international politics and the world economy.

    a. True
    b. False

    Answer: A   Type: T   Page(s): 327-328

Harcourt Brace & Company

Chapter 8

North-South Economic Relations: The Challenge of Development

MULTIPLE CHOICE

1. The regions of the underdeveloped South include

   a. Europe, Latin America & Oceania.
   b. Australia, Africa, and North America.
   c. Latin America, South Asia, and Africa.
   d. North America, China, and Eastern Europe.

   Answer: c Type: M   Page(s): 333

2. Development in the Third World may emphasize which of the following?

   a. Increasing agricultural productivity.
   b. Expanding health services.
   c. Providing for sustainable economic growth.
   d. Producing nuclear weapons.
   e. All of the above.

   Answer: e Type: M   Page(s): 334

3. Which of the following best describes development?

   a. It always focuses on heavy industrialization.
   b. Development is a constantly moving target.
   c. High-technology industries always remain in the same nations.
   d. All of the above.
   e. None of the above.

   Answer: b Type: M   Page(s): 334

Harcourt Brace & Company

4. The gap between the "haves" and the "have nots" in modern times

   a. Has dramatically widened.
   b. Has significantly decreased.
   c. Has remained fairly constant.
   d. Is irrelevant, since different standards must be used.

   Answer: a   Type: M   Page(s): 334

5. Development typically begins at which of the following stages?

   a. Huge migration of labor to the cities.
   b. Rural-urban cleavages.
   c. Industrialization.
   d. Subsistence agriculture.

   Answer: d   Type: M   Page(s): 335

6. Rural-urban cleavages are likely to occur

   a. If food prices remain too high.
   b. If food prices remain too low.
   c. If there is a huge migration of labor from rural to urban areas.
   d. All of the above.
   e. None of the above.

   Answer: d   Type: M   Page(s): 335

7. The two most important factors which influence successful development are

   a. High-tech and low-tech industry.
   b. Trade and exchange-rates.
   c. Domestic political and social factors and the international environment.
   d. Liberalism and Marxism.

   Answer: c   Type: M   Page(s): 338

8. The Third World is best characterized as

   a. Consisting of the former communist nations of Eastern Europe and the Soviet Union.
   b. Heavily dependent on the export of one or a few commodities.
   c. Involved in the export of manufactured products and services.
   d. Producing most of the world's gross national product.

   Answer: b   Type: M   Page(s): 336

9. Modernization theory contends that the most important factors contributing to underdevelopment can be found

a. In the underdeveloped states themselves.
b. In the policies of the developed nations.
c. In forces beyond anyone's control.
d. In the Cold War.

Answer: a Type: M   Page(s): 338

10. The fundamental obstacle to development according to modernization theory is

a. Imperialism.
b. Communism.
c. Traditional cultures.
d. Market economies.

Answer: c Type: M   Page(s): 338

11. Traditional societies are dominated by

a. Market economies.
b. Rigid social structures.
c. Urban dwellers.
d. Rapid innovations.

Answer: b Type: M   Page(s): 338

12. According to modernization theorists, what kind of political system best promotes development?

a. Communism.
b. Authoritarianism.
c. Traditionalism.
d. Democracy.

Answer: d Type: M   Page(s): 339

North-South Economic Relations: The Challenge of Development

13. Which of the following economic practices do modernization theorists stress is important
for development?

    a. Free markets.
    b. Foreign investment.
    c. Foreign aid.
    d. All of the above.
    e. None of the above.

    Answer: d Type: M Page(s): 339

14. Demographic transition refers to

    a. Changes in the birth and death rates.
    b. Changes in the level of democracy.
    c. Changes in the rural-urban cleavage.
    d. Changes in the geography of a country.

    Answer: a Type: M Page(s): 339

15. The infant mortality rate of underdeveloped nations is generally ____ in developed
nations.

    a. Lower than
    b. Higher than
    c. About the same as
    d. Less important than

    Answer: b Type: M Page(s): 339

16. When modern drugs are introduced into developing nations

    a. The death rate falls dramatically.
    b. There is a population explosion.
    c. Infant mortality rates fall.
    d. All of the above.
    e. None of the above.

    Answer: d Type: M Page(s): 340

Harcourt Brace & Company

17. Fertility rates tend to decline

    a. When more women go to work.
    b. Where states emphasize subsistence agriculture.
    c. In the lowest-income countries.
    d. When the mortality rate increases.

    Answer: a   Type: M   Page(s): 340

18. The lowest population growth rates are found in

    a. The OECD countries.
    b. The Third World.
    c. The former communist nations.
    d. The newly industrializing nations.

    Answer: a   Type: M   Page(s): 340

19. Which of the following characterizes rapid population growth in the early stages of demographic transition?

    a. Most of the population consists of the elderly.
    b. There are tremendous resources for investment from the burgeoning population.
    c. Few economies can generate jobs fast enough to employ workers.
    d. It is a consequence of government intervention in the economy.

    Answer: c   Type: M   Page(s): 342

20. Which of the following statements does not characterize urbanization?

    a. It involves rural migrants settling in urban areas.
    b. Third World nations possess all the necessary services to meet urban needs.
    c. The rate of urban population growth is often greater than the population growth.
    d. Urban areas are often poor and crime-ridden.

    Answer: b   Type: M   Page(s): 344

21. Modernization theory has been criticized because

    a. Some question whether the path to economic development taken by the North can be duplicated in the South.
    b. The structure of the international trading system is biased against the North.
    c. There is a lack of international competition to spur these nations to work harder.
    d. Third World economies tend to be too diversified.

    Answer: a   Type: M   Page(s): 344

22. Dependency theory emphasizes that the causes of underdevelopment are a result of

    a. The policies of underdeveloped nations.
    b. Marxism.
    c. The international system.
    d. Impersonal forces.

    Answer: c Type: M   Page(s): 345

23. Dependency theory is most closely associated with

    a. Liberalism.
    b. Marxism.
    c. Realism.
    d. Mercantilism.

    Answer: b Type: M   Page(s): 345

24. According to dependency theory, the role of the periphery is to

    a. Provide manufactured goods.
    b. Provide professional services.
    c. Industrialize.
    d. Provide raw materials.

    Answer: d Type: M   Page(s): 345

25. Primary products would include

    a. Steel.
    b. Computers.
    c. Timber.
    d. Highways.

    Answer: c Type: M   Page(s): 346

26. Which of the following is an example of a country whose exports are dominated by a single commodity?

    a. Saudi Arabia.
    b. Brazil.
    c. France.
    d. Japan.

    Answer: a Type: M   Page(s): 346

Harcourt Brace & Company

27. Among the problems faced by countries that are dominated by a single export commodity is

    a. Boom and bust cycles.
    b. The development of substitutes or alternatives.
    c. Sensitivity to price fluctuations.
    d. Difficulty in long-term planning.
    e. All of the above.

Answer: e Type: M   Page(s): 346-347

28. Unequal terms of trade refers to

    a. Currency exchange-rates.
    b. Urban-rural cleavages.
    c. Ratio of export prices to import prices.
    d. Ratio of labor investment to capital investment.

Answer: c Type: M   Page(s): 347

29. Monopsony refers to

    a. A condition where there are more buyers than sellers of a product.
    b. State control of industry.
    c. Boom and bust cycles.
    d. A condition where there are more sellers than buyers of a product.

Answer: d Type: M   Page(s): 348

30. Which of the following is a multinational corporation?

    a. The United Nations.
    b. IBM.
    c. NATO.
    d. The North American Free Trade Agreement.

Answer: b Type: M   Page(s): 348

31. Modernization theorists argue that MNCs

    a. Are harmful to the Third World.
    b. Promote dependence on export commodities.
    c. Provide capital to Third World countries.
    d. All of the above.
    e. None of the above.

Answer: c Type: M   Page(s): 348

Harcourt Brace & Company

32. Dependency theorists contend that MNCs

    a. Provide capital, technology, and training in Third World nations.
    b. Engage in transfer-pricing in order to disguise profits.
    c. Transfer only the most backward technology to the Third World.
    d. Do not utilize local capital to fund their projects.

    Answer: b Type: M   Page(s): 349

33. Capital-intensive technology

    a. Does not require skilled workers.
    b. Is utilized only in the North.
    c. Is appropriate technology for most of the Third World.
    d. All of the above.
    e. None of the above.

    Answer: e Type: M   Page(s): 349

34. Dependency theorists charge that MNCs

    a. Are worse than colonial powers.
    b. Are better than colonial powers.
    c. Are better than communism.
    d. Are of great assistance to the Third World.

    Answer: a Type: M   Page(s): 350

35. Which of the following serves as an example of the possibility of economic growth in the South?

    a. Africa.
    b. The Middle East.
    c. The East Asian "Tigers".
    d. The United States.

    Answer: c Type: M   Page(s): 350

36. What do we actually know about terms of trade between the developed and developing nations?

    a. Terms of trade always favor the developed nations.
    b. Terms of trade tend to fluctuate more for the developing nations.
    c. Terms of trade have been increasing for everyone.
    d. Only the developed nations have experienced declining terms of trade.

    Answer: b Type: M   Page(s): 351

37. Which of the following is not one of the trading strategies the Third World has used to pursue development?

   a. Emphasis on one export commodity.
   b. Collective bargaining.
   c. Import-substitution industrialization.
   d. Export-led industrialization.

   Answer: a Type: M   Page(s): 354

38. Import-substitution industrialization involves

   a. Encouraging greater self-sufficiency.
   b. Protectionist trade policies.
   c. Encouraging the manufacturing of products otherwise imported from abroad.
   d. All of the above.
   e. None of the above.

   Answer: d Type: M   Page(s): 354-355

39. Import-substitution industrialization often leads to

   a. Great success in boosting export earnings.
   b. Initial growth followed by heavy borrowing and severe indebtedness.
   c. Long-term economic development.
   d. Decreased reliance on capital from the Northern nations.

   Answer: b Type: M   Page(s): 355

40. The export-led industrialization strategy involves

   a. Commodity cartels.
   b. Buffer stocks.
   c. Intensive state intervention in the economy.
   d. Dependency theory.

   Answer: c Type: M   Page(s): 356

41. Which nation followed an export-led industrialization strategy?

   a. Tanzania.
   b. Nicaragua.
   c. South Korea.
   d. Russia.

   Answer: c Type: M   Page(s): 356

42. Export-led industrialization strategies are most closely related to

    a. Modernization theory.
    b. Dependency theory.
    c. Commodity cartels.
    d. Collective bargaining.

    Answer: a   Type: M   Page(s): 356

43. Some argue that export-led industrialization will not work for most nations because

    a. They are too poor.
    b. Successful NICs have crowded out other potential nations from the global market.
    c. Foreign investment capital will not be attracted to economically risky Third World nations.
    d. Such strategies only work in Asia.

    Answer: b   Type: M   Page(s): 358

44. Which of the following did not undermine the power of OPEC?

    a. The switch to alternative energy sources.
    b. Disagreements among OPEC members.
    c. Discovery of other oil sources.
    d. The 1973 Yom Kippur War.

    Answer: d   Type: M   Page(s): 358

45. The nations that belong to the New International Economic Order advocate

    a. Collective bargaining.
    b. Export-led industrialization.
    c. Import-substitution industrialization.
    d. Foreign investment.

    Answer: a   Type: M   Page(s): 359

46. Which of the following is typical of a collective bargaining organization?

    a. The United Nations.
    b. The United States.
    c. The Organization of Petroleum Exporting Countries.
    d. The World Bank.

    Answer: c   Type: M   Page(s): 361

47. The problem with commodity cartels was that

    a. The resources they typically involved were much too valuable.
    b. There were too few nations involved in them.
    c. They did not involve nationalization of industry.
    d. Their commodities were not nearly as valuable as something like oil.

Answer: d Type: M   Page(s): 361-362

48. Bilateral aid is

    a. Aid given by one nation directly to another.
    b. Aid given to Europe.
    c. Aid given by the former communist nations.
    d. Aid given by international institutions.

Answer: a Type: M   Page(s): 362

49. The Marshall Plan is an example of

    a. Multilateral aid.
    b. Bilateral aid.
    c. Private aid.
    d. All of the above.
    e. None of the above.

Answer: b Type: M   Page(s): 362

50. Multilateral aid is given by

    a. Individual states.
    b. Charitable organizations.
    c. International organizations.
    d. Multinational corporations.

Answer: c Type: M   Page(s): 363

51. Which of the following is not an example of multilateral aid?

    a. Aid given by the United States.
    b. Aid given by the United Nations.
    c. Aid given by the International Monetary Fund.
    d. Aid given by the World Bank.

Answer: a Type: M   Page(s): 363

52. Bilateral aid may cause problems in developing nations because

    a. It usually forces nations to quickly enact economic reforms.
    b. It encourages privatization.
    c. It discourages incentives to develop local production.
    d. It does not subsidize the bureaucracies and elites who govern.

    Answer: c Type: M   Page(s): 363

53. Bilateral aid is often

    a. Used to support local bureaucratic and governmental elites.
    b. A great portion of a country's GNP.
    c. Viewed with great skepticism in the United States.
    d. All of the above.
    e. None of the above.

    Answer: d Type: M   Page(s): 363

54. The debt crisis of the 1980s was brought about in part by

    a. The Marshall Plan.
    b. Soaring oil prices in the late 1970s.
    c. Declining terms of trade.
    d. Structural adjustment.

    Answer: b Type: M   Page(s): 364

55. When money is lent with certain strings attached, this is known as

    a. Conditionality.
    b. Multilateral aid.
    c. Dependency.
    d. Comparative advantage.

    Answer: a Type: M   Page(s): 364

56. Structural adjustment policies include

    a. Increasing government spending.
    b. Increasing state ownership of industry.
    c. Opening markets to exports.
    d. Overvaluing currency.

    Answer: c Type: M   Page(s): 365

Chapter 8

57. Which of the following best characterizes structural adjustment policies?

a. They are extremely popular in the Third World.
b. They discourage free market reforms.
c. Private investment is most attracted to countries that refuse to implement structural adjustment policies.
d. All of the above.
e. None of the above.

Answer: e Type: M Page(s): 365

58. Non-governmental organizations typically emphasize

a. Structural adjustment programs.
b. Humanitarian aid.
c. Declining terms of trade.
d. Military assistance.

Answer: b Type: M Page(s): 366

59. Which of the following is not an example of a non-governmental organization?

a. World Bank.
b. Doctors Without Borders.
c. CARE.
d. Red Cross.

Answer: a Type: M Page(s): 366

60. Which type of aid is most likely to be focused around assisting victims of natural disasters?

a. Bilateral aid.
b. Multilateral aid.
c. Private aid.
d. Military aid.

Answer: c Type: M Page(s): 366

61. Bilateral aid programs typically emphasize

a. Humanitarian aid.
b. AIDS prevention and treatment.
c. Natural disaster relief.
d. Military aid.

Answer: d Type: M Page(s): 366

North-South Economic Relations: The Challenge of Development

62. Major U.S. aid recipients include

a. Israel.
b. Egypt.
c. Turkey.
d. All of the above.
e. None of the above.

Answer: d Type: M   Page(s): 366

63. U.S. foreign aid mostly emphasizes

a. Humanitarian projects.
b. Import-substitution strategies.
c. Commodity cartels.
d. Political and strategic interests.

Answer: d Type: M   Page(s): 366-367

64. Developing nations often criticize aid programs because

a. Foreign aid is spread too evenly among recipients.
b. Not enough military assistance is given to the developing world.
c. Bilateral aid is often tied to the purchase of products from the donor country.
d. Aid does not often go toward the development of big projects.

Answer: c Type: M   Page(s): 367

65. Large, highly visible aid projects are criticized because

a. They often win out over less visible projects.
b. They are never funded by donor nations.
c. They do not increase the prestige of either the donor or the recipient.
d. They are not important.

Answer: a Type: M   Page(s): 367

66. Among the current problems involving North-South trade is/are

a. The end of the Cold War.
b. Protectionism among many wealthy nations.
c. Political and social costs of free trade in the North.
d. All of the above.

Answer: d Type: M   Page(s): 368

Harcourt Brace & Company

67. One of the major problems in the U.S.-China relationship has been

a. China's MFN status.
b. China's import-substitution strategy.
c. China's commodity cartel.
d. Chinese economic reforms.

Answer: a   Type: M   Page(s): 369

68. NAFTA was opposed by many in the United States for all except which of the following reasons?

a. Mexican labor unions are controlled by the government.
b. Mexican environmental standards are too strictly enforced.
c. Mexican wages are much lower than American wages.
d. Mexican health and safety standards are much lower than in the U.S.

Answer: b   Type: M   Page(s): 370

69. Mexico has what kind of government?

a. Communist.
b. One-party.
c. Multi-party democracy.
d. Mercantilist.

Answer: b   Type: M   Page(s): 372

70. International trade will make nations increasingly

a. Isolationist.
b. Authoritarian.
c. Interdependent.
d. Poor.

Answer: c   Type: M   Page(s): 372

TRUE/FALSE

71. Development is one of the most ambiguous terms in social science.

a. True
b. False

Answer: A   Type: T   Page(s): 334

72. Subsistence agriculture typically involves a small percentage of farmers who are responsible for feeding the nation.

   a. True
   b. False

   Answer: B   Type: T   Page(s): 335

73. The Third World is quite uniform in terms of economic growth.

   a. True
   b. False

   Answer: B   Type: T   Page(s): 334-335

74. The OPEC nations are among the most wealthy of the Third World nations.

   a. True
   b. False

   Answer: A   Type: T   Page(s): 337

75. Modernization theorists contend that the nations of the South should follow their own paths to development.

   a. True
   b. False

   Answer: B   Type: T   Page(s): 338

76. Modernization theory contends that the global trading system can be a great help to development.

   a. True
   b. False

   Answer: A   Type: T   Page(s): 339

77. Traditional societies generally have very low birth and death rates.

   a. True
   b. False

   Answer: B   Type: T   Page(s): 339

Harcourt Brace & Company

78. The fertility rate tends to be highest in low-income nations.

    a. True
    b. False

    Answer: A   Type: T   Page(s): 340

79. Urbanization often results from demographic transition and industrialization.

    a. True
    b. False

    Answer: A   Type: T   Page(s): 342

80. According to Dependency theorists, the poor nations of the Third World belong to the Core.

    a. True
    b. False

    Answer: B   Type: T   Page(s): 345

81. The exports of many Southern countries are dominated by a single commodity.

    a. True
    b. False

    Answer: A   Type: T   Page(s): 346

82. Multinational corporations typically have their headquarters in the Third World.

    a. True
    b. False

    Answer: B   Type: T   Page(s): 348

83. The sales of some MNCs exceed the gross national products of some industrialized nations.

    a. True
    b. False

    Answer: A   Type: T   Page(s): 348

Harcourt Brace & Company

84. In actuality, both developing and developed nations have experienced periods of declining terms of trade.

a. True
b. False

Answer: A   Type: T   Page(s): 351

85. The New International Economic Order was based on the ideas of liberal economics and modernization theory.

a. True
b. False

Answer: B   Type: T   Page(s): 360

86. Many successful commodity cartels have been established to regulate the prices of primary products.

a. True
b. False

Answer: B   Type: T   Page(s): 361-362

87. Bilateral aid has enjoyed unqualified success in the Third World.

a. True
b. False

Answer: B   Type: T   Page(s): 362-363

88. Currently, the U.S. devotes a greater share of its GNP to foreign aid than any other nation.

a. True
b. False

Answer: B   Type: T   Page(s): 363

89. Structural adjustment programs often meet with strong opposition from citizens of developing nations.

a. True
b. False

Answer: A   Type: T   Page(s): 365

90. Often, aid in the developing nations is tied to the purchase of products from the donor country.

    a. True
    b. False

    Answer:
    A

    Type: T   Page(s): 367

91. The massacre in Tiananmen Square led many in the U.S. to call for the withdrawal of China's MFN status.

    a. True
    b. False

    Answer: A   Type: T   Page(s): 369

92. The North American Free Trade Agreement is the first treaty that has attempted to link First and Third World economies.

    a. True
    b. False

    Answer: A   Type: T   Page(s): 369

93. The development strategy pursued by most nations today is export-led industrialization.

    a. True
    b. False

    Answer: A   Type: T   Page(s): 372

94. Most experts agree that industrialization should not be the cure for the poverty and misery of the Third World.

    a. True
    b. False

    Answer: B   Type: T   Page(s): 373

95. For Southern countries, development is not an option, but an imperative.

    a. True
    b. False

    Answer: A   Type: T   Page(s): 374

Chapter 9

International Law and Organizations

1. Which event best illustrates many of the problems international organizations have in responding to crises?

   a. The Iraqi invasion of Kuwait.
   b. The war in Bosnia-Herzegovina.
   c. The North American Free Trade Agreement.
   d. The Korean War.

   Answer: b Type: M   Page(s): 380

2. The one crucial difference between international and domestic politics is that international politics is

   a. Democratic.
   b. Governed by a central authority.
   c. Anarchic.
   d. More peaceful.

   Answer: c Type: M   Page(s): 380

3. The "law of nations" reflects

   a. The decentralized nature of the international system.
   b. The centralized power of the international sovereign.
   c. The power of the United Nations legislative body.
   d. The lack of reciprocity among nations.

   Answer: a Type: M   Page(s): 381

Harcourt Brace & Company

4. Reciprocity in relations among nations implies

   a. The presence of a centralized international power.
   b. The presence of an international sovereign.
   c. The presence of a single international institution with coercive powers.
   d. One state treating another as it would hope to be treated in return.

   Answer: d Type: M   Page(s): 381

5. International law is ultimately based on

   a. Anarchy.
   b. An international sovereign.
   c. Reciprocity.
   d. Distrust.

   Answer: c Type: M   Page(s): 381

6. Which of the following statements most accurately describes the extent to which states obey international law?

   a. States are more apt to comply with international laws than violate them.
   b. States rarely, if ever, comply with international laws.
   c. Only the major powers obey international laws.
   d. States always obey international laws.

   Answer: a Type: M   Page(s): 385

7. States obey international law because

   a. There is an international sovereign enforcing law.
   b. They fear sanction or reprisal.
   c. They all agree on its meaning and intent.
   d. All of the above.
   e. None of the above.

   Answer: b Type: M   Page(s): 385

8. International law may be enforced by reciprocity because

   a. The long-term benefits of observing international law outweigh the short-term advantages of violating it.
   b. States are encouraged not to practice "tit for tat" behavior.
   c. It promotes an environment in which cheaters prosper.
   d. It encourages the behavior of pariah states.

   Answer: a Type: M   Page(s): 385

9. Which of the following is a good example of a pariah state?

   a. Switzerland.
   b. Sweden.
   c. Japan.
   d. North Korea.

Answer: d Type: M Page(s): 386

10. The Dutch jurist who is often considered to be the first international lawyer was

   a. Vincent Van Gogh.
   b. John Locke.
   c. Hugo Grotius.
   d. Kurt Waldheim.

Answer: c Type: M Page(s): 382

11. International law is derived from

   a. The World Legislature.
   b. Customary practices.
   c. The United States.
   d. Pariah states.

Answer: b Type: M Page(s): 382

12. Which of the following best describes the nature of customary practices in international law?

   a. They have been regarded as binding even on those states that never expressly consented to them.
   b. They are of relatively recent origin.
   c. They are the results of pariah states.
   d. They lack the element of reciprocity.

Answer: a Type: M Page(s): 382

13. Treaties involve which of the following?

   a. Written contracts that impose obligations on only the states that sign them.
   b. Bilateral agreements.
   c. Multilateral agreements.
   d. All of the above.
   e. None of the above.

Answer: d Type: M Page(s): 383

14. Multilateral treaties involve

a. Written contracts that impose obligations even on those states that never expressly consented to them.
b. Agreements between only two nations.
c. Only pariah states.
d. All of the above.
e. None of the above.

Answer: e Type: M   Page(s): 384

15. National sovereignty holds that

a. The international sovereign is responsible for all law.
b. States are required to defer customary practices.
c. Individual states are the ultimate authorities within their own countries.
d. Individual states may not act independently in international relations.

Answer: c Type: M   Page(s): 386

16. Which of the following is not an example of states contesting sovereignty over territory?

a. The Falkland Islands War.
b. The 1979 Iranian takeover of the U.S. embassy.
c. The Vietnamese invasion of Cambodia.
d. The Iraqi invasion of Kuwait.

Answer: b Type: M   Page(s): 387

17. Personal sovereignty allows governments that do not face democratic constraints on thei power

a. To punish pariah states.
b. To invade other countries.
c. To practice diplomatic immunity.
d. To ignore the human rights of their own citizens.

Answer: d Type: M   Page(s): 387

18. The idea of a social contract

    a. Confers rights as well as obligations on citizens and their rulers.
    b. Encourages governments to ignore the rights of their citizens.
    c. Was developed after World War II.
    d. Is a product of the world's increasing globalization.

    Answer: a Type: M   Page(s): 388

19. According to positive law

    a. States should only do good things for their citizens.
    b. Human action is the foundation of law and laws are meaningless without sovereign
       authority to enforce them.
    c. International treaties are the highest form of law.
    d. Certain human rights derive from a higher law that cannot be taken away by
       governments.

    Answer: b Type: M   Page(s): 388

20. The Nuremberg Trials were held in response to

    a. The Soviet invasion of Czechoslovakia.
    b. German responsibility for starting World War I.
    c. The United States' arming of the Nicaraguan contras.
    d. Nazi war crimes during World War II.

    Answer: d Type: M   Page(s): 389

21. The international organization most responsible for turning principles of human rights
    into international agreements has been

    a. The United Nations.
    b. The United States.
    c. The International Monetary Fund.
    d. Amnesty International.

    Answer: a Type: M   Page(s): 389

22. During the Cold War, the issue of human rights

    a. Was rarely mentioned.
    b. Took precedence over state sovereignty.
    c. Became highly politicized.
    d. Was used only by the West against the communist nations.

    Answer: c Type: M   Page(s): 390

23. The United Nations has faced tremendous problems in stopping ethnic cleansing in which nation?

    a. France.
    b. Chile.
    c. The former Yugoslavia.
    d. Czechoslovakia.

    Answer: c Type: M   Page(s): 391

24. Under the UN Charter, states are allowed to use force

    a. When they feel threatened.
    b. To promote human rights.
    c. Only after the UN authorizes it.
    d. In self-defense.

    Answer: d Type: M   Page(s): 391

25. Nations have attempted to regulate the conduct of war by

    a. Setting limits on the methods of warfare.
    b. Banning chemical weapons.
    c. Protecting the rights of prisoners and wounded combatants.
    d. All of the above.
    e. None of the above.

    Answer: d Type: M   Page(s): 391-392

26. Which of the following was not one of the conflicts that marked the 1992 Rio Earth Summit?

    a. North-South relations.
    b. Problems between capitalists and communists.
    c. How to protect the environment and maintain economic growth.
    d. Financial aid and the transfer of technology.

    Answer: b Type: M   Page(s): 394

27. In the 1990s, which state was most opposed to reductions on carbon dioxide emissions?

    a. The United States.
    b. Russia.
    c. Japan.
    d. Brazil.

    Answer: a Type: M   Page(s): 394

28. In order to preserve the earth's ozone layer, international agreements have called for reducing the level of

    a. Nuclear testing.
    b. Acid rain.
    c. Automobile emissions.
    d. Chlorofluorocarbons.

    Answer: d Type: M Page(s): 393

29. Those most opposed to efforts to preserve the earth's ozone layer include

    a. The United States.
    b. The underdeveloped nations.
    c. The developed nations.
    d. Those closest to the two polar regions.

    Answer: b Type: M Page(s): 393

30. Those opposed to efforts to preserve the earth's ozone layer argue that

    a. There is no danger to the ozone.
    b. Sustainable development can take place with a reduced ozone layer.
    c. Underdeveloped nations should not be denied the opportunity to economically modernize without costly regulations.
    d. The industrialized nations have been unfairly overburdened with the cost of regulating.

    Answer: c Type: M Page(s): 393

31. Which continent has been the site of significant environmental cooperation?

    a. Antarctica.
    b. Australia.
    c. America.
    d. Africa.

    Answer: a Type: M Page(s): 393

Harcourt Brace & Company

32. Which of the following statements best characterizes policy over the uses of the ocean

    a. The most developed nations have advocated international control of the oceans' resources.
    b. The less developed nations have advocated international control of the oceans' resources.
    c. The United States has been a staunch supporter of the international management of th mining of ocean-floor minerals.
    d. The treaty has been readily accepted by all nations of the world.

    Answer: b   Type: M   Page(s): 396

33. Which of the following plays a vital role in the success or failure of international agreements?

    a. How well-liked the agreement is.
    b. Who has been responsible for the agreement.
    c. How long the agreement has been in existence.
    d. How effective the enforcement of the agreement is.

    Answer: d   Type: M   Page(s): 397

34. Intergovernmental organizations include all but which of the following?

    a. Amnesty International.
    b. The United Nations.
    c. The North Atlantic Treaty Organization.
    d. The World Bank.

    Answer: a   Type: M   Page(s): 397-398

35. Nongovernmental organizations would include which of the following?

    a. Greenpeace.
    b. The Red Cross.
    c. Amnesty International.
    d. All of the above.
    e. None of the above.

    Answer: d   Type: M   Page(s): 398

Harcourt Brace & Company

36. Which of the following best describes nongovernmental organizations?

    a. They have traditionally been ineffective in changing governments' policies.
    b. They include states in their membership.
    c. They would not include such groups as Amnesty International.
    d. All of the above.
    e. None of the above.

    Answer: e Type: M   Page(s): 398

37. Intergovernmental organizations have become increasingly important because

    a. States realize they cannot address all problems plaguing the international system.
    b. They are so few in number.
    c. They involve only the most important nations.
    d. It is agreed that the world needs one centralized government to manage its problems.

    Answer: a Type: M   Page(s): 398

38. One of the first intergovernmental organizations was

    a. The United Nations.
    b. The World Bank.
    c. The European Union.
    d. The Concert of Europe.

    Answer: d Type: M   Page(s): 399

39. The League of Nations resulted from

    a. The end of the Napoleonic wars.
    b. The end of World War I.
    c. The end of World War II.
    d. The end of the Cold War.

    Answer: b Type: M   Page(s): 400

40. Which nation's absence from the League of Nations severely hindered any chance it had for success?

    a. Great Britain.
    b. France.
    c. The United States.
    d. China.

    Answer: c Type: M   Page(s): 400

41. The League of Nations attempted to prevent international conflict by what method?

    a. Collective security.
    b. Foreign investment.
    c. Balance of power.
    d. Hegemony.

    Answer: a   Type: M   Page(s): 400

42. Which of the following problems did not plague the League of Nations?

    a. Great Britain and France continued to practice balance-of-power politics.
    b. Germany and Japan withdrew from its membership.
    c. The United States dominated almost all the League's policies.
    d. Some major powers were excluded from its membership.

    Answer: c   Type: M   Page(s): 400-401

43. The League of Nations often found it difficult to act because

    a. Any member could block a decision to take action.
    b. It was difficult to enforce its decisions.
    c. Most of the major decisions were watered down to the point of meaninglessness.
    d. All of the above.
    e. None of the above.

    Answer: d   Type: M   Page(s): 401

44. The United Nations was created

    a. After the defeat of Germany and Japan in World War II.
    b. In response to the North Korean invasion of South Korea.
    c. After decolonization began in the Third World.
    d. In response to the end of the Napoleonic wars.

    Answer: a   Type: M   Page(s): 402

45. Which of the following statements best summarizes the impact of the United Nations?

    a. The United Nations has been successful in stopping almost all acts of aggression.
    b. The United Nations has been responsible for decolonization in the Third World.
    c. The United Nations has mainly been an arena for political grandstanding and
       competition.
    d. The United Nations has not worked nearly as well as the League of Nations.

    Answer: c   Type: M   Page(s): 402

46. Voting in the United Nations General Assembly is based on

    a. A state's population.
    b. One state, one vote.
    c. A state's contribution to the UN's operating budget.
    d. Possession of nuclear weapons.

    Answer: b Type: M   Page(s): 404

47. What is required to pass a resolution in the Security Council?

    a. A majority vote.
    b. The support of either the United States or the Soviet Union.
    c. Unanimity.
    d. The support of only one nation.

    Answer: c Type: M   Page(s): 405

48. The United Nations has authorized military action on which of the following occasions?

    a. During the Vietnam War.
    b. During World War II.
    c. During the Soviet intervention in Afghanistan.
    d. All of the above.
    e. None of the above.

    Answer: e Type: M   Page(s): 405-406

49. Which of the following best describes the power of the Secretary General?

    a. He/She can veto any action taken by the Security Council.
    b. He/She has little power to act independently of the Security Council or General
       Assembly.
    c. He/She appoints nations to the Security Council.
    d. He/She is in charge of all UN peacekeeping operations.

    Answer: b Type: M   Page(s): 407

50. The Security Council has been dominated by

    a. Conflict between the United States and the Soviet Union.
    b. Conflict between the developed and underdeveloped nations.
    c. Conflict over the admission of states to the General Assembly.
    d. Conflict between the Soviet Union and China.

    Answer: a Type: M   Page(s): 406

Harcourt Brace & Company

51. The United Nations headquarters is located in

    a. Geneva, Switzerland.
    b. Paris, France.
    c. New York, New York.
    d. Washington, D.C.

    Answer: c Type: M   Page(s): 406

52. Which of the following best describes the powers of the World Court?

    a. Its decisions are not formally binding between the parties concerned.
    b. It has no formal mechanism to enforce its rulings.
    c. State sovereignty has significantly enhanced its powers.
    d. All of the above.
    e. None of the above.

    Answer: b Type: M   Page(s): 410

53. Which of the following is not one of the United Nations' subsidiary agencies?

    a. The North Atlantic Treaty Organization.
    b. The World Health Organization.
    c. The Universal Postal Union.
    d. The International Children's Emergency Fund.

    Answer: a Type: M   Page(s): 411

54. Disputes over the United Nations' subsidiary agencies have involved

    a. Conflicts that involve state sovereignty.
    b. Conflicts that involve the Universal Postal Union.
    c. Conflicts that involve the Food and Agriculture Organization.
    d. All of the above.
    e. None of the above.

    Answer: a Type: M   Page(s): 412

55. The three types of collective security missions the UN undertakes include all except which of the following?

    a. Observer missions.
    b. Nation-building missions.
    c. Peacekeeping missions.
    d. Peace-enforcement missions.

    Answer: b Type: M   Page(s): 414

176

56. Peacekeeping missions differ from peace-enforcement missions because

 a. Peacekeeping missions do not involve the Security Council members, while peace-enforcement missions do.
 b. Peace-enforcement missions require the permission of the countries where the UN forces have operated, while peacekeeping missions do not.
 c. Peace-enforcement missions do not involve the use of military force while peacekeeping missions do.
 d. Peacekeeping missions are designed to prevent combat, while peace-enforcement missions usually involve combat.

Answer: d Type: M   Page(s): 414

57. UN peacekeeping missions have taken place in which of the following countries?

 a. Yugoslavia.
 b. Cambodia.
 c. Somalia.
 d. All of the above.
 e. None of the above.

Answer: d Type: M   Page(s): 414

58. The end of the Cold War has had what effect on UN peacekeeping missions?

 a. It has dramatically increased them.
 b. It has significantly decreased the need for them.
 c. It has allowed ethnic conflicts to continue unnoticed.
 d. It has had no effect.

Answer: a Type: M   Page(s): 414

59. The biggest challenge facing UN peacekeeping missions in the future is

 a. The absence of any need for them.
 b. The lack of political support for them.
 c. The lack of financial support for them.
 d. The lack of support from the Security Council for them.

Answer: c Type: M   Page(s): 415

60. The founders of the United Nations envisioned that peace would be kept by

    a. Debating the great issues in the General Assembly.
    b. The presence of nuclear weapons.
    c. Economic prosperity.
    d. The efforts of the great powers.

    Answer: d   Type: M   Page(s): 419

61. The UN mission against Iraq may best be characterized as a(n)

    a. Peace-enforcement mission.
    b. Peacekeeping mission.
    c. Observer mission.
    d. Peaceful mission.

    Answer: a   Type: M   Page(s): 414

62. General purpose intergovernmental organizations include

    a. The North Atlantic Treaty Organization.
    b. Organization of American States.
    c. Amnesty International.
    d. Multinational corporations.

    Answer: b   Type: M   Page(s): 423

63. The Commonwealth of Independent States would best be characterized as a

    a. Specialized intergovernmental organization.
    b. Nongovernmental organization.
    c. Multinational corporation.
    d. General-purpose intergovernmental organization.

    Answer: d   Type: M   Page(s): 423

64. The Conference on Security and Cooperation in Europe would best be characterized as a

    a. Specialized intergovernmental organization.
    b. Nongovernmental organization.
    c. Multinational corporation.
    d. General-purpose intergovernmental organization.

    Answer: a   Type: M   Page(s): 424

65. The International Red Cross would best be characterized as a

a. General-purpose intergovernmental organization.
b. Multinational corporation.
c. Nongovernmental organization.
d. Specialized intergovernmental organization.
e. None of the above.

Answer: c Type: M   Page(s): 427

66. Multinational corporations would include which of the following?

a. The Irish Republican Army.
b. McDonald's.
c. The International Red Cross.
d. The Organization of Economic Cooperation and Development.

Answer: b Type: M   Page(s): 426

67. International laws and organizations have sometimes failed in their purposes for all but which of the following reasons?

a. They have been poorly designed.
b. Weakness of leadership.
c. The ready willingness of states to give up sovereignty.
d. Weakness of ethics of those running them.

Answer: c Type: M   Page(s): 428

68. Ultimately, the international environment is mostly

a. Governed by the United Nations.
b. Dominated by multinational corporations.
c. No longer based on sovereignty.
d. Anarchic.

Answer: d Type: M   Page(s): 428

69. Which of the following nations is not a member of the UN Security Council?

a. France.
b. Japan.
c. Russia.
d. China.

Answer: b Type: M   Page(s): 413

70. The current (1997) secretary general of the U.N. is

    a. Kurt Waldheim.
    b. Boutros-Boutros Ghali.
    c. Javier Perez de Cuellar.
    d. Kofi Anan.

    Answer: d   Type: M   Page(s): 410

71. In recent decades, the rights of which group have acquired a special place in international human rights laws?

    a. Women.
    b. Military.
    c. Minorities.
    d. Homosexuals.

    Answer: a   Type: M   Page(s): 390

72. The main components of the League of Nations included all of the following *except*:

    a. The Assembly.
    b. The Council.
    c. The Secreteriate.
    d. The Chair.
    e. The World Court.

    Answer: d   Type: M   Page(s): 401

73. The former Warsaw Pact members who sought membership in NATO and were invited to join i 1997 were:

    a. Poland, Hungary, the Czech Republic.
    b. Poland, Romania, Hungary.
    c. The Czech Republic, Romania, Poland.
    d. Hungary, Romania.

    Answer: a   Type: M   Page(s): 424

74. This document focuses on Women's Rights in the 21st century

    a. The Beijing Declaration.
    b. The Human Rights Declaration.
    c. The Women's Rights Protocol.
    d. The Human Rights Protocol.

    Answer: a   Type: M   Page(s): 422

75. The First African and First Arab to lead the U.N. was:

    a. Boutros-Boutros Ghali.
    b. Kofi Anan.
    c. Kurt Waldheim.
    d. Abraham Ayaan.
    e. None of the above.

Answer: a Type: M   Page(s): 410

TRUE/FALSE

76. Only in the last few years have efforts been made to establish authority in the international system.

    a. True
    b. False

Answer: B   Type: T   Page(s): 380

77. All international organizations are forces for globalization.

    a. True
    b. False

Answer: A   Type: T   Page(s): 380

78. It is not in the best interest of nations to preserve international order.

    a. True
    b. False

Answer: B   Type: T   Page(s): 385

79. Diplomatic immunity refers to extending freedom from arrest to all foreigners visiting a nation.

    a. True
    b. False

Answer: B   Type: T   Page(s): 382-383

Harcourt Brace & Company

80. Conflicts over which nations have sovereignty over a certain territory are almost alway decided peacefully.

    a. True
    b. False

    Answer: B   Type: T   Page(s): 387

81. The idea that sovereign governments ought to be subject to international legal constraints to prevent them from violating the human rights of their citizens is a relatively new phenomenon.

    a. True
    b. False

    Answer: A   Type: T   Page(s): 388

82. One of the most important controversies over international human rights agreements has been between those nations which stress individual rights and those which stress collective economic rights.

    a. True
    b. False

    Answer: A   Type: T   Page(s): 390

83. Efforts to regulate the conduct of warfare have been extremely successful.

    a. True
    b. False

    Answer: B   Type: T   Page(s): 392

84. The Law of the Sea governs the use of the continent of Antarctica.

    a. True
    b. False

    Answer: B   Type: T   Page(s): 396

85. The most numerous actors in international relations are international organizations.

    a. True
    b. False

    Answer: A   Type: T   Page(s): 407

Harcourt Brace & Company

36. All international organizations are concerned with developments in the entire world.

    a. True
    b. False

    Answer: B   Type: T   Page(s): 399

37. The Concert of Europe grew out of the Napoleonic wars.

    a. True
    b. False

    Answer: A   Type: T   Page(s): 399

38. The United States never belonged to the League of Nations.

    a. True
    b. False

    Answer: A   Type: T   Page(s): 400

39. The United States began to lose influence in the United Nations General Assembly after decolonization.

    a. True
    b. False

    Answer: A   Type: T   Page(s): 404

40. Since the end of the Cold War, United States influence in the United Nations General Assembly has severely declined.

    a. True
    b. False

    Answer: B   Type: T   Page(s): 404

41. The United Nations was able to intervene in Korea in the early 1950s because the Soviet Union was boycotting its meetings.

    a. True
    b. False

    Answer: A   Type: T   Page(s): 406

92. The UN Educational, Scientific and Cultural Organization has been accused of having an anti-Western bias.

    a. True
    b. False

    Answer: A   Type: T   Page(s): 412

93. The UN Blue Helmets received a Nobel Peace Prize for their peacekeeping work.

    a. True
    b. False

    Answer: A   Type: T   Page(s): 414

94. The unwillingness of many nations to give up sovereignty has been a major obstacle to conflict resolution.

    a. True
    b. False

    Answer: A   Type: T   Page(s): 420

95. General Motors is not a multinational corporation since it has its headquarters in the United States.

    a. True
    b. False

    Answer: B   Type: T   Page(s): 426

96. The founder of the International Red Cross was also the founder of the YMCA.

    a. True
    b. False

    Answer: A   Type: T   Page(s): 427

97. France is not a member of the UN Security Council.

    a. True
    b. False

    Answer: B   Type: T   Page(s): 413

Harcourt Brace & Company

98. The fundamental principle of national sovereignty was first set forth in the United Nations Charter.

    a. True
    b. False

    Answer: B Type: T   Page(s): 429

99. If peaceful means fail, the Security Council can impose harsh sanctions on a nation or even launch military actions:

    a. True
    b. False

    Answer: A Type: T   Page(s): 405

00. The U.N. was created to bring about world peace, and it has been successful in doing so.

    a. True
    b. False

    Answer: B Type: T   Page(s): 421

Harcourt Brace & Company

Chapter 10

Global Issues

1. As the ties that bind countries become more numerous and stronger

   a. States have found more to agree than disagree about.
   b. States have found more to disagree about.
   c. Interdependence has declined.
   d. The number of important global issues has remained about the same.

   Answer: b Type: M   Page(s): 433

2. Global issues include which of the following?

   a. Population movements.
   b. Environmental problems.
   c. Terrorism.
   d. All of the above.

   Answer: d Type: M   Page(s): 434

3. What makes an issue a global issue?

   a. When it affects many people.
   b. When a problem is widespread.
   c. When there is transnationality of cause and effect.
   d. When many people take action to address the issue.

   Answer: c Type: M   Page(s): 434

4. The last doubling of the world's population took approximately how many years?

   a. 40 years.
   b. 75 years.
   c. 150 years.
   d. 1000 years.

   Answer: a Type: M   Page(s): 434

5. Which of the following best describes population growth in the developed world?

    a. The birth rate has rapidly overtaken the death rate.
    b. Population growth has leveled off.
    c. The developed world has a greater population because of long-term growth.
    d. The population of the developed world is relatively young and fast-growing.

Answer: b   Type: M   Page(s): 436

6. Replacement fertility involves

    a. Maintaining population growth only in areas that can sustain more people.
    b. Allowing families which are capable of having children to have more offspring than infertile families.
    c. Maintaining population growth where two parents are replaced by only two children.
    d. Forbidding parents from having any more children than they can afford to.

Answer: c   Type: M   Page(s): 436

7. Which of these statements about family planning programs is true?

    a. Programs in developing nations, while strapped for cash, maintain complete and effective programs.
    b. Government support automatically leads to successful program implementation.
    c. Economic opportunities for women tend to lower birthrates.
    d. All of these statements are correct.

Answer: c   Type: M   Page(s): 437

8. One of the most effective ways of curbing rapid population growth is

    a. Increasing immigration.
    b. Increasing the world's food supply.
    c. Family planning programs.
    d. Advanced medical technology.

Answer: c   Type: M   Page(s): 437-438

9. The most controversial aspect of family planning is

    a. Replacement fertility.
    b. Abortion.
    c. Migration.
    d. Its effect on the environment.

Answer: b   Type: M   Page(s): 438

10. Which of the following best describes migration?

    a. It is an effective method of dealing with the population growth rate.
    b. It is entirely motivated by the need to better oneself economically.
    c. It generally involves people from poorer regions moving into the wealthier parts of the world.
    d. It has been outlawed by the United Nations.

Answer: c Type: M   Page(s): 438

11. Most immigrants coming to the U.S. come from

    a. Asia.
    b. Europe.
    c. Canada.
    d. The former Soviet Union.

Answer: a Type: M   Page(s): 439

12. Which of the following best describes the plight of refugees today?

    a. Their numbers have been declining as the UN has taken a more active role in world affairs.
    b. Refugees may be displaced within their own countries or flee to neighboring states or regions.
    c. Refugees come equally from the developed and developing world.
    d. All of the above.
    e. None of the above.

Answer: b Type: M   Page(s): 440

13. Which of the following countries has been affected by refugee problems?

    a. The Philippines.
    b. Iraq.
    c. Yugoslavia.
    d. Mozambique.
    e. All of the above.

Answer: e Type: M   Page(s): 441

Harcourt Brace & Company

14. Nativist movements are in favor of

    a. Allowing more immigration into their countries.
    b. Creating new jobs for immigrants.
    c. Restricting immigration.
    d. Allowing only natives of a country to immigrate.

    Answer: c Type: M Page(s): 441

15. Which of the following most accurately describes nativist movements?

    a. They have been on the decline since early in this century.
    b. They are often motivated by economic downturns.
    c. They have been politically ineffective.
    d. All of the above.
    e. None of the above.

    Answer: b Type: M Page(s): 441

16. Racist violence against immigrants has been particularly noticeable in which European nation?

    a. Germany.
    b. Sweden.
    c. Spain.
    d. The Netherlands.

    Answer: a Type: M Page(s): 443

17. The United States is most apt to accept immigrants from what countries?

    a. Those with which it has friendly relations.
    b. Those closest to the U.S.
    c. Those with which it has unfriendly relations.
    d. Those which are experiencing severe economic problems.

    Answer: c Type: M Page(s): 443

Harcourt Brace & Company

18. Which nations would be most likely to accept international agreements protecting the rights of immigrants?

a. The wealthier nations of the world.
b. Those nations to which people immigrate.
c. Third World nations.
d. All of the above.
e. None of the above.

Answer: c Type: M Page(s): 445

19. Repatriation involves

a. Returning refugees to their homelands.
b. Providing immigrants with economic support in their new countries.
c. Refusing to allow immigrants into a country.
d. Relocating immigrants to refugee camps.

Answer: a Type: M Page(s): 445

20. The most important challenge in feeding the world's population is

a. A shortage of food.
b. Food distribution.
c. Feeding refugees.
d. Discrimination.

Answer: b Type: M Page(s): 445

21. Which of the following limit(s) access to food?

a. Wars.
b. Poverty.
c. Natural disasters.
d. All of the above.

Answer: d Type: M Page(s): 446

22. To what African nation did the United Nations send military forces to distribute food in 1992?

a. Ethiopia.
b. Cuba.
c. Somalia.
d. India.

Answer: c Type: M Page(s): 447

Harcourt Brace & Company

23. The United States imposed a grain embargo against what nation in 1979?

    a. China.
    b. Haiti.
    c. Ethiopia.
    d. The Soviet Union.

Answer: d Type: M   Page(s): 447

24. Famine-relief efforts have been criticized for

    a. Focusing on food supply rather than food distribution.
    b. Promoting policies that often lead to environmental degradation.
    c. Not emphasizing the need to bring more land under cultivation in famine-stricken nations to grow food.
    d. Focusing too often on long-term needs.

Answer: b Type: M   Page(s): 448

25. The best solution to world hunger is

    a. Increasing the food supply.
    b. Focusing on short-term needs.
    c. Economic development.
    d. Bringing more land under cultivation.

Answer: c Type: M   Page(s): 448

26. Which of the following is the primary cause of deforestation?

    a. Lumber company clearcutting.
    b. War.
    c. Natural processes.
    d. Human settlement and agriculture.

Answer: d Type: M   Page(s): 449

27. Which of the following is not one of the consequences of deforestation?

    a. Loss of wildlife.
    b. Loss of arable land.
    c. Topsoil erosion.
    d. Increased emissions of carbon dioxide.

Answer: b Type: M   Page(s): 449-450

28. Industrial pollution

    a. Is evident only in industrailized nations.
    b. Is not a contentious issue, as all nations have attempted to reduce pollution levels.
    c. Creates tention between nations (i.e. Canada and the U.S.).
    d. Only affects the environment.

    Answer: c Type: M   Page(s): 451

29. Chlorofluorocarbons reduce the amount of

    a. Carbon emissions.
    b. Deforestation.
    c. Ozone.
    d. Air pollution.

    Answer: c Type: M   Page(s): 450-451

30. Many scientists argue that increased emission of greenhouse gases increases

    a. Desertification.
    b. Global warming.
    c. Global cooling.
    d. Urbanization.

    Answer: b Type: M   Page(s): 453

31. Which of the following best characterizes the debate over acid rain?

    a. The U.S. government blames Canada for the acid rain which falls in the United States.
    b. Acid rain is a direct cause of global warming.
    c. The technology necessary to stop acid rain is inexpensive and easy to implement.
    d. All of the above.
    e. None of the above.

    Answer: e Type: M   Page(s): 451

32. Which of the following best describes which nations are most responsible for atmospheric pollution?

    a. Currently, the Third World is responsible for most atmospheric pollution.
    b. Currently, the industrialized nations are most responsible for atmospheric pollution.
    c. Energy consumption is growing fastest in the industrialized nations.
    d. In the future, the Third World will be responsible for less pollution than the industrialized nations.

    Answer: b Type: M   Page(s): 451

Global Issues

33. During the late 1960s and early 1970s environmental conferences

    a. Did not make significant progress in finding solutions to environmental problems.
    b. Did not raise awareness of environmental problems.
    c. Found little link between economic development and environmental degradation.
    d. All of the above.
    e. None of the above.

    Answer: a   Type: M   Page(s): 452

34. Some of the most effective efforts to preserve the environment have been carried out by

    a. The United Nations.
    b. The United States.
    c. Nongovernmental organizations.
    d. The World Bank.

    Answer: c   Type: M   Page(s): 454

35. Which of the following has taken an active role in efforts to preserve the environment?

    a. American Forestry Association.
    b. The World Conservation Union.
    c. The Sierra Club.
    d. The United Nations Environmental Program.
    e. All of the above.

    Answer: e   Type: M   Page(s): 452-454

36. Environmental programs within states can prove successful only if

    a. the UN provided economic incentives.
    b. developing and developed nations adopt long term perspectives.
    c. more feasible, short-term perspectives on the ecosystem are adopted.
    d. the policies catered to the benefits of production and consumption.

    Answer: b   Type: M   Page(s): 455

37. Tropical diseases include which of the following?

    a. AIDS.
    b. Measles.
    c. Malaria.
    d. Polio.

    Answer: c   Type: M   Page(s): 455

Harcourt Brace & Company

38. In Africa, AIDS is transmitted primarily through

    a. Homosexual contact.
    b. Heterosexual contact.
    c. Insect bites.
    d. Intravenous drug usage.

    Answer: b Type: M   Page(s): 456

39. Which of the following is transmitted primarily by contaminated water?

    a. AIDS.
    b. Cholera.
    c. Measles.
    d. Tetanus.

    Answer: b Type: M   Page(s): 456

40. The World Health Organization projects by the year 2000 that

    a. There will be a cure for AIDS.
    b. The number of AIDS cases will have significantly decreased.
    c. There will be between 30 and 40 million cases worldwide of AIDS.
    d. There will be between 300 and 400 million cases worldwide of AIDS.

    Answer: c Type: M   Page(s): 456

41. The international organization responsible for immunization of diseases is

    a. The World Bank.
    b. WHO.
    c. IMF.
    d. UNCTAD.

    Answer: b Type: M   Page(s): 457

42. Efforts to deal with AIDS have concentrated primarily on

    a. Prevention.
    b. Cure.
    c. Immunization.
    d. Eradication.

    Answer: a Type: M   Page(s): 457

43. Which of the following best characterizes the response of individual governments toward AIDS?

    a. It has exacerbated international conflict.
    b. Many nations have denied they even have a problem.
    c. Many nations blame foreigners for the spread of AIDS.
    d. All of the above.
    e. None of the above.

    Answer: d Type: M   Page(s): 458

44. The global community has been most successful in treating which of the following?

    a. AIDS.
    b. Malaria.
    c. Smallpox.
    d. Cholera.
    e. None of the above.

    Answer: c Type: M   Page(s): 457

45. Until recently, efforts to deal with the international drug trade have focused on

    a. Curbing supply.
    b. Decreasing demand.
    c. Declining terms of trade.
    d. Sustainable crop yields.

    Answer: a Type: M   Page(s): 458

46. Which of the following is not one of the areas of the world in which narcotics production is concentrated?

    a. Southeast Asia.
    b. South America.
    c. The Middle East.
    d. Europe.

    Answer: d Type: M   Page(s): 458-459

47. The world's main source of opium is in

    a. The Middle East.
    b. The Golden Triangle.
    c. Latin America.
    d. Russia.

Answer: b Type: M   Page(s): 459

48. The country which produces the greatest amount of marijuana is

    a. Lebanon.
    b. The United States.
    c. Mexico.
    d. Columbia.

Answer: c Type: M   Page(s): 459

49. Cocaine is most produced in what part of the world?

    a. South America.
    b. The Golden Triangle.
    c. Lebanon.
    d. The United States.

Answer: a Type: M   Page(s): 459

50. The one region of the world the international drug trade has yet to reach is

    a. Africa.
    b. Russia.
    c. Asia.
    d. All of the above.
    e. None of the above.

Answer: e Type: M   Page(s): 461

51. Which of the following best characterizes policy toward illegal drugs in the United States?

    a. Americans have traditionally focused on drug treatment and drug abuse prevention.
    b. Americans have traditionally focused on drug interdiction.
    c. Americans have traditionally denied the U.S. has a drug problem.
    d. The U.S. government has not sought the cooperation of other nations in drug eradication.

Answer: b Type: M   Page(s): 462

Harcourt Brace & Company

52. U.S. attempts to reduce drug production in Latin America have been stymied by all except which of the following?

    a. The drug trade is a major source of employment in the U.S.
    b. Lack of legal alternative employment for coca and marijuana growers.
    c. Political violence and intimidation by the drug cartels in Latin America.
    d. Latin American resistance to Yankee imperialism.

    Answer: a   Type: M   Page(s): 462

53. The international drug trade has had which of the following effects in the drug-producing nations?

    a. It has led to declining drug usage.
    b. It has reduced environmental damage by encouraging the growth of alternative crops.
    c. It generates a large percentage of their export earnings.
    d. It has led to a severe economic downturn for these nations.

    Answer: c   Type: M   Page(s): 460-463

54. The United States has recently shifted money for the war on drugs to

    a. Crop substitution programs.
    b. Bilateral efforts and programs.
    c. UN-sponsored programs.
    d. Environmental programs.

    Answer: b   Type: M   Page(s): 464

55. Which of the following most accurately reflects the problem of terrorism?

    a. Terrorism has been steadily increasing in recent years.
    b. Terrorists have had little to do with the international drug trade.
    c. Terrorists have rarely been successful.
    d. Distinguishing between terrorism and legitimate political violence is often subjective.

    Answer: d   Type: M   Page(s): 467

Harcourt Brace & Company

56. Groups that perpetrate terrorism include which of the following?

a. Nationalist groups.
b. Religious groups.
c. Government-affiliated groups.
d. All of the above.
e. None of the above.

Answer: d Type: M   Page(s): 469-472

57. While terrorism is evident throughout the world, which area of the globe experiences the most terrorist attacks?

a. The United States.
b. Western Europe.
c. Southease Asia.
d. The Middle East.

Answer: d Type: M   Page(s): 467

58. According to the U.S. Department of State, which nation is not a sponsor of terrorism?

a. Cuba.
b. Syria.
c. South Korea.
d. Sudan.

Answer: c Type: M   Page(s): 468

59. Terror instigated by nationalist separatists

a. Has emerged only recently, as a response to ever-increasing globalization.
b. Is the only means by which nationalist organizations spread their message.
c. Tend to have clear ethnic, cultural, or religious overtones.
d. All of the above.

Answer: c Type: M   Page(s): 469

60. Ideological terrorism

a. Stems from the desire to overthrow oppressive governments or express anti-imperalist sentiments.
b. Had completely disappeared following the collapse of the Soviet Union.
c. Is evident only in developing countries.
d. All of the above.

Answer: a Type: M   Page(s): 472

61. Which statement concerning religious terrorism is false?

    a. Countering religious terrorism is difficult due to the fervent commitment of their believers.
    b. Religious radicalism has declined along with violence instigated by ideological terrorists.
    c. Religious terrorists typically regard violence as morally justified.
    d. All of the statements are correct.

    Answer: b Type: M   Page(s): 472-473

62. Abu Nidal was once affiliated with which cause?

    a. The Shining Path.
    b. The Irish Republican Army.
    c. The Red Brigades.
    d. The Palestine Liberation Organization.

    Answer: d Type: M   Page(s): 471

63. There have been few effective, global efforts to combat terrorism because

    a. It affects relatively few people.
    b. It has declined dramatically in recent years.
    c. Many governments support or engage in terrorism.
    d. The Soviet Union has now disintegrated.

    Answer: c Type: M   Page(s): 473

64. Efforts to coordinate action against terrorism can be organized

    a. Bilaterally.
    b. Regionally.
    c. Internationally.
    d. All of the above.
    e. None of the above.

    Answer: d Type: M   Page(s): 473

Harcourt Brace & Company

65. A developing society would be most likely to consume what kind of energy resource?

    a. Oil.
    b. Coal.
    c. Wood.
    d. Natural gas.
    e. All of the above.

Answer: e Type: M Page(s): 480-482

66. Much of the recent increase in demand for energy has come from

    a. The United States.
    b. The developed world.
    c. The poorest nations of the world.
    d. The developing world.

Answer: d Type: M Page(s): 479

67. The first major oil crisis was precipitated by which event?

    a. The Yom Kippur War.
    b. The overthrow of the Shah of Iran.
    c. The Gulf War.
    d. World War II.

Answer: a Type: M Page(s): 480

68. The International Energy Agency is designed to

    a. Replace OPEC as the world's dominant oil producer.
    b. Monitor the nuclear power plants of countries suspected of having developed nuclear weapons.
    c. Protect member states from economic difficulties due to oil shortages.
    d. Be the official voice of OPEC in international organizations.

Answer: c Type: M Page(s): 480

69. In 1986, there was a severe nuclear accident in what country?

    a. The United States.
    b. The Soviet Union.
    c. France.
    d. Iraq.

Answer: b Type: M Page(s): 482

70. The energy resource that contributes most to electricity generation is

    a. Oil.
    b. Nuclear power.
    c. Natural gas.
    d. Coal.

    Answer: d Type: M   Page(s): 481

71. Which of the following is a renewable energy resource?

    a. Coal.
    b. Oil.
    c. Hydroelectricity.
    d. Natural gas.

    Answer: c Type: M   Page(s): 482

72. Conflict over water has been particularly severe in which region of the world?

    a. Asia.
    b. Africa.
    c. The Middle East.
    d. Europe.

    Answer: c Type: M   Page(s): 484

73. One nation which has a great deal of influence over water, particularly from major rivers, in the Middle East is

    a. Syria.
    b. Turkey.
    c. Iraq.
    d. Iran.

    Answer: b Type: M   Page(s): 485

74. In the search for consensus on global issues, which of the following statements is most accurate?

    a. States have few common interests.
    b. States have relied most on the UN to solve their problems.
    c. The North and the South agree on the solutions for most global problems.
    d. The anarchic nature of the international environment means that states must generall work among themselves to solve problems.

    Answer: d Type: M   Page(s): 486

Harcourt Brace & Company

75. The defining feature of the world as it enters the twenty-first century is likely to be

    a. Conflict.
    b. Cooperation.
    c. Interdependence.
    d. All of the above.

Answer: d Type: M   Page(s): 486-487

TRUE/FALSE

76. The current world population is expected to double by the end of this century.

    a. True
    b. False

Answer: B Type: T   Page(s): 434

77. Once a population gains access to improved medical services, the birth rate quickly overtakes the death rate.

    a. True
    b. False

Answer: A Type: T   Page(s): 436

78. The world's fastest-growing regions are usually its richest.

    a. True
    b. False

Answer: B Type: T   Page(s): 436

79. Women constitute a small, nearly insignificant portion of economic migrants.

    a. True
    b. False

Answer: B Type: T   Page(s): 440

Harcourt Brace & Company

80. Refugees are classified as those who are forced to flee their home countries for reasons not related to their economic standard of living.

    a. True
    b. False

    Answer: A   Type: T   Page(s): 440

81. Refugees tend to be from poorer parts of the world.

    a. True
    b. False

    Answer: A   Type: T   Page(s): 440

82. The United States is more apt to accept refugees from nations with which it has friendly relations than unfriendly relations.

    a. True
    b. False

    Answer: B   Type: T   Page(s): 443

83. The developed nations consume diets vastly superior in quantity and quality from those of the developing nations.

    a. True
    b. False

    Answer: A   Type: T   Page(s): 446

84. The problem of world hunger is probably the least contentious and most easily solvable global issue.

    a. True
    b. False

    Answer: A   Type: T   Page(s): 448

85. International attention first began to focus on environmental issues during the 1992 Earth Summit in Brazil.

    a. True
    b. False

    Answer: B   Type: T   Page(s): 452

86. Long term perspectives are often the best way to address problems of pollution and deforestation.

    a. True
    b. False

    Answer: A Type: T   Page(s): 455

87. On average, people in the developed world live an average of sixty-two years longer than those in poorer nations.

    a. True
    b. False

    Answer: B Type: T   Page(s): 455

88. Tropical diseases have claimed more victims than AIDS.

    a. True
    b. False

    Answer: A Type: T   Page(s): 456

89. The malaria virus was eradicated by 1980.

    a. True
    b. False

    Answer: B Type: T   Page(s): 457

90. The drug dealers in the Middle East are also heavily involved in politics and the sale of arms.

    a. True
    b. False

    Answer: A Type: T   Page(s): 461

91. Drug cartels have come to resemble multinational corporations in terms of their size and complexity.

    a. True
    b. False

    Answer: A Type: T   Page(s): 460

Harcourt Brace & Company

92. The United States has generously supported alternative employment for former coca and marijuana growers in order to reduce the drug supply.

    a. True
    b. False

    Answer: B Type: T   Page(s): 462

93. Terrorism is a relatively recent phenomenon.

    a. True
    b. False

    Answer: B Type: T   Page(s): 465

94. Terrorism has been declining in recent years.

    a. True
    b. False

    Answer: A Type: T   Page(s): 467

95. The United States has never been the scene of an international terrorist attack.

    a. True
    b. False

    Answer: B Type: T   Page(s): 467

96. Decreased economic activity usually results in increased oil usage.

    a. True
    b. False

    Answer: B Type: T   Page(s): 479

97. The International Energy Agency was formed to help cope with international oil crises.

    a. True
    b. False

    Answer: A Type: T   Page(s): 480

Harcourt Brace & Company

98. Oil is often preferred over nuclear power because it is cheaper.

    a. True
    b. False

    Answer: B Type: T   Page(s): 482-483

99. Almost all energy sources, apart from fossil fuels, are too expensive for developing nations.

    a. True
    b. False

    Answer: A Type: T   Page(s): 483

100. Globalization will make world politics far less conflictual.

    a. True
    b. False

    Answer: B Type: T   Page(s): 487

Harcourt Brace & Company

Chapter 11

Security

1. The security dilemma involves

   a. Deciding in which kinds of weapons to invest.
   b. States increasing each other's insecurity by measures taken to bolster their own security.
   c. Attempting to compel another nation to undertake some action.
   d. Deciding how much money should be invested in the military and how much should be spent on social needs.

   Answer: b Type: M   Page(s): 492

2. External threats to security

   a. Differ according to geopolitical factors.
   b. Are generally the same for most nations.
   c. Typically originate in domestic problems.
   d. Are responsible for all international conflict.

   Answer: a Type: M   Page(s): 493

3. Now that the Cold War is over, more attention has been given to what kinds of security threats?

   a. Population pressures.
   b. Environmental pollution.
   c. Terrorism.
   d. All of the above.
   e. None of the above.

   Answer: d Type: M   Page(s): 493

Harcourt Brace & Company

4. Since its independence, Israel has been in a

   a. Low-threat situation with a secure perception of its security.
   b. Low-threat situation with an insecure perception of its security.
   c. High-threat situation with a secure perception of its security.
   d. High-threat situation with an insecure perception of its security.

   Answer: d Type: M   Page(s): 495

5. The two types of strategies states use to protect their national security include

   a. Deterrence, defense.
   b. Security dilemma, defense.
   c. Defense, flexible response.
   d. Compellence, security dilemma.

   Answer: b Type: M   Page(s): 499

6. Deterrence involves

   a. Dissuading a challenger from attacking a state's own territory.
   b. Discouraging a challenger from attacking an ally or partner.
   c. Credibility.
   d. All of the above.
   e. None of the above.

   Answer: d Type: M   Page(s): 499

7. Deterrence requires which of the following for success?

   a. Forcing a challenger to reverse or undo some action already taken.
   b. Reducing an enemy's capability to do damage.
   c. Commitment to punish or retaliate.
   d. Nuclear weapons.

   Answer: c Type: M   Page(s): 499

8. A long-term strategy designed to discourage serious consideration of any challenge to one's core interests by an adversary is known as

   a. General deterrence.
   b. Immediate deterrence.
   c. Primary deterrence.
   d. Extended deterrence.

   Answer: a Type: M   Page(s): 499

Harcourt Brace & Company

9. A response to a specific and explicit challenge to a state's interests is known as

    a. General deterrence.
    b. Immediate deterrence.
    c. Primary deterrence.
    d. Extended deterrence.

Answer: b Type: M   Page(s): 499

10. Which of the following is a strategy designed to dissuade a challenger from attacking one's own territory?

    a. General deterrence.
    b. Immediate deterrence.
    c. Primary deterrence.
    d. Extended deterrence.

Answer: c Type: M   Page(s): 500

11. Which of the following is a strategy aimed at discouraging a challenger from attacking an ally or partner?

    a. General deterrence.
    b. Immediate deterrence.
    c. Primary deterrence.
    d. Extended deterrence.

Answer: d Type: M   Page(s): 500

12. A strategy that attempts to reduce an enemy's capability to do damage or take something away from the defender is known as

    a. Defense.
    b. General deterrence.
    c. Immediate deterrence.
    d. Compellence.

Answer: a Type: M   Page(s): 500

13. Which of the following strategies is primarily psychological?

    a. Defense.
    b. Deterrence.
    c. All of the above.
    d. None of the above.

Answer: b Type: M   Page(s): 500

14. The phrase, "War is nothing but the extension of politics by other means" was coined by

    a. Napoleon.
    b. Joseph Stalin.
    c. Carl Von Clausewitz.
    d. Richard Nixon.

    Answer: c Type: M Page(s): 498

15. Credibility involves

    a. Defining to an opponent behavior that one considers unacceptable.
    b. Demonstrating willingness to carry out a commitment.
    c. Developing the capability to punish an attacker.
    d. Compellence.

    Answer: b Type: M Page(s): 502

16. The concept of deterrence assumes that decision makers are

    a. Ignorant.
    b. Irrational.
    c. Intelligent.
    d. Rational.

    Answer: d Type: M Page(s): 505

17. Commitment involves

    a. Defining to an opponent behavior that one considers unacceptable.
    b. Demonstrating willingness to carry out a commitment.
    c. Developing the capability to punish an attacker.
    d. Compellence.

    Answer: a Type: M Page(s): 502

18. It is important that commitments be

    a. Open ended.
    b. General enough to keep the adversary guessing.
    c. Definite and specific.
    d. All-encompassing.

    Answer: c Type: M Page(s): 502

Harcourt Brace & Company

19. What is important in maintaining the credibility of a threat?

    a. Reputation.
    b. Past behavior.
    c. Image.
    d. All of the above.
    e. None of the above.

Answer: d Type: M   Page(s): 503

20. When the United States failed to convince Saddam Hussein that it would oppose an Iraqi invasion of Kuwait, it demonstrated a failure of

    a. The security dilemma.
    b. Commitment.
    c. Capability.
    d. Primary deterrence.

Answer: b Type: M   Page(s): 502

21. Because of the incredible destructive power of nuclear weapons

    a. Credibility is easy to maintain.
    b. Credibility is irrelevant.
    c. Credibility is more difficult to maintain.
    d. Capability is all that is important.

Answer: c Type: M   Page(s): 503

22. When Israel chose not to retaliate after being attacked by Iraqi Scud missiles during the Gulf War, many Israelis believed this damaged Israel's

    a. Credibility.
    b. Capability.
    c. Extended deterrence.
    d. Compellence.

Answer: a Type: M   Page(s): 503

23. One major problem with a deterrent strategy is that

    a. It rarely works.
    b. It is difficult to tell when it works.
    c. It assumes decision makers are irrational.
    d. It does not emphasize credibility.

Answer: b Type: M   Page(s): 505

24. To determine if deterrence has succeeded one would need to know

    a. How much capability the defender possessed.
    b. The strength of the commitment.
    c. Whether the challenger intended to commit the action.
    d. Whether the challenger possessed primary deterrence.

    Answer: c Type: M   Page(s): 505

25. One nation may misperceive another's resolve if

    a. The challenger is strongly intent on taking a course of action.
    b. The challenger believes the defender is bluffing.
    c. The challenger underestimates the defender's capabilities.
    d. All of the above.
    e. None of the above.

    Answer: d Type: M   Page(s): 505-506

26. According to deterrence advocates, rationality requires

    a. Decision makers to make choices without emotion.
    b. Decision makers to make comparisons among choices and rank them.
    c. Credibility.
    d. Clarity of perception.

    Answer: b Type: M   Page(s): 505

27. Critics of deterrence theory argue that the rationality assumption is faulty because

    a. Humans have a limited capacity to obtain and process information.
    b. It rests too heavily on credibility.
    c. It ignores the importance of capability in shaping decision makers' expectations.
    d. All of the above.
    e. None of the above.

    Answer: a Type: M   Page(s): 505

28. The history of military technology can be interpreted as a struggle between

    a. The Soviet Union and the United States.
    b. Deterrence and compellence strategies.
    c. Offense and defense.
    d. Perception and misperception.

    Answer: c Type: M   Page(s): 523

Harcourt Brace & Company

29. When the offense is dominant

    a. Wars are more likely to occur.
    b. Wars are likely to be less destructive.
    c. Wars are likely to be of shorter duration.
    d. All of the above.
    e. None of the above.

Answer: d Type: M   Page(s): 523

30. When the defense is dominant

    a. Wars are more likely to occur.
    b. Wars are likely to be less destructive.
    c. Wars are likely to be shorter.
    d. Wars are less likely to occur.

Answer: d Type: M   Page(s): 523

31. The introduction of the tank and aircraft on the battlefield

    a. Made the defense dominant.
    b. Made the offense dominant.
    c. Created an offense-defense stalemate.
    d. Meant the end of the blitzkrieg attack.

Answer: b Type: M   Page(s): 524

32. The scientist who was in charge of development of the atomic bomb was

    a. Albert Einstein.
    b. Edward Teller.
    c. Robert Oppenheimer.
    d. Franklin Roosevelt.

Answer: c Type: M   Page(s): 508

33. Atomic weapons were developed during which war?

    a. World War I.
    b. Korean War.
    c. Vietnam War.
    d. World War II.

Answer: d Type: M   Page(s): 524

34. A state possesses a first-strike capability if

    a. It launches its missiles first.
    b. It can destroy the defender's retaliatory capability.
    c. It can launch a preemptive strike.
    d. It can survive a nuclear attack by an adversary.

    Answer: b   Type: M   Page(s): 507

35. A state possesses a second-strike capability if

    a. It launches a nuclear attack after being attacked by nuclear weapons itself.
    b. It can launch a preemptive strike.
    c. It can destroy the defender's retaliatory capability.
    d. It has enough nuclear weapons to survive a nuclear attack and inflict unacceptable levels of damage on its adversary.

    Answer: d   Type: M   Page(s): 507

36. For stable mutual deterrence each side must possess

    a. A second-strike capability.
    b. A first-strike capability.
    c. Tactical nuclear weapons.
    d. A nuclear triad.

    Answer: a   Type: M   Page(s): 507

37. The U.S. nuclear triad consists of

    a. First-strike capability, second-strike capability and mutual assured destruction.
    b. Bombers, intercontinental ballistic missiles, and submarine-launched ballistic missiles.
    c. Air defenses, anti-ballistic missiles and early-warning radar.
    d. Long-range, medium-range and short-range nuclear weapons.

    Answer: b   Type: M   Page(s): 509

38. Which of the following is destabilizing in a nuclear relationship?

    a. Submarine-launched ballistic missiles.
    b. A second-strike capability.
    c. Vulnerable population centers.
    d. Defensive weapons systems.

    Answer: d   Type: M   Page(s): 510

39. A functioning Strategic Defense Initiative or Star Wars may increase the probability of

    a. A second-strike capability.
    b. A first-strike capability.
    c. Mutual assured destruction.
    d. Multiple Independently Targeted Reentry Vehicles.

Answer: b Type: M   Page(s): 510

40. Which of the following most accurately describes military planning in both the United States and the Soviet Union in the latter years of the Cold War?

    a. Both sides increasingly emphasized nuclear weapons over conventional weapons.
    b. Both sides increasingly emphasized conventional weapons over nuclear weapons.
    c. Both sides moved toward acceptance of the doctrine of massive retaliation.
    d. Both sides stopped increasing their weapons arsenals.

Answer: b Type: M   Page(s): 511

41. Which of the following is not an acknowledged nuclear power?

    a. France.
    b. China.
    c. Russia.
    d. Germany.

Answer: d Type: M   Page(s): 514

42. Arms control during the Cold War was characterized primarily by the search for

    a. Disarmament.
    b. Nuclear proliferation.
    c. Strategic stability.
    d. Massive retaliation.

Answer: c Type: M   Page(s): 527

43. The Kellogg-Briand pact attempted to

    a. Outlaw war.
    b. Remove intermediate-range nuclear weapons from Europe.
    c. Address the Soviet advantage in conventional forces in Europe.
    d. Promote nuclear nonproliferation.

Answer: a Type: M   Page(s): 527

44. The Baruch Plan was an attempt to

    a. Ban the production or use of chemical and biological weapons.
    b. Forbid the development or deployment of anti-ballistic missile systems.
    c. Outlaw war.
    d. Place atomic weapons and energy activities under international control.

    Answer: d   Type: M   Page(s): 527

45. The Strategic Arms Limitation talks accomplished which of the following?

    a. Removed nuclear weapons from Europe.
    b. Prohibited the proliferation of nuclear weapons.
    c. Placed ceilings on the number of nuclear weapons the superpowers could possess.
    d. Required the superpowers to destroy a substantial number of nuclear weapons.

    Answer: c   Type: M   Page(s): 528

46. Weapons of mass destruction include which of the following?

    a. Nuclear weapons.
    b. Chemical weapons.
    c. Biological weapons.
    d. All of the above.

    Answer: d   Type: M   Page(s): 534

47. One of the most important loopholes left by the Strategic Arms Limitation Treaty I was

    a. Its failure to limit the number of nuclear warheads per launcher.
    b. Its failure to limit the deployment of anti-ballistic missile systems.
    c. Its failure to place ceilings on the number of strategic nuclear missiles the superpowers were allowed to have.
    d. It left the United States with far more ICBMs than the Soviet Union.

    Answer: a   Type: M   Page(s): 529

48. Which of the following best describes the Anti-Ballistic Missile Treaty?

    a. It forbade all ABM sites.
    b. It forced both the U.S. and Soviet Union to make tremendous strategic adjustments.
    c. It prohibited the deployment of space-based ABM systems.
    d. It was never ratified by the U.S. Senate.

    Answer: c   Type: M   Page(s): 529

Harcourt Brace & Company

49. Which of the following does not describe the SALT II treaty?

    a. It was never ratified by the U.S. Senate.
    b. Each side generally adhered to the guidelines of the treaty.
    c. It forced the superpowers to disarm a considerable number of nuclear weapons.
    d. It placed limitation on MIRVs.

Answer: c   Type: M   Page(s): 529

50. Which of the following best describes Multiple Independently Targeted Reentry Vehicles?

    a. They have never been covered by arms control treaties.
    b. They increase the temptation for an aggressor to strike first with nuclear weapons.
    c. They are national technical means of verification.
    d. They were ignored in both the SALT I and SALT II treaties.

Answer: b   Type: M   Page(s): 529

51. The START I treaty was begun under which president?

    a. Carter.
    b. Nixon.
    c. Bush.
    d. Reagan.

Answer: d   Type: M   Page(s): 529

52. The START I treaty accomplished which of the following?

    a. It mandated reductions in the number of strategic arms.
    b. It banned the deployment of MIRV missiles.
    c. It outlawed the use of chemical and biological weapons.
    d. It forbade the development of anti-ballistic missile systems.

Answer: a   Type: M   Page(s): 529

53. In the START II treaty, the United States and Russia agreed to reduce their strategic nuclear arsenals to

    a. Less than 100 warheads each.
    b. 10,000 warheads each.
    c. Between 500 and 750 warheads.
    d. Between 3000 and 3500 warheads each.

Answer: d   Type: M   Page(s): 530

54. The Intermediate-Range Nuclear Forces Treaty accomplished which of the following?

    a. It eliminated all MIRV missiles.
    b. It banned an entire class of nuclear weapons.
    c. It banned the deployment of tactical nuclear weapons.
    d. It banned the deployment of anti-ballistic missile systems.

    Answer: b Type: M   Page(s): 530

55. The INF treaty was signed under which president?

    a. Bush.
    b. Carter.
    c. Reagan.
    d. Ford.

    Answer: c Type: M   Page(s): 530

56. The Nuclear Nonproliferation Treaty provided for which of the following?

    a. It prevented states which possessed nuclear weapons from helping other states acquire
       them.
    b. Nonnuclear weapons states were forbidden from manufacturing nuclear weapons.
    c. The peaceful use of nuclear energy was encouraged.
    d. All of the above.

    Answer: d Type: M   Page(s): 531

57. Which of the following best characterizes the success of the Nuclear Nonproliferation
    Treaty?

    a. All states that have signed it have lived up to its requirements.
    b. The only states that have not signed it are ones that have never possessed nuclear
       weapons.
    c. Only the United States remains a holdout from the treaty.
    d. All of the above.
    e. None of the above.

    Answer: e Type: M   Page(s): 532

Harcourt Brace & Company

58. Which category of weapons is banned by an international convention?

   a. Ballistic missiles.
   b. Chemical weapons.
   c. Space-based weapons.
   d. Laser weapons.

Answer: b Type: M   Page(s): 532

59. A person who holds a "Star Wars" image of international relations is most likely to believe which of the following?

   a. Money spent on national security is mostly wasted and ineffective.
   b. Money spent on national security would be better spent on reducing famine, violence and environmental problems.
   c. Resources devoted to national security are necessary and beneficial.
   d. All of the above.
   e. None of the above.

Answer: c Type: M   Page(s): 537

60. The Conventional Forces in Europe Treaty was signed under what president?

   a. Carter.
   b. Reagan.
   c. Bush.
   d. Clinton.

Answer: c Type: M   Page(s): 536

61. Which of the following nations have made efforts to build or acquire nuclear weapons?

   a. North Korea.
   b. Iran.
   c. Pakistan.
   d. Israel.
   e. All of the above.

Answer: e Type: M   Page(s): 531-532

Harcourt Brace & Company

62. Military power includes which of the following:

    a. Armed forces.
    b. Quality & quantity of weaponry.
    c. Training & organization.
    d. All of the above.

    Answer: d Type: M   Page(s): 492

63. Weapons for germ warfare are also called:

    a. Chemical weapons.
    b. Biological weapons.
    c. Nuclear weapons.
    d. Conventional weapons.

    Answer: b Type: M   Page(s): 493

TRUE/FALSE

64. Most nations agree on a common meaning of the term, "national security."

    a. True
    b. False

    Answer: B Type: T   Page(s): 494

65. External and internal threats to security are rarely interrelated.

    a. True
    b. False

    Answer: B Type: T   Page(s): 495

66. There are both objective and subjective components in a state's definition of national security.

    a. True
    b. False

    Answer: A Type: T   Page(s): 500

Harcourt Brace & Company

67. The more powerful a country becomes, the more secure it feels.

    a. True
    b. False

    Answer: B Type: T   Page(s): 503

68. Extended deterrence is more likely to fail than immediate deterrence.

    a. True
    b. False

    Answer: A Type: T   Page(s): 504

69. If a state does not have enough capability to deter an aggressor, it should still try to convince an opponent it is strong enough.

    a. True
    b. False

    Answer: A Type: T   Page(s): 506

70. Deterrence may fail even though a defender clearly signals the credibility of its commitment.

    a. True
    b. False

    Answer: A Type: T   Page(s): 524

71. We know that the United States successfully deterred the Soviet Union during the Cold War.

    a. True
    b. False

    Answer: B Type: T   Page(s): 507

72. The blitzkrieg was made possible by the introduction of the tank and aircraft on the battlefield.

    a. True
    b. False

    Answer: A Type: T   Page(s): 509

73. First-strike capabilities are stabilizing factors during a crisis.

    a. True
    b. False

    Answer: B Type: T   Page(s): 511

74. According to mutual assured destruction, cities should remain vulnerable to nuclear attack.

    a. True
    b. False

    Answer: A Type: T   Page(s): 526

75. The trend toward the end of the Cold War was a movement away from reliance on nuclear weapons.

    a. True
    b. False

    Answer: A Type: T   Page(s): 528

76. The primary aim of arms control has been strategic stability.

    a. True
    b. False

    Answer: A Type: T   Page(s): 529

77. As a result of a number of treaties, the testing of nuclear weapons everywhere has been banned.

    a. True
    b. False

    Answer: B Type: T   Page(s): 529

78. There are international treaties outlawing chemical and biological weapons.

    a. True
    b. False

    Answer: A Type: T   Page(s): 530

Harcourt Brace & Company

79. The SALT II treaty was never ratified by the U.S. Senate.

    a. True
    b. False

    Answer: A Type: T   Page(s): 530

80. The START I treaty represented the first time that an entire class of nuclear weapons had been banned.

    a. True
    b. False

    Answer: B Type: T   Page(s): 531

81. Richard Nixon successfully concluded the START II treaty.

    a. True
    b. False

    Answer: B Type: T   Page(s): 529

82. No new nations have demonstrated the capability to produce nuclear weapons since the signing of the Nuclear Nonproliferation Treaty.

    a. True
    b. False

    Answer: B Type: T   Page(s): 512

83. States have not attempted to reduce the spread of ballistic missile technology.

    a. True
    b. False

    Answer: B Type: T   Page(s): 515

84. Leadership is a quantitative factor of military power

    a. True
    b. False

    Answer: B Type: T   Page(s): 520

Security

85. Three important aspects of technological advances include breakthroughs, lead times, a▮ cost.

    a. True
    b. False

    Answer: A   Type: T   Page(s): 521

Harcourt Brace & Company

Chapter 12

Levels of Analysis

1. The system level of analysis examines influences on world politics that are

   a. External to states.
   b. Internal to societies.
   c. Within states.
   d. Based on the individual.

   Answer: a Type: M Page(s): 546

2. Which of the following schools of thought emphasizes power politics and the amoral nature of humans in shaping interstate relations?

   a. Idealism.
   b. Realism.
   c. Collective security.
   d. Marxism.

   Answer: b Type: M Page(s): 548

3. The most important factor in the realist paradigm is

   a. Economics.
   b. International institutions.
   c. National security.
   d. Interdependence.

   Answer: c Type: M Page(s): 548

Harcourt Brace & Company

4. Structural realists are most concerned with

   a. Economics.
   b. Great powers.
   c. Interdependence.
   d. Collective security.

   Answer: b Type: M   Page(s): 548

5. According to structural realists, states cooperate

   a. Rarely.
   b. Frequently, but only on security matters.
   c. On almost all issues.
   d. When there is an equal distribution of power.

   Answer: a Type: M   Page(s): 549

6. The parity school argues that peace is most likely to occur when

   a. There is an unequal distribution of power.
   b. One state enjoys a preponderance of power.
   c. There is an equal distribution of power.
   d. There is an international collective security arrangement.

   Answer: c Type: M   Page(s): 551-552

7. The preponderance school argues that peace is most likely to occur when

   a. There is an imbalance of power.
   b. No state enjoys a preponderance of power.
   c. There is an equal distribution of power.
   d. The international system is bipolar.

   Answer: a Type: M   Page(s): 554-555

8. According to the balance-of-power model, when one state threatens to become too powerful, the other states will

   a. Try to appease the aggressor.
   b. Make war upon one another.
   c. Work to create a bipolar system.
   d. Form a counterbalancing coalition.

   Answer: d Type: M   Page(s): 551

Harcourt Brace & Company

9. A balance-of-power system encourages

    a. States to identify permanent enemies and friends.
    b. States to exercise moderation and restraint in international relations.
    c. The formation of international organizations.
    d. Movement toward system disequilibrium.

Answer: b Type: M   Page(s): 552

10. One of the problems associated with balancing against a preponderant power through alliances is

    a. States may not always make reliable allies.
    b. They are slow to form.
    c. States may try to force responsibility for confronting aggression on other states.
    d. All of the above.
    e. None of the above.

Answer: d Type: M   Page(s): 553-554

11. An example of the "buck-passing" phenomenon occured in:

    a. World War I.
    b. The Korean War.
    c. Yugoslavia.
    d. The Persian Gulf War.

Answer: c Type: M   Page(s): 608

12. An example of the "chain-ganging" phenomenon in alliances occurred before which war?

    a. World War I.
    b. The recent wars in Yugoslavia.
    c. The Franco-Prussian War.
    d. The Persian Gulf War.

Answer: a Type: M   Page(s): 554

13. If a state "bandwagons," it does which of the following?

    a. It joins with the coalition opposing a preponderant power.
    b. It joins forces with the preponderant power.
    c. It waits for other states to take responsibility for confronting aggression.
    d. It gets dragged into a war which it has no interest in fighting.

Answer: b Type: M   Page(s): 554

Harcourt Brace & Company

14. Those who believe that an international system characterized by power preponderance is more conducive to peace argue that

    a. Peace will result because no state will challenge the hegemon.
    b. An equality of power will make all states acceptant of the status quo.
    c. States will join together in collective security arrangements to protect themselves.
    d. Hegemons will engage in buck-passing to keep the peace.

    Answer: a Type: M   Page(s): 554-555

15. According to power transition theorists, wars are most likely to occur when

    a. There is an unequal balance of power.
    b. Collective security arrangements fail.
    c. There is no hegemon.
    d. An emerging state encroaches upon a dominant power's position.

    Answer: d Type: M   Page(s): 555

16. Which of the following is not one of the responsibilities of a hegemon?

    a. Establishing and enforcing a set of rules that govern the international system.
    b. Providing military and economic aid.
    c. Deciding which other powers will take responsibility for stopping aggression.
    d. Maintaining global commitments.

    Answer: c Type: M   Page(s): 555

17. The four stages of long-cycle theory include

    a. Global war.
    b. World power.
    c. Delegitimation.
    d. Deconcentration.
    e. All of the above.

    Answer: e Type: M   Page(s): 555-556

18. Those who believe bipolar systems are more peaceful argue that in a multipolar system

    a. Undetected imbalances of power can occur.
    b. There is a greater likelihood of miscalculating a rival's strength and intentions.
    c. There is a greater chance of friction and antagonism.
    d. All of the above.
    e. None of the above.

    Answer: d Type: M   Page(s): 557

19. Those who believe multipolar systems are more peaceful argue that

    a. Increasing state interaction increases antagonisms.
    b. State interaction increases unnecessary risk-taking.
    c. Multipolar systems are zero-sum games.
    d. All of the above.
    e. None of the above.

    Answer: e Type: M   Page(s): 557-558

20. If stability is encouraged by the potential destructiveness of nuclear weapons, then

    a. Bipolar systems will be more stable.
    b. Multipolar systems will be more stable.
    c. Hegemonic systems will be more stable.
    d. The number of great powers will no longer make a difference,

    Answer: d Type: M   Page(s): 558

21. The school of thought that argues that the anarchy and violence of the international system can be overcome by international institutions promoting cooperation is called

    a. Liberalism.
    b. Collective security.
    c. Balance of power.
    d. World system.

    Answer: a Type: M   Page(s): 558

22. Arms races exemplify what kind of international problem?

    a. Collective security.
    b. Prisoner's dilemma.
    c. Free riders.
    d. Balance of power.

    Answer: b Type: M   Page(s): 559

23. Which of the following is not a strategy designed to overcome the prisoner's dilemma?

    a. Tit for tat.
    b. International regimes.
    c. The balance of power.
    d. Economic interdependence.

    Answer: c Type: M   Page(s): 559-562

Harcourt Brace & Company

24. The purpose of the tit for tat strategy is to

    a. Demonstrate your willingness to cooperate with your opponent.
    b. Establish international regimes.
    c. Create prisoner's dilemmas in international relations.
    d. Provide for economic interdependence.

    Answer: a Type: M   Page(s): 559-560

25. The domestic level of analysis mostly stresses which of the following?

    a. The process by which national leaders make foreign policy.
    b. The balance of power.
    c. The number of poles in the international system.
    d. The personality traits of individual leaders.

    Answer: a Type: M   Page(s): 563

26. Statist theories focus on the foreign-policy implications of

    a. Public opinion.
    b. A state's overall form of government.
    c. Domestic interest groups.
    d. The international distribution of power.

    Answer: b Type: M   Page(s): 564-565

27. Societal theories focus on the foreign-policy implications of

    a. A state's overall form of government.
    b. Regime type.
    c. The international distribution of power.
    d. Domestic interest groups.

    Answer: d Type: M   Page(s): 571

28. In authoritarian regimes, the state is

    a. More constrained in its behavior than a democratic regime.
    b. More likely to be affected by public opinion.
    c. Less likely to go to war than a democratic regime.
    d. Less constrained in its behavior than a democratic regime.

    Answer: d Type: M   Page(s): 565

Harcourt Brace & Company

29. Regime type determines which of the following?

    a. The extent to which public opinion can affect government.
    b. The extent to which domestic interest groups can affect government.
    c. The extent to which economic policy is managed by the government.
    d. All of the above.
    e. None of the above.

Answer: d Type: M Page(s): 565

30. Which of the following statements is most accurate?

    a. Democracies are less likely to make war on each other.
    b. Democracies are less likely to be involved in war than any other regime type.
    c. Authoritarian regimes are most likely to be involved in war.
    d. Regime type makes little difference in involvement in war.

Answer: a Type: M Page(s): 578

31. In which country would one most likely expect the legislature to have significant influence over foreign policy?

    a. Iraq.
    b. The former Soviet Union.
    c. Israel.
    d. China.

Answer: c Type: M Page(s): 568

32. Which model holds that foreign-policy outcomes are the result of political competition among government agencies?

    a. Bureaucratic politics.
    b. Organizational process.
    c. Rational actor.
    d. Regime type.

Answer: a Type: M Page(s): 569-570

Harcourt Brace & Company

33. The final outcome of foreign-policy decisions in the bureaucratic politics model reflects

    a. The preferences of one organization.
    b. The preferences of the president.
    c. The preferences of many organizations.
    d. The national interest.

    Answer: c Type: M   Page(s): 569

34. The societal approach views state institutions as

    a. Autonomous.
    b. Disinterested.
    c. Reflective of the interests of powerful groups.
    d. Closed and focused exclusively on interstate relations.

    Answer: c Type: M   Page(s): 571

35. Interest groups would include all but which of the following?

    a. Military organizations.
    b. Veterans' groups.
    c. Business groups.
    d. The United Nations.

    Answer: d Type: M   Page(s): 571-572

36. The relationship between public institutions and private interests has been particularl strong in

    a. Environmental issues.
    b. The defense establishment.
    c. The maritime industry.
    d. The electronics industry.

    Answer: b Type: M   Page(s): 573

37. Which of the following best characterizes the role of public opinion in foreign-policy making?

   a. Public opinion is important only in open, democratic regimes.
   b. Public opinion has become important only with the introduction of modern polling techniques.
   c. Public opinion often constrains the options open for decision makers.
   d. Politicians allow public opinion to dictate their policies.

   Answer: c Type: M   Page(s): 575

38. Public support is most important when

   a. Foreign-policy budgets are being made.
   b. A government decides to go to war.
   c. A government joins an international organization.
   d. A government signs a trade treaty.

   Answer: b Type: M   Page(s): 575

39. Political culture may influence a nation's foreign policy by

   a. Creating a cultural vision of its proper role in the world.
   b. Shaping its standard operating procedures.
   c. The "rally-around-the-flag" effect.
   d. Forming a "bully pulpit".

   Answer: d Type: M   Page(s): 577

40. Political parties are noted for

   a. Making little difference in a state's foreign policy.
   b. Often behaving quite similarly.
   c. Having little interest in foreign policy.
   d. Being more interested in the national interest than support from voters and interest groups.

   Answer: b Type: M   Page(s): 568

41. In states where there are many strong political parties, foreign policy is

   a. Likely to be more complicated.
   b. More likely to vacillate.
   c. More difficult to formulate.
   d. All of the above.

   Answer: d Type: M   Page(s): 568-569

Levels of Analysis

42. In authoritarian states

   a. There are usually multiple political parties.
   b. The party and the state are essentially identical.
   c. There are no political parties.
   d. There are usually just two political parties.

Answer: b Type: M   Page(s): 565-566

43. Ideology refers to

   a. Belief systems on which states and groups within states base their actions.
   b. Coalitions of groups seeking control over the political process.
   c. A consensus among members of diverse groups to stand behind a tough foreign policy.
   d. The national style of politics and policy making.

Answer: a Type: M   Page(s): 576

44. Which of the following is not one of the domestic political institutions that shape the preferences and behavior of states?

   a. Public opinion.
   b. Regime type.
   c. Bureaucracies.
   d. Executive-legislative relations.

Answer: a Type: M   Page(s): 565-578

45. Societal approaches would examine all but which of the following?

   a. Public opinion.
   b. Political culture.
   c. Regime type.
   d. Interest groups.

Answer: c Type: M   Page(s): 571-580

46. Those who study systemic or domestic factors in international relations argue that these forces

   a. Create the context for decisions on foreign policy.
   b. Can predict decisions that will be made.
   c. Are so important that individuals have little if any impact in international relations.
   d. Are largely eclipsed by the influence of powerful leaders.

Answer: a Type: M   Page(s): 581

Harcourt Brace & Company

47. Operational codes are

    a. A system of beliefs and a guide to action.
    b. Found only in national elites.
    c. A product of public opinion.
    d. Influenced primarily by Marxism.
    e. All of the above.

    Answer: a   Type: M   Page(s): 592-593

48. Which of the following best characterizes the operational codes of early Bolshevik leaders in the Soviet Union?

    a. Leaders were led to distrust their opponents.
    b. Leaders were generally pessimistic.
    c. Leaders were generally risk-averse.
    d. All of the above.
    e. None of the above.

    Answer: a   Type: M   Page(s): 592

49. American leaders' operational codes during the Cold War were based on

    a. The utility of unlimited war and unconditional surrender.
    b. Risk-acceptance.
    c. Integrative complexity.
    d. Dissociative reactions.
    e. None of the above.

    Answer: e   Type: M   Page(s): 592

50. The greatest amount of stress on decision makers is typically caused by

    a. Protracted negotiations.
    b. Crises.
    c. Integrative complexity.
    d. Nuclear weapons.

    Answer: b   Type: M   Page(s): 593

51. Stress often leads to all but which of the following?

    a. It reduces the ability to evaluate information and options.
    b. It increases dissociative reactions.
    c. It increases integrative complexity.
    d. It reduces the ability to respond more flexibly to new situations.

    Answer: c Type: M   Page(s): 593-594

52. Crises are characterized by

    a. Surprise.
    b. Quick decision time.
    c. Threats to important values and interests.
    d. All of the above.

    Answer: d Type: M   Page(s): 594

53. Decision makers seeking to maintain cognitive consistency are likely to

    a. See the world as it really is.
    b. Be influenced by dissociative reactions.
    c. Consider large amounts of information and respond flexibly to information.
    d. Assimilate information according to their beliefs and images.

    Answer: d Type: M   Page(s): 595

54. Individuals try to maintain cognitive consistency in order to

    a. Obtain more information to reach better decisions.
    b. Better understand their opponents and adversaries.
    c. Resolve tensions between beliefs and information.
    d. Achieve greater cognitive and integrative complexity.

    Answer: c Type: M   Page(s): 595

55. Cognitive restructuring involves

    a. Increasing the amount of information in order to reach decisions more expeditiously.
    b. Stringing decisions out over a long period of time.
    c. Increasing the attractiveness of a preferred option.
    d. Turning aside information that aggravates a value conflict.

    Answer: d Type: M   Page(s): 595

56. Attribution theory considers decision makers to be

    a. Consistency seekers.
    b. Problem solvers or naive scientists.
    c. Procrastinators.
    d. Irrational and unstable.

Answer: b Type: M   Page(s): 595

57. A fundamental attribution error involves

    a. Applying double standards.
    b. The overuse of heuristics.
    c. Bolstering.
    d. Defensive avoidance.

Answer: a Type: M   Page(s): 596

58. When one makes a fundamental attribution error

    a. One's own inappropriate behavior is attributed to character and fundamental goals.
    b. An opponent's inappropriate behavior is attributed to character and fundamental goals.
    c. One's own appropriate behavior is attributed to circumstances beyond one's control.
    d. An opponent's appropriate behavior is attributed to character and fundamental goals.

Answer: b Type: M   Page(s): 596

59. When U.S. foreign-policy makers criticized Soviet control over Eastern Europe and ignored U.S. domination over Latin America, they were

    a. Engaging in defensive avoidance.
    b. Seeking to maintain cognitive consistency.
    c. Bolstering.
    d. Making a fundamental attribution error.

Answer: d Type: M   Page(s): 596

60. Heuristics are

    a. Double standards used in evaluating foreign policy.
    b. Rules of thumb or mental shortcuts.
    c. Fundamental errors of attribution.
    d. Methods by which decision makers delay taking action.

Answer: b Type: M   Page(s): 597

61. Which of the following is not a type of heuristic?

   a. The availability heuristic.
   b. The representativeness heuristic.
   c. Defensive avoidance.
   d. Schemas.

   Answer: c Type: M   Page(s): 597

62. When American foreign-policy makers believed that Iraq's invasion of Kuwait closely resembled the aggressive behavior of Adolph Hitler, they were using what heuristic?

   a. The representative heuristic.
   b. The personal experience heuristic.
   c. The defensive avoidance heuristic.
   d. The consistency-seeking heuristic.

   Answer: a Type: M   Page(s): 597

63. Schemas are

   a. A type of heuristic.
   b. The use of historical analogies in diagnosing a new situation.
   c. Generic concepts stored in an individual's memory that refer to objects, events or people.
   d. All of the above.

   Answer: d Type: M   Page(s): 597

64. Which of the following is a drawback to using schemas?

   a. They do not provide an economical means of storing memories.
   b. They do not allow an individual to go beyond the information given to make inference about a present situation.
   c. Important pieces of information may be lost.
   d. Individuals cannot envision a sequence of actions to achieve a goal when using them.

   Answer: c Type: M   Page(s): 597

65. The tendency of decision makers to believe the next war will be like the last one is an example of

    a. Defensive avoidance.
    b. Overuse of schemas.
    c. Cognitive complexity.
    d. Pragmatism.

Answer: b Type: M   Page(s): 597

66. Anwar Sadat accomplished which of the following while president of Egypt?

    a. Defeated Israel in the Six-Day War.
    b. Travelled to Jerusalem to make peace with Israel.
    c. Nationalized the Suez Canal.
    d. Brought Egypt back into a position of leadership in the Arab world after the peace with Israel.

Answer: b Type: M   Page(s): 586-587

67. Leonid Brezhnev accomplished which of the following while leader of the Soviet Union?

    a. Signed the Strategic Arms Limitation Talks treaty.
    b. Established the Warsaw Pact.
    c. Removed Soviet troops from Afghanistan.
    d. Placed Soviet nuclear missiles in Mexico.

Answer: a Type: M   Page(s): 589

68. Generational experiences are

    a. Examples of defensive avoidance.
    b. Crisis-induced dissociative reactions.
    c. Events that have a powerful impact on particular age groups.
    d. Generic concepts stored in an individual's memory that refer to objects, events or people.

Answer: c Type: M   Page(s): 590

69. The generational experience of World War I led many European policy makers

    a. To develop a foreign policy of peace through strength.
    b. To fear another Vietnam.
    c. To rush headlong into another war.
    d. To try to appease Hitler.

Answer: d Type: M   Page(s): 590

70. During the Cold War, Western foreign-policy makers often used which of the following to justify their policies?

    a. The Munich analogy.
    b. Appeasement.
    c. Pan-Arabism.
    d. The need for a buffer zone of states.

    Answer: a   Type: M   Page(s): 727

TRUE/FALSE

71. The realist school of international relations theory is of relatively recent origin.

    a. True
    b. False

    Answer: B Type: T   Page(s): 548

72. When there is movement in the international system toward an equal distribution of power, this is known as preponderance.

    a. True
    b. False

    Answer: B Type: T   Page(s): 549

73. According to the balance-of-power model, states should fight rather than pass up a chance to increase capabilities.

    a. True
    b. False

    Answer: A Type: T   Page(s): 551

74. According to long-cycle theory, the first global hegemon in modern history was Great Britain.

    a. True
    b. False

    Answer: B Type: T   Page(s): 555

75. A hegemon is the dominant military and economic power in the international system.

    a. True
    b. False

    Answer: A   Type: T   Page(s): 555

76. Not all power transitions result in global war.

    a. True
    b. False

    Answer: A   Type: T   Page(s): 555

77. Those who believe that multipolar systems are more peaceful argue that cross-cutting concerns moderate state behavior.

    a. True
    b. False

    Answer: A   Type: T   Page(s): 557-558

78. A zero-sum game is one in which there are no benefits for any state, just losses.

    a. True
    b. False

    Answer: B   Type: T   Page(s): 558

79. Bureaucracies and legislatures may adopt foreign policies that do not reflect the interests of the nation as a whole.

    a. True
    b. False

    Answer: A   Type: T   Page(s): 569

80. Regime type refers to the influence exerted on government by domestic interest groups.

    a. True
    b. False

    Answer: B   Type: T   Page(s): 565

Harcourt Brace & Company

81. Democratic regimes rarely make war against any other nations.

    a. True
    b. False

    Answer: B Type: T   Page(s): 578

82. The organizational process model stresses the importance of competition among government agencies.

    a. True
    b. False

    Answer: B Type: T   Page(s): 569-570

83. The bureaucratic politics model argues that bureaucrats place the interests of departments and agencies above the national interest.

    a. True
    b. False

    Answer: A Type: T   Page(s): 569-570

84. The societal approach argues that the national interest is determined by governmental institutions.

    a. True
    b. False

    Answer: B Type: T   Page(s): 571

85. The influence of the military-industrial complex is only felt in open, democratic societies.

    a. True
    b. False

    Answer: B Type: T   Page(s): 575

86. Public opinion only matters in foreign-policy making in open, democratic regimes.

    a. True
    b. False

    Answer: B Type: T   Page(s): 575-576

Harcourt Brace & Company

87. Political parties often make a major difference in a state's foreign policy.

    a. True
    b. False

    Answer: A Type: T   Page(s): 568

88. Ideologies are often used to justify a nation's foreign policy.

    a. True
    b. False

    Answer: A Type: T   Page(s): 576

89. Not all levels of stress are harmful to individuals' decision-making abilities.

    a. True
    b. False

    Answer: A Type: T   Page(s): 593

90. Increasing cognitive consistency generally leads to more effective decision making.

    a. True
    b. False

    Answer: B Type: T   Page(s): 594-595

91. When one makes a fundamental attribution error, one's own inappropriate behavior is attributed to character and fundamental goals.

    a. True
    b. False

    Answer: B Type: T   Page(s): 596

92. Heuristics are identical to fundamental errors of attribution.

    a. True
    b. False

    Answer: B Type: T   Page(s): 597

93. The availability heuristic suggests that policy-makers are prone to expect a situation outcome that is most easily remembered on the basis of past experience.

   a. True
   b. False

   Answer: A Type: T   Page(s): 597

94. Harry Truman had tremendous prior experience in foreign policy before becoming U.S. president.

   a. True
   b. False

   Answer: B Type: T   Page(s): 582

95. George Bush preferred to focus on foreign rather than domestic policy.

   a. True
   b. False

   Answer: A Type: T   Page(s): 583

96. Nikita Krushchev initiated the Soviet invasion of Afghanistan.

   a. True
   b. False

   Answer: B Type: T   Page(s): 588

97. George Bush was unlike Reagan in that he did not promote a sweeping vision of America's role in the world.

   a. True
   b. False

   Answer: A Type: T   Page(s): 583

98. Under Nikita Khrushchev's leadership, the USSR temporarily took the lead in the "space race" by orbiting Sputnik.

   a. True
   b. False

   Answer: A Type: T   Page(s): 588

Harcourt Brace & Company

99. To understand variations on or deviations from a consistent theme in a state's foreign policy may require an approach that combines several levels of analysis.

    a. True
    b. False

    Answer: A   Type: T   Page(s): 600

00. Each level of analysis used to study international relations provides a different type of explanation for events.

    a. True
    b. False

    Answer: A   Type: T   Page(s): 598

Harcourt Brace & Company

Chapter 13

The Future of International Politics

MULTIPLE CHOICE

1. Which of the following are important to the future, from the systemic perspective?

   a. Ability of regimes to regulate conflict.
   b. States' capabilities of promoting cooperation.
   c. States' abilities to maintain their sovereignty in the economic and security spheres.
   d. All of the above.

   Answer: d Type: M   Page(s): 606

2. When states attempt to escape the trend of global integration by insisting on their own systems,

   a. Capital moves elsewhere with the speed of the Internet.
   b. They escape all the negative effects of interdependence and ultimately may gain hegeminic status.
   c. They can make new trading partners.
   d. None of the above.

   Answer: a Type: M   Page(s): 607

3. Which of the following is considered a rogue state that refuses to play by the rules of the international system?

   a. Japan.
   b. Brazil.
   c. Libya.
   d. Russia.

   Answer: c Type: M   Page(s): 607

Harcourt Brace & Company

4. As integration increases, the relative importance of natural resources is expected to

   a. Increase steadily.
   b. Decrease steadily.
   c. Increase a little.
   d. Decrease a little.

   Answer: b Type: M   Page(s): 608

5. The most influential in the 21st century may be:

   a. Large territories with many citizens.
   b. States which export critical natural resources.
   c. "Virtual states" (trade and financial capitals with hardly any territory).
   d. "Rogue states" that ignore international law.

   Answer: c Type: M   Page(s): 608

6. Which of the following is a characteristic of the EU?

   a. It is moving toward common environmental regulations.
   b. It is moving toward common safety regulations.
   c. It is developing a common currency and social charter.
   d. All of the above.

   Answer: d Type: M   Page(s): 609

7. In which of the following areas has cooperation been the most difficult to achieve?

   a. Social institutions.
   b. Security.
   c. Environmental changes.
   d. None of the above.

   Answer: b Type: M   Page(s): 609

8. According to Greider and other labor advocates, the newly integrated world will have what effect on labor?

   a. Decreased health and safety protection for workers.
   b. Increased health and safety protection for workers.
   c. Decreased safety but increased health protection for workers.
   d. About the same standard of living, and health and safety protection for workers.

   Answer: a Type: M   Page(s): 609

9. Globalization will likely

   a. Increase total output and efficiency.
   b. Result in heightened economic inequality between workers and investors.
   c. All of the above.
   d. None of the above.

   Answer: c   Type: M   Page(s): 609

10. How can free trade increase purchasing power even when monetary wages decline?

    a. Creates jobs in other countries.
    b. Workers get a tax break.
    c. Gives consumers access to less expensive imports.
    d. None of the above.

    Answer: c   Type: M   Page(s): 609

11. The German law Reinheitsgebot was recently repealed by the EU. What did this law measure the quality of?

    a. Beer.
    b. Cars.
    c. Cheese.
    d. Meat.

    Answer: a   Type: M   Page(s): 610

12. Realists are skeptical of a newly interdependent world because

    a. In reality there is no true interdependence.
    b. The system was efficient before, why change it?
    c. Power remains a significant issue.
    d. Nations can feel more secure in such a world.

    Answer: c   Type: M   Page(s): 611

13. Which of the following could not currently be described as an economic power?

    a. Japan.
    b. The EU.
    c. China.
    d. Brazil.

    Answer: d   Type: M   Page(s): 611

14. Which nation may come to dominate East Asia militarily?

    a. Taiwan.
    b. Japan.
    c. China.
    d. Korea.

    Answer: c Type: M   Page(s): 611

15. Which of the following might help to moderate conflict and stabilize the international system?

    a. A creation of a "concert of powers".
    b. Increased money spent on defense by powers such as the U.S. and China.
    c. Less integration.
    d. Less collective security.

    Answer: a Type: M   Page(s): 612

16. Which philosopher argued that shared values, goals, procedures, and habits of democracy would cause democratic states to refrain from war against each other?

    a. Nietzsche.
    b. Kant.
    c. Hume.
    d. Mill.

    Answer: b Type: M   Page(s): 613

17. Problems with which nation's inability to accept norms of human rights could lead to a second cold war?

    a. South Korea.
    b. Malaysia.
    c. China.
    d. Brazil.

    Answer: c Type: M   Page(s): 615

Harcourt Brace & Company

18. Which scenario postulates that the shared cultural values of civic democracy will promote cooperation?

    a. Perpetual Peace.
    b. One World Ready or Not.
    c. Clash of Civilizations.
    d. Forward into the Past.

    Answer: a   Type: M   Page(s): 615

19. Which cultural gap is likely to cause the most major problems in the clash of civilizations scenario?

    a. Catholics vs. Protestants.
    b. Western culture vs. Far-Eastern culture.
    c. Islamic culture vs. Western culture.
    d. African culture vs. Far-Eastern culture.

    Answer: c   Type: M   Page(s): 616

20. Cultural compromise always includes

    a. Abandonment of fundamental values.
    b. Loss of economic power.
    c. Loss of security.
    d. None of the above.

    Answer: a   Type: M   Page(s): 617

21. According to the Darwinian view of international politics, in the long run the only way to deal with the threat from rival civilizations is to

    a. Convert them or destroy them.
    b. Let them be as they are.
    c. Refuse to acknowledge their existence.
    d. None of the above.

    Answer: a   Type: M   Page(s): 617

22. Which of the following leaders met at the Congress of Vienna in 1815?

    a. Metternich.
    b. Talleyrand.
    c. Casltereagh.
    d. All of the above.

    Answer: d   Type: M   Page(s): 619

The Future of International Politics

23. At the Vienna conference, the Concert of Europe was created because

    a. The three major leaders believed the Napoleonic Wars were caused by domestic problems.
    b. The three major leaders believed the Napoleonic Wars were caused by international problems.
    c. Nations feared the economic implications of peace.
    d. None of the above.

    Answer: a Type: M Page(s): 619

24. The arrangements made at Vienna were eventually undermined by

    a. The Industrial Revolution.
    b. Demographic changes.
    c. The unification of Italy and Germany.
    d. All of the above.

    Answer: d Type: M Page(s): 619

25. Civil Wars in nations such as Bosnia, Somalia, Chechnya, and Rwanda have made it clear that collective security

    a. Does not work.
    b. Can be utilized to stop any aggression.
    c. Must be limited in order to be effective.
    d. None of the above.

    Answer: c Type: M Page(s): 620

26. Theorists from the individual level can tell us what about leaders in the 21st century

    a. What type of leaders will be in power.
    b. How they can make a difference.
    c. What system of government they will use.
    d. All of the above.

    Answer: b Type: M Page(s): 622

27. Increased diversity among leaders will

    a. Help to build new systems that are not centered on narrow elitist views.
    b. Create tension between leaders and hurt diplomacy.
    c. Lead to inefficiency.
    d. Make interdependence more difficult.

    Answer: a Type: M Page(s): 622

28. According to theorists from the individual level, which of the following most affects international politics

    a. Ideologies.
    b. Institutions.
    c. Culture.
    d. Individuals.

    Answer: d   Type: M   Page(s): 622

29. Every person affects world politics by acting

    a. As producers and consumers.
    b. As beneficiaries of cultural traditions.
    c. As guardians of environmental heritage.
    d. All of the above.

    Answer: d   Type: M   Page(s): 623

30. Which of the following will play a major role in world politics in the 21st century?

    a. Trade.
    b. The environment.
    c. Weapons of mass destruction.
    d. All of the above.

    Answer: d   Type: M   Page(s): 624

TRUE/FALSE

31. According to William Greider, the scenario for the future of world politics, economic interdependence has already increased past the point where nation states can control their own trade and investment policies.

    a. True
    b. False

    Answer: A   Type: T   Page(s): 607

32. In the Information Age, the most important factor of production--information itself--is not very mobile.

    a. True
    b. False

    Answer: B   Type: T   Page(s): 607

33. Transfer of sovereignty is likely to apply only to economics and trade.

   a. True
   b. False

   Answer: B Type: T   Page(s): 607

34. Large populations may only mean increased concerns for states.

   a. True
   b. False

   Answer: A Type: T   Page(s): 608

35. There is little evidence of the "once world" scenario.

   a. True
   b. False

   Answer: B Type: T   Page(s): 609

36. There have been few difficulties for regional groups such as ASEAN, MERCOSUR, and NAFTA

   a. True
   b. False

   Answer: B Type: T   Page(s): 609

37. It is likely that the wages of unskilled and semiskilled workers have increased because of the huge pool of labor available in developing nations.

   a. True
   b. False

   Answer: B Type: T   Page(s): 609

38. Manufacturers may cut back on environmental safety to increase export profits.

   a. True
   b. False

   Answer: A Type: T   Page(s): 610

39. According to the realist perspective, globalization has a rosy future.

   a. True
   b. False

   Answer: B Type: T   Page(s): 610-611

40. The EU, Japan, and China are all threats to U.S. hegemony.

   a. True
   b. False

   Answer: A Type: T   Page(s): 611

41. It is impossible for the world ever to revert to a multipolar system.

   a. True
   b. False

   Answer: B Type: T   Page(s): 612

42. Many optimists believe that if democratic ideals had been stronger in Germany's Weimer Republic, Hitler never would have emerged.

   a. True
   b. False

   Answer: A Type: T   Page(s): 614

43. Non-democratic states will receive assistance from democratic nations simply because they have similar cultures.

   a. True
   b. False

   Answer: B Type: T   Page(s): 614

44. The strength of a democratic peace would be determined by the strength of democracy in influential and pivotal states.

   a. True
   b. False

   Answer: A Type: T   Page(s): 615

Harcourt Brace & Company

45. Muslim clerics believe that integration is important and are willing to give up their cultural identity.

    a. True
    b. False

    Answer: B Type: T   Page(s): 616

46. In the Clash of Civilizations scenario, there is no guarantee that any one civilization will eventually triumph.

    a. True
    b. False

    Answer: A Type: T   Page(s): 618

47. According to the individual level, the evolution of world politics is a punctuated equilibrium, wherein one system exists until it suffers a profound shock and then it collapses into chaos.

    a. True
    b. False

    Answer: A Type: T   Page(s): 618-619

48. The treaty designed by leaders at the end of World War I was clearly more efficient than the one designed at the end of the Napoleonic Wars.

    a. True
    b. False

    Answer: B Type: T   Page(s): 619

49. Leaders such as Margaret Thatcher and Boris Yeltsin, were never able to use the UN as an institution for containing and managing conflict in a manner similar to that intended by the organization's founders.

    a. True
    b. False

    Answer: B Type: T   Page(s): 620

50. The strengthening of the EU and the WTO established a trend toward international governance on translational issues, especially in the economic sphere.

a. True
b. False

Answer: B Type: T Page(s): 620-621